Just Wonder

JUST WONDER

Shifting Perspectives in Tradition

Edited by
Pauline Greenhill and Jennifer Orme

UTAH STATE UNIVERSITY PRESS
Logan

© 2024 by University Press of Colorado

Published by Utah State University Press
An imprint of University Press of Colorado
1580 North Logan Street, Suite 660
PMB 39883
Denver, Colorado 80203-1942

All rights reserved

 The University Press of Colorado is a proud member of the Association of University Presses.

The University Press of Colorado is a cooperative publishing enterprise supported, in part, by Adams State University, Colorado State University, Fort Lewis College, Metropolitan State University of Denver, University of Alaska Fairbanks, University of Colorado, University of Denver, University of Northern Colorado, University of Wyoming, Utah State University, and Western Colorado University.

ISBN: 978-1-64642-583-9 (hardcover)
ISBN: 978-1-64642-584-6 (paperback)
ISBN: 978-1-64642-585-3 (ebook)
https://doi.org/10.7330/9781646425853

Library of Congress Cataloging-in-Publication Data

Names: Greenhill, Pauline, editor. | Orme, Jennifer, editor.
Title: Just wonder : shifting perspectives in tradition / edited by Pauline Greenhill and Jennifer Orme.
Description: Logan : Utah State University Press, [2024] | Includes bibliographical references and index.
Identifiers: LCCN 2024003047 (print) | LCCN 2024003048 (ebook) | ISBN 9781646425839 (hardcover) | ISBN 9781646425846 (paperback) | ISBN 9781646425853 (ebook)
Subjects: LCSH: Justice—Folklore. | Justice in literature. | Fairy tales—Social aspects. | Fairy tales—Europe—History and criticism. | Awe—Folklore. | Wonder—Folklore. | Hope—Folklore. | Hope in literature. | Mass media and folklore.
Classification: LCC GR877 .J87 2024 (print) | LCC GR877 (ebook) | DDC 398.2—dc23/eng/20240129
LC record available at https://lccn.loc.gov/2024003047
LC ebook record available at https://lccn.loc.gov/2024003048

Cover illustration: "Mothercraft," © Winnie Truong, winnietruong.com

Contents

Acknowledgments vii

Introduction: Just Wondering about Hope
  Jennifer Orme and Pauline Greenhill 3

SECTION 1: ENACTING JUSTICE

1. Our Own Way of Walking: Reflecting Physical Difference in Icelandic Yule Tradition
   Eva Þórdís Ebenezersdóttir and Stekkjastaur 19

2. Transformations of Wonder in the BBC series *Detectorists*
   Marek Oziewicz 40

3. The Problem with Justice
   Veronica Schanoes 59

4. Making a Mountain Mundane: Social Media and the Mundanity of Wonder in the Struggle to #ProtectMaunakea
   Bryan Kamaoli Kuwada 69

SECTION 2: RE/VIEWING JUSTICE

5. Defending Happily Ever After: Seanan McGuire's *Indexing* Serial
   Andrea Braithwaite 93

6. Disabled Bodies, Hurting Emotions: Suicide and Toxic Masculinity in *The Fall*
   Heidi Kosonen   115

7. Post-Traumatic Soldier Stories: Speaking to Survive with Hope
   Jack Zipes   136

8. Reimagining Evil: Justice and Magic in Disney's Fairy-Tale Live-Action Remixes
   Ming-Hsun Lin   152

SECTION 3: SEEKING JUSTICE

9. Queer Kinship in the Grimms' "The Three Spinning Women": Challenging the Binary
   Kay Turner   175

10. Dead-End Genres, Hidden Wolves, and Misrecognition: Reading *Promising Young Woman* through "Little Red Riding Hood"
    Anne Kustritz   196

11. Margery's Miscellany; or, What "All the World Must Allow": Children's Citizenship, Goody Two-Shoes, and the Fairy-Tale Public Sphere
    Allison Craven   217

12. The Horror of Crime: Representing (In)Justice in Canadian Indigenous Crime Films
    Steven Kohm   241

    Afterword
    Jennifer Orme and Pauline Greenhill   263

    Index   267
    About the Authors   283

Acknowledgments

Our first debt of gratitude is to the contributors. These things always take time, and we appreciate their patience and kindness. We also thank the press's readers for their appreciation, keen eyes, and helpful suggestions.

The work was supported by the Social Sciences and Humanities Research Council of Canada, Insight Grant 435-2019-0691, Fairy-Tale Justice in Old and New Media: Transforming Wonder. In addition, from the University of Winnipeg we received invaluable funding from: the Marsha Hanen Global Dialogue and Ethics Award, the Work-Study Programme, and the Office of Research. We thank in particular Jino Distasio, Vice President of Research and Innovation; and Lead Program Officer, Research Partnerships, and Research Goddess, Lauren Bosc.

We are grateful for research and editorial assistance from Jazmin Foster, Hannah Paterson, and Em Penner and for research consultation with Danielle Bitz. We thank our colleagues in The. Best. Department. Ever., Women's and Gender Studies at the University of Winnipeg, for their ongoing support.

Finally, this book literally would not have been possible without the friendly helpful staff at the University Press of Colorado. Laura Furney and Dan Pratt were always on our side. Copyeditor Robin DuBlanc caught some infelicities and lacunae. We thank especially editor in chief Rachael Levay, our acquisitions editor at Utah State University Press.

Just Wonder

Introduction

Just Wondering about Hope

JENNIFER ORME AND PAULINE GREENHILL

Where does hope reside in a time of climate disaster, social and political upheaval, and factionalism amid a deadly global pandemic? Spending time with the internet's catastrophic fantasies and echo chambers, so-called doomscrolling, an ever-vigilant urge to know the latest in calamity, does not seem to lead to betterment. Conversely, an avoidance mode that wallows in the shallows of baby animal videos and funny memes provides escape into the adorable, the enjoyable, and the just plain silly, but gives little in the way of hope for the now or the future. Feet-on-the-ground activism, letter-writing campaigns, volunteering, and giving what money one can afford to causes all offer valid forms of protest and action for change. But creating, teaching, reading, and imagining what justice looks like and highlighting the injustices too often ignored in the face of the status quo and normalized dominance also suggest forms of resistance. They all begin with wondering, shifting one's view, questioning the way things are to see if they might be otherwise. All change begins with someone (or a bunch of someones) *just wondering*: what if . . .

---

https://doi.org/10.7330/9781646425853.c000

Here we find hope in popular texts and folkloric traditions that point to injustices and/or envision forms of redress. Making a problem known, dramatizing it, encourages visualizing possible solutions. If fair resolutions could come easily in the current "globally dominant, largely white, market-oriented, human supremacist, settler-colonial and extractivist, growth-addicted, Euro- and North American–oriented culture" (as contributor Marek Oziewicz puts it in his chapter), surely they would have been implemented by now. But justice remains complex and very difficult, so we do not expect the source texts described here—or, indeed, the contributors' chapters—to provide ready solutions. Nevertheless, we remain convinced, along with feminist theorists like Patricia Hill Collins, who says "the path to individual and collective empowerment lies in the power of a free mind" (2000, 204), that imagination is a first step toward liberation. Following that step, any work to defy injustices done to populations of humans, nonhuman animals, and ecological systems also moves toward hope.

We believe in wonder as a force not only for personal transformation in an individual's moment of awe, but for collective power as well. Openness to wonder provides potentially critical social, cultural, and individual stances that have a role to play in reconceptualizing the past, present, and future. Tales and traditions can illustrate and support ways of creating more just and equitable worlds in diversity. But if narratives of wonder offer hope, they have also been used to validate inequality, inequity, and discrimination. This book offers readers ways of looking critically as well as wondering creatively to expand possibility, resist oppression, and seek justice.

Folklorists and folkloristics have long explored issues around social justice (see, e.g., Fivecoate, Downs, and McGriff 2021). And while some maintain a qualitative distinction between folklore/traditional culture on the one hand, and popular/mass culture on the other (e.g., Foster 2016), we decline to do so (see Kosonen and Greenhill 2022, 351). We consider here materials pretty conventionally understood as folklore, like tales from the Grimms' collections or the Icelandic Yule Lads; revisions of traditional ideas and figures in film, television, novels, and social media; and ideas based on and inspired by traditional cultures and remixes thereof. We don't concern ourselves with whether or not a text under examination would be understood as folkloric by nineteenth-, twentieth-, or even twenty-first-century folklorists. Instead, we want to examine its significance and meaning as a popular intervention into discourses around the forms and meanings of justice in many senses.

One of these meanings is the familiar notion of "fairy-tale justice," which refers to the perceived simplistic punishments and rewards of some of the best-known tales. So prevalent is the concept that it is the title of a comedy sketch on *RuPaul's Drag Race: All Stars* (season 7, 2022), in which contestants, in the roles of well-known fairy-tale characters, participate in a courtroom reality show. Such courtroom sketches parody the perceived criminal acts of fairy-tale and nursery-tale characters such as the wolf or Goldilocks while simultaneously ridiculing American court TV shows and the American justice system (Mieder 2016). Indeed, fairy tales provide themes, characters, and plots for a plethora of procedural television shows dealing with justice granted and denied (see Rudy and Greenhill 2021, 159–206). Cinematic variations of "Little Red Riding Hood" in particular, whether live-action or animated, dramatic or comedic, for adult or child audiences, explore fairy tales, crime, and justice (Greenhill and Kohm 2010, 2013; Kohm and Greenhill 2011, 2014). But not all chapters in this volume deal with traditional fairy tales or with criminal contexts. They do, however, concern justice and the just.

JUST

Just can minimize. As a synonym for *only* or *merely*, the title might suggest that this book concerns wonder and nothing else, or mere wonder, the unimportant, simple escapism. We recognize that for many people wonder, fairy tales, magic, and even awe are indeed just imaginary flights of fancy. As the unreal, they may be pleasurable, entertaining, enchanting, even, but they lack the gravitas of allegedly true events or realistic depictions of the world. Yet the interpenetration between reality and magic has long concerned scholars of fairy tales as well as creators working with the form in various media (see, e.g., Greenhill 2020).

In contrast, when challenged as lies and/or harmful, especially to children, fairy tales become all too serious. Consider, for example, mid-twentieth-century feminists' concerns that fairy tales sold girls in particular a damaging heteronormative narrative with the unrealistic expectation that they would marry a handsome prince and live happily ever after. And while fairy tales and other wonder genres are not and have never been only or even primarily for children, as contributors Eva Þórdís Ebenezersdóttir and Stekkjastaur, Heidi Kosonen, and Allison Craven explore, even work consumed by or created for children can respect their capability for complex thought, their culture, and their personhood. Infantilization of the young, especially in combination with issues of gender, ethnicity, class, and/or physical embodiment, transforms the objects of discussion into mere children—just kids—whom the dominant (adult) subject must watch over, control, protect, and speak for, for their own good. This tactic excuses unjust treatment of individuals and groups, but pointing to its construction and who benefits from its normalization highlights resistance to its power.

Our most pointed usage of *just* means equitable, right, correct, fair in relation to judgments (legal or moral), or actions and behaviors—to be on the side of justice. The chapters concern ways of thinking that relate to what contributor Craven calls "the fairy-tale public sphere" ("the role of wonder in arenas of public debate") broadly conceived, but also to more personal and private struggles. Our international collaborators (from Australia, Canada, Finland, Hawai'i, Iceland, Netherlands, Taiwan, and the continental US) self-identify from different subjectivities and locations and come from a range of inter/disciplines in the arts, humanities, and social sciences: children's studies, communications, criminal justice studies, ethnology, film studies, folkloristics, Indigenous studies, languages, literary studies, media studies, performance studies, and women's and gender studies. This diversity makes for a variety of approaches and considerations of justice and wonder in traditional and popular culture.

Justice is itself a multivalent and complex term. As contributor Veronica Schanoes asks, "If justice means undoing harm, it truly is impossible, and there is no such thing. Nothing restores lives lost and families destroyed. If justice means making unfair things fair, it again is impossible and there is no such thing. . . . Is justice acknowledging the harm done? But who would be doing the acknowledging?" Contributors engage with *social justice* (seeking a just and fair society with equal opportunities and treatment in institutions and cultures) and *restorative justice* (repairing communities); they reflect on their own art and activism, and on the ethics of narrative production today. They may focus on representations implicating crimes (unlawful actions) and harms (damage to individuals, society, and environments often not criminalized) as well as responses to these wrongs. Chapters explore both *procedural* (fair process) and *substantive* (fair outcome) justice in fictional texts.

Andrea Braithwaite's, Ming-Hsun Lin's, Anne Kustritz's, and Steven Kohm's chapters implicate Nicole Rafter's (2007) concept of popular criminology (see Kohm 2017), an approach that uses "film, television, literary, and other cultural representations of crime and criminal justice as analytical as well as textual sources" (Kohm and Greenhill 2011, 196), to address crimes and harms and the responses to them. Schanoes, Kosonen, Jack Zipes, Lin, and Kustritz address the traumatic aftermath of injustice and the ways wonder can address and, sometimes, redress. And solidarity and the creation of community figure as tools and key aspects of struggles for justice focus Ebenezersdóttir and Stekkjastaur's, Bryan Kamaoli Kuwada's, and Kay Turner's chapters. Oziewicz, Kuwada, and Kohm deal with ecological justice, and show how art, storytelling, and activism use wonder to open pathways to human and nonhuman relations that question, and sometimes explicitly reject, the ethics and inevitability of a hierarchical relationship in which humans picture ourselves as naturally inhabiting the dominant position. Each approach figures acts of storytelling, sometimes in doing harm and other times in voicing responses to harms done. Competing stories and storytelling techniques highlight injustices, and voicing one's own story offers a path for seeking justice—even if it is not yet attained.

WONDER

As with *just*, *wonder* has more than one meaning. Its verb form invokes open curiosity, questioning, testing, and playing with ideas, a capacity fundamental to all scholarship and art, and where they begin. But it also provides a key to seeking justice. Change comes about from questioning the status quo and pondering alternatives. As a noun, a quality or an emotion, it allows feelings of awe, of marvel, or of surprise in a way that, even if only momentarily, causes one to apprehend the world differently. This does not mean that wonder is necessarily rare or that one must go far and wide to seek it. As Kuwada's chapter demonstrates, it can manifest in the mundane and quotidian, as when one suddenly notices the beauty of the land or of weather patterns. A glimpse of the moon or clouds or a gliding hawk out of an apartment window has the power to make one pause, admire, and revel in these sights as marvels. The mundane need not be ordinary or unnoticed. In order for a thing to be wonder*ful(l)* it must have some degree of surprise or aspect of the unexpected. And this is the way that wonder in narrative often works.

A number of chapters engage specifically with fairy tales—primarily European in origin and manifestation. But we prefer to use the term *wonder* for opening up and aligning with other groups and stories, to respect and acknowledge the situatedness of traditional and popular narratives of wonder and the marvelous. In addition to discussions of fairy tales, we include considerations of other forms of wonder: in folk traditions, popular literature, realistic television, Indigenous knowledge, personal experience, fantasy, and horror.

Wonder's association with particular types of stories means that it "names the marvel, the prodigy, the surprise as well as the responses they excite, of fascination and inquiry; it conveys the active motion towards experience and the passive stance of enrapturement" (Warner 1994, 3). Acknowledging that the term *fairy tale* comes from the French conte de fées,[1] Marina Warner notes: "The word *Wundermärchen* was adopted by the Romantics in Germany and the Russian folklorists to characterise the folk tale or fairy tale. It is a useful term, it frees this kind of story from the miniaturised whimsy of fairyland to breathe the wilder air of the marvellous" (3). We would add that wonder also brings us back to activism and away from the infantilizing and dismissal too often linked to fairy tales. Instead, with Cristina Bacchilega (2013), we advocate for a politics of wonder.

Further, fairy tales were used as language and enculturation tools in colonial and postcolonial sites (Naithani 2010; Bacchilega and Naithani 2018; Hearne 2017). Transporting fairy tales from Europe to colonial settings has deleterious effects. For example, in Australia: "The uniqueness of the Australian landscape and its flora and fauna—from the European perspective—allowed the actual environment to fulfill the role of a fairy realm, but the fairies themselves emigrated from England and arrived in this realm in their European diaphanous gowns and fashionable hair" (Do Rozario 2011, 14). Fairy tales take up room and subsume or supplant Indigenous narratives, taking those tales out of context, ignoring their cultural functions, and placing a foreign understanding upon them while also relegating them to the nursery (Bacchilega and Naithani 2018).

Daniel Heath Justice notes that "'fantasy' . . . presumes a kind of arrogant certainty over what is real and unreal, true and false, legitimate and delusional. 'Wonder,' on the other hand, is a word rooted in meaningful uncertainty, curiosity, humility; it places unsolvable mystery, not fixed insistence, at the heart of engagement" (2018, 153). He explains, "'Fantasy' as it's commonly understood is dangerous, because it's so deeply entangled in settler-colonial logics of dead matter, monolithic reality, and rationalist supremacy"; thus he prefers the term "wonderworks" (152). "These works remind us that there are other ways of being in the world than those we've been trained to accept as normal. They offer us hopeful alternatives to the oppressive structures and conditions we're continually told are inevitable material 'reality'" (155).

We don't conflate wonder tales and Justice's Indigenous wonderworks, as we seek to avoid reprising settler-colonialism's appropriation of Indigenous narrative traditions. Bacchilega and Orme carefully point out that "while Euro-American wonder tales are not to be confused with what Daniel Heath Justice calls 'Indigenous wonderworks,' both speculative genres participate in 'imagining otherwise' as a 'moral imperative'" (2021, xx). Instead, our title's and contents' wonder seeks to ensure that the situatedness of texts that come from traditions beyond Euro-American fairy tales are not subsumed by them (see also Bacchilega 2007, 2013, 2018, 2019; Bacchilega and Naithani 2018; Haase 2010, 2019; Naithani 2010). We seek to reflect these concerns in our three sections: "Enacting Justice"—taking activist approaches to traditions; "Re/Viewing Justice"—exploring shifts in fictional representations; and "Seeking Justice"—focusing on perspectives of those who have been harmed by injustice and redressing their situations. Readers may note that the texts that offer our contributors inspiration and are gathered together in these sections are often quite disparate. Our point is that similar processes—enacting, re/viewing, and seeking justice—happen in a broad range of locations.

ENACTING JUSTICE

These contributions reflect upon the relations between wonder and activism and take an activist stance themselves. They examine and challenge long-held assumptions and offer alternate approaches to a wide variety of traditions and texts that have misrepresented, dominated, and/or ignored some human communities and/or the nonhuman world. We open with a chapter coauthored by a human and her writing partner of trollish descent, showing the role the Jólasveinn (Yule Lad) Stekkjastaur and his family have in Iceland's Christmas traditions. Ebenezersdóttir and Stekkjastaur reflect on their shared experiences as a disabled human and a supernatural being with physical impairment to center their mutual understanding in tradition and society. Stekkjastaur is now considering becoming a spokeslad for disability awareness.

Next, Oziewicz's chapter contends that a contemporary "fantasy for the Anthropocene" must attend to the climate crisis and other ecological disasters. He challenges common portrayals of the natural world in fantasy, and argues for an emphasis on nonhuman kinship in both the genre and society. He draws on the BBC television show *Detectorists* to explore ideas of ecoliteracy and how connections to the nonhuman world allow wonder to inhabit an otherwise realistic text to bring attention to human-created eco-disasters and imagine other ways of being in the world.

Schanoes then moves us toward problematizing particular stories. Her chapter explores the history of antisemitism in the Grimms' fairy tales, demonstrating the personal harm that they cause by normalizing such narratives. She explores the damage that reimagining them might cause, as it potentially brings forth harms and risks as a result of erasing the historical impact of antisemitism in folktales. She raises questions about how fairy tales define justice—and whether or not justice is possible within a corpus of texts so deeply informed by hate speech.

This section concludes with an examination of the Hawaiian-led occupations of Maunakea on the Big Island of Hawai'i between 2015 and 2019, and how Indigenous land protectors fought to defend the mountain from ecological harm. Kuwada explores how social media offers an effective tool for Hawaiian activists to communicate with each other and the world. He considers how social media can share tales of wonder, shaping individuals' connections to traditional stories and the land while also redefining understandings of relations between wonder and the mundane.

RE/VIEWING JUSTICE

These chapters consider fictional cinematic and literary representations of criminal injustices and harms and those texts' possible just responses to them. They address the traumatic aftermath of injustice and the ways that characters turn to wonder to address and redress harms done to them, sometimes offering models for action in the world and sometimes explicitly rejecting potential alternatives. The section begins with Braithwaite's chapter on Seanan McGuire's *Indexing* duology, which investigates how understandings of the true-crime genre and fairy-tale form shift when they are brought together. By combining the two, *Indexing* urges readers to reimagine the representation of justice and who or what defines it in a world literally dominated by narrative tropes.

Next, Kosonen examines director Tarsem Singh's exploration of wonder tale–telling by unequal narrator participants and how storytelling becomes tied to the taboo of suicide and its relations to gender, age, disability, and ethnicity. She demonstrates how *The Fall*'s primary male character embodies ideas of toxic masculinity, violence, and disability and juxtaposes them against the girl child co-narrator's positionings.

Then we move to a critical examination of soldier stories from six folklorists of the nineteenth century and how they criticize principles of war, trauma, and justice. Zipes argues that these narratives reveal the trauma that soldiers experience from war, and offers critiques of the military as an institution. He reflects upon texts for children and adults and concludes with a call to scholars to study the power of soldier stories more deeply.

We close the section with an exploration of how Disney's live-action remixes of their earlier animated features challenge ideas of justice, good, and evil in the corporation's fairy-tale universe. Lin points out that these remixed stories reposition villains as being incapable of love and transforms otherwise problematic characters who do demonstrate care—parental or heterosexual—as merely misunderstood. In doing so, the remixes portray magic as a diminishing force or as a moral test that must be overcome.

SEEKING JUSTICE

These chapters engage with difficult questions raised by traditional verbal and recent cinematic texts. They counter invisibility and erasure by training their gaze on and through the perspectives of queer kinship; victims of sexual violence; dismissed young, female, activist voices; and discriminatory power structures between white settler-colonial and Indigenous communities. In the chapter that opens the section Turner explores the fairy-tale portrayal of homosocial and queer relations, showing how the Grimms' versions of "The Three Spinning Women" challenge heterosexual binaries through the title characters' triad bond and their relations to other female characters. She highlights the importance of women's friendship and bonding as means of overcoming personal and social struggles caused by gendered oppression.

Kustritz's chapter draws narrative connections between "Little Red Riding Hood" and the film *Promising Young Woman* to critically examine how women rarely receive justice for the acts of harm against them. Kustritz reflects on the patriarchal pervasiveness of unredressed sexual violence against women in both the real and fairy-tale worlds.

Craven then turns to the long-lasting legacy of the character and book of Goody Two-Shoes, examining how since the eighteenth century stories and fairy tales have modeled values of citizenship and morality to children, despite their being disallowed active participation in society. Craven applies ideas from what she calls "the fairy-tale public sphere" to examine how media continually demean and dismiss today's young women activists in response to their work as protesters and global citizens.

The section concludes with Kohm's interrogation of the films *Clearcut* and *Blood Quantum*, portraying the impacts of intergenerational trauma, colonialism, and racism against Indigenous peoples in Canada. Both draw on the true-crime and horror genres, using preternatural figures to reflect on the ways that Canada's colonial legacy continues to haunt Indigenous peoples. While both films employ Indigenous actors in Indigenous roles, Kohm points to some of the crucial differences between the white-settler-written and -directed *Clearcut* and the Indigenous-written and -directed *Blood Quantum*.

We hope that this volume contributes to and advances interdisciplinary discussions of justice, wonder, and traditions, but we also hope that our readers will respond to its calls to action. Curiosity, questioning, and intellectual wondering are essential to finding solutions and routes to a more just society. This is where we began this project and the contributors began each of their chapters: by pondering, daydreaming, picking at, thinking deeply, and venturing beyond limits. That is always a great place to start. As you take in these chapters and ideas, we urge you too to *Just Wonder*.

NOTE

1. In consultation with contributors, and as an expression of decolonizing solidarity, we do not italicize non-English-language words. In correspondence, Kuwada noted, "Most, if not all, Hawaiian scholars try to avoid [italicizing Hawaiian words] because we are making the claim that our language is not foreign to us" (2022). Though this practice is by no means entirely uncontroversial, "over the last decade, there has been a shift away from enforcing italics on non-English words in publishing. And the decision to italicize or not has prompted authors and editors to ask for whom they're writing, and to question assumptions about the experience of reading" (Ha 2018). Further, "the practice of italicizing . . . [non-English] words is a form of linguistic gatekeeping; a demarcation between which words are 'exotic' or 'not found in the English language,' and those that have a rightful place in the text: the non-italicized" (Barokka 2020). The journal *AlterNative*, for example, has as its house style: "As a rule, do not italicize Indigenous or other non-English words" (n.d.).

We note, however, in contrast, that Gregory Younging, in a standard work on Indigenous style, makes no such recommendation. Indeed, he raises the opposite concern, about the *lack* of italicizing that marks assimilation into English. He notes that the Collins, Merriam-Webster, and Oxford dictionaries leave unmarked words like canoe, hammock, igloo, kayak, and maize. He says, "I regret that English has swallowed these words. These words bear witness to the history of Indigenous Peoples in contact with Europeans. They often represent technologies and foods that Indigenous People introduced to Europeans. Their presentation as 'English' terms fails to acknowledge the contributions Indigenous Peoples have made to mainstream culture and the English language, and fails to educate readers who may not be aware of these contributions" (2018, 87). However, we see not italicizing as appropriate in this context and now, although we note that practices may change over time.

REFERENCES

AlterNative. n.d. "AlterNative House Style." Accessed December 24, 2022. https://www.sagepub.com/sites/default/files/alternative_house_style.pdf.

Bacchilega, Cristina. 2007. *Legendary Hawai'i and the Politics of Place*. Philadelphia: University of Pennsylvania Press.

Bacchilega, Cristina. 2013. *Fairy Tales Transformed? Twenty-First Century Adaptations and the Politics of Wonder*. Detroit: Wayne State University Press.

Bacchilega, Cristina. 2018. "Where Can Wonder Take Us?" *Journal of the Fantastic in the Arts* 28 (1): 6–25.

Bacchilega, Cristina. 2019. "'Decolonizing' the Canon: Critical Challenges to Eurocentrism." In *The Fairy Tale World*, edited by Andrew Teverson, 33–44. New York: Routledge.

Bacchilega, Cristina, and Sadhana Naithani. 2018. "Colonialism/Postcolonialism/Decolonization." In *The Routledge Companion to Media and Fairy-Tale Cultures*, edited by Pauline Greenhill, Jill Terry Rudy, Naomi Hamer, and Lauren Bosc, 83–90. New York: Routledge.

Bacchilega, Cristina, and Jennifer Orme, eds. 2021. *Inviting Interruptions: Wonder Tales in the Twenty-First Century*. Detroit: Wayne State University Press.

Barokka, Khairani. 2020. "The Case against Italicizing 'Foreign' Words." *Catapult*, February 11. https://catapult.co/stories/column-the-case-against-italicizing-foreign-words-khairani-barokka.

Collins, Patricia Hill. (1990) 2000. *Black Feminist Thought: Knowledge, Consciousness, and the Politics of Empowerment*. Rev. 10th anniversary ed. Abingdon, UK: Routledge.

Do Rozario, Rebecca-Anne C. 2011. "Australia's Fairy Tales Illustrated in Print: Instances of Indigeneity, Colonization, and Suburbanization." *Marvels & Tales* 25 (1): 13–32.

Fivecoate, Jesse A., Kristina Downs, and Meredith A. E. McGriff, eds. 2021. *Advancing Folkloristics*. Bloomington: Indiana University Press.

Foster, Michael Dylan. 2016. "Introduction: The Challenge of the Folkloresque." In *The Folkloresque: Reframing Folklore in a Popular Culture World*, edited by Michael Dylan Foster and Jeffrey A. Tolbert, 3–33. Logan: Utah State University Press.

Greenhill, Pauline. 2020. *Reality, Magic, and Other Lies: Fairy-Tale Film Truths*. Detroit: Wayne State University Press.

Greenhill, Pauline, and Steven Kohm. 2010. "'Little Red Riding Hood' Crime Films: Criminal Themes and Critical Variations." *Annual Review of Interdisciplinary Justice Research* 1: 77–93.

Greenhill, Pauline, and Steven Kohm. 2013. "*Hoodwinked!* and *Jin-Roh: The Wolf Brigade*: Animated 'Little Red Riding Hood' Films and the Rashômon Effect." *Marvels & Tales* 27 (1): 89–108.

Ha, Thu-Huong. 2018. "Bilingual Authors Are Challenging the Practice of Italicizing Non-English Words." *Quartz*, June 24. https://qz.com/quartzy/1310228/bilingual-authors-are-challenging-the-practice-of-italicizing-non-english-words#:~:text=In%20the%20late%201990s%2C%20the,%2C%20Otravez%2C%E2%80%9D%20were%20not.

Haase, Donald. 2010. "Decolonizing Fairy Tale Studies." *Marvels & Tales* 24 (1): 17–38.

Haase, Donald. 2019. "The Fairy Tale Canon." In *Teaching Fairy Tales*, edited by Nancy Canepa, 54–66. Detroit: Wayne State University Press.

Hearne, Joanna. 2017. "'I Am Not a Fairy Tale': Indigenous Storytelling on Canadian Television." *Marvels & Tales* 31 (1): 126–46.

Justice, Daniel Heath. 2018. *Why Indigenous Literatures Matter*. Waterloo, ON: Wilfrid Laurier University Press.
Kohm, Steven. 2017. "Popular Criminology." In *Oxford Research Encyclopedia of Crime, Media, and Popular Culture*, edited by Nicole Rafter and Michelle Brown, n.p. https://oxfordre.com/criminology/page/crimemedia/the-oxford-encyclopedia-of-crime-media-and-popular-culture.
Kohm, Steven, and Pauline Greenhill. 2011. "Pedophile Crime Films as Popular Criminology: A Problem of Justice?" *Theoretical Criminology* 15 (2): 195–216.
Kohm, Steven, and Pauline Greenhill. 2014. "Little Red Riding Hood Crime Films: Critical Variations on Criminal Themes." *Law, Culture and the Humanities* 10 (2): 257–78.
Kosonen, Heidi, and Pauline Greenhill. 2022. "'Something's Not Right in Silverhöjd': Nordic Supernatural and Environmental and Species Justice in *Jordskott*." *Folklore* 133 (3): 334–56.
Kuwada, Bryan Kamaoli. 2022. Email to Pauline Greenhill and Jennifer Orme, August 15.
Mieder, Wolfgang. 2016. "Cartoons and Comics." In *Folktales and Fairy Tales: Traditions and Texts from Around the World*, edited by Anne E. Duggan and Donald Haase, 173–76. Santa Barbara, CA: Greenwood.
Naithani, Sadhana. 2010. *Story-Time of the British Empire: Colonial and Postcolonial Folkloristics*. Jackson: University Press of Mississippi.
Rafter, Nicole. 2007. "Crime, Film and Criminology: Recent Sex-Crime Movies." *Theoretical Criminology* 11 (3): 403–20.
Rudy, Jill Terry, and Pauline Greenhill. 2021. *Fairy-Tale TV*. New York: Routledge.
RuPaul's Drag Race: All Stars. 2022. Season 7, episode 4. United States: World of Wonder Productions.
Warner, Marina. 1994. *Wonder Tales*. Oxford: Oxford University Press.
Younging, Gregory. 2018. *Elements of Indigenous Style: A Guide for Writing by and about Indigenous Peoples*. Toronto: Brush.

SECTION ONE

Enacting Justice

1

Our Own Way of Walking

Reflecting Physical Difference in Icelandic Yule Tradition

EVA ÞÓRDÍS EBENEZERSDÓTTIR AND STEKKJASTAUR

The lifelong comradery of a disabled human being and a supernatural being with physical impairment reveals a tradition that reflects and changes with the community. The custom in question, an Icelandic Yuletide (Christmas) one, involves a large family of mischievous gift givers of a trollish persuasion. This lively tradition is beginning to show signs of reflecting ideas of human diversity and disability, even if those signs are not recognized by all. Through the lens of the personal, including embodied experiences, and with an analyzing gaze of folkloristics and disability studies, we reveal the wonderful transformation that we see in the lore and the potential empowerment and social justice it can bring for disabled Icelandic children and adults. First, though, because as authors our backgrounds and our bodies are paramount to our understanding, we begin by introducing ourselves.

Eva Þórdís, a PhD student in folkloristics at the University of Iceland, researches disability understanding in archived Icelandic legends and lore. When she was born it was clear that her body was different from most people's; her left leg was, and is, shorter than the right. From the time she started walking she has used a prosthetic brace that is locked at the knee and extends from her hip down. As she often states, it is so she can reach all the way to the ground, since from the sole of her left foot to the floor there are about twenty-seven centimeters.

The second author, Stekkjastaur,[1] is a Jólasveinn, a Yule or Christmas being who lives with his family in the wild mountains of Iceland. He comes to visit human towns and cities in the middle of December, bringing gifts to Icelandic children. Most believe that Stekkjastaur has staur[-]fætur (literally, pole or post legs), which are referred to in his name: Stekkjastaur could be understood to be the poles or posts used to mark stekkir, the area where sheep were kept in nineteenth-century Icelandic farmsteads (Jónasson 2010, 167–69). There are varying opinions of what is meant by staurfætur, since drawings and pictures of Stekkjastaur show his legs in various ways. Some show them as flesh-and-bone legs with unbending knees, others as wooden peg legs, but it seems clear that, like his coauthor, he has a physical impairment. Many of the Jólasveinar use walking sticks but none as much as Stekkjastaur, who is rarely shown without the aid of a sturdy staff. It is important to Stekkjastaur that all versions of his body be considered, as each image is true to form within the belief and imagination of the creator. According to Stekkjastaur, all accounts of his body are correct.

From early in her undergraduate studies in folklore, Eva Þórdís has combined folkloristics and disability studies. She realized then that Stekkjastaur has been her constant folkloric and disability companion throughout her life. This comradeship, and now research partnership, became more focused at the beginning of Eva Þórdís's PhD studies, when she named Stekkjastaur her research's supernatural representative. Thus, our connection and partnership are based on the fact that we both have physical leg impairments that in context with environment and society can lead to disability. We share the experience of unbending knees, the use of prosthetics, and the unique walking style that comes with our bodies. We also share a love/hate relationship with the sometimes-disabling snow in Iceland's winters and with the damage to prosthetics that eventually wear out from the active lifestyles of a PhD student and a Yule Lad. Last but certainly not least, we share the joy of sitting down for a rest after a long walk, to take those prosthetics off and put ointments and Band-Aids on skin that has been rubbed raw on long walks.[2]

One author is a creature of folklore and belief, a supernatural being who some might say does not exist and therefore could not be either a participant in or an author of academic works. So this chapter, an academic and activist experiment, combines our embodied experience of disability and ownership of the tradition, what Stephen Olbrys Gencarella calls critical folklore studies, an approach that "forefronts the development of new coalitions, subjectivities, and hegemonic order for social change, while pinpointing the need for relations with local demands and articulations" (2011, 268). In addition, our activist stand, similarly to Vivian Labrie's work with fairy and wonder tales (2018, 101–2), consciously uses the legends and images of Stekkjastaur to spark discourse and demand social justice of recognition and cultural participation for disabled people and creatures, bringing us out from the invisible margins into the center of tradition and society.

The basis for Stekkjastaur's role as coauthor also comes from critical and cultural perspectives of disability, and the disability movement's slogan "Nothing About Us Without Us." Social understanding of disability makes a distinction between impairment (the physical) and disability (a social construction), a dualism that can be a helpful starting point when rejecting the general perspective of disability as a deficit and physical flaw that needs fixing. From the perspective of critical and cultural disability studies, the sociocultural construction of disability, more than a simple dyad, is a complex intersection of context, culture, the personal, the political, and the relation between body, environment, and society (e.g., Kafer 2013, 4–8). "Nothing About Us Without Us," used by activists for the last few decades, demands that disabled people have a voice and power in discussions and decision making that have to do with our lives (e.g., Traustadóttir 2006; 2009, 6; United Nations 2003–2004). Encompassing both the simpler, dualist understanding of disability and the complexity of critical disability studies, the slogan is equally important for disability rights movements and in academia.

In the realm of research, "Nothing About Us Without Us" evokes the ethical approach of disability inquiry that is with and by disabled people, not on and about us. This call has been answered methodologically with, for example, inclusive methods and a transformative paradigm. In inclusive research methods, academically trained people and disabled people (often those with intellectual impairments), who are too often excluded from academic training because of their impairments, collaborate. Papers are coauthored by all collaborators, academically trained and not (e.g., Atkinson and Walmsley 2010, 280–82). We do not claim that this chapter falls under inclusive research as Stekkjastaur's status as a supernatural being prevents him from such academic requirements as giving his signature and explicit consent for participation (McKee and Porter 2012, 66–68). We do, however, work in the same spirit. Stekkjastaur's contribution lies in his numerous depictions in the Icelandic cultural sphere, as well as the connection inherent in the two authors' parallel embodiment. By approaching his representations as narratives of an actual being we lean toward the ethical approach of inclusive research (Ebenezersdóttir and Ólafsdóttir 2021, 77).

Perhaps not as controversial in our method is what John Creswell calls an advocacy worldview, and Donna M. Mertens refers to as a transformative paradigm in research design. Advocacy and transformative research combine a focus on working with people from marginalized groups, addressing social issues, and having an individual impact on the researchers as well as a push for changes and reformation of the group's social situation (Mertens 2010, 21–25; 2017, 20; Creswell 2014, 9–10). These approaches highlight that the personal is not only political, it's also a base for knowledge. In addition, Mertens points out that intuition, feelings, and emotions are integral to transformative research (2017, 22), all of which are part of the embodiment of difference and prosthetics use the authors know well.

In the end there are three clear reasons we find it appropriate, important, and just for Stekkjastaur to coauthor this work. One is that he has a different body and, as we will discuss below, is increasingly being viewed as a disabled person. Another is that he is part of an old, living, and ever-changing tradition, and although disability is a modern concept, people with different bodies and minds have always been part of both humanity and the supernatural (Ebenezersdóttir 2013, 71–72; 87–89; 2014, 30–38; Sigurjónsdóttir and Rice 2021, 5–7; Sigurjónsdóttir, Jakobsson, and Björnsdóttir 2013, 18–20). Third, and perhaps most important, is that according to children in Iceland, Stekkjastaur is a real living person. With these three points in mind, the demand of disability studies, activism, and advocacy, "Nothing About Us Without Us," firmly gives Stekkjastaur the right of official participation in academic work about him. Regarding the slogan's impact on academia, we take a step further in disability studies, showing that a disabled academic and a disabled nonacademic who is also *a supernatural being* can collaborate on transformative research about embodied experiences of difference and disability in the folklore of both authors.

THE PRACTICE OF THE LIVING LORE

The Icelandic Jólasveinar, or Yule Lads, are thirteen brothers, the sons of Grýla and (likely) Leppalúði, who live in the mountains of Iceland and lie low for most of the year. On the eve of December 11, the first brother, Stekkjastaur, roams the land on foot, placing small presents in children's shoes that have been put on their bedroom windowsills for this purpose. In the days leading up to Christmas the other brothers come, one each night, out of the darkness of winter, both to scare us and to treat us with their company in the Advent of Christmas and the Winter Solstice. After December 24[3] and the time of gift giving, they leave town, one each night, the last one departing on the thirteenth night of Christmas, January 6. These Lads also travel to other countries, bringing shoe gifts to Icelandic children living abroad. The thirteen nights before and after Christmas are a time of belief and magic for Icelandic children, who await the arrival of the brothers and firmly believe in their power to visit every window and every shoe, each small present solidifying their belief.[4]

The Lads and their extended family are an intricate part of our Advent and Christmas traditions and an important social performance and theater that everyone participates in (Schechner 2020, 334–335). Younger children's belief in the brothers is strong; they know that if they want a good gift, they must brush their teeth and be on their best behavior, otherwise they will wake up to find a raw potato in their shoe. However, around eight years of age, many children start wavering in their belief, doubting that the Lads can deliver all those gifts and wondering if perhaps it was their parent(s) who were sneaking around their bedroom window the night before.[5] When children express their doubt, a private conversation takes place between them and the adults in their family. Perhaps the wavering of belief, and then being brought into the social drama to help preserve the belief of younger children, is a coming-of-age (van Gennep 1960, 3, 54–55) moment, as they are let in on one of the nation's most important public secrets. They become members of the group of older, siblings, parents, and grandparents, all participating and contributing to the social drama that is the belief in Jólasveinar. Doubting the existence of the Lads is not done in public. Beyond that private conversation they are real, they do exist, they bring every child a present in one night, and if you have not been on your best behavior, they bring a raw potato rather than a piece of chocolate, a tangerine, a few coins, or a small gift.

THE YULE FAMILY HISTORY

The Lads come from a peculiar family with a complicated legend history that Árni Björnsson, folklorist and a pioneer in the field of folklore in Iceland, covered extensively in his *Saga Jólanna* (The Saga/History/Tale of Christmas/Yule) (2006). In addition to manuscripts and legend collections of the past, he also built on the National Museum's archival folklife collection. According to Björnsson, most Jólasveinar came from the mountains, although some came sailing on skin boats from unknown lands to scare and steal from God-fearing people during the darkest time of the year.

The Lads are first mentioned in writing in the seventeenth century, as the trollish offspring of the matriarch Grýla (Björnsson 2006, 66–73; Gunnell 2001, 33–35). She is mentioned in the Icelandic sagas as well as in poems from the fifteenth and sixteenth centuries onward, where she is described as a mean, vicious, human-eating troll with a taste for misbehaving children. She has had many mates and lovers during her life and has allegedly eaten at least one of them (Björnsson 2006, 70; Jónsdóttir 2021; Valgeirsson 2021). Grýla has a strong presence in Icelandic folklore, but according to folklorist Terry Gunnell she is also part of the northern European tradition of horrific female midwinter deities and creatures (2021). For most children and their parents, she now only pretends that she wants to eat children and does so in accordance with phrases such as "I could just eat you up," commonly used by elderly aunts as they comment on the cuteness of young children.

For the adults, the question of the Lads' paternity is also a topic of discussion. Leppalúði, Grýla's current mate, is said to be the father of the Thirteen Lads, and according to the children, he is. However, considering Grýla's relationship history, the adults do wonder what results a paternity test involving Leppalúði and the Lads would yield (Icelandic Web of Science 2020).

Around 1860, Jón Árnason gathered legends about Jólasveinar as part of his project to arrange, edit, and publish the first legend collection in Iceland. The first volume of *Íslenzkar þjóðsögur og ævintýri* (Icelandic Folk and Fairy

Tales) was published in 1862 (Árnason 1954). In addition to legends about Jólasveinar and Grýla, Árnason received numerous lists naming Grýla's children. The senders came from various places around the country, indicating well-established local traditions about the Yule invaders. Following Árnason's collection, others also included names of Jólasveinar and Jólameyjar (Yule Lads and Lasses). In these older archives the total number of names exceeded 80 (Björnsson 2006, 76–78); all in all, there are likely around 100 (Jónsdóttir 2021; Valgeirsson 2021). Many names describe the role and function of the individual Lads, indicating that they are mischievous and food driven. They come to the homestead to steal food in the dead of winter, Bjúgnakrækir (Sausage-Swiper) and Skyrgámur (Skyr[6]-Gobbler), being obvious examples. Those who are not after food are utterly shameless, such as Gluggagægir (Window-Peeper) and Faldafeykir, who lifts the hems of women's skirts.

In 1932, Jóhannes úr Kötlum published *Jólin Koma: Kvæði Handa Börnum* (Christmas Is Coming: Verses for Children) (2012), a small book of poems based on old tales and beliefs about the Yule creatures. Reprinted multiple times, it has become a Christmas classic in Iceland. We do not know when Icelandic children began to get gifts in their shoes or why the thieving Jólasveinar took it upon themselves to deliver them. Stekkjasatur's memory is a bit vague on specific dates, but he finds it likely that it was sometime after the family heard about the Danish Yule Nissar. The Nissar are nice little creatures who do not steal. They are given rice pudding on Christmas, and in return they bestow gifts on children. Apparently the Danish Nissar made an impact in the Icelandic mountains, and after much discussion the Lads started to change their behavior to nicer and more modern ways. This seems to have been the beginning of global influences on our band of Lads and their adaptation to new ideas in the society that would become the structured twenty-first-century Christmas tradition (Björnsson 2006, 76–88).

Just as the Lads were inspired by the Danish Nissar, they have been globally affected by the fashion of St. Nicholas, as well as the Coca-Cola Santa and other red-coat-wearing Christmas influencers. Traditionally the Lads wear Icelandic wool clothing, although they do feel just as comfortable in the well-known red and white Santa costume, apart from using rubber boots and woolly socks rather than fancy leather boots.[7] As active participants in our society, they have gradually been adapting to the worldview and technology of the twenty-first century. The Lads attend scheduled events of the present day, such as Christmas balls and smaller gatherings in schools and kindergartens, and show up at Christmas markets, bringing tangerines and candy for children of all ages. They also attend television programs and are featured in news outlets and social media. In December 2021, the Icelandic Meteorological Office reported specific weather forecasts on its Facebook page, giving each Lad his own forecast for the night he was to appear (Veðurstofa Íslands 2021).

And then there is the peculiar case of the folklorist who became a referee on national radio. Sometime in the 1960s, some children, but not all, were getting gifts in December. Some got something every day, while others got perhaps only one, and some of the gifts were big and expensive while others were minimal. This created a big problem in the society as the children felt the effect of their families' class and economic status, and this disparity was heatedly debated on the national radio. The Icelandic National Broadcasting Service, a cultural institution with responsibilities to society, felt the need to call in an expert to settle the matter. They contacted Björnsson, asking him to go on air to clarify this conundrum about the Jólasveinar and the shoe gifts. A young folklorist at the time, somewhat bewildered, he went on air saying that he had it on good authority from the Jólasveinar themselves that they agreed this matter was getting out of hand. On behalf of the Yule family, he declared that the Thirteen Lads from the poem by Kötlum would come, one a night, on the last days before Christmas, and place a small gift or treat in children's shoes.[8] The aftermath was twofold: Björnsson became for decades thereafter the authority on all things old, Icelandic, and Yule, and the tradition of the Thirteen placing gifts in children's shoes was solidified. However, despite the power of the folklorist to quantify the gifts to thirteen, the debate about the size and cost of shoe gifts is repeated every few years, with rumors of affluent children getting iPhones or video games in their shoes, reflecting the general discussion of different social statuses in society.

To this day the Jólasveinar are as food oriented as they always were, but in times of plenty, they do not need to steal food, as we gladly share our treats with them. Some children leave, for example, a pot of skyr in the window for Skyrgámur, a piece of cured meat for Ketkrókur, or a hot dog for Bjúgnakrækir. The brothers can still be a bit naughty, but they have stopped the horrifying shenanigans that made them infamous in the nineteenth century. Their main goal now is to bring gifts and keep young minds occupied in the rising excitement for Christmas. And despite the globalism of the current age, the lore has its regional specifics. Children who live in Reykjavík know that the Yule family lives in the mountain Esja, which is seen from all the municipalities in the area, while those who live on the other side of the country know just as well that the family resides in Dimmuborgir, a fantastical landscape of lava in the northern part of Iceland. According to Stekkjastaur, they also live in other mountains and landscapes in the vicinities of towns all around the country.

At the same time as the Lads participate in our personal lives in homes, schools, and social media, part of the modernization of their lifestyle is their connection to the commercial and capitalist spirit of the current holidays. The Lads can be found everywhere as Christmas approaches, including in pictures of them on packaging of everyday groceries like milk and seasonal produce such as Christmas beer. It is perhaps telling of today's society that the capitalist influence on the tradition is important in keeping it alive. The marketing and usages of the folklore do bring to light some of the old and forgotten Lads. A good example is Froðusleikir, or Foam-Licker, a Lad whose name likely originally referred to his taste for the foam of new milk but is today the name of an alcohol-free Christmas beer.

STARING AT STEKKJASTAUR

The lively and mixed-genre usage of the Yule family lore gives it the flexibility to mirror the mindset of contemporary society. The lore constantly changes. New Lads come and go; some stick around while others disappear—for example, the so-called fourteenth Lad, Kortaklippir or Card-Clipper, has been around for many years now. Kortaklippir arrives in February to destroy the credit cards that were maxed out in December to pay for Christmas. However, more than food and capitalism reflect the lore; the family also mirrors the increasing awareness of human diversity in society, although these gift bringers are still all Caucasian old men, and some little hints point to them being heterosexual and cis as well. Stekkjastaur, who doesn't wish to out any of his brothers, is silent on the topic.

At the same time, although old Yule Lasses (Jónsdóttir 2021; Valgeirsson 2021) have been brought to the attention of society, and new Lasses have popped into existence to address the obvious gender imbalance in the family, there is a clear and present need to bring these Lasses further into the spotlight. People have also wondered if Hurðaskellir might have ADHD (attention deficit hyperactivity disorder) as he seems to have no control over his door slamming. The best (in the authors' humble opinion) example of the diversity mirror is how modern Icelanders are beginning to see Stekkjastaur and his different body as a representation of disability in the group of Lads. From the time he was portrayed as having stiff legs, his body was recognized as different, and he moved differently than his brothers. Today he is becoming contextualized with disabled people, presenting his body and embodiment in the light of diversity.

To see Stekkjastaur in this way, it is necessary to look, to *stare*, at his body and the lore around him. Being stared at is an everyday reality for those of us with different bodies. As disability scholar Rosemarie Garland-Thomson discusses, staring is a complex biological, social, and cultural phenomenon. It is often uncomfortable for both starer and staree. On the one hand, it is impolite to stare, and on the other hand being stared at is an invasion of privacy, and unwanted attention. However, staring also serves the purposes of information gathering; to build an understanding of what we find different, we must take a close look (Garland-Thomson 2009, 3–6, 47–49). Garland-Thomson discusses how photographs and images can be used as a safe space; the starer can look their fill without making the staree uncomfortable. This is a double-edged sword, however, as photographs of disabled people too often tell a demeaning narrative. But when disabled folks willingly create images specifically to tell a strong positive story, they truly can allow a starer to learn something new (79–83), with permission to look at their differences with an open and curious mind.

Garland-Thomson's discussion is solely based on the visual, but a safe staring space can also be created through written, spoken, or otherwise performed narration. At the beginning of this chapter, we created a safe staring space by putting ourselves forward and describing our bodies for the reader to be able to recognize our physical differences. We do this openly and willingly to lead readers into a space where they can stare not only at our bodies but also at the tradition in question and what it implies. We are thus doing what disability scholar Tanya Titchkosky calls reading the cultural material in another way and revealing cultural ideas about disability (2007, 3–6, 108–11). We now invite you to use that space and stare even closer at Stekkjastaur.

It may come as a surprise that Stekkjastaur is rarely children's favorite Lad, even though he is the first to arrive every year. This might be because Icelanders have not used sheep milk for over a century and today's children do not know the taste of Stekkjastaur's favorite food. As has been discussed, most of the Lads are food driven and their names often represent, or refer to, their favorite. Stekkjastaur is no exception, as in the old days he used to go into the sheep huts for a sip of milk from the ewes. Admittedly he did have some trouble with this: ewes are in heat in the middle of December and do not have any milk to give, so accessibility to the warm drink is difficult. Moreover, sheep are built quite low to the ground, and the narrow and dark sheep huts do not accommodate his stiff, unbending legs.[9]

As a child Eva Þórdís had a connection to the strange pole-legged Lad, even if she did not understand why. She has no recollection of a conversation with grown-ups about the resemblance between her own body and Stekkjastaur's, but she remembers a feeling of a kind of obligatory connection to him. When she was asked who her favorite Lad was, she would say it was Stekkjastaur even though it was really Stúfur. Stekkjastaur does remember meeting a five-year-old girl who mirrored his own specific way of walking, and it is likely that the feeling Eva Þórdís remembers was established in that moment of cultural and physical mirroring of what a walk is supposed to look like. In the world of children's TV, movies, and literature, images of positive characters with different bodies are few and far between (Sigurjónsdóttir and Sigþórsdóttir 2013, 204–6). In fact, they are so rare that many of us, Eva Þórdís included, never experience seeing a body in popular culture that we can identify with. It is therefore no wonder that she did not understand the mirroring between her and Stekkjastaur. Today, Eva Þórdís wholeheartedly acknowledges Stekkjastaur as her favorite without any reservations, built on a strong bond of recognition, respect, and comradery in being physically different from most others, and experiencing hurdles both in nature and society.

We have asked ourselves why it took so long for Eva Þórdís to realize that Stekkjastaur, a disabled counterpart in the public imagination and Yuletide folklore, had been with her all her life. Because the Yule family and the folklore around them are a vital part of Icelandic society, we Icelanders tend to take them for granted, not always recognizing what is right in front of us. In recent years newsletters and online posts intended for tourists and the English-speaking public have portrayed Stekkjastaur in a more impairmentesque light than native Icelanders are used to. For example, in 2014 the tourist-oriented *Reykjavík Grapevine* reported the following:

> **Sheep-Cote Clod Turns Down Össur Prosthetic**
>
> Stekkjastaur (Sheep-Cote Clod), the first of the 13 Icelandic Yule Lads, has turned down a generous offer from pioneering prosthetic company Össur to help him with his leg condition.
>
> For centuries Sheep-Cote Clod's daily life has been inhibited by a rare medical condition that causes his legs to be stiff as wood, making it hard for him to bend down or kneel.
>
> "Well it can be tough," said Sheep-Cote Clod. "Sneaking onto farms isn't what it used to be. With all the security measures and electric fences, it's hard work. Then once I finally reach the sheep, I barely have the energy to harass them and there's no chance of me bending down to suckle from their teats with my legs being what they are."
>
> The news comes as a blow to Össur as well. The company had already built a prototype for Sheep-Cote Clod to try on when he travelled down from the mountains this morning.
>
> "Yes it was a disappointment," a representative of Össur told the Grapevine. "Sheep-Cote Clod had expressed an interest in our work and we were excited to collaborate with him and help restore a more natural gait through our bionic technology. His rejection came as quite a surprise."
>
> When asked why he had rejected the prosthetic, Sheep-Cote Clod was less forth-coming, at first citing "troll reasons." Upon further questioning the Yule Lad conceded he couldn't work out how to use the device remote. (Árnadóttir 2014)

Two years later a blogger for the travel guide *Iceland 24* gave a very detailed description of Stekkjastaur's unbending knees: "He walks as though they were made of wood, and he has to use a long walking stick to be able to walk properly. Some folk art portrays him as having two wooden prosthetic limbs, but I go more for him just having long, straight legs" (Berglind 2016). In the example from *Reykjavík Grapevine*, the emphasis on his body and the context of modern, technologically advanced prosthetic braces catapult Stekkjastaur into the contemporary group of disabled people. It is even clearer since the international company Össur is known for developing high-tech prosthetics, from running blades for athletes to artificially intelligent knee joints and exoskeleton support braces, but it also makes prosthetic limbs domestically in Iceland. It seems that describing Stekkjastaur in another language, for guests getting to know the traditions around the Yule family, draws the native eye to Stekkjastaur's body and disability.

But Icelanders are also starting to see Stekkjastaur's disability. Recently the *Horses of Iceland* webpage posted a story about Stekkjastaur befriending a horse during his night of gift giving to get some rest and aid on his long walk. This experience turned out to be a bit more of an adventure than Stekkjastaur had anticipated, and after a wild ride he decided to keep to his stiff walking rather than risk physical injury on horseback (Horses of Iceland n.d.). Finally, a few years ago artist Egill Hjaltalín drew Stekkjastaur with modern running blades such as pro athletes use. According to Hjaltalín the idea for this image came as he was being consulted about knee braces by a friend who worked at Össur at the time. Talking to this friend and learning about some of the advancements within the company inspired Hjaltalín to draw Stekkjastaur thus (Hjaltalín, Facebook message to author, February 10, 2022).

What all these accounts have in common is that they are created by Icelanders who were raised in the traditions of the Yule family, and Stekkjastaur's physical difference is just now rising to the surface of their stories. At the same time, the creators find it difficult to define Stekkjastaur as disabled; he does not fit common, stereotypical understandings of disabled people as inadequate, lacking, dependent, and so on. Without realizing it, the people behind these narratives are, in fact, defying common understandings of disability as deficit and dependency by showing us that Stekkjastaur has always had an impairment, but we do not think he is any the less because of it.

Eva Þórdís began staring fixedly at her friend via the analytical lens of disability folklore, and in 2017 produced a poster that was a first attempt to tell the story of Stekkjastaur in a disability context (see figure 1.1). Stekkjastaur himself was not part of the process but became intrigued with the concept and the story Eva Þórdís brought forth, and with his interest came his participation. On the poster is a drawing by disabled artist Fannar Örn Karlsson of Stekkjastaur with wooden peglegs. He carries a burlap sack on his back holding a startled-looking sheep. Around the image are short statements: "Stekkjastaur was and is the first"; "Is representative of supernatural creatures and folk belief in DbD";[10] "Is a fighter for human rights;" "Was

FIGURE 1.1. The poster Eva Þórdís made in 2017, featuring a picture of Stekkjastaur drawn by artist Fannar Örn Karlsson. The image depicts Stekkjastaur walking with the use of prosthetics across a road, carrying a sheep in a sack around his shoulder. The poster includes Icelandic sayings discussing the portrayal of disability in folklore.

mischievous and horrid"; "Was alone in the group of Jólasveinar"; "Is one of many in the group of disabled people"; "Meets ableism"; "Is underestimated sometimes and overestimated in piles of snow";[11] "Deals with skin rubbed raw and pain"; "Is in constant contact with orthotists"; "Is neither a weakling nor is he remarkably efficient"; and "He loves sheep milk and pecorino cheese." Every phrase is a miniature narrative drawn from Stekkjastaur's history and contemporary imagery, showcasing his interests, body, and embodiment. The poster was given to colleagues, friends, and family in the form of a Christmas card. The orthotist who designs and makes Eva Þórdís's prosthetic, Guðmundur Magnússon, works for a company called Stoð (Support), and as a long-standing client she also brought them a copy of the poster, which was displayed in the staff's coffee room. Despite most of the recipients being known to Eva Þórdís, the response to the poster and its messages can be contextualized as staring.

The first part of staring occurs when something different catches our eye and we turn to look. After that come varying reactions, including that as soon as we realize that what has caught our eye is a person, social rules take hold and we become ashamed of our rudeness, look away, and get flustered (Garland-Thomson 2009, 71–76). Nothing on the poster altered the familiar representation of Stekkjastaur's body; it simply placed him in the context of prosthetics and embodied disability. For most of the poster viewers, being offered the opportunity to freely look at his body in this way was confrontational, almost like pointing a finger at a body and saying, "Look, he is different," a highly rude and intrusive action. The result is a flustered response of surprise, hesitant smiles, nervous chuckles, and mumbling, "Oh, well, yes, I suppose so!" No one claimed the representation was not plausible, but it was clear that for many it was uncomfortable to be confronted with Stekkjastaur's body in this light. As people realized that the poster was intended as a safe space to stare, they relaxed and, in the end, could not deny that part of his existence is an image and narration of disability. Eventually the uncomfortable emotion eased as the flustered mumble turned into recognition and exclamations of "Why did I not see that before!?" and they accepted the disability narrative of the poster as positive.

We continue to show the poster and talk to people whom we encounter about the disability narrative of Stekkjastaur, be they academics, students of folklore and disability studies, or disabled people or their children and parents. Among them are the previously mentioned Magnússon and other orthotists who work at Stoð. These are specialists who work with disabled people every day and are aware of the myriad ways disability is narrated and embodied. Before seeing the poster they had not seen Stekkjastaur in this light nor wondered who might be making his legs. If we ask them today, they either all take credit for Stekkjastaur's prosthetics or other walking aids, or claim "No comment" because they take their clients' confidentiality seriously.

Stekkjastaur appreciates all the orthotists and has an appointment on the afternoon of December 11 in preparation for his evening's activities and again on the morning of December 12 to fix and renew what has worn out during the long walk the previous night.[12] Not only do the orthotists like the disability narrative of Stekkjastaur, they find it obvious as soon as it has been pointed out and are astonished that they had not spotted it before. Those who work with disabled children plan to include Stekkjastaur in their prosthesis discussion with them from now on, especially in December. Stekkjastaur is happy to lend a leg in building a positive and empowered body image for Icelandic children, disabled or not.

THE REFLECTION

Much of disability related folklore is negative, harmful, and even violent as negative understanding hides under the cover of conservative tradition. Being a disabled folklorist, Eva Þórdís is in a significant position to engage with critical folklore and disability studies by using her insight to reveal disability in folklore, and actively proposing how such lore can be developed for positive social change. It is not always possible to have a research partner who is themself a part of folklore, but such a partnership is invaluable. By becoming the human and academic representative of the Yule family in the 1960s, Björnsson set a precedent for a close working relationship between folklorists and supernatural beings, although he never took his partnership from the public to the academic sphere. Incorporating important traits of academic work (courage and imagination), we have adjusted his example to the current academic and ethical standard of participation and inclusion.

By developing this partnership from the 1960s to the 2020s we are calling for and answering the invocation of "Nothing About Us Without Us" in all research, folkloristics included (e.g., Blank and Kitta 2017; Goldstein and Shuman 2016). Some might say that as Stekkjastaur is a supernatural being, our application of the slogan positions us in line with the age-old practice of dehumanizing disabled people. We reject such a statement, as Stekkjastaur is not, never has been, nor ever will be human, and we are not claiming that disabled people are Yule Lads—far from it. In our minds the status of disability reaches beyond the realm of the human body into the supernatural, human imagination, belief, and wonder. Denying Stekkjastaur's engagement with the slogan is to ignore his different body and silence the power he has in the representation of disability in the twenty-first century; it would mean exclusion based on his supernaturality at the cost of his impairment and disability. Including supernatural beings with differences and disabilities can only strengthen disabled people's claim for social justice and participation in society and culture.

Through the combined academic, social, and cultural power of the disabled folklorist and the disabled supernatural being we have purposefully focused on the positive narratives of the Yule family tradition. We tell the story of Stekkjastaur in a contemporary disability context with the intent to use the Icelandic Yuletide tradition as a platform for positive change in the way people understand and narrate disability, for as Gunnell says, "The stories people tell change things" (2018, 27). In *Feminist, Queer, Crip* disability activist and scholar Alison Kafer imagines a future where disability is seen as valuable and integral in society (2013, 3). By realizing that our lifelong comradery is one of shared experience of disability and narrating that partnership in a valuable way, we strive to manifest a little bit of Kafer's desirably disabled future in coming Yule times. We can tell such a story because the tradition is an integral part of our society; as Icelanders we partake in making sure that the belief is safe and alive, and as disabled Icelanders we live and breathe it. It is our embodied story to tell anew and to evoke discussion about social and cultural reality of disabled people, and supernatural beings, in our society.

In the everyday lives of Icelandic children in December, Stekkjastaur is as real and tangible as disabled people, and he is slowly becoming a recognizable mirror of diversity in Iceland. If people are open to different human beings in children's lives, they should be equally open to different supernatural beings. We believe that when we raise awareness about Stekkjastaur as a disabled Lad, children will develop a stronger connection to him because they may recognize his different body and disability better than his taste for sheep-milk products. The question remains if Stekkjastaur himself should be a disability activist. Our answer is no. It is important for him to represent and be what everyone wants him to be and as such, he cannot take a political stance. He will continue to be simply the funny oddball who loves sheep milk. Nevertheless, he will also lend a leg to human disability activists when needed. And if they want, he will gladly become a companion for disabled children, walking with them in their own way, highlighting the beauty of human diversity.

NOTES

1. In English he is often called Sheep-Cote Clod, which highlights his love of sheep but leaves out any reference to staurfætur or pole legs. The first mention of

Sheep-Cote Clod seems to have been in the *White Falcon*, a newsletter of the Keflavík US Naval Air Station, in 1982.

2. Using embodied experience of disabilities as analytical viewpoint in folkloristics is not common, but to name two: Amanda Leduc discusses fairy tales via her own embodied experience of disability in *Disfigured: On Fairy Tales, Disability, and Making Space* and by doing so brings attention to depiction, narration, and understanding of disability in fairy tales (2020). And Anand Prahlad uses his folkloric training to tell his story of embodied experience of Asperger's (Autism Spectrum Disorder) in *The Secret Life of a Black Aspie: A Memoir* (2017).

3. In Iceland Christmas starts on the evening of December 24 with a family meal, sitting around the Christmas tree, and opening presents.

4. Many examples given about the Lads and their family are common knowledge in Icelandic general discourse.

5. Stekkjastaur has never seen any parents skulking in windows when he is doing his rounds on the evening of December 11.

6. Skyr is a fresh cheese, eaten today in a similar fashion to yogurt.

7. A case of practicality over fashion when it comes to footwear suitable to wet Icelandic snow, which is quick to ruin beautiful leather boots.

8. Some years ago, Björnsson gave a lecture on Christmas traditions for the Icelandic folklore society. During the discussions after his presentation, he told this story with a gleam in his eye and in a hushed voice, so as not to break the sanctity of the belief; you never know when small ears are listening to the grown-ups.

9. He claims that he now recognizes the biological lack of milk from ewes in December, but in recent years and with increased imports of cheese he admits to sneaking into shops (much more accessible than sheep huts) and stealing some pecorino. This fact is, alas, not widely known beyond dedicated cheese lovers.

10. DbD, or Disability before Disability, was a research project that marked the beginning of Eva Þórdís's doctoral studies.

11. The words *sometimes* and *snow pile* rhyme in Icelandic.

12. During the process of writing, Stekkjastaur has realized that he might also benefit from a few sessions with a physiotherapist both before and after his round. In the last few years, Eva Þórdís has been a guest lecturer in the department of physiotherapy at the University of Iceland, where she introduces the students to cultural understandings of disability and has used the poster as an example. Stekkjastaur plans to seek out some of her former students, now practitioners, for some much-needed physio.

REFERENCES

Árnadóttir, Nanna. 2014. "Sheep-Cote Clod Turns Down Össur Prosthetic." *Reykjavík Grapevine*, December 12. https://grapevine.is/news/2014/12/12/sheep-cote-clod-turns-down-ossur-prosthetic/.
Árnason, Jón. 1954. *Íslenzkar þjóðsögur og ævintýri*. 6 vols. Edited by Árni Böðvarsson and Bjarni Vilhjámsson. Reykjavík: Þjóðsaga.
Atkinson, Dorothy, and Jan Walmsley. 2010. "History from the Inside: Towards an Inclusive History of Intellectual Disability." *Scandinavian Journal of Disability Research: SJDR* 12 (4): 273–86. https://doi.org/10.1080/15017410903581205.
Berglind. 2016. "Stekkjarstaur—Icelandic Yule Lads (December 12th)." *Iceland 24*, December 12, https://www.iceland24blog.com/stekkjarstaur-icelandic-yule-lads/.
Björnsson, Árni. 2006. *Saga Jólanna*. Ólafsfjörður: Tindur.
Blank, Trevor J., and Andrea Kitta. 2017. "Introduction: The Anatomy of Ethnography: Diagnosing Folkloristics and the Conceptualization of Disability." In *Diagnosing Folklore: Perspectives on Disability, Health, and Trauma*, edited by Trevor J. Blank and Andrea Kitta, 3–19. Jackson: University Press of Mississippi.
Creswell, John W. 2014. *Research Design: Qualitative, Quantitative and Mixed Methods Approaches*. 4th ed. Los Angeles: SAGE.
Ebenezersdóttir, Eva Þórdís. 2013. "Umskiptingar, börn og samfélög." In *Fötlun og menning: íslandssagan í öðru ljósi*, edited by Hanna Björg Sigurjónsdóttir, Ármann Jakobsson, and Kristín Björnsdóttir, 71–94. Reykjavík: Social Science Research Institute and Centre for Disability Studies.
Ebenezersdóttir, Eva Þórdís. 2014. "Haltrað í tveimur heimum: Skilningur á fötlun og skerðingum í íslenskum þjóðsögum fyrir 1900." MA thesis, University of Iceland. Hdl.handle.net/1946/17315.
Ebenezersdóttir, Eva Þórdís, and Sólveig Ólafsdóttir. 2021. "From a Life with a Different Body to a Recreated Folklore of Accentuated Difference: Sigríður Benediksdóttir versus Stutta-Sigga." In *Understanding Disability throughout History: Interdisciplinary Perspectives in Iceland from Settlement to 1936*, edited by Hanna Björg Sigurjónsdóttir and James G. Rice, 76–94. London: Routledge. https://doi.org/10.4324/9781003180180.
Garland-Thomson, Rosemarie. 2009. *Staring: How We Look*. New York: Oxford University Press.
Gencarella, Stephen Olbrys. 2011. "Folk Criticism and the Art of Critical Folklore Studies." *Journal of American Folklore* 124 (494): 251–71. https://doi.org/10.5406/jamerfolk.124.494.0251.
Goldstein, Diane E., and Amy Shuman, eds. 2016. *The Stigmatized Vernacular: Where Reflexivity Meets Untellability*. Bloomington: Indiana University Press.
Gunnell, Terry. 2001. "Grýla, Grýlur, 'Gröleks' and Skeklers: Medieval Disguise Traditions in the North Atlantic?" *Arv: Nordic Yearbook of Folklore* 57: 33–54.

Gunnell, Terry. 2018. "The Power in the Place: Icelandic Álagablettir Legends in a Comparative Context." In *Storied and Supernatural Places: Studies in Spatial and Social Dimensions of Folklore and Sagas*, edited by Ülo Valk and Daniel Sävborg, 27–41. Helsinki: Finnish Literature Society.

Gunnell, Terry. 2021. "Riders on the Storm; Riders at the Door: The Nordic Legends of the Wild Ride." Paper presented at "Encountering Emotions in Folk Narrative and Folklife," the 18th ISFNR Congress, Institute of Ethnology and Folklore Research, September 5, Zagreb.

Horses of Iceland. n.d. "Stekkjastaur fær far með hesti." *Horses of Iceland*. Accessed January 21, 2022. https://www.horsesoficeland.is/is/samfelag/sogur/stekkjastaur-faer-far-med-hesti/1074.

Icelandic Web of Science. 2020. "Eru Grýla, Leppalúði og jólakötturinn til í dag?" *Vísindavefeur*. Accessed January 21, 2022. https://www.visindavefur.is/svar.php?id=80740.

Jónasson, Jónas. 2010. *Íslenzkir þjóðhættir*. 4th ed. Reykjavík: Opna.

Jónsdóttir, Dagrún Ósk. 2021. "Jólasveinarnir eru ekki þrettán heldur um hundrað." Interview by Brynja Þorgeirsdóttir. *Kastljós*, RÚV [The Icelandic National Broadcasting Service]. December 30. https://www.ruv.is/frett/2021/12/30/jolasveinarnir-eru-ekki-threttan-heldur-um-hundrad.

Kafer, Alison. 2013. *Feminist, Queer, Crip*. Bloomington: Indiana University Press.

Kötlum, Jóhannes úr. (1932) 2012. *Jólin Koma: Kvæði Handa Börnum*. Reykjavík: Mál og menning.

Labrie, Vivian. 2018. "Activism: Folktales and Social Justice: When Marvelous Tales from the Oral Tradition Help Rethink and Stir the Present from the Margins." In *The Routledge Companion to Media and Fairy-Tale Cultures*, edited by Pauline Greenhill, Jill Terry Rudy, Naomi Hamer, and Lauren Bosc, 93–103. New York: Routledge. https://doi.org/10.4324/9781315670997.

Leduc, Amanda. 2020. *Disfigured: On Fairy Tales, Disability, and Making Space*. Toronto: Coach House Books.

McKee, Heidi A., and James E. Porter. 2012. "The Ethics of Archival Research." *College Composition and Communication* 64 (1): 59–81.

Mertens, Donna M. 2010. *Research and Evaluation in Education and Psychology: Integrating Diversity with Quantitative, Qualitative, and Mixed Methods*. 3rd ed. Los Angeles: SAGE.

Mertens, Donna M. 2017. "Transformative Research: Personal and Societal." *International Journal for Transformative Research* 4 (1): 18–24. https://doi.org/10.1515/ijtr-2017-0001.

Prahlad, Anand. 2017. *The Secret Life of a Black Aspie: A Memoir*. Fairbanks: University of Alaska Press.

Schechner, Richard. 2020. *Performance Studies: An Introduction*. 4th ed. Edited by Sarah Lucie. London: Routledge.

Sigurjónsdóttir, Hanna Björg, Ármann Jakobsson, and Kristín Björnsdóttir. 2013. "Inngangur: Rannsóknir á fötlun og menningu." In *Fötlun og menning: íslandssagan í öðru ljósi*, edited by Hanna Björg Sigurjónsdóttir, Ármann Jakobsson, and Kristín Björnsdóttir, 7–26. Reykjavík: Social Science Research Institute and Centre for Disability Studies.

Sigurjónsdóttir, Hanna Björg, and James G. Rice. 2021. "Introduction." In *Understanding Disability throughout History: Interdisciplinary Perspectives in Iceland from Settlement to 1936*, edited by Hanna Björg Sigurjónsdóttir and James Rice, 1–12. London: Routledge. https://doi.org/10.4324/9781003180180.

Sigurjónsdóttir, Hanna Björg, and Guðrún Sigþórsdóttir. 2013. "Spegill, spegill herm þú mér: Fötlun í barnabókmenntum." In *Fötlun og menning: íslandssagan í öðru ljósi*, edited by Hanna Björg Sigurjónsdóttir, Ármann Jakobsson, and Kristín Björnsdóttir, 189–210. Reykjavík: Social Science Research Institute and Centre for Disability Studies.

Titchkosky, Tanya. 2007. *Reading and Writing Disability Differently: The Textured Life of Embodiment*. Toronto: University of Toronto Press.

Traustadóttir, Rannveig. 2006. "Convention on the Rights of Persons with Disabilities." *Treaty Series* 2515: 3.

Traustadóttir, Rannveig. 2009. "Disability Studies, the Social Model and Legal Developments." In *The UN Convention on the Rights of Persons with Disabilities: European and Scandinavian Perspectives*, edited by Oddný Mjöll Arnardóttir and Gerard Quinn, 3–16. Boston: Martinus Nijhoff.

United Nations. 2003–2004. "'Nothing About Us, Without Us' International Day of Disabled Persons, 2004." Accessed January 21, 2022. https://www.un.org/esa/socdev/enable/iddp2004.htm.

Valgeirsson, Arnar Tómas. 2021. "Landshlutaskipting jólasveinanna og þróun þeirra í gegnum árin eru til umræðu í erindi Dagrúnar Óskar Jónsdóttur á Landnámssýningunni í dag." *Fréttablaðið*, December 21. https://www.frettabladid.is/lifid/lungnaskvettir-og-flotnos/.

van Gennep, Arnold. (1918) 1960. *The Rites of Passage*. Translated by Monika B. Vizedom and Gabrielle L. Caffee. Chicago: University of Chicago Press.

Veðurstofa Íslands [Icelandic Met Office]. 2021. "Í dag verða sagðar jólasveina veðurfréttir. Stekkjastaur mun leggja af stað um landið aðfaranótt 12. Desember." Facebook post. December 11. https://www.facebook.com/Vedurstofan/photos/a.431284043605831/4746267495440776/?type=3&eid=ARByJMWTdWpj3QFcjb29i4vTUhMShvx-ImyT3aEBo8VnoMk8aOwbUXKL5_odYRVqXJTtMclzHHJdF5jL.

White Falcon. 1982. "Yuletide Lads assist Santa." *White Falcon*, December 17. https://timarit.is/page/6060683.

2

Transformations of Wonder in the BBC Series *Detectorists*

MAREK OZIEWICZ

The story system called fantasy exists in a precarious relationship with its own history, with the evolving interpretations of that history, and with the larger cultural trends of the present that propel it into the future. In all its forms, fantasy is predicated on "imagined wonder," which J.R.R. Tolkien famously identified as "the primal desire at the heart of the Faërie" (1947, 7). Like everything else in our world, however, wonder—the feeling of "being moved by what is at least in some point or aspect above us, above our measure" (Tolkien 2000, 298)—is an experience that evolves. It takes new forms in response to new challenges faced by each generation. One of these recent challenges has been to understand how articulations of wonder position fantasy to engage with the urgencies of the Anthropocene: the most widely used, albeit contested, term for the current era of human-driven devastation of the Earth's life-support systems (Oziewicz 2022b, 2–3). This chapter opens with a provocation: that the fantasy we are used to—the fantasy whose story grammar and hero models are imbricated with dominance, separation, conquest, and anthropocentric focuses—may not be the fantasy we need going forward.

https://doi.org/10.7330/9781646425853.c002

I argue that the fantastic operates at once as a genre and an imagined order; that new forms of the fantastic arising within emerging imagined orders challenge traditional forms by exposing their limitations; and that all of these changes can be theorized as transformations of wonder geared to enable us to better respond to what is above and larger than us: specifically, the hyperobjectivity of climate change. *Hyperobjects* is a term introduced by Timothy Morton to describe entities so extremely complex and so "massively distributed in time and space relative to humans" that we are unable to wrap our minds around their totality or even specific aspects (2013, 1). Climate change, of course, is a Mortonian hyperobject par excellence. It is not just massive and dispersed relative to humans. It is also nonlocal—present everywhere and nowhere at once (54), interobjective—never merely itself but a mesh of various phenomena (83), and viscous—revealing itself to be more entangled with everything the more we learn about it (32). At the current moment of catastrophic climate change and biodiversity loss, transformations of wonder in literary and filmic fantasy may thus include the emergence of the fantastic wonder in narratives that appear to be eminently realistic. I make the case for this new "fantasy for the Anthropocene" (Oziewicz 2022a, 58) using the example of the BBC TV series *Detectorists* (three seasons, 2014–2017). I contend that the fantastic wonder is essential for reimagining our relationship with the biosphere which, in turn, is essential for the much-needed transition to an ecological civilization.

Critiques of traditional fantasy structures—especially its core components of the hero narrative and the subjugation of the nonhuman—can be traced back at least to Joseph W. Meeker's 1972 *The Comedy of Survival*. They have since received sustained attention in the work of feminist, postcolonial, Indigenous, and environmental scholars. By the late 1990s, critical reflection, including Ursula K. Le Guin's "The Carrier Bag Theory of Fiction" (1989), Riane Eisler's *The Chalice and the Blade* (1987), Brian Attebery's *Strategies of Fantasy* (1992), and Margery Hourihan's *Deconstructing the Hero* (1997), had demonstrated that the master story of Western civilization is one of exploitation and violence: "the killer story," in Le Guin's terms (1989, 168). More recent reflection explores the far-reaching social, racial, and cultural implications of this master story model (Attebery 2014; Thomas 2019; Oziewicz, Attebery, and Dědinová 2022). Similar narrative structures—ones that perpetuate and legitimize colonialist, gender, racial, and environmental violence—inform the dominant grammar of science fiction too (Rieder 2008, 2021; Higgins 2021). It is beyond the scope of this chapter to offer a comprehensive summary of this vast and growing body of scholarship. However, an emerging consensus suggests that much of fantasy's traditional imagery, language, logic, and narrative tropes—conceptual engines that continue to mold the way readers think and behave—is deeply entangled with ecocidal epistemologies at the heart of Western storytelling traditions (Oziewicz, Attebery, and Dědinová 2022).

How do we reverse this trajectory? How do we extricate fantastic wonder from the trap of what I have elsewhere called the "ecocidal unconscious": a refusal to acknowledge ourselves as agents of ecocide, psychologically repressed and narratively reinforced by our story systems whose deep grammar is anchored in ecocidal ontologies and infects them with anthropocentric myopia (Oziewicz 2022a, 59)? My suggestion is that it might be productive to allow fantasy to be something different than what it has been so far. One interesting development in this space is the emergence of new forms of the fantastic in narratives designed—for all means and purposes—as purely realistic.

Having recently coedited a collection, *Fantasy and Myth in the Anthropocene* (Oziewicz, Attebery, and Dědinová 2022), I want to start with two important distinctions from this project that have a direct bearing on the current argument. The first is the difference between fantasy as a literary genre and fantasy as an imagined order. As a literary genre—and largely in visual formats as well—fantasy refers to "a type of story that presents the magical, the supernatural, and the wondrous as a fact in the world of the narrative—whether or not it makes any ontological claims about the world of the reader's direct experience" (Oziewicz 2022b, 7). Genre fantasy operates through several distinct subgenres and in their combinations, with structural similarities among individual narratives indicating their level of kinship. Attebery's fuzzy set theory is perhaps the best descriptive framework for fantasy genres proposed to date (2014, 33–36).

Fantasy as an imagined order is a whole different thing. I have borrowed the term "imagined order"—constructed as the opposite of "natural order"—from Yuval Noah Harari, who uses it to refer to sets of collectively shared beliefs that enable humans to create societies and maintain social cohesion (2015, 111). Fantasy has long functioned as an imagined order. On this level, in fantasy scholarship, the notion of imagined order overlaps with Attebery's "mode"—"a stance, a position on the world as well as a means of portraying it" (2014, 1)—and with what John Clute calls "fantastika": a larger, culturally maintained system of stories through which we tell ourselves what is possible or impossible (2023). Fantasy as an imagined order manifests as "stories we tell ourselves about ourselves and the world, stories that might imagine the fulfillment of our desires or the realization of our fears, a kind of storytelling that pervades everyday life and profoundly shapes social interaction at every level" (Rieder 2022, 137). The point here is not just that fantasy genres exist in a dynamic relationship with imagined orders, shaping them while being shaped by them at the same time. It is also that the emergence of new imagined orders—say, visions of a post-carbon ecological civilization—at once reveal the structural limitations of the genre conventions (and forms of wonder) within *dominant* imagined orders and engender a search for new conventions (and forms of wonder) capable of driving progressive change within the *emerging* imagined orders.

The other distinction is that between the fantasy *of* the Anthropocene and fantasy *for* the Anthropocene (Oziewicz 2022a, 64). The former is an imagined order reflecting a belief that humans are masters of this planet. The latter is my shorthand term for the emergent forms of the fantastic that assert our nonmasterly kinship with all life, helping audiences creatively engage with the urgencies of the Anthropocene and perhaps even imagine hope. Fantasy of the Anthropocene is the opposite of hope. It is the analogue of what environmental sociologist Eileen Crist calls "the discourse of the Anthropocene": "a blend of interweaving and recurrent themes" that legitimize the expansion of human impacts and the market economy, the domestication of the planet, the uniqueness of humans, human separation from nature and other life forms, and human destiny to rule them all (2016, 15). As I have argued elsewhere, much of literary and filmic fantasy to date has played—often unintentionally—into this fantasy of the Anthropocene (Oziewicz 2022a, 60–61). In this sense, genre fantasy has been complicit in creating the imagined order called the fantasy of the Anthropocene.

To turn this around, we need to reimagine the way we use wonder and the fantastic. My suggestion is that fantasy for the Anthropocene will succeed only insofar as it pushes against the fantasy of the Anthropocene. The key challenge for humanity today is what the Intergovernmental Panel on Climate Change's February 2022 report calls "transformational adaptation"

(IPCC 2022, 42), otherwise known in common speech as *a rapid transition to an ecological civilization*. Extrapolating from this imperative, the key challenge for fantasy in the twenty-first century is to help us imagine fantastic alternatives to ecological collapse and other forms of devastation actively driven by the operations of an imagined order called the global market economy. Indeed, what can be more fantastic today than visions of biocentric, sustainable communities on a vibrant, living planet? What can be more radically fantastic than stories about ordinary people taking ordinary steps in their ordinary lives that help us dream about the possibility of an ecological civilization: a good life on this green Earth?

This is where *Detectorists* comes in. The show follows two amateur metal detectorists, Andy (Mackenzie Crook) and Lance (Toby Jones), as they search for Saxon treasures in their little pocket of Essex. Interacting with their detectorist clubmates and partners, coping with everyday challenges, and sparing no effort to defend their hobby against misperceptions, Andy and Lance are quirky but thoroughly ordinary characters. So too is their world. "The show plays off stereotypical Englishness," writes Phil Emmerson. "It shows the awkwardness of the 'typical' English man's psyche. It is full of dry English humour. And of course, it is set in idyllic English arable landscapes" (2020, 208). As Innes M. Keighren and Joanne Norcup put it, the series speaks "to the significance of the rural environment at a time of ecological crisis" (2020, 15), stressing "the relationship between landscape and forms of identity and belonging" (16). Likewise for James Delingpole, *Detectorists* celebrates "quintessentially English things—middle-aged male friendship; pub banter; blokeish hobbies; the sleepy, boring, slightly down-at-heel village; [and] folk music" (2017). Most commentary stresses the show's small-town realism and "self-mocking comic character" (Howell 2021, 7) as the key sources of its appeal. Based on the reviews, the show might initially appear to be as far removed from anything evoking wonder or fantasy as it possibly could be.

While the small-town realism appeal claim is correct, there is more to *Detectorists* than quirky realism, and it is the series' increasing engagement with wonder through fantasy tropes, concepts, and framings. With each subsequent season, the story evolves in a direction that requires more fantasy and makes fantasy more central to how the story works.

Specifically, the series increasingly relies on the fantastic as it moves away from purely anthropocentric concerns into a broader ecocentric framework, where human lives are recognized as strands in the larger historical-biological tapestry of life. It relies on the fantastic to communicate that understanding one's responsibility to the past, present, and future is intimately tied to an understanding of one's responsibility to the nonhuman world writ large. And it relies on the fantastic in showing how the two eccentric-going-ecocentric protagonists, as they roam across meadows and plowed fields, acquire practical ecoliteracy and learn to "hear" the land around them. The series increasingly reinforces their emerging insights with episodes of wonder, flow, fairy-tale justice, and reciprocal connection with, at once, nature and the distant historical past. This ecospheric embeddedness that emerges through ecoliteracy—what Keighren and Norcup identify as "the opportunity for new ways of seeing and knowing the world" (2020, 18)—becomes central to the series. While not fantasy in the traditional sense, *Detectorists* thus exemplifies the kind of wonder that lies at the heart of fantasy for the Anthropocene. The series showcases how essential the fantastic is for reimagining our relationship with the biosphere even in narratives that purport to be realistic. It highlights the potential of wonder and fantasy to not only bridge the past with the present, but to imagine ways toward a sustainable future.

There is very little wonder in season 1. In fact, all things fantastic are actively mocked in the character of Lance's ex-wife Maggie (Lucy Benjamin), who runs a New Age shop called—surprise, surprise—Crystal Enigma. Maggie is perhaps the least sympathetic character in the series. She abandoned Lance for Tony (Adam Riches), a Pizza Hut manager, but sticks around because she knows Lance has won the lottery and she wants his money. Maggie, pretending to love Lance, regularly uses him to run her errands and take care of her mother. She buys "spiritual stuff" by weight and flaunts her alleged spirituality, which is an appalling mixture of ignorance, self-importance, and self-indulgent New Age confusion. Lance seems to be aware of this, but he is still in love with her. He often stops by the shop to chat with Maggie, and he tries to impress her by performing a song he wrote for her, "New Age Girl," at the White Horse pub—she doesn't even show up. He also minds the store when Maggie needs to leave, inventing ridiculous explanations to ridiculous questions asked by a curiously ignorant customer. Fantasy, for Lance and the audience, is bollocks. Only close to the season's ending does Lance wake up to Maggie's motives. He refuses to loan her money and Maggie moves away.

At the same time, there are deeper fantasies at play even in season 1. These personal imagined orders include the fantasy of virgin land—a detectorists' dream of an unsearched land that comes true when Andy and Lance are given permission to detect on Larry Bishop's (David Sterne) farm. Another is the fantasy of winning Maggie back, for Lance; and for Andy the fantasy of personal validation—being admired by a newbie detectorist Sophie (Aimee-Ffion Edwards) or becoming president of the Danebury Metal Detecting Club (DMDC). Ruling them all are fantasies about finding treasure: especially the mythical ship-burial site of King Sexred of the East Saxons. Throughout season 1, Lance and Andy traverse the land looking for their own Sutton Hoo[1] and they seem to be the only ones who believe that the ship burial exists. In a bitter twist, they give up this belief in the last episode of season 1, though they are actually standing directly above the buried ship. After Lance declares the site empty, the camera sinks into the soil, showing the wonder of coins, bracelets, bones, and other artifacts of a royal burial. Lance and Andy then walk away, while the camera zooms up to show the ship's outline in the meadow. One message this closing scene communicates is that their fantasy was true. They just gave up on it too soon.

This narrative strategy of showing the audience part of the story hidden from the characters—what producer Adam Tandy has come to call "Treasurecam shots" (2020, 101)—is also used in seasons 2 and 3. Season 2 opens with a scene showing a Saxon monk burying a Bible and a golden aestel—a jeweled handle for a wooden pointer rod used for following words when reading a book—to protect the objects from drunken knight raiders. The hidden artifacts deteriorate over time in what the camera's eye suggests is a fast-forward to the present. When the camera rises from the ground, we see Andy and Lance detecting on a nearby meadow. This strategy creates an expectation that is sustained throughout the season: the first minute of each episode includes a shot of the aestel waiting to be discovered. Adding to this perfectly realistic preview, season 2 introduces philosophical questions about the nature of wonder and about what should be discovered, when, and by whom. This larger theme is developed partly through the character of Peter (Daniel Donskoy), a young German who asks the DMDC for help in locating the remnants of his grandfather's plane but eventually turns out to be a nighthawk—a treasure hunter—in search of Nazi gold. This theme is also developed in Lance's and Andy's personal lives, as each of them finds something else—and better—than they were looking for.

When most of the other characters get involved in Peter's search, Lance declares, "If it's not forgotten, I'm not interested" (season 2, episode 2). This notion of being interested in what is forgotten brings up a new dynamic: how forgotten things want to be found and how what is hidden wants to come to light. These questions play out in the character's lives. Lance is contacted by a daughter, Kate (Alexa Davies), who he knew existed but had never seen, and then he scares her away. Worried that he might have mucked the interaction up, Lance leaves Kate a message—"I want to be part of your life, even a tiny part, just don't disappear. I don't think I could stand that" (season 2, episode 6)—after which Kate returns. She is the treasure he was looking for without knowing it.

For Andy, this theme develops as life—in the form of his wife Becky (Rachael Stirling)—pushes him to apply for an archeology job in Botswana. Despite being terrified of Africa and feeling utterly incompetent, Andy is offered the job and then loses the offer letter. Looking for reasons not to go, he tells Lance: "It's a sign." "There's no such thing as signs," Lance replies. "There are," Andy retorts, "if you want them to be" (season 2, episode 5). This sentiment is confirmed in reverse when Becky finds the letter, confronts Andy, and announces that she is going to Africa anyway—with or without him. Andy feels trapped, like the entire universe is conspiring against him. Eventually, he sees this discovery as a sign—a sign working in reverse to what he thought it meant—that he has to go. He and Becky reconcile and their trip to Africa is a find of a lifetime that cements their relationship. This teleological framing of the characters' story arcs—as opposed to things happening at random—is a fantastic device the show employs to invoke wonder: the wonder of seeing that events happen because they are meant to lead to specific outcomes.

The fantasy element in season 2 is most pronounced, however, when Lance finds the aestel. By that point Andy has found a gold aureus coin of Septimius Severus in season 1—a coin he gives Becky when he proposes—and Lance is frustrated, thinking that he will never find any gold at all. Episodes of season 2 had already signaled that he is "worthy" of the find, when Lance increasingly pronounces detecting is a kind of animistic spiritual activity that puts one in touch with the land and history. Although Lance has no word for it, this form of knowing is recognized in Indigenous traditions as "extra-cognitive," "sacred," and centered around—as Australian Aboriginal author Tyson Yunkaporta explains—"the messages that land and Ancestors bring to us" (2020, 137). In the English context the message comes in the form of a premonition. In the very last minutes of the last episode, Lance and Sophie say good-bye to Andy, who is about to leave for Africa. Sophie draws a cross on the ground, saying that the three of them should meet here a year from now. At that point Lance hears horses neighing—the same horses the audience had seen wild knights riding a thousand years ago. Lance heeds the hunch, turns his detector on, and finds the aestel. The shock of the improbable find takes their breath away. The effect is amplified by the camera zooming up and out to a wide panoramic shot, as if blown away by the force of wonder unleashed by the discovery.

When Lance hears the horses across centuries and then unearths the aestel, the story takes a sharp fantastic turn. One gets a sense that—even if only for a moment—a portal to another time has been opened; Lance does not so much find the aestel as help rescue it from the robbers. This fantastic framing is amplified and reinforced in the show's Christmas special, which starts with Lance visiting the aestel in the British Museum. It is there because, by British law, all finds of potential historical importance must be reported, evaluated, and become state property if deemed to be part of the country's cultural heritage—with adequate financial compensation paid to the landowner (50 percent) and to the finder (50 percent). Lance has someone take his picture by the aestel display. When he shows it at the club, Sheila (Sophie Thompson) asks, "Who's that? Behind you?" As the characters look closer, they see a black-hooded monk standing behind the glass case with the aestel, looking at Lance. Before they have time to process this image, the projector bursts into flames and the slide is gone forever.

The club members move to the pub to discuss the event. Drawing on detectorist lore, they speculate whether Lance may be under the curse of the gold—a concept he at first vehemently denies. At the same time, Lance admits that ever since finding the aestel several months back he had not found anything else. "No, no," he clarifies in response to questions. "You don't understand. I have found *nothing* since then. Not a ring pull, not a buckle, not a scrap. I get phantom signals that disappear when I start to dig" (season 2, episode 7). Lance has also been experiencing other unexplained things: stumbling into nettles, tripping over roots or rocks, being bitten by a wasp in December. Worse yet, he has not been able to hear any sounds of nature: wind, birdsong, the buzz of insects. It is like the world had shut him off. And every time anyone mentions the reward money—the finder's check for £25,000 he is about to receive—bad things happen.

As the episode unfolds, Lance comes to grips with his initial perception that the aestel in the glass case "looks like a wild animal locked in a cage" (season 2, episode 7); that he is, indeed, under the curse of the gold. According to detectorist lore, the only way to break the curse of the gold is to return the treasure or die. Lance travels back to London, intending to break the aestel out. Fortunately, he stumbles into a conversation with a museum historian who understands Lance's sense of guilt—apparently common among detectorists whose finds end up in museums as state property. The historian suggests that Lance make a donation to the museum, that he "give something back" (season 2, episode 7). Lance latches onto this idea, but in his own way. We see him walk into a numismatics store in London to emerge with a pouch of newly minted gold coins. His reward for finding the aestel is £25,000 and the audience is made to understand that he spends it all on these new gold coins. The following day, Lance buries the gold in the field. Then, as he stands listening, suddenly the trees around him sway in a gale and a blackbird sings. Lance smiles. His gift has been accepted; the curse is lifted.

All of these fantastic strategies are then applied in season 3. In the opening episode, Andy finds a brass hawk whistle. When he cleans and blows it, the whistle's song appears to rewind time itself. Andy and Lance shiver in a sudden gust of wind. When they turn to walk back to the pub, the landscape begins to change. Again, as with the aestel, this preview is shown only to the audience, not to the characters. Trees grow smaller until a few seconds later there is a Roman-era adolescent girl with the whistle, standing in the same meadow with the burial of a family member happening behind her. The camera shows a burial urn with gold coins and other offerings being placed in the ground, a priest reciting prayers, and the family standing in a circle. The scene then quickly winds forward through the ages, showing an eighteenth-century couple walking past the meadow, then a mid-twentieth-century farmer plowing the field with a tractor, gold coins spilling out from the furrows.

Most important, the time-rewind shot introduces magpies—across centuries—hopping about the place where coins pop up from the ground. All this is shown against a haunting chant of a traditional nursery rhyme about magpies: "One for sorrow, two for joy, three for a girl, four for a boy, five for silver, six for gold, seven for a secret ne'er to be told" (season 3, episode 1). The magpies had watched the Roman burial and in season 3 they are now watching Lance and Andy. Even as the story sets magpies up as guardians of secrets, additional suspense is created when the characters learn that the farm has been sold. It will be converted into a solar farm within six weeks. "I always thought there was something good there, something significant," Lance sighs. "I thought this was the year we find it" (season 3, episode 1).

When in episode 2 Andy finds shards of a cremation urn, this intuition is confirmed. There *was* a Roman burial here. In episode 3 Lance finds a gold coin but before he can take a picture of it in situ, a magpie swoops down and snatches it away. Lance is devastated. He begins to suspect that the magpies have been watching this place for centuries because they know there is more gold here. He also figures that the magpies are hoarding the gold in one place. Indeed, in the last scene of episode 4 the camera zooms up for a treasure shot, showing a massive nest full of gold in the oak under which Andy and Lance are camping. The question the series now raises is whether they will prove worthy of finding the treasure.

This theme of being worthy of the gift of a find was introduced in season 2 and is now explored not just in Andy and Lance's main story line but in three parallel subplots. In one, Maggie seeks the treasure by sneaking into Lance's apartment to find his money, but her cheating is exposed and Kate throws her out. In another, Lance seeks the treasure of a relationship with Toni (Rebecca Callard), and he proves his commitment after he admits to the small, cowardly lies he had told in the process. Finally, Andy seeks the treasure of having a home for his family, which miraculously happens after he stands up for other beings' homes too: there are episodes in which he gives a home to a rescued hedgehog and saves the home spot of the oak he and Lance had sat under all these years.

The oak story, developed in episodes 5 and 6, starts when Lance and Andy learn that all trees on Church Farm will be removed to make place for solar panels. They are sad to hear this, but particularly upset at the thought that their favorite oak will be cut down. "We should probably save it," Andy remarks. As they contemplate available options, Andy and Lance agree that traditional forms of protest, like chaining themselves to a tree, are embarrassing and impractical. Until, that is, Andy comes up with the idea of installing a bat box to make the tree untouchable. Apparently trees where bats roost are of special interest and under special environmental protection. When they return to the meadow, however, the tree is already sealed off with tape and marked for removal.

It is at this moment that Andy breaks the law: in a comic heroic act of ecotage, he sneaks under the tape, climbs the tree, and installs the bat box anyway. Again, he is less than three feet from the gold-filled nest, watched by magpies. As the two walk back, Lance rejoices, "Feels good, being an activist, right?" "We're like ninjas," Andy exults, "environmental ninjas. But when do the bats move in?" (season 3, episode 5). They had not considered that question at all. When Lance calls a bat action helpline they find, to their horror, that the volunteers who are able to assist them are their detectorist competitors, Paul (Paul Casar) and Phil (Simon Farnaby). The pair are authorized by the Bat Action Trust to post preservation orders on any tree. In return, however, Paul and Phil demand access to the field that Lance and Andy had guarded so closely these past five years.

This is probably the greatest sacrifice Lance and Andy make in the series. In the last episode they open up their field to a detectorist rally with Paul and Phil, all members of the DMDC, and guests. Yet the day brings no finds. The rally closes and the group heads out to a pub. Lance and Andy stay behind to contemplate their dashed hopes. "I don't know why we do it," Andy says, resigned. "I do," Lance replies. "Time travel" (season 3, episode 6). He goes on to explain that "metal detecting is the closest you get to time travel" and that their hobby differs from archeology in that they "unearth the scattered memories, mine for stories, and fill in the personality. Detectorists. We're time travelers" (season 3, episode 6). This reflection loops back to the larger theme of one's relationship to time—the past and the future—that had been central throughout the series and revolves around the core concepts of embeddedness and stewardship. As they start walking toward the car, the oak, as if nodding in agreement with these sentiments, sways in the wind. Gold coins start rolling down its trunk. The gift is given. Lance and Andy approach in wonder. As they realize what is happening, the camera zooms up and out to a wide panoramic shot of the beautiful living Earth. This too is a gift. Everything is a gift.

The way that wonder in season 3 is projected into the world of nature is the culmination of a transition from the primarily anthropocentric concerns of season 1 to the larger ecocentric framework dominating seasons 2 and 3. In this framework "being able to see through time depends upon understanding the language in which the landscape's story is written" (Keighren 2020, 33). Human lives are important not in themselves but only as part of a larger historical and biological tapestry of life that works through circles of reciprocity: giving and taking, taking and returning, finding and losing, and most of all: giving back. This ecocentric gift economy plays out particularly intensely in season 3 when Lance's curse is lifted after he returns gold to the Earth.

Throughout the series we see Andy saving little animals and living beings. In season 1, for example, he picks up a frog from a grass patch in the middle of the A414 highway. In season 3 we even see him saving weeds on the shoulder of a road when he sprays them with water instead of a weed killer. Most important for the plot, in season 3 Andy saves a hedgehog and the oak—both of which events, in a spectacular display of wonder, prompt nature to literally return the gifts. The hedgehog shows Andy the cottage that he and his family will make their home. As he picks up the hedgehog on the highway and takes it away, Andy walks into a clump of trees that surround the ruined Tatterdown Cottage, which is soon going up for auction. Andy releases the hedgehog and looks around. He is then asked by one of the workers to help carry boards inside—a way for him to be introduced to the place. While it may be hard to frame the cottage as hedgehog's gift, without the animal Andy would never have found the property in the first place. Then, at the end of season 3, the oak showers Andy with gold at the time when he needs it most: Andy and Becky have just bought the cottage with borrowed money.

None of these events are fantastic in themselves. When put together, though, they communicate serendipity, purpose, even intention that is a source of wonder. Improbable coincidences happening to the right person at the right time are the language of enchantment at the heart of the fantastic. They require reciprocity and a relationship, including that with the nonhuman world central to an ecocentric worldview. In the words of Patrick Curry, enchantment is an experience of wonder that emerges when we enter, even for a moment, into a relationship with another and recognize that other being as a person. "Whether the other party is technically human or not, or even alive or not, is unimportant" (2019, 14); what matters is the sense of deep relationality with the other, accompanied by "fearless receptivity" in which we recognize the constitutive power of this relationship (16).

In *Detectorists*, this relationship is with the land writ large, a collective Gaian entity. The Gaia concept was proposed by James Lovelock in 1972 and has since become a shorthand term for the living Earth framework, which sees the planet as "the superorganism composed of all life tightly coupled with air, the oceans, and the surface rocks" (2000, xii). The many close-up shots of insects, flowers, birds, trees, and living landscapes that pepper this series are not gratuitous interludes between human-centered scenes. They are conversations of their own kind, grounding the human characters in the land they walk on, but also showing humans as part of a larger exchange happening among everything that lives or lived in the past. The close-ups and panoramic shots communicate that there is always more to life, if only we care to notice; that the human is not a measure of all things. Lance and Andy, who appear huge and far more important than the ladybirds and beetles they walk past in one shot, are dwarfed to specks in another shot that shows a bird's-eye view of a local landscape of which humans are but a tiny part of a larger web of life.

There is a large ecocritical tradition—including, most notably, Morton's *Hyperobjects* (2013), Timothy Clark's *Ecocriticism on the Edge* (2015), and Morton's *Dark Ecology* (2016)—that sees the problem of scale as a fundamental challenge for ecological thinking. The argument is that the human mind is unable to grasp scales that are much smaller and much vaster than the narrow human range: a species-related myopia that renders most climate issues and environmental impacts at once imperceptible and/or insurmountable. *Detectorists* navigates this challenge by showing how different scales exist in one place at the same time—including temporal scales—and how things big and small, human and nonhuman, past and present interact at the nexus of wonder and meaning in ways that are almost impossible to describe as reality yet equally impossible to dismiss as fantasy. Instead, in *Detectorists* as in life, things are both at once. For instance, the many scenes set under the oak—probably the most frequent site of Lance and Andy's conversations—emerge, from the perspective of season 3, as conversations in which the oak has always been a third partner: listening, accepting, and welcoming. Although the characters never explicitly say so, it is this personal relationship with the oak that spurs Andy to save it in season 3—and be saved in return as well.

This connection with and responsibility to the nonhuman world that Andy and Lance develop is probably best described by the term *ecoliteracy*:

an embodied understanding of one's being part of the larger living world even as we appear to be agentially separate from it. Isla Forsyth describes this silent learning as representing "a continual and gentle confrontation with transience and impermanence" (2020, 54). While this is true, in my reflection on this show the endless hours Andy and Lance spend outside—listening to the land through their detectors but also developing a sense of openness to the many and unpredictable voices of nature—emerge as a quintessential example of what environmental educator David Sobel calls "place-based education": the process of actively thinking about the Earth through "hands-on, real-world learning experiences" (2013, 11) that transform Lance and Andy into endemic species within their environments. Ecoliteracy is an antidote to the logic of separation and domination, requiring instead a focus on connection, community, and interdependence—with both human and nonhuman communities.

Does place-based education and ecoliteracy make Andy and Lance into climate or environmental activists? I do not think so. What we are shown instead is a sort of local action *with* (not *for*) the environment by people who have become endemic species, rather than acting as a force external/superior to nature. Theirs is a form of action that navigates past the label of activism, a label uncomfortable for many people, including Andy and Lance, yet achieves tangible results. While this message is merely implied, I feel it has powerful resonance to the questions we are facing at a time when all of us are complicit in the systemic demolition of the planet. Ecophilosopher Joanna Macy, describing the "Great Turning"—her term for a cognitive and spiritual shift from the industrial growth society to a life-sustaining civilization based on embracing "our interdependence, . . . mutual belonging, . . . [and] recognition of our essential non-separateness from the world" (2021, 188)—suggests that this work has three dimensions: holding actions, structural change, and shift in consciousness.

Holding actions, or slowing down the destruction through blockades, boycotts, and civil disobedience, is what most people associate with activism. This work can be exhausting, and Lance and Andy feel awkward and uncomfortable at the very thought of engaging in it. Structural change, which includes creating ecovillages, cooperatives, and other forms of alternative structures and systems, is a more exciting form of activism but requires more social skills and larger community coordination, for which neither Andy nor

Lance feel the calling. The third dimension, shift in consciousness, happens at once on individual and collective levels. It is open to everyone, "awakening perceptions and values" that show us "the beauty and power that can be ours as conscious, responsible members of the living body of Earth" (Macy 2021, 195). And while the philosopher Lance often discounts ideas he calls "mystic," it is on this level that the characters grow most throughout the series. As they become more rooted in the land, Andy, Lance, and other detectorists in the show come to exemplify a connection to nature and a form of ecoliteracy in which the object and the subject become part of a larger organic and quotidian whole. Particularly in season 3, their actions exemplify positive change toward Earth connectedness that is local and executed in everyone's own capacities as part of what they already do. This practical ecoliteracy, and the very possibility of it in ordinary circumstances, is one of the wonders that the series offers.

In 2020, a reviewer called "theknownames" posted the following on the IMDb site: "I am so drawn to this [series]; the colors, the lighting, the artistry, complexity, even the music. How does a sci-fi, plot-twisted, mind-bending, action lover come to watch a show like this? And have it quickly become my go to show?" I have been considering the same question. *Detectorists* is the only show whose all three seasons I have watched three times in a row and within about a week. It was a very different experience from what I am used to in fantasy, yet it also felt like fantasy on so many levels. The wonder lens is one possible explanation, with magical wonder being, by the series' producer's admission, "more subtle and pervasive in the narrative than other plot mechanics" (Tandy 2020, 97).

Detectorists is not a work of fantasy. Yet, its appeal hinges on an evocation of fantastic wonder that is particularly needed today. That wonder, in the words of Curry, is "the Earthly origin and nature of enchantment" (2019, 26): the wonder communicating that the greatest treasure we're looking for is not gold but a connection to everything around us. This connection to the wondrous aliveness of the world is something that the globally dominant, largely white, market-oriented, human supremacist, settler-colonial and extractivist, growth-addicted, Euro- and North American–oriented culture—otherwise known as the global "we" drivers of the climate emergency—had taken for granted or failed to notice until the last ten years or so, when the world's aliveness is seriously threatened by the operations of our global ecocidal civilization. Writing about the series' central theme, Tandy says that *"Detectorists* is about two men searching for their hearts' desire," except that the golden treasures they are looking for are really "metaphors for their real searches for emotional happiness" (2020, 104). While this is correct, I want to make a more specific suggestion: *Detectorists'* larger claim to cultural importance resides in the series' performance of the ecocentric wonder that lies at the heart of fantasy for the Anthropocene. This wonder helps us articulate dreams of reintegration with the biosphere that are gentle, local, grounded, and understated to the point of almost being overlooked. We have never needed such narratives more than we do today.

NOTE

1. Sutton Hoo is the seventh-century Anglo-Saxon Great Ship burial site near the English town of Woodbridge, Suffolk. Excavated by an amateur archeologist in 1938, the site yielded a wealth of artifacts, from gold and garnet cloisonné jewelry to musical instruments and everyday objects. Sutton Hoo is considered the most important Anglo-Saxon archeological discovery ever made, now alongside the Staffordshire Hoard of Anglo-Saxon gold and silver that was unearthed by a metal detectorist in a farmer's field in 2009 (for more see National Trust UK 2022).

REFERENCES

Attebery, Brian. 1992. *Strategies of Fantasy*. Bloomington: Indiana University Press.
Attebery, Brian. 2014. *Stories about Stories: Fantasy and the Remaking of Myth*. New York: Oxford University Press.
Clark, Timothy. 2015. *Ecocriticism on the Edge: The Anthropocene as a Threshold Concept*. London: Bloomsbury Academic.
Clute, John. 2023. "Fantastika." In *The Encyclopedia of Science Fiction*. June 5. https://sf-encyclopedia.com/entry/fantastika.
Crist, Eileen. 2016. "On the Poverty of Our Nomenclature." In *Anthropocene or Capitalocene? Nature, History, and the Crisis of Capitalism*, edited by Jason Moore, 14–33. Oakland, CA: PM.
Curry, Patrick. 2019. *Enchantment: Wonder in Modern Life*. Edinburgh: Floris Books.
Delingpole, James. 2017. "Television: The Pleasures of *Pointless/Detectorists*." *Spectator*, November 25. https://www.proquest.com/docview/1967375881?accountid=14586&parentSessionId=SESXAw8GYdjS6o2UthLjSN6IA6vkMTHS2fMtFpe7Wbg%3D.

Detectorists: Complete Collection. 2018. Directed by Mackenzie Crook. United Kingdom: Acorn Media.

Eisler, Riane. 1987. *The Chalice and the Blade: Our History, Our Future*. San Francisco: Harper & Row.

Emmerson, Phil. 2020. "Review of *Landscapes of Detectorists*." *Cultural Geographies* 28 (1): 208–9.

Forsyth, Isla. 2020. "Hoarding the Everyday—The Disquieting Geographies of the *Detectorists*." In *Landscapes of Detectorists*, edited by Innes M. Keighren and Joanne Norcup, 42–55. Axminster, UK: Uniformbooks.

Harari, Yuval Noah. 2015. *Sapiens: A Brief History of Humankind*. New York: HarperCollins.

Higgins, David M. 2021. *Reverse Colonization: Science Fiction, Imperial Fantasy, and Alt-Victimhood*. Iowa City: University of Iowa Press.

Hourihan, Margery. 1997. *Deconstructing the Hero: Literary Theory and Children's Literature*. London: Routledge.

Howell, Philip. 2021. "Review of *Landscapes of Detectorists*." *AAG Review of Books* 9 (3): 7–8. doi:10.1080/2325548X.2021.1921444.

IPCC. 2022. *Sixth Assessment Report: "Impacts, Adaptation and Vulnerability."* Accessed January 4, 2023. https://www.ipcc.ch/report/ar6/wg2/.

Keighren, Innes M. 2020. "'When I look at this landscape, I can read it': Practices of Landscape Interpretation in *Detectorists*." In *Landscapes of Detectorists*, edited by Innes M. Keighren and Joanne Norcup, 24–38. Axminster, UK: Uniformbooks.

Keighren, Innes M., and Joanne Norcup. 2020. "Introduction." In *Landscapes of Detectorists*, edited by Innes M. Keighren and Joanne Norcup, 14–21. Axminster, UK: Uniformbooks.

Le Guin, Ursula K. 1989. *Dancing at the Edge of the World*. New York: Grove.

Lovelock, James. (1972) 2000. *Gaia: A New Look at Life on Earth*. Rev. ed. New York: Oxford University Press.

Macy, Joanna. (1991) 2021. *World as Lover, World as Self: Courage for Global Justice and Planetary Awakening*. Edited by Stephanie Kaza. Berkeley, CA: Parallax.

Meeker, Joseph W. (1972) 1974. *The Comedy of Survival: Studies in Literary Ecology*. New York: Charles Scribner's Sons.

Morton, Timothy. 2013. *Hyperobjects: Philosophy and Ecology After the End of the World*. Minneapolis: University of Minnesota Press.

Morton, Timothy. 2016. *Dark Ecology: For the Logic of Future Coexistence*. New York: Columbia University Press.

National Trust UK. 2022. *Sutton Hoo*. Accessed January 4, 2023. https://www.nationaltrust.org.uk/sutton-hoo.

Oziewicz, Marek. 2022a. "Fantasy for the Anthropocene: On the Ecocidal Unconscious, Planetarianism, and Imagination of Biocentric Futures." In *Fantasy and Myth in the Anthropocene: Imagining Futures and Dreaming Hope in Literature and*

Media, edited by Marek Oziewicz, Brian Attebery, and Tereza Dědinová, 58–69. London: Bloomsbury Academic.

Oziewicz, Marek. 2022b. "Introduction: The Choice We Have in the Stories We Tell." In *Fantasy and Myth in the Anthropocene: Imagining Futures and Dreaming Hope in Literature and Media*, edited by Marek Oziewicz, Brian Attebery, and Tereza Dědinová, 1–11. London: Bloomsbury Academic.

Oziewicz, Marek, Brian Attebery, and Tereza Dědinová, eds. 2022. *Fantasy and Myth in the Anthropocene: Imagining Futures and Dreaming Hope in Literature and Media*. London: Bloomsbury Academic.

Rieder, John. 2008. *Colonialism and the Emergence of Science Fiction*. Middletown, CT: Wesleyan University Press.

Rieder, John. 2021. *Speculative Epistemologies: An Eccentric Account of SF from the 1960s to the Present*. Liverpool: Liverpool University Press.

Rieder, John. 2022. "Kim Stanley Robinson's Case for Hope in New York 2140." In *Fantasy and Myth in the Anthropocene: Imagining Futures and Dreaming Hope in Literature and Media*, edited by Marek Oziewicz, Brian Attebery, and Tereza Dědinová, 136–47. London: Bloomsbury Academic.

Sobel, David. 2013. *Place-Based Education: Connecting Classrooms and Communities*. Great Barrington CT: Orion Society.

Tandy, Adam. 2020. "Afterword." In *Landscapes of Detectorists*, edited by Innes M. Keighren and Joanne Norcup, 95–105. Axminster, UK: Uniformbooks.

theknownames. 2020. "Gentle Entertainment?" *IMDb*, 22 July. https://www.imdb.com/title/tt4082744/reviews/?ref_=tt_ql_urv.

Thomas, Ebony Elizabeth. 2019. *The Dark Fantastic: Race and the Imagination from "Harry Potter" to "The Hunger Games."* New York: NYU Press.

Tolkien, J.R.R. 1947. "On Fairy Stories." *Cool Calvary Files*. Accessed October 6, 2023. https://coolcalvary.files.wordpress.com/2018/10/on-fairy-stories1.pdf.

Tolkien, J.R.R. (1981) 2000. "[Letter] To Walter Allen, *New Statesman*." In *The Letters of J.R.R. Tolkien*, edited by Humphrey Carpenter, with the assistance of Christopher Tolkien, 296–99. New York: Houghton Mifflin.

Yunkaporta, Tyson. 2020. *Sand Talk: How Indigenous Thinking Can Save the World*. New York: HarperOne.

3

The Problem with Justice

VERONICA SCHANOES

Fairy tales contain rough justice, everybody knows that: Cinderella's stepsisters slice off their toes, cut off their heels, and have their eyes gouged out by pigeons; Snow White's stepmother dances to her death in red-hot iron shoes; Perrault's Little Red Riding Hood is gobbled up for her misstep.

Fairy tales contain no justice, fairy-tale experts know that: Donkeyskin's incestuous father recovers from his "madness" and attends his daughter's wedding; the thirteenth fairy leaves Sleeping Beauty's christening unharmed; Hansel and Gretel's father lives a life of luxury with the children he abandoned. Fathers are forgotten and unpunished even if they are not forgiven in tales ranging from "The Armless Maiden" (ATU 706) to "Rumpelstiltskin" (ATU 500).

In S. J. Rozan's novel *Winter and Night*, her narrator, a world-weary private eye, comments, "That's the problem with justice. There's no such thing" (2002, 388). As the above examples attest, this turns out to be true even, or perhaps especially, in fairy tales.

In "The Jew in the Thornbush" (ATU 592), a stouthearted young peasant is granted three magical wishes and uses them to torment and eventually lynch a passing Jew. In "The Good Bargain" (ATU 1642), a conniving Jew tries to trick a good peasant out of some money and is flogged for his trouble. In "The Bright Sun Will Bring It to Light" (ATU 960), a tailor murders a Jewish pedlar and, years later, is hanged for it, but the pedlar stays dead. In "The Bronze Ring" (ATU 560), which opens the original edition of Andrew Lang's *The Blue Fairy Book* (1889), the antagonist of the fairy tale is a wicked Jewish sorcerer who ends up tied to the tail of a donkey loaded with nuts until his bones are broken into as many pieces as there are nuts.

As far as I know, there are no European gentile fairy tales that feature Jewish characters as heroes. A 1782 German literary variant of "Snow White" (ATU 709), "Richilde," written by Johann Karl August Musäus, involves a Jewish physician who initially aids the wicked queen in poisoning the Snow White character, but ends up betraying her in order to save Blanca. Interestingly, the final lines of the tale as translated in 1791 by William Thomas Beckford concern the physician:

> Godfrey of Ardenne and the beautiful Blanca lived as happy as Adam and Eve in Paradise; they amply rewarded Sambul the physician, who, contrary to the practice of his colleagues, refused to kill where he safely might. Moreover, his integrity was recorded in heaven for a blessing. His race flourishes still, after an hundred generations: one of his posterity, the Jew Samuel Sambul, stands exalted, like a cedar of the house of Israel, in the presence of his Majesty the Emperor of Morocco; and in the character of prime minister he lives to this day, in happiness and honour, bating [excepting] a few bastinadoes [beatings] on the soles of his feet. (Musäus 1791/2010, 89)

The final image this tale leaves us with is of a Jew being tortured. I cannot help but notice that aside, "contrary to the practice of his colleagues," and wonder whether his "colleagues" are meant to be understood as physicians, Jews, or the intersection of both. Knowing the European Christian image of Jews (see in particular the work of Joshua Trachtenberg 1943/1983), I cannot help but suppose that the colleagues who "kill where [they] safely might" are meant to be Jews, notwithstanding the positive depiction of Sambul himself.

These stories are part of a long cultural tradition of antisemitism in Europe, hundreds of murderous years culminating in the Holocaust in the mid-twentieth century. But they are, after all, only a few stories. What harm could they do?

I don't know the answer to that. I do know that the English and American children who grew up reading about the villainous Jew in "The Bronze Ring" and the torture and death of the Jew in "The Jew in the Thornbush" and, to pick another children's book, the portrayal of the Jewish moneylender in E. Nesbit's *The Story of the Treasure Seekers* (1899/2013), became adults in countries that refused entrance to Jews trying desperately to flee the Nazis in the years leading up to World War II, who accepted Jewish children on the kindertransport, but not their parents, dooming them. How much responsibility does any one cultural text bear for those actions? Probably very little. But cumulatively, when the cultural tradition is taken as a whole, quite a lot. And fairy tales have been complicit.

In the contemporary United States, when Jews encounter fairy tales that actively partake of antisemitic discourse, it does personal harm, of course. Those of us who love the European fairy-tale tradition experience a betrayal.

What would justice look like for Jews in the European fairy-tale tradition? Could there be any such thing? Who could provide it? And in the end, would it matter?

If justice means undoing harm, it truly is impossible, and there is no such thing. Nothing restores lives lost and families destroyed. If justice means making unfair things fair, it again is impossible and there is no such thing. What would "fair" look like in this case? The construction of a dominant Jewish society that vilifies gentiles in its fairy tales? Turnabout may be fair play, but here it is impossible, and I don't think it would be desirable either.

Is justice acknowledging the harm done? But who would be doing the acknowledging?

To begin with, I would suggest that we as scholars and aficionados of fairy tales need to acknowledge the harm our beloved tale traditions have been complicit in. In his casebook on the blood libel, Alan Dundes writes: "If one were to poll most folklorists as to whether or not folklore was on the whole a positive force in human culture, I suspect there would be considerable consensus that indeed it was. . . . Yet it is important to keep in mind that there is some folklore which is highly pernicious and even life-threatening. . . . [I]t is my contention that one can make a convincing case for the label 'evil folklore' for selected individual items of tradition" (1991, 336–37).

I agree with Dundes: most of us who study folklore and fairy tales do so because we love them; life is too short, after all, and the opportunities and pay in folkloristics too meager to warrant studying them if we do not love them. And out of love, we owe the field our honesty about the role folklore and fairy tales have played in propping up pernicious and deadly ideologies.

But we are a small community. And our reach, while in some ways greater than that of other scholars due to the popular appeal of fairy tales, is still limited.

Perhaps that's why I wrote "Among the Thorns" and "Burning Girls." The first story is a sequel to "The Jew in the Thornbush," and the second is a retelling of "Rumpelstiltskin" set among Jewish immigrants to New York City at the turn of the twentieth century (Schanoes 2021). (While "Rumpelstiltskin" does not, in my research, appear to encode antisemitism in its own historical context, it has been read as an antisemitic story in the present day by readers as diverse as Jane Yolen, who wrote the story "Granny Rumple" as a response [1994], and Naomi Novik, author of *Spinning Silver* [2019], on the one hand, and white supremacists posting to Stormfront, a well-known neo-Nazi website, on the other.)

In "What Can We Do About Fagin? The Jew-Villain in Western Tradition," Leslie A. Fiedler concludes with a call to counter antisemitic myths by "build[ing] rival myths of our meaning for the Western world, other images of the Jew to dispossess the ancient images of terror" (1949). Is that justice? I do not conceive of my stories as attempts to "dispossess" antisemitic stereotypes; I know too well how revision works to believe that. I argued in my first book (Schanoes 2014), with respect to feminist rewritings of fairy tales, that revision not only reemphasizes the earlier tale from which it is born, it actually depends on it to fully develop its meaning. By writing and publishing "Among the Thorns," was I not perpetuating and reinscribing "The Jew in the Thornbush" into the public consciousness, or at least that part of it belonging to readers of my work?

Well, perhaps that's part of justice as well. Whom does it benefit if a harm is forgotten? That, after all, is what happened to "The Bronze Ring." Sometime between 1937 and 1943 (I have been unable to pinpoint the year with any greater specificity), Longman, the original publisher of *The Blue Fairy Book*, decided to replace the word *Jew* in "The Bronze Ring" with the words *man* and *sorcerer* (see Lang 1935, 1943). They didn't alter the full-page antisemitic illustration of the wicked sorcerer, with his dark skin, full lips, and large nose, but changing the words seems to have done the trick. Even the Dover editions that claim not a word has been altered from the original 1889 text reproduce the redaction. Whom did that change benefit?

I suppose it benefited me, as it allowed me to grow up loving Lang's colored fairy books, unaware that he chose for the opening story of what was mainly a collection of classic European tales (it was not until later books that he expanded his sources) an obscure tale whose fairy-tale villain was neither a witch nor an ogre, but a Jew. But what about that illustration? With the antisemitism tacit instead of clearly labeled, it becomes all the easier for stereotyped Jewish features to become associated with wickedness without the reader even noticing. And the change obscures our understanding of Lang's project by whitewashing his editorial decisions. It benefits the perpetrators and supporters of the harm, not the targets of it, and allows tacit representations of antisemitism to go unremarked.

What, after all, are we to make of Disney's representation of Mother Gothel in *Tangled* (2010)? The word *Jew* is never used, but she is an overbearing, smothering mother, she looks like me—dark curly hair and a big nose—and she kidnaps a blonde baby princess in order to use her body for magic purposes. On the other hand, what are we to make of the character of Isaac Heller, a recurring explicitly Jewish antagonist on the television show *Once Upon a Time* (2011–2018)? Once again we are child stealers and villains—is this justice? Did we ever get to be the heroes and heroines?

Perhaps keeping the older stories in consciousness is part of the process of justice. Redacting them can make them incomprehensible as well. In the 1970s, Perry Nodelman encountered a Penguin edition of Edgar Taylor's translations of the Grimms that changed "The Jew in the Bush" to "The Miser in the Bush" (1979). How can you tell someone is a miser when he's just standing by the side of a road looking at a bird? And how does being a miser make it acceptable to torture someone and get him killed?

Letting the stories fall away allows white gentiles to forget how recently open hostility toward Jews was considered acceptable among them, allows them to imagine their tradition as more welcoming and benevolent than it really was, and thus occludes the harm done. Letting them fall away also supports the assimilation of white Jews into white gentile society, thus encouraging us to forego identification with people of color and other oppressed peoples in favor of identifying with the dominant culture. I do not think that either of these effects contributes to larger projects of justice.

What else is part of the process of justice? Making a place for anger. When I workshopped "Among the Thorns," far and away what made readers most uncomfortable was that the narrator, the daughter of the Jew in "The Jew in the Thornbush," is not punished for seeking and taking revenge. She does not have to dig two graves. She does not regret her actions when she murders the peasant who had her father killed. That reaction on the part of early readers of the story seems to me to be a very pointed commentary on who is allowed to even *fantasize* about violent revenge in this culture (how many movies, after all, are about a white man taking revenge on the bad guys who have harmed *his* woman?) and who is required to uphold nonviolence as the only legitimate resistance to harm, even in the imagination. I am reminded of the segment in Disney's *Cinderella* when the heroine chastises her dog for *dreaming* about chasing and catching her stepmother's loathsome cat—"That's bad!" she says (1950). Why does the specter of anger, of violence on the part of wronged peoples seem so horrifying? Is it because the Western world knows what it has coming if that anger is unleashed?

So I think justice means sitting with the anger and the discomfort it causes. I am *angry* that my beloved fairy tales could never be about *me*, that stories of European princes and princesses would never mean me. I am *angry* that as a reader of fairy tales I have to put up with the knowledge that "The Jew in the Thornbush" exists and that my fond memories of *The Blue Fairy Book* are now tainted by knowing that Lang surely never envisioned young Veronica among the children reading his volume. If I have to bear this knowledge and feel this anger, then yes, justice is making sure that other people carry this knowledge and have to sit with this anger.

But what about my current academic project, a book-length study of Jewish representation in the English-language fairy-tale tradition? Does that function the same way as my fiction? Does it too have a role to play in seeking justice for these fairy-tale injuries?

What, after all, can I expect from a scholarly project? Especially when odds are it will reach a much smaller audience even than my fiction? I don't confuse scholarship with activism; if I had wanted to become an activist, I would have become a labor organizer instead of an academic, a path that was at one point open to me. I don't think scholarship *can* restore or repair damage. I don't think that's what it's for. Scholarship doesn't provide justice; it asks, and sometimes answers, questions. My questions are, in light of this representation, what relationship can and do Jews have with the European fairy-tale tradition? How do we interact with it, as characters, as writers, as readers, in order to create enough justice to go on? What does that justice look like?

It looks like coming to grips with "The Bronze Ring" and the antisemitism it crystallizes; but it also looks like paying critical attention to the work of nineteenth-century folklorist and polymath Joseph Jacobs—his fairy-tale collections as well as his advocacy work for the Ashkenazim displaced by pogroms. How did his enthusiastic collection and promotion of fairy tales and folk narratives mesh with his tireless work in and for Jewish communities? Moving to the twentieth century, why does more than one novel about the Holocaust use fairy tales to structure its narrative, and why are most of those novels written by gentiles? How do Jewish and Jewish-descended writers such as Yolen, Novik, and myself work with fairy tales today?

I'm writing this project in part to judge, a word that has the same etymological root as justice. To judge the tradition, yes, and to judge and understand Jewish relationships to it. "History will judge," says common wisdom at the same time as it tells us, "Don't judge, it was a different time." Well, I am here, the time is now, and I am judging. Perhaps that's as close as we can get to justice.

Fairy tales have long been the topic of feminist arguments about their portrayals of gender and female characters. But women, while subordinated and oppressed under patriarchy, not only play a vast range of roles in the long history of fairy tales that many feminist scholars have brought back into public consciousness, but also do not comprise a subcommunity in the contemporary United States, Canada, or United Kingdom. It is long past time we look unflinchingly at the ways fairy tales and folktales affect and are inflected by discourses of race, religion, and sovereignty, the roles they play in constructing mainstream representations of marginalized communities. It is almost too obvious to be worth noting that the Grimms' and Disney's "Snow White" tales equate beauty with white skin—but surely we should not dismiss or gloss over this reading in a time when plenty of viewers are in an uproar over the casting of Halle Bailey as Ariel in Disney's live-action *The Little Mermaid*.

Of all the tales to adapt for his first feature-length film, why did Disney choose "Snow White," the tale that emphasizes the importance of white skin? Unlike the mother in the tale, Disney could not have been particularly taken by the visual possibilities of the color combination red, black, and white, as his first sketches of the character made her a blonde. What does it tell us about contemporary fairy-tale culture that the American behemoth that is Disney's princess industry is based on the valorization of whiteness? Disney has tried in recent years to add some princesses of color into the mix. Tiana, in *The Princess and the Frog* was indeed a Black young woman, but she spent most of the movie as a frog. The story of Pocahontas is an American legend rather than a fairy tale proper. But it was adopted by Disney and made into one of their "princess" tales as part of that legend's function of romanticizing and prettifying the actual history of Matoaka, captured at seventeen by the English and dead at twenty-one, and by extension the history and ongoing situation of the settler-colonialism of the United States and Canada.

I am far from the first scholar whose work addresses the issues marginalized communities face with respect to European and/or American fairy tales. Kimberly Lau (2016, 2021) is doing amazing work at the intersection of racism and fairy tales. Michelle J. Smith and Rebecca-Anne C. do Rozario (2016) survey racialized representations of the Beast in Victorian theatrical productions of "Beauty and the Beast" and explicate their connections to the newly published theories of Charles Darwin. These analyses are part of a reckoning in fairy-tale studies, of understanding the racial and ethnic ideologies encoded in our culture's beloved tales.

But analysis is not the same thing as justice, is it? What would justice look like for Rochelle Smith, writer of an essay about the longing for a Black princess on Disney's movie screen that went unfulfilled in her childhood (2016)? Does it look like Halle Bailey's Ariel? Does this much-belated arrival make whole that which was damaged by the fairy tales of a white supremacist society? It seems to me that justice requires a sustained effort, not a one-off. We need an ocean of representations. It also seems to me that justice requires truth, requires our society to look squarely at its history and its fairy tales, admit its cruelties and injustices, and commit to rectifying them. I will be honest and say that I'm not holding my breath for that. But justice, if it exists, and even if it doesn't, can be thought of as "the work" in the oft-cited quotation from Pirkei Avot ("Ethics of Our Fathers" is the general translation) from the Mishnah: "It is not your responsibility to finish the work, but neither are you free to desist from it (2:21)." Justice has that in common with scholarship: neither is ever finished, and yet we persist.

REFERENCES

Cinderella. 1950. Directed by Clyde Geronimi, Hamilton Luske, and Wilfred Jackson. United States: Walt Disney Productions.

Dundes, Alan. 1991. "The Ritual Murder or Blood Libel Legend: A Study of Anti-Semitic Victimization through Projective Inversion." In *The Blood Libel Legend: A Casebook in Anti-Semitic Folklore*, edited by Alan Dundes, 336–76. Madison: University of Wisconsin Press.

Fiedler, Leslie. 1949. "What Can We Do About Fagin? The Jew-Villain in Western Tradition." *Commentary*, May. https://www.commentary.org/articles/leslie-fiedler/what-can-we-do-about-faginthe-jew-villain-in-western-tradition/.

Lang, Andrew. 1889. *The Blue Fairy Book*. London: Longmans, Green.

Lang, Andrew. 1935. *The Blue Fairy Book*. New York: Longmans, Green, and Co.

Lang, Andrew. 1943. *The Blue Fairy Book*. New York: Longmans, Green, and Co.

Lau, Kimberly. 2016. "Imperial Marvels: Race and the Colonial Imagination in the Fairy Tales of Madame d'Aulnoy." *Narrative Culture* 3 (2): 141–79.

Lau, Kimberly. 2021. "Power: The Archeology of a Genre." In *A Cultural History of Fairy Tales in the Modern Age*, edited by Andrew Teverson, 181–96. London: Bloomsbury Academic.

The Little Mermaid. 2023. Directed by Rob Marshall. United States: Walt Disney Pictures.

Musäus, Johann Karl August. (1791) 2010. "Richilda." Translated by William Thomas Beckford. In *Sleeping Beauties: Sleeping Beauty and Snow White Tales from around the World*, edited by Heidi Anne Heiner, 67–89. Nashville: SurLaLune with CreateSpace.

Nesbit, E. (1899) 2013. *The Story of the Treasure Seekers and the Wouldbegoods*. London: Palgrave Macmillan.

Nodelman, Perry. 1979. "The Case of the Disappearing Jew." *Children's Literature in Education* 10 (1): 44–48.

Novik, Naomi. 2019. *Spinning Silver*. New York: Del Rey.

Once Upon a Time. 2011–2018. Created by Edward Kitsis and Adam Horowitz. United States: ABC Studios.

Pirkei Avot. Ethics of Our Fathers. Pirkei Avot 3.1. Mishnah. sefaria.org. https://www.sefaria.org/Pirkei_Avot.3.1?ven=Open_Mishnah&lang=bi&with=Translations&lang2=en.

The Princess and the Frog. 2009. Directed by Ron Clements and John Musker. United States: Walt Disney Animation Studios.

Rozan, S. J. 2002. *Winter and Night*. New York: Minotaur Books.

Schanoes, Veronica. 2014. *Fairy Tales, Classical Myth, and Psychoanalytic Theory: Feminism and Retelling the Tale*. Farnham, UK: Ashgate.

Schanoes, Veronica. 2021. *Burning Girls and Other Stories*. New York: Tordotcom.

Smith, Michelle J., and Rebecca-Anne C. do Rozario. 2016. "Race, Species, and the Other: 'Beauty and the Beast' in Victorian Pantomime and Children's Literature." *Nineteenth Century Contexts* 38 (1): 37–53.

Smith, Rochelle. 2016. "Wonder Tale." *Callaloo* 39 (3): 531–36.

Tangled. 2010. Directed by Nathan Greno and Byron Howard. United States: Walt Disney Studios Motion Pictures.

Trachtenberg, Joshua. (1943) 1983. *The Devil and the Jews: The Medieval Conception of the Jew and Its Relation to Modern Antisemitism*. Philadelphia: Jewish Publication Society of America.

Yolen, Jane. 1994. "Granny Rumple." In *Black Thorn, White Rose*, edited by Ellen Datlow and Terri Windling, 204–16. New York: William Morrow.

4

Making a Mountain Mundane

Social Media and the Mundanity of Wonder in the Struggle to #ProtectMaunakea

BRYAN KAMAOLI KUWADA

In July 2015, Hawai'i was in the midst of a sweltering summer. Honolulu set or matched record highs twenty times in the first half of the month (Gima 2015). Beaches were packed; people went to the movies just to sit in the air-conditioning. It was hot and muggy. And then it snowed.

The summit of Maunakea was covered in an inch and a half of snow (Big Island Video News 2015), and while snow in the middle of summer was not unprecedented there, it was definitely rare. The snow generated some local news stories and coverage from national travel outlets because of the incongruity, though meteorologists essentially explained it away as "weird, but it happens" (Gima 2015).

Many Hawaiians, however, had a different reading of the situation. From 2014 and into 2015, kia'i, or protectors, from the Hawaiian community blockaded the construction of the Thirty Meter Telescope (TMT), an eighteen-story structure with an eight-acre footprint (Kahea n.d.) to be sited in a conservation district at the peak of one of our sacred mountains. Pushing for the construction of the TMT was a multinational consortium made up of the California

https://doi.org/10.7330/9781646425853.c004

Institute of Technology, the University of California, and institutions from Japan, China, India, and Canada (TMT 2022) with the cooperation of the University of Hawai'i and the State of Hawai'i. Previous telescope construction had heavily damaged fragile cultural and ecological systems at the summit, so kia'i camped out and used their bodies to keep the construction vehicles from reaching the building site. On that July day, the 113th of the occupation of Maunakea, often referred to as just the Mauna (the Mountain), there was a day of pule, or prayer and ceremony, done in conjunction with Indigenous peoples in other parts of the Pacific. That evening, it began to snow and the summit was closed, ensuring that the Mauna was safe from construction again.

Rather than seeing this as a mere meteorological anomaly, many Hawaiians, occupying the Mauna or not, saw it as confirmation that the kia'i standing against the TMT had the support not only of our ancestors but of the land itself, which had clearly joined the fight. The Protect Maunakea Instagram account, with over 100,000 followers, posted a picture of the snow-covered telescopes: "#PoliahuProtectingMaunakea." This story of wonder was not a defining moment of the struggle, but instead merely one among hundreds and even thousands of moments of wonder that crop up when we enter into proper relations, relationships of wonder, with 'āina ("that which feeds," referring to what might be called the land and sea, though we also refer to the ocean as moana). In fact, there is a certain mundanity to wonder that is foundational to Hawaiian understandings of our connection to 'āina. This does not mean that wonder loses any of its wondrousness or that it cannot still be sublimely transporting or truly terrifying at times, only that when we put ourselves in relationship with the 'āina and the world around us, we also allow ourselves to grasp the wonder that is inherent in it and recognize that the elements and beings around us have life and mana, the power that resides in all things.

STRUGGLE FOR WONDER / RELATIONSHIP OF WONDER

The struggle over Maunakea, the tallest mountain in the world when measured from the seafloor, has come to a head in recent years over the Thirty Meter Telescope. If it were to be built, it would be the second-largest telescope on the planet, the tallest building on the island, and require the excavation of 64,000 cubic yards of the summit (Kahea n.d.), all in a conservation district. Far from having the minimal impact that many telescope proponents asserted, the final permissions that the Hawai'i State Supreme Court granted for the construction of the TMT in 2018 were based on the sheer amount of damage already done to the Mauna. In his dissenting opinion, Justice Michael D. Wilson, who opposed the permissions, referred to the basis of the Supreme Court's decision as "the degradation principle," the idea that the summit of Maunakea had already been so damaged by previous astronomy activity and construction to a degree termed a "substantial adverse impact" that the building of the TMT could not have a further substantial adverse impact (2018, 1).

For so long, the fight over the telescope was carried out in the state's and the TMT's terms. They framed the argument as culture versus science and made the seemingly reasonable claim that both culture and science could coexist on the mountain, implying that Hawaiians who opposed the TMT were anti-science. Another front in this battle, again using their terminology, was whether Maunakea was "sacred" to Hawaiians or not. Yet for Hawaiians, culture and science are not separate entities that can be set into opposition with each other. The argument over the sacredness of the mountain misses the point that we consider all land sacred, though some places could indeed accrue more mana than others. This framing by the state and the TMT was strategic; it portrays the struggle in a light favorable to them by creating a false binary between science and culture that only they are willing to balance. Perhaps ironically, it also points to the absence of a relationship of wonder with the 'āina, not only on the part of those making the arguments, but also for much of the general public who accepted the arguments on those terms.

The relationship that we Hawaiians have with the land is something that we call aloha 'āina, which is an aloha, or love, for the 'āina that is born out of the fact that it is our relative, our elder sibling, in fact. Aloha 'āina is also a highly political relationship because during the tumultuous nineteenth century, when Hawaiians were fighting to keep control of their kingdom, 'āina and kingdom/sovereignty were often seen as synonymous, meaning that our ancestors were motivated by and even referred to as "aloha 'āina." So, aloha 'āina encompasses a myriad of aspects, including what might otherwise be classified as sustainability and ecological protection efforts, cultural recovery efforts, or political demonstrations and marches. Two of the important facets of aloha 'āina that I am interested in here are justice and wonder.

Pono is our conception of justice. As with all linguistic and cultural translation, the concept of justice does not directly map onto the Hawaiian term, but pono is the closest approximation. Pono is the sense that everything is balanced and that our relationships with each other and with the ʻāina are healthy. Pono is supposed to undergird the decisions and actions of our hereditary leaders. It even dictates some of the shapes and sizes of our land divisions. An ahupuaʻa, one of our common land divisions, is sized so that its residents have enough resources—arable land, access to fresh water and the ocean, available materials for building homes and making clothing—to provide for their general needs. Pono, in fact, besides referring to this state of balance, is also used linguistically in places where English speakers might say "need," as in "I need this or that"; in Hawaiian, one would use "pono" and the implication would be that "in order for pono to be achieved, I/we need this or that."

Pono is also what drives aloha ʻāina, always striving to keep things in balance, and within that, wonder is an integral part of pono. Indeed, instilling wonder is arguably one of the goals of aloha ʻāina and the presence of wonder is an indicator of pono. There must be an element of wonder in our interactions with ʻāina for them to be pono. Daniel Heath Justice (Cherokee) describes wonder this way: "Etymologically 'wonder' is of unclear origin, but always keeps astonishment, admiration, and even a bit of mindful fear at its core. Wondrous things are other and otherwise; they're outside the bounds of the everyday and mundane, perhaps unpredictable, but not necessarily alien, not necessarily foreign or dangerous—but not necessarily comforting and safe, either. They remind us that other worlds exist; other realities abide alongside and within our own" (2017). While I will argue later that the true place of wonder, at least from a Hawaiian cultural standpoint, is squarely within the mundane, Justice makes clear that the concept is uncontainable within the bounds of how Western society has taught us to interact with the world. This uncapturable aspect of wonder is something that ensures possibilities.

Cristina Bacchilega, in speaking of the poetics of wonder she finds in activist fairy-tale adaptations, points to where this power comes from: "The experience of wonder springs from awe and inspires curiosity; compounds fear and desire; it is unsettling and thus transformative.... As a state of being and an action, wonder is both the trigger and the product of transformation, ours and the world's. Its connective power invites humans to be and act humbly in a world that is continuously transforming itself and us, to become more attuned to the world's and our aliveness" (2017, 8). Though, as Bacchilega also points out, Indigenous literatures and oratures are distinct from fairy tales, the connective power she mentions, along with the invitation provided by wonder, plays a large role in Hawaiian moʻolelo (story/history/account/tale), particularly ones oriented toward pono.

This relationship between wonder and pono that Justice and Bacchilega gesture toward undergirds so many stories that have come out of the recent struggles to protect the Mauna. In fact, one of my foundational understandings of wonder in the Hawaiian context came from Bacchilega. I had been part of a team translating a book-length version of one of our traditional moʻolelo published in nineteenth-century Hawaiian-language newspapers. In it, we had been translating akua—a term that covered everything from what some might call goddesses to natural elements to spirits—as "supernatural," trying to allow for their many manifestations. When asked for feedback on the translation, Bacchilega asked if that was the best translation for akua, since it implied that they were "super"—above, beyond, or outside—natural when akua seemed to her understanding to be very much a part of the natural. This was such a revelation, as I had been unknowingly interpreting/translating our Hawaiian understandings of aloha ʻāina and the relationships of wonder that we have through a Western lens that held people, ʻāina, and akua not as living beings in relationships of care with each other, but as separate unrelated and mainly unliving things.

A lack of wonder most noticeably characterizes mainstream Western understandings of land, where it is real estate or a resource to be exploited, and where the ocean is a dumping ground for satellites, nuclear waste, and the plastic detritus of our modern lifestyles. One of the most pernicious yet often invisible effects of colonialism has been to take people out of relationships of wonder with their own ʻāina. It makes sense then that many of the stories of Hawaiians awakening to anticolonial understandings have to do with them returning to this relationship of wonder with the ʻāina, recognizing it as our elder sibling the way that our ancestors did, and also coming to understand the reciprocal relationship we have with it.

As the younger sibling of the ʻāina, that which feeds, people are expected to reciprocate the ʻāina's generosity by caring for it in turn. This understanding is something that the colonizing forces occupying Hawaiʻi tried to eradicate from Hawaiian thinking over the last two centuries, and while this connection to land was never completely lost, it was not until the Hawaiian Renaissance of the 1960s and 1970s that there was a resurgence of this connection to land, all driven by a push for pono. The Renaissance coincided with and was influenced by many of the prominent social movements of the time, but was at its heart a distinctly Hawaiian reawakening. A renewal of pride in things Hawaiian intertwined with a revitalization of cultural practices such as hula, chant, music, long-distance ocean navigation, and Hawaiian language as well as political and activist movements around ʻāina use and access. Thus it was through reconnection with ʻāina, identity, and culture, and the cultivation of sometimes neglected relationships of wonder that many Hawaiians were reintroduced to aloha ʻāina.

ALOHA ʻĀINA AND MUNDANE WONDER ON SOCIAL MEDIA

Though aloha ʻāina has come to be foundational to the Hawaiian sovereignty movement and much of our linguistic and cultural revitalization/ renormalization efforts over the last four decades, individual stories today still echo the themes of rediscovering that relationship of wonder inherent in aloha ʻāina that those of the Hawaiian Renaissance experienced. One thing that has changed, however, is the near ubiquity of digital and social media and the means to create in these genres. Prior to 2015, most of the battle to protect Maunakea had been relatively successfully waged in the courts by community activists and advocates. In 2015, however, those efforts spilled out into the literal streets, as kiaʻi blocked the Maunakea Access Road, keeping construction vehicles from the proposed telescope site. Lanakila Mangauil, one of the young leaders of the movement, recalled the July day in 2015 when it snowed, posting about it on Facebook a year later: "I remember this day, people from all around Polynesia aligned with prayers for MaunaKea, and I remember the mana because later the evening of this pic, I woke up in my car to hear metal dragging on the rd again, the rangers put up the rd closed sign because a 'winter storm' came and it was snowing!! In July! Poliahu heard the combined prayers!" (2017).

Mangauil, along with many of those who commented on the post, attributed the wondrous occasion of a winter storm appearing in summer and protecting the mountain from construction to Poliʻahu, our akua who spreads her white cloak of snow over the mountains. Poliʻahu is one of four "sister-deities of Maunakea: with . . . Lilinoe of the mists, Waiau of the lake, and Kahoupokāne of the thunder and lightning" (de Silva 2006). She is also sometimes referred to as "ka wahine noho mauna" (She Who Dwells on the Mountain) (Haleʻole 1863). As Hiʻilei Hobart asserts in her analysis of this unexpected snowfall and what she calls "elemental agency": "Attributing the snow to Poliʻahu, an important akua (god) of the cold who is known to reside at the top of Maunakea, many Kānaka Maoli recognized the event to be an exercise of her desire to protect the sacred mountain from desecration. The snow and reactions to it importantly signal Kānaka Maoli perspectives on the agential forces of the elements as not just atmosphere, precipitation, and temperature but as intention, ancestor, and spirit" (2019, 30).

The agentic aspects Hobart describes are what people begin to recognize when we enter or reenter these relationships of wonder with the ʻāina.

The 2014–2015 stand was successful in keeping the telescope from being built as it resulted in the TMT's conservation district use permit being vacated, revoking their permission to build and requiring them to apply all over again. When permission was finally granted by the Hawaiʻi Supreme Court near the end of 2018, justified as described earlier by the "degradation principle," kiaʻi mounted a highly organized and successful occupation to again prevent construction.

The kiaʻi set up what would grow from a small caravan of vehicles in the parking lot of Puʻuhuluhulu, a native tree sanctuary across from the entrance to the Maunakea Access Road, to become a large encampment of thousands of people, giving the kiaʻi a strategic advantage in terms of proximity and mobilization. One of the main events that kicked off the occupation, however, was when eight kiaʻi chained themselves to a cattle guard built into the access road. They remained locked to the cattle guard for nearly twelve hours (Dayton and Hurley 2019), though law enforcement officers had placed them under arrest in the early morning.

The wonder tale that came out of this event, besides the moving story of kiaʻi putting themselves through the hardship of chaining themselves to the cattle guard in the bitter cold, was that the police mobile command center sent to coordinate law enforcement's presence as well as the removal of the kiaʻi chained to the grate sputtered out right in front of the encampment and the blockade, and the kiaʻi themselves helped to push the stalled vehicle safely off to the side of the road. And then the extraction vehicle that was on its way to take the arrested kiaʻi from the cattle guard also died coming up the mountain.

When a cell phone video was posted on Facebook of the mobile command center being helped to the side of the road by kiaʻi, it got over 17,000 views. Shares of the video included comments such as: "The Mauna is sacred" (Young 2019), "That's the Mauna for you" (Neemia 2019), "What prayers can do . . . and the humor of ancestors" (Mendoza 2019), "Hōʻailona!!!" (Fo 2019), "The Ancestors at work!!" (Desha 2019), "The Akua are surely having a say . . . and look, our Kiaʻi helping them [law enforcement] out. That's some aloha radiating out" (Aki 2019), and "When the #mana works! And of course the protectors gotta help #powerofprayers" (Ishibashi 2019). As both Young and Neemia point out in their posts, it is very matter-of-fact that the breakdowns happened. That kind of thing is to be expected when you are trying to mistreat the ʻāina. The other commenters point out the influence of the ancestors, our akua, and the power of our pule/oli/hoʻokupu/protocols, and so on to make things like this happen. The hōʻailona that Fo mentions are signs that we receive, usually in the natural world, from our ancestors and the akua indicating where we are in regard to pono. Fo's post thus indicates that the breakdown of the mobile command center and the extraction van are hōʻailona that we are on the right path.

If the TMT struggle had gotten the Hollywood treatment, either of these two happenings would be the wondrous climaxes of the movie, the miraculous deus ex machina replete with swelling orchestral music and hero shots of the kiaʻi who have witnessed the sublime delight of finding out that there are divine forces at play in the world that are beyond our understanding. Yet the truth of the matter is that when Hawaiians retell the story of the fight to protect the Mauna, these happenings are generally not included as major drivers of the narrative. They are brought up more as sidenotes, not because kiaʻi don't think that Poliʻahu or our ancestors had actually taken an active role in the struggle, but because these kinds of things happen all the time.

If we are open to the idea that the land is our actual sibling and that akua are not supernatural but a part of our natural world, then we will see these things happening more and more around us. So the stories of these happenings are related with the same sense of awe and wonder as stories of the mist coming down at a particular time or of nēnē geese flying in formation during the offering of pule. This does not make the individual stories less wondrous—rather, it makes the world itself even more wondrous because it is filled with these kinds of happenings. And to accept a world where we are surrounded by wonder is to open ourselves to aloha ʻāina, but also to come to understand the mundanity of wonder in such a world.

Although "mundane" has come to mean boring or lackluster, making it seem like the opposite of wonder, "mundane" also has to do with being of the mundus, of the world, and rooting wonder back into the mundane world actually creates more possibilities rather than limiting them. The potential for possibility is conveyed through what Justice calls "wonderworks," and how wonder is "a term that gestures, imperfectly, to other ways of being in the world, and it reminds us that the way things are is not how they have always been, nor is it how they must be. It's in Indigenous wonderworks that some of the best models of different, better relationship are being realized, and it's these stories that give me hope for a better future even in these scary times" (2017). When our relationships with the ʻāina and moana are not limited by the flat understanding of what can happen in the alleged "real" world held by mainstream Western understandings, there is much more room for possibility and thus transformation and change.

INVITING CONNECTION THROUGH SOCIAL MEDIA

It is no surprise that much of the impact of the two wondrous happenings mentioned above came via social media, now one of the major tools of social movements. One of the things that stood out about the 2019 stand for Maunakea compared with the 2015 stand and other Indigenous land struggles is the way that the kiaʻi controlled the narrative. They had a dedicated grassroots media team made up of a large and sometimes loose collective of photographers, videographers, writers, content creators, and artists who volunteered their time to create short-form documentaries, poetry performances, informational posts, press statements, travelogues, photo essays, and art pieces.

As one of the core members of the media team, Ryan "Gonzo" Gonzalez states, "We're at a point in time where technology is making it easier for us to make connections" (Kuwada and Revilla 2020a, 647). This sentiment goes against the often-prevailing understanding of social media and sometimes technology in general as disconnecting us from each other and from nature. Teacher, songwriter, musician, and Hawaiian-language advocate Kainani Kahaunaele described how people connected with the movement through social media:

> Social media platforms have helped open up our efforts to the world in real time, garnering tremendous support from individuals and native cultures around the world. People around the globe were simultaneously participating in the ceremony through the livestream, tuning in to the press conferences, Puʻuhuluhulu University classes [Puʻuhuluhulu University is a grassroots school with daily classes taught by professors, public and private school teachers, cultural experts, elders, and other knowledgeable people], music performances, and recording the development and rise of our self-discipline, determination, and leadership. . . . The lāhui's [Hawaiian nation/people/community] daily posts kept a close pulse on what we were training for, celebrating, lamenting, and learning from. It's hard to imagine how the course would have been altered without digital technologies and instant access to information. (2020, 549)

Not only were people from other parts of the world able to connect with the movement, but even people on other islands in Hawaiʻi or those who just couldn't be up on the Mauna were able to follow the situation. In the early days of the 2019 struggle, tens of thousands of people were watching the livestreams of the blockade (and anything else that was going on) on Facebook and Instagram from accounts like Kākoʻo Haleakalā (formed in response to attempts to build a telescope on Haleakalā) and Kanaeokana (a network of Hawaiian culture-, language-, and ʻāina-based schools and organizations). Indigenous people and supporters from far and wide were able to witness what was going on, but local people also used the streams to make sure that their friends and family up on the Mauna were safe.

As can be imagined, social and digital media cannot put someone in an actual, hands-on relationship with ʻāina. Though 3D cameras and virtual reality have advanced to a great degree, there is no substitute for being on the ʻāina and feeling the dirt or being in the ocean and feeling the swells lift you. But the stories told through these media can *invite* you to ʻāina; they can bring you to want to have a relationship of wonder with the land. Tagé

Cho Hudän scholar and visual artist Lianne Marie Leda Charlie talks about how a particular kind of story can invite you to ʻāina, particularly "stories about our ancestors' stories—tales of wonder—that awaken our inherent curiosity and a deep-seated ancestral desire to be back out on the land" (2016, 23). This feeling, when transmitted through the social media tales of wonder coming from the Mauna, also engendered a concomitant desire to protect the land.

Gonzalez recalls the differences between the 2015 and 2019 stands; in the latter "more were on social media and whatnot. People could connect. And once people made those connections, you had people who maybe wouldn't have supported in the past being able to support because they had access to that" (Kuwada and Revilla 2020a, 647). The wide array of approaches and means of interactive presentation enabled through social media (text, image, video, audio, etc.) meant that there were many ways for people to engage, including, as Gonzalez mentions, people who might not have supported the cause otherwise.

An important distinction to make here has to do with who is getting to tell the stories. The media coming from and/or inspired by the Mauna were a combination of highly curated content with high production values that came from the volunteer kiaʻi media team and tens of thousands of posts from anyone with the slightest connection to or interest in Maunakea. While the broad accessibility of social media did sometimes result in the spread of odd rumors (like the TMT using nuclear power) or misinformation about law enforcement or kiaʻi plans, the fact that anyone could say just about anything meant that the media team and the Hawaiian community at large had many opportunities to post and share about aloha ʻāina in ways that mainstream media tended not to report or value.

Kēhaunani Abad, a longtime activist and community visionary who was very involved in the media team, talks about the importance of kiaʻi being able to drive the narrative through a powerful social media presence: "We didn't have to worry about what twenty-second bite they were going to give us on the six o'clock news. There was an opportunity for us to get to a large number of people. And all of the other platforms that had been built as well, Kākoʻo Haleakalā, Protect Maunakea, everybody's platforms, oh gosh, in terms of strategy, that turned out to be one of the most important things. . . . It was one gigantic media team. If someone had to contract all those folks out there who were volunteering their time, it would have been crazy expensive" (Kuwada and Revilla 2020b, 675).

Platforms like Kākoʻo Haleakalā and Protect Maunakea, along with Kanaeokana, brought with them tens and hundreds of thousands of followers and had already cultivated an ethos of trust because they had activists, community organizers, cultural practitioners, historians, and Hawaiian-language experts all contributing to their content. For example, Kanaeokana was a network of over sixty ʻāina-, culture-, or language-based schools and related organizations, so their social media was created by people who were known to the community and who had expertise in language, history, culture, traditional mele, and more. Through their platform alone, at the height of the 2019 struggle, a single post could reach over 400,000 people. Kanaeokana also produced or shared videos through their channels, and the general public watched over 5.5 million minutes of media team–produced video during that time (Kanaeokana 2020). Their *Fifty Years of Mismanaging Mauna Kea* video (2018), based on the Office of Hawaiian Affair's Maunakea lawsuit, information from Kāhea: The Hawaiian-Environmental Alliance, and some of my own research, reached over 1 million people just on its own.

Although it is hard to measure the impact of a narrative, and polls can be unreliable for a number of reasons, local reporter Kevin Dayton described a twenty-point swing in the polls regarding support for the TMT, and talked about how Governor David Ige "noted the flurry of anti-TMT activity on social media in recent months, and acknowledged the poll shows support for the project dropped amid that cacophony" (2019). The use of "flurry" and "cacophony" hides the organization and skill behind the kiaʻi-authored narratives of the pro-Mauna media campaign, but Colin Moore, director of the Public Policy Center at the University of Hawaiʻi at Mānoa, was more sanguine when he said: "You're talking about people changing their mind about an issue, which is an incredibly hard thing to achieve. It's not as if the TMT is a new idea that no one has ever heard before. I mean, people had years to form opinions on this, so it goes to show in some ways the brilliance of the protest campaign" (quoted in Dayton 2019).

Abad points to one of the ways the "protest campaign" put that brilliance into practice, by using the flexibility of social media to bypass mainstream media: "We started the news cycles, basically. We didn't wait for something else to happen. We created that narrative, so we were pretty much always ahead of where TMT and [Governor] Ige guys were in the narrative, so they were always playing catch up" (Kuwada and Revilla 2020b, 675). And the narrative being created was one that pointed to the importance of having this relationship of wonder with ʻāina.

Abad continues on to describe the role that ʻāina and our relationship with it plays in the works created: "Some of the most important effective pieces we did placed ʻāina as the main character in them. . . . There are large parts of [the] work where you don't have any narrative at all, you're just seeing the night sky, you're just seeing the Mauna, you're just seeing the mist. . . . The vast majority of what's in the view is not about people. It's about the place, and what you're framing was really the place, so the Mauna is taking up most of the screen on purpose" (Kuwada and Revilla 2020b, 677). In this manner, even the videography and composition of the shots operate to indicate that the Mauna, and by extension the ʻāina, is not the backdrop for human activity but an active part of what is going on. A large part of the media team's works were also created directly on the Mauna itself, with media team members huddled around a propane heater working on their laptops until the small hours of the morning and accessing the internet through mobile hotspots to get their videos and images uploaded and statements released to the press.

Gonzalez also talks about the various dimensions the team used to feature ʻāina in the pieces they created: "I always like to save a pretty large space to make sure that ʻāina is represented in some fashion in terms of the soundscape because it has its own voice. And it's communicating. . . . There's also the sound that's created by the dynamic between kānaka and the space that was there, that kind of just reverberates in my head" (Kuwada and Revilla 2020a, 643). The unseen soundscape reinforces the feeling of connecting with ʻāina grounding these pieces, and as Gonzalez's comment shows, the understanding of ʻāina as a living being is not always pushed in an overt fashion, but is an obvious starting place for telling stories from the Mauna. So whether the piece is an *MTV Cribs*–style walkthrough of all of the features of the kiaʻi encampment, such as free health care and food, an art tent, and the free university, or a discussion about the historical mismanagement of the Mauna, or a poetry performance put on at Puʻuhuluhulu, both kānaka and ʻāina are on the screen and in the audio together as interconnected and related beings. And in that manner, each post, video, and tweet seeds possibility and pono out into the social media landscape, becoming a tale of wonder, what Justice would call a "wonderwork," because an understanding of ʻāina as a living being is at their core.

The use of digital and social media also serves another narrative purpose: to locate these tales of wonder as very much rooted in the present and looking toward the future. Kiaʻi have been referred to by astronomers and science writers as "wanting to return to the Stone Age" (Herman 2015) or as being involved in a turn "back towards the dark ages" (Johnson 2014), and have been continually painted as "anti-science" (despite the number of Hawaiian scientists who are kiaʻi), with the TMT and Hawaiʻi's governor Ige framing their own efforts as trying to find a way for science and Hawaiian culture to coexist on Maunakea (Ige 2019). When put in these terms, Hawaiian cultural concerns are distinct from science, and by implication, modernity and progress. Therefore, when kiaʻi and the volunteer media team used digital and social media in ways that were culturally relevant and creatively and technically savvy, they pretty resoundingly outmaneuvered the TMT's highly paid public relations firm and provided a powerful narrative. Being in a relationship of wonder with ʻāina was presented as a pono way of moving into the future, rather than Hawaiians being stuck in the past.

Not all the social media posts about the Mauna were explicitly talking about tales of wonder, but oftentimes they were. Among people's everyday experiences on or with the Mauna, posts about mundane wondrous experiences were often shared. One common type of post was about hōʻailona, the signs from akua or ancestors saying that we were on the side of pono. A university student spoke of how the light showers that came while they performed a certain song at the University of Hawaiʻi at Mānoa, or the gusts of wind, or even the intense heat of the sun that day were all signs validating our protest actions, and he ended the post with a plea: "Listen to our ʻāina. Listen to our rain. Listen to our sun. Listen to the wind. Listen to the ocean. Listen to the hōʻailona that are made manifest to you" (Kapuni-Reynolds 2019).

A kumu hula (teacher/leader of a traditional hula school) and professor of Hawaiian Studies posted an image of a full rainbow above the Puʻuhonua with the caption: "Lā 2 ma ka mauna [Day 2 on the Mauna]: woke up to this! #hoailona" (Basham 2019). Many others shared pictures of white rainbows, nighttime rainbows, double rainbows, all with captions mentioning them being hōʻailona (Kapa Radio 2015; Pisciotta 2019; Moniz 2019; Apana 2019; Hoopii 2019). In a Hawaiian understanding, rainbows and fragments of rainbows serve as indicators of danger or that someone of akua or chiefly status is near, and often appear in our traditional moʻolelo around wondrous happenings such as the birth of akua or influential aliʻi (the women and men who lead Hawaiian society due to their genealogy and training). The preponderance of rainbows around events dedicated to the Mauna or at the Mauna itself are seen as clear hōʻailona that the kiaʻi are acting in a way that is pushing for pono, and the ʻāina itself is often thought to be manifesting these hōʻailona as ways of communicating. As Gonzalez expresses: "For me that was my journey ... trying to understand what people mean when they say the ʻāina is alive, and it's very much living. She's living, she breathes, she sleeps, she weeps. She embraces us, she also rejects us. She also tells us when we're not being good family members to her. She lets us know, but it's a matter of what we do when she gives us those signals" (Kuwada and Revilla 2020a, 639). Thus, all of the wonder tales shared through social media, although brief, reinforce the idea that standing for the Mauna against the TMT is the pono path, and it is through the relationship of wonder and being open to receiving hōʻailona that one is made aware of pono.

When people in this relationship of wonder with ʻāina speak about the hōʻailona they receive or the interventions from akua that they witness, their tones are of course reverent, but also very matter-of-fact. After the mid-July snowfall, Mangauil, one of the leaders of the kiaʻi, posted: "Just talked to uncle, everyone was evacuated off of the mauna at about 1am, Eo Poliahu ka wahine kapa hau anu o MaunaKea" (2015). The Hawaiian sentence at the end translates into something like "Poliʻahu, the woman of Maunakea with the cloak of freezing snow, has called out/answered." No exclamation mark, no superlative language. Just a statement of what happened.

The Hawaiian community commemorates the return of Hawaiʻi's sovereignty in 1843 after a rogue British ship captain took over for six months. On the holiday in 2019, Hawaiian flags were raised at the highest point of Maunakea, and Kalani Flores, an educator and community leader, wrote: "It was magical as the flags were raised, Lilinoe and ancestral guardians of this sacred mountain surrounded us in this mist so that no telescopes and other obstructions could be seen at this time" (2019). Again, the tone is very matter-of-fact. It is a report. Flores does not exclaim or exalt about Lilinoe's presence, merely states that she showed up as if it were a daily occurrence. Which it is.

That is what the mundanity of wonder is about; magical/spiritual/powerful events are recognized but also commonplace if you are open to their existence. In a Hawaiian understanding of the world, the akua always surround, and their names are sometimes even synonymous with the physical manifestations of the things they are akua of. For example, Pele is the well-known akua of fire and the volcano, and the Hawaiian word for lava is pele. The word for a particular kind of fine mist is lilinoe, like the name of the akua of the Mauna mentioned above. And people often talk about the snow atop Maunakea as coming from Poliʻahu, but also just refer to the snow itself as Poliʻahu. In that sense, the akua surround us and appear before us every day, but it is only when you understand the ʻāina as living and the world as filled with wonder that you can recognize this.

In that way, when wonder is restored to its mundane status, returned to being very much a part of the world, the world becomes much more filled with possibilities. It is a world where it can snow in Hawaiʻi in July or where our akua are in evidence around us everyday, or where a community of people can stop a $2 billion construction project (Kelleher 2020), or where pono is a driving force for the way we interact with each other and the ʻāina.

AN INVITATION TO WONDER

Part of the possibilities that come from being in a relationship of wonder with the ʻāina is that it is not just you and the land but an entire web of responsibility to other beings and other people. And since everyone has people in their friends or followers list who are not part of the relationship of wonder, these social media posts and narratives of mundane wonder are able to access and influence these people to move into the web of responsibility. Social media is critiqued, often rightly so, for being an echo chamber, but it is also this very power of amplification and reverberation that is so effective for transmitting these tales of wonder and drawing more people into connection with the land and with each other.

There is a recursive power there as well, by which people are influenced by these stories of wonder on social media and then create their own narratives of wonder in turn. In common parlance, this is equated with virality, but rather than a metaphor of disease, what is happening with these wonderworks from the Mauna is more like a healing type of growth, where our connections to each other and to the land are being rediscovered and reinforced. These tales of wonder honor our connections to the land and all of the living entities we share this world with. They are not about opposing some construction project, but instead about trying to push for a way of being in the world. That is why these narratives of wonder are so important; they give people glimpses of what such a world might look like. It is one of the reasons that kiaʻi have been so staunch about calling themselves "protectors" rather than "protesters," because it is both the ʻāina and this way of looking at ʻāina that they are protecting. They are not standing *against* the telescope, but standing *for* wonder.

In the decades after the illegal overthrow of the Hawaiian kingdom in 1893, as Hawaiʻi was absorbed more and more into the United States, both politically and culturally, the concept of aloha ʻāina and the wonder that came with it fell further and further from the mainstream. It is not that Hawaiians no longer practiced it, just that it became much more diffuse and even the phrase itself dropped out of common parlance. But when the Hawaiian Renaissance took place and brought aloha ʻāina back to the public consciousness, wonder began to transform both the individual people involved in the struggle and the larger movement itself.

The movement's initial goal of reparations during the Renaissance began to mean less than the need to return to being in relationships of wonder with ʻāina, and so many of our decolonial/deoccupying/revitalizing/renormalizing efforts have come from that pono. But even then they were using the new media of the time to spread these tales of renascent aloha ʻāina: documentary filmmaking, photography, homegrown newspapers, and flyers. In fact, "new" media has been a vehicle for pono and the wonder of aloha ʻāina for over a century and a half, as kingdom-era Hawaiians had an amazingly powerful media presence through the Hawaiian-language newspapers, of which there were over a hundred from 1834 to 1948, that they used to promote Hawaiian cultural values, keep up with the news and literature from other places, and organize resistance to colonial incursions.

But it was not until nineteenth-century Hawaiians had control of the means of production, actual printing presses, that the newspapers really began to serve Hawaiian aims, and that is what we see happening with social media today. Hawaiians have more access to the tools of content production and storytelling now that people are able to take photos and videos with their phones and social media provides a platform to share their wonder with the world. So as we push for justice/pono both on- and offline, these stories that come through these new media are both the evidence of and catalyst for transformation. They remind us to pay attention to what the rain might say to us, how pono helps us to be in balance with each other and the ʻāina and, most important, to open ourselves up to wonder.

REFERENCES

Aki, Zuri CW Kaapana. 2019. "The Akua." Facebook post, July 15. https://www.facebook.com/groups/hawaiilegalstatus/posts/2288609561238176/.

Apana, Mele. 2019. "A White Rainbow Hoʻailona." Facebook post, July 15. https://www.facebook.com/MentoMele/posts/pfbid038AhNpEQMdWkopoP7Szey-D57s6Fp7tdJTZBwaH2KTn1ntVLPzLVqQGvCuJ96mM4CLl.

Bacchilega, Cristina. 2017. "Where Can Wonder Take Us?" *Journal of the Fantastic in the Arts* 28 (1): 6–25.

Basham, Leilani. 2019. "Lā #2." Facebook post, July 25. https://www.facebook.com/leilani.basham/posts/pfbid0J68KkXuC5FgNJFgSRB2EXJSCTbVyxtbHEEwtUvG2Js7nmhoqcSkrfWeKVsTVGWkhl.

Big Island Video News. 2015. "Hawaii Gets Summer Snow on Mauna Kea." *Big Island Video News*, July 17. http://www.bigislandvideonews.com/2015/07/17/hawaii-gets-summer-snowfall-on-mauna-kea/.

Charlie, Lianne Marie Leda. 2016. "Sók Neyniʼįn." *Marvels & Tales* 30 (1): 22–25.

Dayton, Kevin. 2019. "Public Support for TMT Drops Sharply, According to a New *Honolulu Star-Advertiser* Poll." *Honolulu Star-Advertiser*, September 25. https://www.staradvertiser.com/2019/09/25/hawaii-news/public-support-for-tmt-drops-sharply-according-to-a-new-honolulu-star-advertiser-poll/.

Dayton, Kevin, and Timothy Hurley. 2019. "7 Telescope Opponents Unchained from Mauna Kea Access Road Cattle Guard; No Arrests Made." *Honolulu Star-Advertiser*, July 14. https://www.staradvertiser.com/2019/07/14/breaking-news/gov-david-ige-dispels-rumors-of-impending-sweep-of-protesters-on-mauna-kea/.

Desha, Alika. 2019. "The Ancestors." Facebook post, July 15. https://www.facebook.com/alika.desha/posts/pfbid0XU4k1iw1ypNBnTeCNxZwqdYvBtLcJh-WayZiKVHbmFAnQULT1KUxhR2VLqnfqBWBwl.

de Silva, Kīhei. 2006. "Noho ana ka Wahine (Pauahi ʻo Kalani)." *Kaʻiwakīloumoku: Pacific Indigenous Institute*. Accessed January 4, 2023. https://kaiwakiloumoku.ksbe.edu/article/mele-noho-ana-ka-wahine.

Flores, Kalani. 2019. "Today, July 31, 2019." Facebook post, July 31. https://www.facebook.com/Kanaeokana/photos/a.1898432697058667/2390641251171140/?type=3&eid=ARBaKM-Pf3oPuc_X_kXLRplaVLjuffY5NYwEe5xeVVcRGl8gMBLOX89_pZXkT2AEdCY-Tpa2ojY5u6LH.

Fo, Kaiolohia. 2019. "Hōʻailona!!!" Facebook post, July 16. https://www.facebook.com/kaikai.maitai/posts/pfbid0hREv8phvR3UT5AMRTWZZ3hTfaPU-3VuP5QkibTPpz3Q5cp92A1Ve1gztMp9abyqRbl.

Gima, Craig. 2015. "Snow Falls on Mauna Kea as Temperatures Hit Record Levels." *Honolulu Star-Advertiser*, July 17. https://www.staradvertiser.com/2015/07/17/hawaii-news/snow-falls-on-mauna-kea-as-temperatures-hit-record-levels/.

Haleʻole, S. N. 1863. "Ka Moolelo o Laieikawai, Mokuna XVIII." *Ka Nupepa Kuokoa*. Accessed October 3, 2023. https://nupepa.org/gsdl2.5/cgi-bin/nupepa?e=d-onupepa--00-0-0--010---4-----text---0-1l--1haw-Zz-1---20-about---0003-1-0000utfZz-8-00&a=d&cl=CL2.19&d=HASH01d939cf45af28c85e2b9efd&gg=text.

Herman, Doug. 2015. "The Heart of the Hawaiian Peoples' Arguments against the Telescope on Mauna Kea." *Smithsonian Magazine*, April 23. https://www.smithsonianmag.com/smithsonian-institution/heart-hawaiian-people-arguments-arguments-against-telescope-mauna-kea-180955057/.

Hobart, Hiʻilei Julia. 2019. "At Home on the Mauna: Ecological Violence and Fantasies of Terra Nullius on Maunakea's Summit." *Native American and Indigenous Studies* 6 (2): 30–50.

Hoopii, Torie. 2019. "Mauna Kea Is Hands Down." Facebook post, September 12. https://www.facebook.com/photo.php?fbid=10217336740744598&set=pb.1055661695.-2207520000.&type=3.

Ige, David. 2019. "DYK." Facebook post, August 15. https://www.facebook.com/GovernorDavidIge/photos/a.389461384562593/1379387342236654/?type=3.

Ishibashi, Lana. 2019. "When the #Mana Works." Facebook post, July 15. https://www.facebook.com/lana.ishibashi/posts/pfbid0u6EY9AJqNhaQ7G4tDq6JP7x2Pn8dXU3jXfMqj8PitaKGDT5SkNXcxkCQZNrokyjFl.

Johnson, George. 2014. "Seeking Stars, Finding Creationism." *New York Times*, October 21. https://www.nytimes.com/2014/10/21/science/seeking-stars-finding-creationism.html.

Justice, Daniel Heath. 2017. "Indigenous Wonderworks and the Settler-Colonial Imaginary." *Apex Magazine* 99, August 10. https://apex-magazine.com/nonfiction/indigenous-wonderworks-and-the-settler-colonial-imaginary/.

Kahaunaele, Kainani. 2020. "Mele and ʻŌlelo Hawaiʻi on the Mauna." "We Are Maunakea: Aloha ʻĀina Narratives of Protest, Protection, and Place." Special issue, *Biography: An Interdisciplinary Quarterly* 43 (3): 541–50.

Kahea: The Hawaiian Environmental Alliance. n.d. "Fact Sheet: Massive 18-Story Telescope Complex Proposed for Mauna Kea." Accessed October 10, 2018. http://kahea.org/issues/sacred-summits/sacred-summits-documents/fact-sheet-thirty-meter-telescope-tmt/at_download/file.

Kanaeokana. 2018. *Fifty Years of Mismanaging Mauna Kea.* Facebook video, October 30. https://fb.watch/dnH1EOKRGy/.

Kanaeokana. 2020. "Page Insights." Facebook tool.

Kapa Radio. 2015. "Hōʻailona." Facebook post, November 17. https://www.facebook.com/kaparadio/photos/a.10150724285903939/10153832968353939.

Kapuni-Reynolds, Halena. 2019. "Yesterday." Facebook post, July 18. https://www.facebook.com/hkaprey/posts/pfbid02RrqT7inv2HUmAW0dz3jPGRhQv6GD5uY7WXfkexKqQ6tv3VDZUcKvRVAd7xntYDxMl.

Kelleher, Jennifer Sinco. 2020. "Giant Hawaii Telescope Cost Estimate Increases to \$2.4B." *ABC News*, March 17. https://abcnews.go.com/Technology/wireStory/giant-hawaii-telescope-cost-estimate-increases-24b-69653890.

Kuwada, Bryan, and Noʻu Revilla. 2020a. "'Filling in Puka': Interview with Ryan 'Gonzo' Gonzalez." "We Are Maunakea: Aloha ʻĀina Narratives of Protest, Protection, and Place." Special issue, *Biography: An Interdisciplinary Quarterly* 43 (3): 638–49.

Kuwada, Bryan, and Noʻu Revilla. 2020b. "'We Were Being Who We Are, and That Was the Story': Interview with Kēhaunani Abad." "We Are Maunakea: Aloha ʻĀina Narratives of Protest, Protection, and Place." Special issue, *Biography: An Interdisciplinary Quarterly* 43 (3): 673–81.

Mangauil, Joshua Lanakila. 2015. "Just Talked." Facebook post, July 17. https://www.facebook.com/photo?fbid=10204478923355626&set=a.1531389047183.

Mangauil, Joshua Lanakila. 2017. "I Remember." Facebook post, July 16. https://www.facebook.com/joshua.mangauil/posts/pfbid0Rs4Cnaqj9njbf2zzuc2qjWwAhpcSuSj3cb69dux6L9ZJB7uSwhAvHRXDJf5cgzvql.

Mendoza, Darshan. 2019. "What Prayers." Facebook post, July 15. https://www.facebook.com/permalink.php?story_fbid=pfbid0cCWaSGDkpAF371chnL6hsCiqmjZHRps4ixYAJi5jvNSkD9ijUMkP9C6fGc5zb4dCl&id=100009331554193.

Moniz, Melissa Leinaʻala Haa. 2019. "HŌʻAILONA." Facebook post, August 15. https://www.facebook.com/melissa.moniz.9/posts/pfbid0z7iTQr4DMdS8i5yv62bH1hX40DPSiyGxYXiKErpxRqs1sxZarrvUpELjscZrY29tl.

Neemia, Tracy Leinaala Kapali. 2019. "That's the Mauna." Facebook post, July 15. https://www.facebook.com/mehana.kihoi/posts/pfbid0BizpjzB9sBTRQqrwpLAnbK5SXb6U9QY1wncZ0fe8cY193fswUqDfzNJkcY4wp2Jjl.

Pisciotta, Kealoha. 2019. "Aloha Mauna Kea and Kai Palaoa Ohana." Facebook post, September 9. https://www.facebook.com/photo/?fbid=1291873460983982&set=a.241771435994195.

Protectmaunakea. 2015. "In the Height." Instagram photo, July 17. https://Instagram.com/p/5PyWQIPwJB/.

TMT. 2022. "About." *TMT International Observatory.* Accessed October 3, 2023. https://www.tmt.org/page/about.

Wilson, Michael D. 2018. "Amended Dissenting Opinion." *In the Matter of Contested Case Hearing re Conservation District Use Application (CDUA) Ha-3568 for the Thirty*

Meter Telescope at the Mauna Kea Science Reserve, Kaʻohe Mauka, Hāmākua, Hawaiʻi, TMK (3) 404015:009 SCOT-17-0000777, SCOT-17-0000811, and SCOT-17-0000812: Appeal from the Board of Land and Natural Resources. November 18. https://www.courts.state.hi.us/wp-content/uploads/2018/12/SCOT-17-0000777conam.pdf.

Young, Kalani. 2019. "The Mauna." Facebook post, July 16. https://www.facebook.com/kalani.young.73/posts/pfbid02rprTA8To7kQ9d5Z6XsaxYysoP9rKUU0SGYM6E3ixLnpxx3XD3QXA3Nbw8ogXVuVrl.

SECTION TWO

Re/Viewing Justice

5

Defending Happily Ever After

Seanan McGuire's Indexing *Serial*

ANDREA BRAITHWAITE

Seanan McGuire's *Indexing* (2013) opens on a young woman named Alicia, who is mysteriously unwell and dazedly heading for the hospital. We then jump to a cop grumpy at being woken up early, well before her alarm—a shift between possible victim and her potential savior that is familiar to fans of crime stories. Except Alicia is seeing things, "strange signs and symbols that she couldn't quite understand," and the cop—Henry (Henrietta) Marchen—isn't roused by a phone call but by "half a dozen blue birds beating themselves to death" against her bedroom window, something she's used to but not happy about (McGuire 2013a, 1–2). The beginning of Henry's story is unsettling because she doesn't deal with typical crimes. Henry deals with fairy-tale crimes, and Alicia's story is about to turn into one: "Here's the first thing you need to know: all the fairy tales are true. Oh, the specific events that the Brothers Grimm chronicled and Disney animated may only have happened once, in some kingdom so old that we've forgotten whether it ever really existed, but the essential elements of the stories are true, and those elements are what keep repeating over and over again. We can't stop them, and we can't get rid of them" (5).

https://doi.org/10.7330/9781646425853.c005

The stories that unfold in *Indexing* and its sequel *Indexing: Reflections* (2015) follow this premise that fairy tales are real—and pose a real threat. Henry works for a secret government agency called the ATI Management Bureau, named for the nonfictional Aarne-Thompson (AT) Index used by real-world scholars to map fairy-tale stories and their variations.[1] McGuire's Bureau agents use the index to predict and manage the intrusion of fairy tales into the otherwise ordinary world. Alicia's situation is what the Bureau calls a "memetic incursion": a fairy tale manifesting in an otherwise ordinary person and rewriting her life according to the patterns of the tale itself. As the Bureau's agents have learned, "that's the second, and most important, thing you need to know about fairy tales: once a story starts, it won't stop on its own. There's too much narrative weight behind a moving story, and it wants to happen too badly. It won't stop, unless somebody stops it" (McGuire 2013a, 7). This is even more ominous than it sounds, for fairy-tale experiences are rarely benign—particularly when contrasted to the norms of everyday life. Luckily, Henry and her team of fairy-tale experts are there to help.

Describing her *Indexing* duology as "transformative fan fiction," McGuire treats fairy tales as crime stories and crime stories as fairy tales (2013b, para. 7). By situating the topsy-turvy elements of fairy tales within the orderly, investigative framework of the crime story, McGuire is "remaking the fairy tales we grew up with, trying to turn them into something we feel is still relevant" (para. 8). In doing so, she raises questions about the impact of story patterns and themes. What elements of the fairy tale and the crime story move through—and stick in—our social imagination? How do we (re)produce the ideas of knowledge and authority that mobilize these narratives? How do fairy tales represent issues of autonomy, agency, and gendered identities, and can the crime genre offer us ways to think differently about these issues? The transformative urges of the *Indexing* serial encourage us to revisit fairy-tale fantasies about justice, gender, and happily ever after.

SERIAL STORYTELLING AND THE CRIME GENRE

McGuire wrote both *Indexing* and *Indexing: Reflections* as part of Amazon's short-lived Kindle Serial publishing program. Running from 2012 to 2014, this initiative offered interested readers a subscription to an author's work in progress: subscribers would pay a single price and receive regular installments of the story, pushed directly to their Kindle e-reader. Author participation was by invitation only, and Amazon contracted writers to a rapid release schedule: 10,000 to 15,000 new words every other week for approximately six months. After the story was completed, Amazon rereleased it in its entirety as both an e-book and a physical book through its in-house 47North imprint. *Indexing* and *Indexing: Reflections* clearly bear the marks of this publishing structure. Both move episodically, oscillating between the individual cases Henry and her team are investigating and the slowly unravelling threads of a larger mystery. This makes it possible for readers to jump in (or out) partway through the project and still have a clear sense of the story and its world.

The structure also resembles that of the police procedural, a subgenre of the crime story and a "type of fiction in which the actual methods and procedures of police work are central to the structures, themes, and actions" (Scaggs 2005, 91). Popularized by works like Ed McBain's 87th Precinct novels (a fifty-five-book series) and Ian Rankin's Inspector Rebus series (now at twenty-five books), the police procedural follows a cadre of cops through their daily slog of paperwork and (mostly) minor crimes. With its tendency toward episodic and serial storytelling "suggestive of its place in the larger machine of indefinite, unceasing surveillance and discipline," the procedural is often approached as a persuasive vehicle for normative ideologies (Scaggs 2005, 89; see also Dove 1982; Winston and Wellerski 1992). Such analyses reflect a broader understanding of crime fiction as "a literature of containment, a narrative that 'makes safe'" through its typical focus on identifying threats to the social order and eventually restoring it (Plain 2001, 3). With its emphasis on the minutiae of police work as an effective antidote to everyday crime, the procedural grapples with ideas about safety and the status quo "not only with regard to specific police practices, but also concerning deeper problems of privilege and power" (Raskin 1992, 108).

The fairy tale has similarly been seen as a means of conveying social norms and dramatizing possible repercussions for deviating from them—or for even getting around them (see, e.g., Haase 2000; Warner 1995; Zipes 2006). A "locus of struggle over cultural values and individual desires," fairy-tale justice takes root in our sympathies—or antipathies—for characters' plights, rather than a codified list of rights and wrongs (Haase 2000, 40; see also Short 2018). With persistent themes of societal expectations and personal transformations, fairy tales (especially the popularized versions that are likely the most familiar to contemporary popular fiction readers) are also frequently stories of how to get to a happily ever after imagined as a magical instantiation of the heterosexual marriage plot. The *Indexing* serial's mix of fairy tale and crime fiction "plac[es] the fairy tale in new dynamics of competition and alliance with other genres," as a critical reflection on how idea(l)s of normality, justice, and happiness are perpetuated, and where they can be changed (Bacchilega 2013, 28).

MEMETIC INCURSIONS

The serial, case-style structure of the *Indexing* books underscores how fairy tales obtain and maintain their imaginative power through repetition. In *Indexing* they are instances of what the ATI Management Bureau refers to as *the narrative*, a world-building force that can effect change in the world as it already is: "The narrative is an old, dark force that keeps trying to worm its way back out into the light, and sometimes the only thing that keeps it locked away is knowledge" (McGuire 2013a, 245). The Bureau's language of memetic incursions echoes folklorist Jack Zipes's (2006) discussion of fairy tales as analogous to memes. In *The Irresistible Fairy Tale*, Zipes draws on the work of evolutionary biologist Richard Dawkins, especially Dawkins's (1976) influential concept of the meme as unit of cultural transmission—a vehicle for reproducing and communicating ideologies. Zipes encourages us to think of fairy tales in a similar way, arguing that a "a good example of a meme is a fairy tale, but not just any fairy tale, an individual fairy tale and its discursive tradition" (2006, 5). While fairy-tale scholars are not universally convinced by Zipes's argument, the imaginative implications of his ideas appear throughout the *Indexing* serial in how McGuire depicts and describes fairy-tale incursions into *Indexing*'s storyworld. As the Bureau's remit—it is "an organization dedicated to keeping stories from eating the world" (McGuire 2015, 4)—illustrates, the possibilities of memetic incursions literalize how "a fairy tale as meme is concerned with its own perpetuation and will adapt to changes and conflict in the environment" (Zipes 2006, 15).

Zipes posits that fairy tales stay active by updating to fit different cultural circumstances, to continue feeling familiar and relevant. We can see this, for instance, when Henry's colleague Sloane is casting about for some narrative threads to use to her own advantage during a memetic incursion, hoping that "maybe some kid was already dreaming up a Cinderella remix with guerrilla fighters in place of stepsisters, and she could tap into that sweet vein of potential story" (McGuire 2013a, 377). Fairy tales aren't just sets of stories that we tell, they are also discursive forces that insert themselves into the everyday because "all tales want to stay alive in us" (Zipes 2006, 27). In McGuire's stories this reproductive drive is literal; fairy tales are "capable of rewriting reality in order to get what they want—and what they want is rarely good for anybody who's not on the short list for a happy ending" (McGuire 2015, 4). For Bureau employees like Henry, the lingo they use to describe a story coming to life is "manifesting," and the narrative may start to manifest when it finds even the thinnest points of overlap between its own tropes and ordinary moments so that its story is the way people's lives are lived and told: "The narrative doesn't give a crap about whether it makes sense. The narrative just wants it to *happen*" (McGuire 2013a, 86).

Yet even before it does some people are already "story-touched," existing on the very edges of an imminent story. This includes Henry, who is "halfway into the Snow White mold" thanks to the circumstances of her birth. Her mother, "a four-ten, Sleeping Beauty. She was in a deep coma when my twin brother and I were born, the misbegotten children of the doctor who was supposed to be treating her injuries and wound up taking advantage of her instead" (McGuire 2013a, 6–7).[2] Orphaned and raised by the Bureau, Henry is adept at fairy-tale patterns, skilled at creatively changing their trajectory so that they no longer resonate with the narrative. Leading a team of other story-touched agents, she is tasked with preventing narrative manifestations and saving innocent lives: "The law that we were enforcing wasn't the law of men or countries. It was the law of the narrative, and it was our job to prevent the story from going the way it always had before—impossible as that could sometimes seem" (13).

Following the law of the narrative does not mean following legal norms or even social norms, but instead *story* norms. Generally in fairy tales "those we would regard as victims of crime are simply presented as unlucky, often receiving no recompense, despite experiencing behavior that we would now deem to be unlawful" (Short 2018, 171). To combat this, Henry and her team call upon the logics of the crime story, which insists that threats be contained and order restored. This offers the Bureau agents—and us, as readers—an opportunity to look again at the fates that fairy tales have in store for their protagonists, especially women, through the lens of the crime story. For instance, *Indexing*'s first case, Alicia Connors, turns out to be another fourten, a Sleeping Beauty, and her presence starts putting bystanders to sleep shortly after she arrives at the hospital. In this memetic incursion, the hospital becomes "the modern-day castle where a silly little girl who'd pricked her finger on something she shouldn't have been touching was sleeping through the day that she'd been born for" (McGuire 2013a, 31). Henry and her team manage to thwart the narrative's plans to combine a sleeping sickness with the H1N1 flu: they find and activate a nearby Pied Piper, Demi Santos, because "if it's a disease, it falls under the AT Index for 'vermin,' and if the problem is vermin, we can resolve the story with another story" (19). Demi summons a host of rats, pipes the virus into them, and then directs the rodents to commit suicide. Even more, they also manage to save Alicia from the rest of Sleeping Beauty's story: "She wouldn't need a Prince to save her. She wouldn't sleep through her own rape and pregnancy, or any of the other horrible fates that await the four-tens" (34).

In another case, overworked diner waitress Jennifer Lockwood thinks she's simply dreaming about bears outside her bedroom window—until she sees claw marks and paw prints. Jennifer "looked like the sort of woman who had long since given up wishing for a fairy-tale ending, and was just hoping to make it through the week without collapsing. Too bad for her that the fairy tale hadn't given up so easily" (McGuire 2013a, 72). Her economic precarity sets the narrative in motion, since working back-to-back-to-back shifts in order to make ends meet leaves her so exhausted that she often falls fast asleep within minutes; the narrative uses this opportunity to launch a lesser-known version of "Goldilocks and the Three Bears," in which "Goldilocks didn't initially break into the home of the three bears—they came in *her* home and took it over. Then, when she tried to chase them out, the normal 'larcenous little girl' narrative started to unfold. We're probably looking at one of these home-invasion scenarios" (85). The animals vanish only after Henry and her colleagues have deliberately berated Jennifer for making a prank 911 call and Jennifer anxiously, profusely apologizes, promising never to do it again. In this case, the tendency of crime and cop stories to blame (often female) victims for their own vulnerability draws attention to the ways in which fairy tales routinely disenfranchise their female figures. In their ongoing struggle to prevent or at least mitigate the effects of memetic incursions, Henry and her team regularly rely on the narrative force of the crime drama because "if you're supposed to fight fire with fire, then it made sense to fight narrative with narrative" (6).

COP AND CRIME STORIES

McGuire marshals the patterns of the crime story throughout both books, presenting it as its own powerful, sense-making generic structure in which policing appears "both as a material practice and as a symbolic rhetoric where cultural authority . . . [has] been reenacted and debated" (Wilson 2000, 6). As Henry notes: "People forget law enforcement is a narrative too" (McGuire 2015, 282), and it's one of the only ways memetic incursions can be countered. The tropes of the police procedural are especially effective, for "bureaucracy trumps narrative any day" (7). The ATI Management Bureau relies on the standardized, repetitive nature of everyday policing procedures to predict the narrative's threat to social order. This includes, for instance, carefully monitoring social media accounts for clues that someone may be the site of the next memetic incursion: "She has all the symptoms. Pale skin, dark hair, affinity for small animals—she works in a shelter that takes in exotics, and half the pictures we were able to pull off her Facebook profile show her with birds, rats, or weird-ass lizards hanging out on her shoulders" (McGuire 2013a, 10).

The "stress on the methods and procedures of police investigations that characterizes the police procedural" recurs throughout both *Indexing* and *Reflections*, showcased in part through Henry's begrudging acquiescence to the Bureau's rules and orders (Scaggs 2005, 93). One typical source of friction between Henry and the ATI Bureau is the institution's insistence on thorough documentation of all of its agents' actions—in other words, paperwork, part of the "living folklore of policing" (Smith, Pedersen, and Burnett 2014, 219). We regularly see Henry frustrated by this part of the job, in the police procedural's familiar shift from scenes of high-action crime fighting to slow, tedious office work. As she gripes after returning from another successful intervention: "And my reward for saving her, for granting her a second chance at happy ever after? Paperwork. Oceans and seas and fjords of paperwork. Virtual kingdoms of paperwork, spread out across my desk like the vanguard of an invading army, all needing to be defeated if I wanted to avoid an internal review of my actions" (McGuire 2013a, 34).

Henry's colorful language is also reminiscent of the sardonic voice and vivid metaphors of hard-boiled crime fiction (Christianson 1989). We see this hard-boiled attitude in Henry's pointed observations about another one of the narrative's potential victims when she and her team first arrive on the scene: "She was beautiful in the classical seven-oh-nine way, with sleek black hair and snowy skin that probably burned horribly in the summer" (McGuire 2013a, 13). Like classic gumshoes Philip Marlowe and Sam Spade, for whom "wit is the weapon that enables him to expose people, situations, and institutions for what they are," Henry is similarly cynical about the chasm between law and justice (Porter 1981, 166). Surveying the bodies left behind after a Cinderella turns violent, she ruminates: "I won't say that these women would have deserved to die under normal circumstances, but if they pushed a five-ten-A into going homicidal, then they probably did something unforgivable. She's already paid for this crime in advance" (McGuire 2013a, 136–37). Henry's moral compass is oriented not by the letter of the law but by her own experience with what the narrative portends when it pushes its way into her world, a reframed perspective on fairy-tale tropes that emphasizes the ways in which they turn to tragic rather than happy endings.

This shift is also highlighted by McGuire's substitutions of Aarne-Thompson Index classifications for standard police codes. While police officers use numerical codes as shorthand to quickly communicate the type of incident they're reporting or investigating, the ATI Management Bureau employs the AT number system. Developed by scholar Antti Aarne in the early 1900s as a mechanism for identifying and cataloguing the motifs that appeared across European folklore, the system was updated throughout the mid-1900s by Stith Thompson—its purview expanded and categories modified to include numerical designations for each tale type. Since then, other researchers have iterated on this work, most notably Hans-Jörg Uther, whose *The Types of International Folktales: A Classification and Bibliography* (2004) proposed the now widely accepted ATU Index, which includes more details for many tale types and incorporates stories from across a wider cultural base. Both the AT and the ATU Index list core narrative elements for each fairy tale, as well as common variations and combinations.

In McGuire's work, the index is the backbone of the Bureau's arsenal, and Henry's team brings a paper copy with them on all cases. They use it to determine what they're dealing with by matching the events they encounter with those itemized in the ATI: "We use the Aarne-Thompson Index to map the manifestations as much as we can cross-referencing fairy tales from all over the world. . . . Like any rating system, the ATI has its flaws, but it mostly gets the job done, and it's better than running around in the dark all the damn time" (McGuire 2013a, 6). Henry's colleague Jeffrey is the team's ATI expert, tasked with knowing minute details and histories of each tale type as well as evolving versions and new additions. The latter is especially important on the ground, as we see when Henry is getting ready to head into the Bureau's interrogation room: "The scene felt faintly unreal, like something out of a story, and I made a note to ask Jeff whether the narrative could be making use of modern television tropes as well as urban legends and the like. I didn't particularly want to find myself in the kind of crime drama where someone always gets shot right before the commercial break" (291).

Henry's anxiety here reflects one of the other important uses of the ATI among her team: as a record not just of what stories *were*, but of what they *are now*. A form of institutional storytelling and labor, McGuire's version of the ATI is an evolving document that agents use to capture and define the patterns of people's lives; it is "a policing practice in itself, and does not merely represent reality, but also brings new perspectives on reality" (Smith, Pedersen, and Burnett 2014, 218). This distinguishes it from the "real" AT Index that informs scholarly pursuits, since Jeffrey and other Bureau archivists regularly update the field version to include other stories that have become embedded in popular culture and consciousness. As Henry explains: "Little Mermaids are a relatively recent addition to the Index: technically, they're not listed in the ATI, since the version used by mundane scholars only looks at true folktales and motifs, not stories whose authors have been identified and listed in the public record. Maybe we shouldn't list the voiceless girls and boys either, but our job is hard enough without splitting our best defense into multiple rulebooks" (McGuire 2013a, 304).

In the hands of the ATI Management Bureau, the ATI becomes both a prescriptive and descriptive manual for its agents, and "underlying all of this potential for change to the ATI is the possibility for change to the existing stories and new stories" (Williams 2021, 90). McGuire's use of the crime story to frame encounters with fairy tales creates a struggle between accepted and emergent ways of seeing and being in the world; Henry and her colleagues police this line between how things are and how things could or should be.

DOCUMENTING AND BUREAUCRATIZING FAIRY TALES

That these are competing discourses is underscored by a revelation near the end of *Indexing*, in which another, ancient Snow White scolds Henry for her lack of narrative thinking: "What, you thought one story was somehow more real than all the others, just because it's the one that has the most people living in it? Shit, if it worked that way, all the narratives would focus on quantity over quality, and we'd be buried under something featuring rabbits. What we think of as reality is just the tale type that took over longest ago. The others keep fighting back" (McGuire 2013a, 372).

The revelation that Henry's reality is simply one story of how the world works brings the policing function of the ATI and the ATI Management Bureau into even sharper focus. More than just a resource for identifying tale types, the ATI functions as "common-sense organizational knowledge" (Smith, Pedersen, and Burnett 2014, 220) about this reality, a codification of people into character types and events into outcomes. This information is used not only to manage aberrant behavior in the city's—and even the Bureau's—population, but to predict and preempt it as well. Making these determinations by adding to and updating the ATI is an exercise of institutional authority, for the "documentation implies stability, but as the stories change . . . it is clear that the stability is a product of the documentation or narrative structures, not the stories themselves" (Williams 2021, 84).

Updating the Bureau's official index is a ponderous bureaucratic prerogative limited to a small number of people in the institution's upper echelons, not the agents on the ground who see how memetic incursions—their reality—are adapting. Henry's colleague Sloane bemoans this arduous process during one of their team meetings: "Wasn't there a management discussion like ten years ago about adding—what's it called—urban legends to the Index? Since they're sort of like a new form of memetic incursion that's been getting more codified with every repetition?" (McGuire 2013a, 181). Such decisions are deliberated far above agents' heads, and on a decades-long timeline that is out of step with what they experience every day.

Henry explains that some of it is organizational inertia: "The ATI Management Bureau is the way it is today because it's had centuries to grow and evolve, going from a loose alliance of storytellers and archivists to a governmentally funded agency with ties to law enforcement and media censorship agencies. We don't change quickly" (McGuire 2013a, 155). Today, the

ATI's definitions and categorizations are entrenched forms of hierarchical institutional knowledge, often designed to make the work of administration easier. Now, the index is part of the Bureau's *"symbolic* authority: . . . [the] parts of police power that involve story-making, the mobilization and differentiation of audiences, the engagement with media, the engineering of consent" (Wilson 2000, 12).

Such world-making power can be appealing to those in its proximity, as Henry and her team learn by the end of *Indexing*. Not only do they find themselves sent out on more response calls than usual, but their cases often turn out to be something else—and something worse—than initially reported. The team's archivist Jeff suspects it could be the work of a Storyteller: "There are tale types that include storytellers. . . . The whole Scheherazade class of narratives depend on someone who can tell them—and that's just one grouping. We could be dealing with someone, a person, who can control the narrative. And if that's true . . ." (McGuire 2013a, 223). Jeff's concerns are realized when they figure out that Birdie Hubbard, one of the Bureau's operations agents, has been intervening in memetic incursions, putting Henry and her team in grave danger. Birdie works as a dispatcher, closely monitoring all communication and surveillance traffic in the city and mining it for any clues that a memetic incursion may be imminent.

This is a privileged position within the institution, "important from an organizational context in terms of initiating and perpetuating the social and political dimensions of police knowledge" (Smith, Pedersen, and Burnett 2014, 232) as it connects the day-to-day life of the city to the institutionalized knowledge and militarized response of the Bureau. Birdie is authorized to label everyday occurrences as significant, and in doing so she emboldens the narrative. She is the one behind the quickly changing tales they're attempting to control, part of her larger scheme to bring a different reality into ascendance, as she condescendingly explains to her hired goons: "Yes, dearie, all that 'fairy tale mumbo jumbo' is real, and we're going to help it become even *more* real, because once the rules of the world are rewritten into something more . . . pliant . . . people like me and our benefactor will be as gods" (McGuire 2013a, 385).

Birdie's dream of wielding her own narrative power is amplified by her status as a Mother Goose—the fictional author of a variety of folktales, and a connection initially overlooked since the Bureau's ATI doesn't include Mother Goose, who is a literary figure, or Mother Hubbard, as an authored nursery rhyme. Yet what gets included and excluded from ATI is determined by the interests of those in or near power (like Birdie); much like its real-world counterpart, the ATI "was written by humans.... There can be holes" (McGuire 2013a, 258). These holes in documented, official knowledge make it easier for Birdie to slip through the cracks of the ATI Management Bureau's system, since according to their records Mother Goose doesn't exist and therefore cannot be a threat. Henry and her team know differently, for the "paperwork and the fictional AT index (as well as the real one) imply discrete order whereas the 'lived' experience of the characters demonstrates far more fluidity than the structuralist approach allows" (Williams 2021, 83).

The agents' more fragmented firsthand knowledge means that they have to act in response not to the official documentation of what memetic incursions are, but to the tales as they actually find them—to a world in which Mother Goose is a real and present threat. Without any approved guidelines for how to manage the danger Birdie represents, Henry improvises, using the skills and stories she has on hand: "There's something major about *every* narrative that the Bureau doesn't know.... That's the nature of stories. No one ever gets to know the entire thing. We just get to know the parts we have to deal with right there, right now" (McGuire 2013a, 376). Trapped beside a bomb Birdie planted to take out Henry and her team, Henry deliberately activates her story, becomes both herself and a Snow White—susceptible to the narrative's machinations, yet also able to use its forces to her own ends.

Henry disregards one of the Bureau's foundational rules—to not activate your story—in order to save her team. In doing so, she also starts to rewrite her trajectory: "My story might have started with a spoiled little princess who was scared of her own shadow, but it wasn't going to end that way" (McGuire 2013a, 267). Leveraging Snow White's affinity for nature, Henry calls forth a flood of woodland creatures and packs them into the small space between her team and the bombs Birdie has planted, sacrificing the animals' lives by using them as a shield. With this gruesome act, Henry challenges and changes the story of Snow White, and casts doubt upon the Bureau's claims to knowledge, order, and authority.

NAMING THE STORY-TOUCHED

Henry isn't the first or the only Bureau employee to be an active story. Her acerbic teammate Sloane is also story-touched, and has been for centuries. Older than the Bureau and predating the ATI, Sloane is both inside and outside a story: "Story-struck, yes, but only from the side; the story [she] stepped through was never meant for [her]" (McGuire 2015, 205). Sloane is particularly valuable to the Bureau because she is more finely attuned to narrative forces than most: "There are those who would use me as a form of narrative bloodhound, and they're not entirely wrong in that: I'm a dowsing rod for active stories, shaking them out of the fabric of the world one sentence at a time, until they're pinned to the page before me" (222). The best the Bureau can determine is that Sloane's a "failed Wicked Stepsister," however the Bureau is uncomfortable with her narrative indeterminacy (McGuire 2013a, 35). Because the index is so central to how the organization "use[s] stories as 'sense-making' and 'sense-giving' heuristics and in the social construction of knowledge to create common sense and order in their world and to bring evidential order out of the dramatic and chaotic" (Smith, Pedersen, and Burnett 2014, 231–32), the Bureau is determined to fix her with a tale type as a means of exerting control.

When Henry gets a glimpse of Sloane's past in *Reflections*, we experience Sloane's history for ourselves—not as a tale type, but instead as a young woman determined to break free from the narrative's hold on her family, and forever battling to keep it from overtaking her as well. We also see the context behind the Bureau's constitution, its transition from an ad hoc group of storytellers and story-hunters to a formalized arm of the American government—and its burgeoning organizational mission to have all tales categorized and labeled, including Sloane's:

> "Ah, but you see, we've found the story for you!" The man sounded smugly pleased with himself. "Number three-fifteen, 'The Treacherous Sister.'" Sloane frowned. "Sir, I've read every book of fairy tale and folklore I could find, from all around the world. I have sponsored translations. The story you reference has nothing to do with me. . . . You can't give me a label that doesn't fit. It serves as no true warning." "The stories will be what we say they are," said the man. "That's the point of this exercise. We'll remake them in the image that suits us best." (McGuire 2015, 213–14)

Sloane's centuries of experience and expertise are cast aside in favor of what the Bureau thinks it already knows, and "her story is twisted to fit what already exists in order to preserve the authority of the index and the Bureau" (Williams 2021, 86). Her role in the crime story is often closer to that of an informant, thanks to her deep knowledge of fairy tales and her firsthand experience of the narrative's power. Moreover, Sloane is coerced into working for the Bureau, given a choice between serving its interests or being locked away in its prison, designed specifically to keep the story-touched away from the general public. That her freedom is always only at the Bureau's discretion is heightened by mandatory "therapy" sessions that double as surveillance to see that Sloane does not become a successful Wicked Stepsister. Trapped by the slow, steady churn of power the Bureau represents, Sloane struggles between who she is, who the story tries to turn her into, and who the Bureau wants her to be.

SNOW WHITE MEETS THE CRIME STORY

Sloane's fraught history with the Bureau illustrates how its "classification system can be used to contain stories rather than describe them" (Williams 2021, 85). It also showcases one of McGuire's preoccupations in this series: exploring how fairy tales often limit women's agency and autonomy—or punish them for it. The crime story's "profound investment in dynamics of power inevitably incorporates discourses of gender and sexuality" (Plain 2001, 8), and this structure furthers how the fairy-tale women in *Indexing* grapple with the expectations of their stories by bringing some of crime's own archetypal tropes into the script, like the femme fatale. The femme fatale is a figure of both fascination and fear as she evades the limited roles of victim or damsel in distress most commonly available for women in crime stories, and is especially intriguing to the story's (usually male) detective. A "constellation of tropes and characteristics emerging from concerns about women and power," she typically serves as a cautionary tale about stepping too far from comfortable, accepted forms of femininity (Stacy Gillis, quoted in Farrimond 2018, 4; see also Doane 1991; Grossman 2020; Kaplan 2019).

In *Indexing* this role is played by another Snow White—Adrianna—whose fate has long been used by the Bureau to keep Henry herself in line: "They made me recite her history while I was in school, drumming the failure that she represented deep into the marrow of my bones. Never again. Other stories could turn sour, but not mine: never again" (McGuire 2013a, 147). As we learn in *Reflections*, however, Adrianna's aberrant behavior—a murderous rampage in which she killed more than twenty people—was an act of vengeance for the deaths of her sisters, leaving her angry with "those Bureau bastards who never thought to ask what had set her off and left her to be consumed by rage. They had never once asked how she had grown to adulthood without losing herself to either her temper or her story" (McGuire 2015, 135). Instead of working with her to learn more about her encounters with the narrative, the Bureau tossed her into its prison for fairy tales, where she continued to be berated for not being the right kind of Snow White: *"Bad little girl*, whispered the prison. *Learn your place and be grateful that you have it"* (135).

As a "category that feeds cultural gender fantasies," the femme fatale is clever and manipulative, and poses a threat to the moral integrity of the crime story's hero (Grossman 2020, 19). Henry encounters this side of Adrianna in the Whiteout Wood, an (un)conscious realm where all manifested Snow Whites past and present gather that takes the form of an endless, dreamy forest landscape. When Adrianna tries to pursue Henry the wood shifts and twists, a blizzard making each wintry grove seem identical to the next in a scene reminiscent of the iconic funhouse mirror sequence at the end of director Orson Welles's classic film noir *The Lady from Shanghai* (1947); Henry even escapes by leaping through one of the wood's mirrored doorways that leads back to the waking world. Yet the "flexibility of 'femme fatale' as an evocative rather than a descriptive term" (Farrimond 2018, 3) makes it possible for us to read Adrianna as a figure of resistance.

What begins as a warning about women's agency and duplicity—about the social risks of being something other than or more than the norm—ends up as another rumination on the social institutions and power dynamics that attempt to govern women's behaviors. In hard-boiled detective fiction and film noir, femmes fatale "strive to find meaning outside oppressive social roles" (Grossman 2020, 3). It's through her conflict with Adrianna that Henry starts to see the possibilities for remaking Snow White for herself. Henry's interactions with Adrianna and with the other Snow Whites in the Whiteout Wood are important moments of self-reflection; Henry sees herself in these women, and uses what she sees to think about her own story. In the wood, "the Snow White story was infinitely complex, a canvas defined only by a shared colour and a sketchy common narrative. We would all eat the apple; we would all find ourselves in coffins made of glass. It was the space between those events that mattered, defining us in ways we couldn't explain, but lived through every day" (McGuire 2015, 292).

The gaps between the Snow White story and Snow Whites like Adrianna and Henry draw attention to how fairy tales—and discourses around fairy tales—(re)produce gendered expectations about autonomy and self-determination, and the crime story is central to how Adrianna and Henry make these spaces their own. Just as Adrianna's independence is refracted through the figure of the femme fatale, Henry's detective work helps her see herself as more than a princess: "I could hear voices in the snow. And yes, they spoke of hearth and home and service to others. But what I did for the Bureau was a form of service, wasn't it? Maybe I didn't wash windows, but I saved lives, and that wasn't 'just as good.' That was *better*. I was *better* for my story because of what I did" (McGuire 2015, 306).

While both the police officer and the detective have historically been male-dominated roles in crime stories (see, e.g., Krutnik 1994; Walton and Jones 1999), the increasing prominence of the female detective in pop culture moves Henry beyond the confines of the Snow White story and into another one: the story of the woman investigator. As Deborah Jermyn points out, the "presence of a female detective in itself is no longer worthy of remark, nor an innovation or novelty in itself" (2017, 260; see also Brown 2011, 2015; Mizejewski 2004). Now an expected crime story character, the woman cop is part of the pulse of the law enforcement narrative that Henry calls upon to keep herself in focus after activating her story, as she proclaims: "This wasn't a fairy tale, and I was not a princess in hiding. I was Henrietta Marchen, field agent, and fuck the narrative if it wanted me to be anything else" (McGuire 2013a, 286).

Henry's defiant attitude toward the gendered expectations of the Snow White story echoes the oppositional stance of what Jeffrey Brown (2011, 2015) calls the action heroine: an increasingly popular female character type found in places like crime fictions, who assumes the central agentive, action-oriented role historically reserved for men. In doing so, action heroines "reconfigure the logic of power, privilege, and narrative authority" endemic to their genre or story norms, as Henry's determination to resist the fairy-tale princess's passivity demonstrates (Brown 2011, 17). The action heroine is also typically presented as a neoliberal heroine, her choices embodying the "assumption that each of us is responsible for our own happiness, our success" (Brown 2015, 169; see also Braithwaite 2021; Chen 2013; Rottenberg 2018). We find such a limited sphere of influence in the *Indexing* serial as the stories sketch out a patriarchal, bureaucratic, and carceral system of law and order. The Bureau's coercive exploitative employment practices, for instance, wedge active stories between working for the Bureau or being remanded to Childe, its prison for fairy-tale figures housed in a former asylum.

Childe's compulsion charms act on its inhabitants to keep them docile and obedient—to mute the narrative's influence on their thoughts and actions. Demi, the team's newest recruit, describes her experience in the prison prior to agreeing to become a field agent: "It's supposed to keep us from freaking out and killing each other when we're all locked up together like a big box of stories. All it ever did for me was scramble my brains into pudding" (McGuire 2015, 35). Most of the people trapped in Childe are there only because they are manifested narratives, not because they have committed any particular crime: "This was what the Bureau was doing to all the stories they had in custody. Innocent people whose only crime was being afflicted with an incurable narrative were being kept under the same spells that were used to control and contain real villains" (38–39).

Henry finally experiences the effects of the compulsion charms now that she is an active Snow White, and Jeff encourages her to act on her newfound knowledge, to use her position of leadership and authority to advocate for changes to the Bureau's reliance on incarceration as an employee- and fairy tale–management strategy: "You're one of us now. . . . Maybe management will listen when you say that this is inhumane. They're letting you lead a field team, after all" (McGuire 2015, 35). Yet this system persists beyond the novels' resolution, leaving intact the Bureau's punitive approach to fairy tales it can't incorporate or make use of. Henry's complacency at the end of the series emphasizes how her own happily ever after takes narrative precedence, as she reflects on how "all those things were problems for later. Right now, I was here, I was home, and I was one step closer to the ever after that I deserved. That was what mattered . . . that was all that mattered in the world" (325). Brown notes that "the ideological chasm between a myopic focus on the self and the belief in collective agency" (2015, 178) typifies the work of many action heroines.

Indexing's overarching focus on how Henry tracks down errant Snow White Adrianna makes this tension between individual and collective agency clear, for Henry is pulled between understanding Snow White as part of her own self and seeing the character as an archetype and a narrative trajectory. Her work on behalf of the Bureau to restore the existing social order further complicates her sense of identity: "There were so many things I could have said. Any one of them would have ended the scene, and would have determined who I was going to be hereafter. I swallowed them all, seeing the one that meant Henry Marchen, the one that meant early mornings and late nights and fights with Human Resources and a brother I never saw and a Shoemaker's Elf who might eventually be able to kiss me out of a coma. It wasn't easy. She didn't have as much of a story behind her" (McGuire 2013a, 402).

Henry's nascent story persists beyond these narrative roles, for while the Whiteout Wood offers a communal space for past Snow Whites, it also opens pathways to connect with present ones when they lie unconscious; Adrianna uses these pathways to vanish from the wood and back into the world, into Henry's vulnerable form. To catch up, Henry finds another comatose Snow White and inhabits her body. She is able to convince her coworkers that she is Henry under this skin by describing their shared social lives. While the narrative works hard to homogenize the Snow Whites it creates—"skin bleached into alien pallor by the story that had shaped them" (McGuire 2013a, 270)—the events that follow Henry and Adrianna's body swapping tell us that these women aren't determined by their fairy-tale bodies.

That fairy-tale bodies are not fairy-tale destinies is most fully realized by Henry's twin brother Gerry. Born biologically female like Henry, Gerry "had always been my brother, even if most people refused to understand that. Both of us had always known exactly who we were" (McGuire 2013a, 341). The narrative, in contrast, is focused on "the flesh, not the person inside it," an insistence that made it possible for Gerry to evade the narrative altogether (McGuire 2015, 252). By reclaiming his gender, Gerry not only found himself but also discovered a way out of the plot the narrative had for him: "He didn't get caught in a story, because he was born part of a story that could never have been his . . . the narrative wanted him to be a princess, and the only way to get away from it was to leave everything behind" (75).

In one of the *Indexing* serial's most striking imaginings of "how fairy tales affect the making of who we are and the world we are in" (Bacchilega

2013, 3; see also Butler 1999; Zipes 2006), the repetition that is necessary for a fairy tale's power and persistence also creates the conditions for subverting its expectations. Importantly, Gerry's escape from the narrative's plan also shows his sister Henry that fairy-tale narratives, even revised ones, aren't the only stories out there; his happily ever after means leaving *the* narrative—and *all* narratives—behind. Now a "high school English teacher and purposefully ordinary guy," Gerry is so determined to exist outside the narrative's purview that he distances himself both physically and emotionally from Henry (and Sloane, with whom he'd had an intense fling) (McGuire 2013a, 328). When he and Henry briefly reconnect in *Indexing* he tells her: "Boring has sort of been my life's goal," and by avoiding any generic or storied structure to his life, Gerry is also avoiding any expectations beyond his own of how or who he is supposed to be (354).

"THE STORY CHANGES"

Truths are changeable, Henry learns. Lived experiences, desires, and beliefs have the capacity to shift discursive structures for making meanings. While patterns in some people's lives may make them more susceptible to the narrative, the inverse also holds true: proximity or adjacency to the narrative makes it easier to repurpose its energy to alternate endings—to a different kind of happily ever after. And so after Henry's colleague Jeff kisses her to draw her out of a narrative-induced coma near the end of *Indexing*, they admit their romantic feelings for each other. Part of why their relationship works is *because* it doesn't follow the pattern of either of their stories: "Jeff was no Prince Charming and I was no dainty little maiden . . . while there had been hundreds, if not thousands, of people like us through the years, I was pretty sure we were the first ones to fall into bed together" (McGuire 2015, 3).

At the end of *Reflections* they're happily cohabitating, yet it's an ending far from those the narrative—and even broader social norms—feed upon: "I don't know whether what Jeff and I have is true love, and I don't care. I like him. He likes me. He makes me feel safe. Why should I require 'true love' on top of all that?" (McGuire 2015, 260). By framing fairy tales within the larger trajectory of the crime story, McGuire creates spaces to reflect on and update their traditional expectations of justice and happiness. At the same time, some of the impulses of the crime story simply re-dress these idea(l)s, reinforcing individualistic narratives in which success appears as the apprehension of single antisocial villains, while the larger bureaucratic and carceral systems that prop up the existing social order remain intact. Yet there is no guarantee that even that power is secure, for when she incorporates the life of a fairy-tale princess into the life of a crime-fighting detective, becoming a heroine somewhere in between Snow White and a cynical cop, Henry shows us that "the story *changes*" (McGuire 2015, 310).

NOTES

1. Now replaced, as discussed below, by the Aarne-Thompson-Uther (ATU) index (Uther 2004).

2. Four-ten refers to the number assigned to "Sleeping Beauty" in the tale-type index, AT[U] 410. In contrast to current scholarly convention, McGuire uses "AT" rather than "ATU" for her classifications (as well as a few tale types of her own invention). Moreover, instead of numerals, McGuire writes out the numbers in full—a nod to police call numbers, as I discuss further on. To underscore this aspect of genre mixing, I maintain McGuire's own style throughout.

REFERENCES

Bacchilega, Cristina. 2013. *Fairy Tales Transformed? Twenty-First-Century Adaptations and the Politics of Wonder*. Detroit: Wayne State University Press.
Braithwaite, Andrea. 2021. "Lost Girl: Popular Feminism and Fables." *MAI: Feminism and Visual Culture* 7. June 14. https://maifeminism.com/lost-girl-popular-feminism-and-fables.
Brown, Jeffrey A. 2011. *Danger Curves: Action Heroines, Gender Fetishism, and Popular Culture*. Jackson: University Press of Mississippi.
Brown, Jeffrey A. 2015. *Beyond Bombshells: The New Action Heroine in Popular Culture*. Jackson: University Press of Mississippi.
Butler, Judith. 1999. *Gender Trouble: Feminism and the Subversion of Identity*. New York: Routledge.
Chen, Eva. 2013. "Neoliberalism and Popular Women's Culture: Rethinking Choice, Freedom and Agency." *European Journal of Cultural Studies* 16 (4): 440–52.
Christianson, Scott R. 1989. "Tough Talk and Wisecracks: Language as Power in American Detective Fiction." *Journal of Popular Culture* 23 (2): 151–62.
Dawkins, Richard. 1976. *The Selfish Gene*. Oxford: Oxford University Press.
Doane, Mary Ann. 1991. *Femmes Fatales: Feminism, Film Theory, Psychoanalysis*. New York: Routledge.

Dove, George. 1982. *The Police Procedural*. Bowling Green, OH: Bowling Green University Popular Press.
Farrimond, Katherine. 2018. *The Contemporary Femme Fatale: Gender, Genre and American Cinema*. New York: Routledge.
Grossman, Julie. 2020. *The Femme Fatale*. New Brunswick, NJ: Rutgers University Press.
Haase, Donald. 2000. "Feminist Fairy-Tale Scholarship: A Critical Survey and Bibliography." *Marvels & Tales* 14 (1): 15–63.
Jermyn, Deborah. 2017. "Silk Blouses and Fedoras: The Female Detective, Contemporary TV Crime Drama and the Predicaments of Postfeminism." *Crime Media Culture* 13 (3): 259–76.
Kaplan, E. Ann, ed. 2019. *Women in Film Noir*. London: BFI.
Krutnik, Frank. 1994. *In a Lonely Street: Film Noir, Genre, Masculinity*. London: Routledge.
The Lady From Shanghai. 1947. Directed by Orson Welles. United States: Columbia Pictures.
McGuire, Seanan. 2013a. *Indexing*. Seattle: 47North.
McGuire, Seanan. 2013b. "Once upon an over and over and over again . . ." *LiveJournal*, May 31. https://seanan-mcguire.livejournal.com/512685.html.
McGuire, Seanan. 2015. *Indexing: Reflections*. Seattle: 47North.
Mizejewski, Linda. 2004. *Hardboiled and High Heeled: The Woman Detective in Popular Culture*. New York: Routledge.
Plain, Gill. 2001. *Twentieth-Century Crime Fiction: Gender, Sexuality, and the Body*. Edinburgh: Edinburgh University Press.
Porter, Dennis. 1981. *The Pursuit of Crime: Art and Ideology in Detective Fiction*. New Haven, CT: Yale University Press.
Raskin, Richard. 1992. "The Pleasures and Politics of Detective Fiction." *Clues: A Journal of Detection* 13 (2): 71–113.
Rottenberg, Catherine. 2018. *The Rise of Neoliberal Feminism*. New York: Oxford University Press.
Scaggs, John. 2005. *Crime Fiction*. London: Routledge.
Short, Sue. 2018. "Crime/Justice." In *The Routledge Companion to Media and Fairy-Tale Cultures*, edited by Pauline Greenhill, Jill Terry Rudy, Naomi Hamer, and Lauren Bosc, 171–77. New York: Routledge.
Smith, Robert, Sarah Pedersen, and Simon Burnett. 2014. "Towards an Organizational Folklore of Policing: The Storied Nature of Policing and the Police Use of Storytelling." *Folklore* 125 (2): 218–37.
Uther, Hans-Jörg. 2004. *The Types of International Folktales: A Classification and Bibliography*. Helsinki: Suomalainen Tiedeakatemia.
Walton, Priscilla L., and Manina Jones. 1999. *Detective Agency: Women Rewriting the Hard-Boiled Tradition*. Berkeley: University of California Press.

Warner, Marina. 1995. *From the Beast to the Blonde: On Fairy Tales and Their Tellers*. New York: Farrar, Straus & Giroux.

Williams, Christy. 2021. *Mapping Fairy-Tale Space: Pastiche and Metafiction in Borderless Tales*. Detroit: Wayne State University Press.

Wilson, Christopher P. 2000. *Cop Knowledge: Police Power and Cultural Narrative in Twentieth-Century America*. Chicago: University of Chicago Press.

Winston, Robert P., and Nancy C. Mellerski. 1992. *The Public Eye: Ideology and the Police Procedural*. Basingstoke, UK, Macmillan.

Zipes, Jack. 2006. *The Irresistible Fairy Tale: The Cultural and Social History of a Genre*. Princeton, NJ: Princeton University Press.

6

Disabled Bodies, Hurting Emotions

Suicide and Toxic Masculinity in The Fall

HEIDI KOSONEN

The Fall (henceforth *Fall*) is a 2006 adventure fantasy film directed and co-written by Tarsem Singh (also known as Tarsem) with Dan Gilroy and Nico Soultanakis, based on the 1981 Bulgarian drama film *Yo Ho Ho*. Set in a hospital in early twentieth-century Los Angeles, *Fall* features an unusual friendship between paralyzed Hollywood stunt player Roy Walker (Lee Pace) and a young Romanian girl, Alexandria (Catinca Untaru), who has broken her arm. The movie opens with Roy's accident, depicted over the slow-motion black-and-white opening credits accompanied by the second movement of Beethoven's Symphony No. 7: a man's head emerges from the depths of a river; people dressed as cowboys and Native Americans mill about; workers and bystanders are on a cross-river bridge; a halted train emits steam; a man is pushed away on a trolley; a beautiful woman fondles a heart-shaped locket, as if disturbed from pleasant contemplation; a horse is lifted from the water. Clearly, a stunt jump has gone severely wrong.

As revealed later in the film, Roy was paralyzed, with little hope of recovery, while performing a stunt to impress his former fiancée, the beautiful

https://doi.org/10.7330/9781646425853.c006

woman shown in the opening credits, who abandoned him for her co-actor. Alexandria is in the hospital after sustaining a fall while picking oranges. Five years old, endowed with a vivid imagination but speaking only rudimentary English, she wanders into Roy's hospital room, whereupon he involves her in his suicide plan. To persuade Alexandria to steal a fatal dose of morphine for him, he starts telling the child a heroic story of love and revenge. She introjects herself into the story, with the result that she alters it, eventually also changing Roy and his plans.

Thematically, the film is a study of male suicidality, a topic rarely confronted within Anglophone films without excessive layers of symbolism and distancing (Kosonen 2020a).[1] However, male self-endangerment roots several action genres of cinema with heroic, reckless, or even death-desiring male protagonists witnessed in varied "mortality-testing, death-defying, and martyr-invoking moments" (Aaron 2014, 19). To be specific, *Fall* studies its male protagonist's suicidal ideation in relation to this romanticized martyr-invoking aesthetic as propagated by the films that Roy himself, as a stunt player, is involved with.

The protagonists in Roy's story are a multicultural group of bandits on a quest to vanquish the evil Governor Odious (Daniel Caltagirone), who has committed crimes against all of them. Ex-slave Otta Benga's (Marcus Wesley) brother has died in bondage; one-legged Italian explosives expert Luigi (Robin Smith) has been banished from his home; Indian's (Jeetu Verma) beautiful "squaw" has suicided to save herself from Odious; Charles Darwin (Leo Bill), accompanied by his monkey companion Wallace, has been tauntingly delivered a dead specimen of the rare butterfly he seeks; and the Masked Bandit or Black Bandit (first Emil Hostina, later Pace/Roy himself) seeks to avenge the murder of his brother Blue Bandit (also Hostina). This motley crew is joined in their quest by a shaman called Mystic (Julian Bleach).

As a cinematic tale featuring an oral story co-created by the main protagonists—with a "narrative taleworld" included within the "context storyworld" (Greenhill 2020, 77)—*Fall* offers a great opportunity to examine the power of narrative. The story works as a means for Roy to get Alexandria to do his bidding, while it illuminates the man's struggle with suicide, the backstory featuring the child's accident, and the deepening relationship between the two. It is narrated in Roy's voice yet visually reflects the girl's perspective and responds to her comments, morphing according to her understanding of the world and becoming filled with the staff, patients, and visitors Alexandria encounters as she wanders the hospital's corridors and hides in its nooks. Thus, the tale opens a window onto Roy's death-desiring psyche while reflecting Alexandria's perspective and imagination. Eventually the tale shapeshifts to fulfill the happy ending Alexandria wants, as she struggles to wrest control over the tale from Roy, who has taken a harmful direction in his narration.

Roy's narrative wanders with imaginative twists and turns, involving a doomed love story between the Masked Bandit (henceforth Bandit) and Sister Evelyn (Justine Waddell), who represents both Roy's ex-fiancée and Evelyn, the hospital nurse Alexandria has a crush on; a logic-defying intervention by the Bandit's daughter (also Untaru/Alexandria), in which the child herself enters the story to save the Bandit, who is falling asleep after swallowing a handful of what he thinks are morphine pills; and a homicide of the bandits in a suicidal burst of emotion by Roy, which Alexandria also disrupts. Through these events, but also through Alexandria's love for Roy, whom the girl starts to consider a surrogate father (her father died trying to prevent a horse theft), Roy is forced back to life. Instead of suiciding, Roy recovers and lives. So does Alexandria, who goes back to living at the orange farm with her mother and siblings.

Fall highlights the harmful influences of the (hypermasculine) tales told throughout the millennia in oral storytelling settings and modern media like popular cultural cinema, bringing to the fore subversive stories' transformative powers. The film especially opens a window onto the toxic effects of such cultural scripts of masculinity tied to bodily ability and suppression of emotion. It also tells a different tale of suicide, a death feared as contagious and subjected to both censorship and discourses aimed at alleviating the threats of suicide's representations that might also have marginalizing and stigmatizing effects (Kosonen 2020a, 2020b). As a tale complicating unilateral views of gender and disability and diverging from the ways suicide and suicidal characters are conventionally depicted—one-dimensionally mad, weak, irrational, and feminine—*Fall* can be explored as a narrative that has implications for (social) justice.

Fall is Tarsem's second feature film, preceded by the 2000 science fiction/horror *The Cell*, and followed by the 2011 Theseus epic *Immortals*, the 2012 "Snow White" (ATU 709) adaptation *Mirror Mirror*, and the 2015 science fiction *Self/less*. For television, Tarsem has also directed and produced the 2017

Wizard of Oz modernization *Emerald City*, canceled after its first season. *Fall* is the only film Tarsem not only directed but also cowrote and produced (he was executive producer for Emerald), but it shares elements with his other works. Specifically, *Fall* features a child who disrupts an adult male's violent or murderous masculinity. This topos also appears in *The Cell*, in which the inner child (Jake Thomas) of a schizophrenic mass murderer (Vincent D'Onofrio) works with a child psychiatrist (Jennifer Lopez) to save the murderer's next victim. In *Self/less*, a wealthy businessman (Ben Kingsley) escapes death through a medical operation in which his consciousness overtakes the body of a younger man, Damian Hale (Ryan Reynolds), and becomes a better person by developing sympathy toward Hale's wife (Natalie Martinez) and daughter (Jaynee-Lynne Kinchen).

These films also involve themes of men dealing with death in different ways—not wanting to die, not wanting to live—and so-called toxic masculinity, the many harmful elements of a notion of what it is to be male tied to toughness, aggression, and dominance. Crucial is hegemonic masculinity's denial of emotion, as it is connected to suppressed feeling and idealized bodily strength and ability. In this chapter, I discuss *Fall* and its tale within a tale in relation to these themes dealing with hegemonic masculinity, and in relation to Anglophone cinema, where suicide's representations are frequently gendered—contemporary stories narrating masculinity and honorable or dishonorable death.

FALLEN MEN: DISABLED BODIES, GENDERED EXPECTATIONS

Diegetically, *Fall*'s title refers to the two falls thanks to which the film's two protagonists meet: Roy's failed stunt from the train bridge, and Alexandria's accident at the orange farm. But there are also other falls in the film: Alexandria's nearly fatal one in getting Roy morphine, and several in the story Roy tells: four characters literally fall to their deaths, and several others fall on the battlefield in the conventional metaphorical sense. Symbolically, the title can also be interpreted to signify Roy's loss of face or honor as a man. He has been abandoned—cuckolded—by his fiancée, failed a stunt with crippling effects, and cannot work due to his disability. The connection between these falls—literal and figurative, from honor and to self-willed death—manifests in the film.

In terms of Anglophone suicide cinema, Roy's story relates to two distinct topoi, one commonly related to femininity and the other to masculinity: a suicide because of unrequited or failed love, and a sacrificial suicide while in pain or severely wounded, respectively. These two deaths are frequently differentiated and invested with value according to sociologist Émile Durkheim's classic typology (1966): taboo-laden suicides against society ("egoistic suicides") and sanctioned suicides for society ("altruistic suicides"), which are often gendered (Kosonen 2020a) and unevenly treated in the cinematic imagination (Aaron 2014, 47). But reflecting *Fall*'s accommodation of and fluctuation between Roy's and Alexandria's perceptions, its suicides are simultaneously both and neither; they are egoistic and altruistic, but they are also simply deaths. As Hye Jean Chung argues, "The narrative tension is sustained by a marked contrast between the outer and inner stories in regard to the physical immobility of its characters" (2012, 94).

Several characters in the story Roy tells suicide, sacrificing themselves to save others. Thus the falls in the story, reflecting Roy's patriarchal, masculinist views, are altruistic, glorified, and presented as being for the common benefit. But these deaths, as well as Roy's own intentions, become molded by Alexandria's perception, according to which Roy's suicidality and the taleworld suicides he tells appear egoistic in very negative modes: selfish, collectively harmful, and unnecessary. The film also blurs these suicides' habitual gendering according to strict binaries that view love, emotion, and their expression as feminine and seeks to forbid them to "masculine" men (Kosonen 2020a; Kosonen and Greenhill 2022). *Fall* here exposes several toxic masculine ideals that relate to male self-harm and harmful behavior toward others.

Connecting to the gendered imagination of suicide cinema, Michele Aaron discusses illness and debilitation as frequent motives that underlie one of the recurring ways of representing tabooed suicide.[2] In the case of illness, suicide appears as a method of "avoiding dying" (or suffering) (2014, 45) and secures an "honorable" exit instead of a slow decay from disease or disability. Similarly, Steven Stack and Barbara Bowman recognize this theme in late twentieth-century film, with fatally ill male characters suiciding in the altruistic framework. They cite two Clint Eastwood films featuring male protagonists dying of cancer, the 2000 adventure drama *Space Cowboys* with Colonel William "Hawk" Hawkins (Tommy Lee Jones) flying "an old Russian space shuttle (loaded with atomic bombs and headed for earth) into the moon" to save the entire planet, and the 2008 drama *Gran Torino*, with war veteran Walt Kowalski (Eastwood himself) staging "his own suicide by gang members" in order to save his neighborhood (2009, 107).

Especially, they connect this topos to American Westerns featuring actor John Wayne, whom John M. Clum titles a Hollywood model of "masculine coherence" in the 1940s and 1950s: this "heroic male served as a role model for young boys, and an icon of nostalgia for a lost or threatened ideal of manhood" (2002, 49). Stack and Bowman recognize eight Wayne films (between 1941 and 1976) that feature a male hero in extreme pain, whether battle wound, fatal illness, or psychic pain, and his subsequent altruistic suicide—for example, Howard Hawks's 1966 *El Dorado*, featuring a gunshot wound, and Don Siegel's 1976 *The Shootist*, featuring stomach cancer (2009, 104). Further, they argue: "Possibly Wayne's films reflected this general theme and helped to perpetuate it" (2009, 108).

Fall, with its paralyzed protagonist Roy in extreme emotional pain, can be associated with this topos through its use of Western imagery and Roy's profession as a stunt player in this cinematic style that maintained its heyday as the most popular Hollywood genre from the 1920s to the 1960s. Aaron crystallizes how in films connecting suicide to escape from illness and weakness, "it is not just morality that is at stake . . . but masculinity too" (2014, 45). And similarly, Western films referenced by Stack and Bowman and *Fall* are heavily gendered and *gendering* (Kosonen 2020a), as they are linked with critic Mark Simpson's assertion that films dealing with war and the military are "hardly ever about anything other than what it means to become a man and how to become one" (1994, 212–213).

Michael Kimmel views the cowboy—the hero of most Westerns—as the icon of a compulsive masculinity that must always prove itself and is always in doubt (1987, 237). Kimmel describes a protagonist who is fierce and courageous, all the while being unemotional and unattached, programmed with the singular purpose of conquering nature—his own sensitive nature included. As Clum argues, in John Wayne films, "soft, handsome young men had to be hardened by the dominant image of asexual phallic masculinity," thus offering Americans a "hero who was a man independent of women, of domesticity, of authority, but who, like a cold father, offers only the lesson that life is tough, and men have to be tougher" (2002, 52, 58).

Carla J. McDonough's characterization of "the desire to cling to a certain model of masculinity, even as it fails, and at times destroys, its participants" (1997, 15) illustrates the way this type of independent, strong, and thick-skinned masculinity is not just impossible, but also unhealthy and dangerous, from fueling violence (e.g., Baele, Brace, and Coan 2019; Haider 2016) to leading to reflexive, inward-turned harm (e.g., Inckle 2014; Kalish and Kimmel 2014). In relation to the latter, Raewyn Connell argues that "the constitution of masculinity through bodily performance means that gender is vulnerable when the performance cannot be sustained—for instance as a result of physical disability" (2005, 54; see also Mara 2012, 255). The cultural scripts regarding masculinity and the disability incompatible with it connect to suicide and other forms of premature death, as both Tom Shakespeare (1999, 63) and David Mara (2012, 256–57) describe. Katrina Jaworski (2014), and Silvia Canetto and David Lester (1995) also term masculinist cultural scripts and gender identity as important factors in men's suicides; they are held in a tight loop by the gendered expectations that require them to succeed even when suiciding. This is one of the factors that leads men to assume more violent methods of suicide (Sabo 2010, 254).

Alexandria's drug-induced dream at the film's climax gives cues of the connection between masculinity and bodily ability, and that these are tied to Roy's desire to die, as Alexandria has learned through observation and the story he tells. Sneaking into the hospital's drug cabinet to steal morphine for Roy (her first two attempts have left him disappointed: first she only brings three pills, then a placebo), Alexandria climbs up the shelf, slips, and falls, fracturing her skull. The reality shifts to animated dream, filled with surrealist imageries and a scary soundtrack of breaking glass, ringing, and humming. Pills scatter across the floor; oranges and the Masked Bandit fall in a landscape of vibrant orange trees; a flag with a mask imprinted upon it flutters down; the Bandit screams, holding his injured leg while a one-legged pirate laughs; a leg prosthesis breaks into bits and splinters; warriors in historical costumes and battle scenes get their legs severed by their opponents; the Bandit slumbers while Alexandria runs in a burning landscape screaming: "Papa, they steal our horse; Papa, the angry people burn our home"; Alexandria's father runs after horse thieves while their home burns in the background; Roy falls off his horse. A puppet theater display of Alexandria's head surgery against a soundtrack of her chattering and crying in Romanian signals that all this falling and breaking takes place in Alexandria's mind. But instead of referring to her own dangerous fall, most events seem to relate to Roy: his disability and the transcultural mosaic of heroic, hypermasculine stories he has made use of to lure Alexandria into his suicide plan. It is as if Roy's fall, his pain, and the masculinist worldview he has embraced have swallowed the little girl whole.

These elements also seem to reflect how Roy thinks of himself after the fall, expressed in gendered terms. As mentioned, hegemonic models of masculinity tie it to bodily agency and strength (e.g., Mara 2012, 255–56; Shakespeare 1999, 57). According to Shakespeare, "The traditional account . . . of disabled masculinity rests . . . on the notion of contradiction: femininity and disability reinforce each other, masculinity and disability conflict with each other" (1999, 57). Western masculinity is defined, in opposition to femininity (e.g., Kimmel 1996), as based on rationality, control, strength, invulnerability, and independence, most of which disability appears to deny according to ableist cultural scripts (see Garland-Thomson 2002). These gendered binaries are contradicted and rejected by feminist disability scholarship (e.g., Kafer 2013; Leduc 2020).

Mara describes the interruptions in identity that disability engenders (2012, 255–56). Roy's dialogue shows he considers himself a man expelled from proper masculinity. In his own words (although he speaks of the one-legged taleworld character), he is "half a man." The story he tells Alexandria is filled with feats of male physical heroism he is no longer capable of, with Alexandria alone undermining the traditional gender roles and imageries of male heroism as the Bandit's daughter. And both the stolen and restive horses of Roy and Alexandria's father, opposed to the well-behaved horses of the warriors, as well as the montage of breaking and broken limbs in Alexandria's dream, seem to refer to what Roy has lost: not only his mobility but his manhood too. Horses are a well-known symbol of masculine virility and power (e.g., Weil 2006), and the two things Roy has lost—his horse and able legs—link directly to his suicidality.

TOXIC MASCULINITY: FORBIDDEN AND VOLATILE EMOTIONS

The origin story behind *Fall* is as rich as the film itself: gaining no direct funding, Tarsem travels the world making music videos, and seizes these chances also to shoot scenes for *Fall*, with filming to be completed by the then six-year-old lead actor Untaru (Russell 2020; Wise 2008). The story of a deceitful woman and the ensuing nearly fatal heartbreak, narratively central to the film, is alleged to have autobiographical roots, as film critic Nicholas Russell proposes: "Maybe it's really the product of a bad breakup . . . money once saved for a wedding later used for production costs" (2020). If Roy is suicidal, a discussion overheard by Alexandria verifies that his condition is not really his disability: "The problem is not his back, it's the broken heart. He needs to get over her." Roy's root problem becomes especially evident in the tale he tells, where the damsel in distress whom Bandit rescues breaks his heart. This story—like the cowboy films Roy acts in or the heroic narratives he weaves into in his tale—also represents masculinity overcoming nature. It emphasizes "those traits that separate the cultural concept of man from woman," as Anastasia Salter and Bridget Blodgett describe the popular cultural hero genre with hypermasculine protagonists (2017, 23).

In the film, Roy might wish to die because he is heartbroken, but according to gendered oppositions that differentiate between masculinity and disability, suiciding for love does not belong to the cultural scripts of masculinity. As Canetto describes, in a recurring trope, it is women who are depicted dying for love (1993, 5), while men are represented dying for honor. Further, as Jaworski notes, men are presented as dying for "rational" reasons, women for "irrational" ones (2014, 22), and dying for love, generally perceived as feminine, counts among the many irrational reasons to die. Similarly, in cinema, men's suicides often respond to honor and shame, while women's suicides, for unrequited or failed love or another reason, mark their irrationality, vulnerability, romanticism, or sexual missteps (Kosonen 2020a, 100). Like the bodily weakness denied to Roy by masculinist cultural scripts, suicide for love is something he is denied as a male character.

Robin Lewis and George Shepeard report data according to which male athletes who killed themselves because of a professional failure "were considered more emotionally well-adjusted compared to males who suicided because of a relationship failure and all females" (1992, 187). Reflecting this, *Fall*'s narrative taleworld fluctuates between a story of heartbreak, reflecting what Roy really feels, and a masculinist story of honor and violence, reflecting the gendered sociocultural expectations Roy must meet. As such, the story is also tinged with toxic masculinity. Paul Kivel describes how, "from a very early age, boys are told to 'Act Like a Man.' Even though they have all the normal human feelings of love, excitement, sadness, confusion, anger, curiosity, pain, frustration, humiliation, shame, grief, resentment, loneliness, low self-worth, and self-doubt, they are taught to hide the feelings and appear to be tough and in control. They are told to be aggressive, not to back down, not to make mistakes, and to take charge, have lots of sex, make lots of money, and be responsible. Most of all, they are told not to cry" (2010, 83).

Yet Ingrid Waldron recognizes suppressed emotion as a risk contributing to self-harm (1995, 24). Reflecting a similar understanding, *Fall* seems to tie Roy's suicidality to his suppression of feeling, rather than the breakup or his disability, especially in the tale that he renders a masculinist suicide mission toward the end. Many elements of the film speak of this. Roy's inability to deal with this breakup (or the rather aggressive way he deals with it) manifests in the many precarious emotions he expresses in the tale, which fluctuate unpredictably from self-pity and self-hatred to rage and vengeance toward Bandit's taleworld sweetheart Sister Evelyn, representing his ex-fiancée, and toward Alexandria, his co-narrator. Roy's suppression of emotion also manifests in his use of liquor after Alexandria's fall at the ward. Moreover, *Fall* indicates that these repressed yet volatile emotions inflict psychological and physical harms on Alexandria and are therefore harmful also to others.

These concerns—especially the toxic effects of suppression of emotion in Roy's case—emerge in the succession of key scenes after the midpoint of the film that witness Roy's suicide attempt and its relation to his broken relationships, and lead to the co-created story's conclusion. After Roy has secured from Alexandria what he thinks is a full bottle of morphine, his tale—thus far just an enticement to keep Alexandria coming back—gets personal, almost like a suicide letter. Masked Bandit serves as Roy's surrogate and Sister Evelyn as the replacement for his fiancée, as Bandit confesses his love to the woman whom the bandits have kidnapped from Governor Odious's horse carriage. "I've been on a quest for revenge. You should go. You've captivated my heart. That's why I can no longer keep you in captivity. I've fallen in love with you. But I'm consumed by revenge. I'm not a man that can be loved." As Tom Foster's analysis of suicide notes indicates, "apology/shame (74%)," "love for those left behind (60%)," and "hopelessness/nothing to live for (21%)" count among the most common themes (2003, 323), and Roy/Bandit's dialogue reflects these motivations.

Roy's tale and the context storyworld are next united by an image of a morphine bottle falling, as a consequence of which the pills scatter across the floor. In the storyworld, Roy—who has downed a handful of them—mumbles to Alexandria, "I'm sorry about this. I'm sorry. I don't want you to see me like this." In the story, bordering on dream, the Masked Bandit and Sister Evelyn are wed. With both fantasy-fulfilling elements and warnings against suicide, the scene feels like a stream of consciousness. Darwin translates Mystic's words for Roy: "Suicide is not the answer." He relays to Roy the magic words for warding off evil that Alexandria has learned from the old man sharing a room with Roy—"Googly, googly"—and warns him, "If you fall asleep you will never wake up." The magic words echo in the air as a Gregorian chant, and dervishes spin in their ritual clothes. The wedding ritual is a trap. The following sequence witnesses the bandits being captured by Odious's men, and then saved by the Masked Bandit's daughter, while in the context storyworld Roy falls asleep despite Alexandria's tender attempts to wake him up.

The day after Roy's attempted overdose, Alexandria gets a fright. Looking out the window, she witnesses a body covered with white cloth being carried away on a trolley and, with the audience, she believes the corpse is Roy's. Alexandria rushes to the trolley, but is shooed off by the hospital staff. In a panic, she sprints to Roy's room, pulls open the covers—and sees Roy lying in his bed, slowly waking from slumber. As his neighbor's traumatized account reveals, the dead body is that of another patient in the ward. Alexandria wakes Roy up, crying, "I thought you were dead." But this is exactly what Roy had hoped and expected—instead finding himself waking to see another day, he goes into a rage that brings the nurses to his bed. They forcefully pacify Roy and shoo Alexandria away. As we learn from Roy's desperate screams, the pills stolen by Alexandria from Roy's neighbor's cabinet are just a placebo. Subsequently, Roy's manipulation physically endangers the girl by causing her to fall: worrying about Roy not being able to sleep, Alexandria tries to steal more morphine, fracturing her skull.

As Roy resumes his story, it is again altered: no longer filled with brooding self-pity but outright toxic, with Roy's misogyny toward his ex-lover and hatred of himself spilling over all the characters in his story and Alexandria too. As scholars recognize, human emotions are multidimensional, with their subjective experience differing from their expressive or behavioral side (e.g., Plutchik 1984), and with a natural flow from one to another (e.g., Nussbaum

2018). Considering compulsive masculinity, the limited range of emotions men are allowed to engage in while maintaining their manliness causes many feelings to be outwardly projected as anger and hate (e.g., Kimmel 2018). Or, as Phil Hubbard argues, "Men [are] encouraged to repress particular emotions that are associated with vulnerability rather than strength" (2005, 121).

Especially the "best men," the heroes of popular cultural and other stories, "are cold, calculating, and highly logical. . . . They rarely let moods get the better of them and if they engage in any emotional display they should be angry, occasionally brooding" (Salter and Blodgett 2017, 25). Thus, it is not surprising that after Roy's honest suicide letter–like confession of emotions in thinking he is going to die, these earlier expressions of shame, heartbreak, and love change form and are expressed as uncontrolled anger and rage. Roy's reaction is also facilitated by intoxication from alcohol, a common masculine means to be able to express emotions, and it reveals not only the physical but also the psychological damage Roy's story is inflicting on the girl.

As Alexandria wakes after her accident, Roy sits next to her bed in a wheelchair, his eyes red from crying, or perhaps from liquor, or both. They smile feebly at one another. "I fell again," Alexandria announces, and Roy replies that he heard, that everybody did, and guiltily bursts into tears. If the earlier scene reads like a suicide letter, with difficult emotions poetically expressed under the belief the creator is going to die, the next bit reads like a drunken confession, poetry lacking in Roy's burst of honesty. Alexandria asks Roy to finish his story, but he does not have an ending: "The story was just a trick to get you to do something for me." Roy gets emotional again, takes a sip of liquor, "You should ask someone else, there is no happy ending with me." As Alexandria continues to implore him, Roy tells her to ask Nurse Evelyn. But Alexandria does not want to; just before falling she had seen her in bed with one of the hospital men: "She was just pretending to love you"—Alexandria holds back tears—"Like your girlfriend." "I see" Roy says, looking at Alexandria with an expression hard to decipher.

And then his story continues. The five bandits discover Sister Evelyn has betrayed them; she is with Governor Odious. In the taleworld, Masked Bandit gulps down a large mouthful of liquor, imitating Roy's acts by the bedside, and says roughly: "We don't need her. She can't be trusted. You give them your heart, but all they really want is your wallet. Sooner or later she's gonna leave him for a richer man." This is not the only scene tinted with misogyny.

In an earlier sequence Roy's tale has featured Bandit shooting Sister Evelyn because she is someone else's fiancée, the fatality of the act avoided only because her heart-shaped locket stops the bullet.

Roy's hatred also spills over onto Alexandria, who has taken up the topic of Roy being betrayed by his girlfriend, and in Alexandria's imagination also by Nurse Evelyn. After a suicide letter and a confession, Roy's tale here takes the form of a masculinist hero legend filled with violence. Roy's emotion is manifested by the Bandit's breaking voice in the taleworld, but according to gendered limitations to expressing feelings, Roy circumvents his vulnerability by instead starting to tell a story of mass death, of a glorified and violent male mission of altruistic suicides the five bandits now venture on. Alexandria does not understand the term. "What is suicide?" the Bandit's daughter asks the Indian in the taleworld, and he mimics cutting his throat.

A fatal battle ensues in front of Odious's palace; Roy is killing off all the characters. Wallace dies of a bullet wound. As Bandit's daughter studies Wallace blacking out in Darwin's lap with a puzzled face, Alexandria sobs in the background, "Does he really . . . died?" He does. Darwin screams in sorrow, and Odious's men step out to ambush them in huge numbers. Bandit's daughter screams at Darwin to leave, but he does not. He is shot to death by Odious's men. Now Roy's muted voice sobs: "He died too." Back to reality, at the hospital ward, Alexandria looks at Roy and cries, "Did he really died?" with Roy responding insensitively: "Yeah. . . . It's the natural order of things." And the camera cuts back to the taleworld, where the bandits are running through the streets of Odious's citadel, interrupted by Roy's voice-over: "All things must die." His statement witnesses wounded Luigi falling back from the other bandits and, in an act of self-sacrifice, immolating himself and Odious's warriors in an explosion. Next Mystic gets afflicted, without a visible reason. And still escaping from Odious's troops, Masked Bandit stops, grimacing with pain, as Alexandria's voice-over, still sobbing, intervenes: "I don't like this, I don't like this story." And yet Roy goes on, as if taking revenge on the girl for understanding, perhaps better than he does, the heartbreak, betrayal, and shame at the root of his death wish.

In this scene, Alexandria asks the vital question whose answer is needed to understand Roy's suicidality: "Why did Luigi kill himself?" The camera cuts frantically between the withering Mystic and the Masked Bandit, sipping his liquor like Roy. And with his cracking voice, Roy utters, "He was half a man. He couldn't do that, he gave up. Not very satisfying, is it?" He is clearly talking of himself, seeing himself in the character with the leg prosthesis. But from his self-pity, another montage of violent scenes ensues, accompanied by epic music. Otta Benga dies to save the Bandit's daughter, arrows piercing his body, and then the Indian heroically cuts the rope suspending both himself and Odious's men so that Bandit and his daughter may escape.

Here we have classic altruistic on-screen suicides, far removed from Roy's self-pitying death wish, as if they represent a glorified version of his reality. Now only Masked Bandit and his daughter remain. But the latter tears her hand from his, as she cries, "No no no no." The camera cuts to the reality, with Alexandria looking at Roy with tear-filled eyes, and Roy looking back at her with red-rimmed ones. "Why are you killing everybody?" "It is my story!" Roy barks, but Alexandria, still weeping, resists: "Mine too!" Roy breaks into tears. Alexandria is of course right, and her words reveal Roy's egoism and selfishness in thinking his actions and words have no consequences for the girl he has woven into his suicide plan, and into his toxic masculinist tale of violence and revenge.

It is eventually Alexandria who disrupts this tale. As Roy proceeds to tell the story of the Bandit's final battle with Odious, her voice-over starts babbling changes and additions to his narration. And, influenced by her, the story morphs to reflect the heartbreak underlying Roy's actions and death wish. Odious is dressed in a contemporary suit to show he is the man who in diegetic real life came to replace Roy in his fiancée's heart, and Alexandria's earlier comment about his girlfriend only pretending to love Roy repeats in the air. Roy tries to resist. He tells Alexandria/Sister Evelyn to shut up, and self-loathingly tries to narrate Bandit's defeat at the hands of Odious, while Alexandria pleads. They both cry. "Don't kill him," Alexandria begs, and, grunting, Roy rests his head on her bed. Alexandria makes him promise. And so, submerged in a pool of blood, Bandit regains his strength. He punches Odious, but does not kill him, following Alexandria's wish. Instead of completing Bandit's death, according to Roy's violent plans, the story has a happy ending. Bandit gives up his revengeful suicide mission to tend to his "daughter." The love triangle is resolved: Bandit tosses away the heart-shaped locket, telling Sister Evelyn to follow her heart. And as Alexandria's voice-over tells at the end of the film, ever since their encounter, she sees Roy in every familiar stunt trick done in the history of cinema.

THE POWER OF STORIES

The Fall is a film about stories. Not only does it feature the tale within the tale both Roy and Alexandria shape, his occupation as a Hollywood stunt player positions the film in a continuum of oral stories told by a fireplace or at the agora—or by a sickbed, where Roy and Alexandria's storytelling sessions take place. The story itself is unique but generic: it is built around a heroic quest, and includes a main hero, an evil villain, a damsel in distress (turned femme fatale), and a motley crew of helper figures. As a co-creation of the fictive early twentieth century—by characters Roy, a white American man in his thirties, and Alexandria, a Romanian girl of five—the tale can be seen as reflecting a mosaic of transcultural stories told in different contexts over years, centuries—even millennia. The Roman soldiers, fourteenth-century pirates, "Indians," and bandits are all from the films Roy has acted in yet are shaped by Alexandria's perspective—all kinds of heroes and anti-heroes appear side by side in the tale and in her imagination. All these stories, especially the one told by disabled, cuckolded, and suicidal Roy, carry potentially harmful messages about gender and masculinity, suicide, and honorable and dishonorable death.

As Salter and Blodgett describe the hypermasculine heroes of popular cultural media, their characteristics can be broken into two general groups: physical traits and acts, and behavioral, emotional, and thought patterns (2017, 22–23). In both domains, hegemonic masculinist scripts cause the paralyzed, heartbroken Roy's suicidality and the violent toxicity of his tale. This is important to recount in the context of the power of stories because, as Connell notes, masculinities are not just personal but institutionalized and organized practices, learned from sources such as the state, the family, and the media (1993). They are learned from stories, films included, stored in individuals' affective embodiment (Ahmed 2014) and materially performed through their actions (Butler 2011). Salter and Blodgett note the "tug of war" between male characters' individuality and their generically hypermasculine traits, arguing that this conflict "is particularly true for those the story identifies as the hero or main characters" (2017, 22–23)—the character who tends to be the most desirable for identification and self-modeling in many films, yet in *Fall* is shown as having a bad influence over the young girl. Roy's story testifies to the power of stories over individuals also as it weaves together influences from tales of heroism and displays his fluctuation between varied states of vulnerability and compulsive masculinity, of needing to compensate for his wounded manhood.

Stories about suicide are frequently gendered and imbued with ideas of heroic male agency and feminine irrationality. As Jaworski notes, "In stark contrast to women's overexcited sensibilities, male deaths were associated with heroism, bravery and courage" (2014, 431; on cinema, see Kosonen 2020a). There is a toxic side also to stories of altruistic male suicide, as illustrated by Roy and his selfish manipulations: he would rather die, like the heroes whose violent deaths he forces Alexandria to imagine, than live in a half-paralyzed but functioning body expelled from the imageries of hypermasculine physical ability. Roy might consider his death altruistic, benefiting others and restoring his honor, like the several suicides he recounts in his tale.

As Thomas Joiner and colleagues propose, the perception of being a burden is one of suicide's central predictors (Conner et al. 2007; Joiner 2005). Stack and Bowman connect this concept of burdensomeness directly to the notion of altruism, noting how, in the minds of people seeing themselves as financial, emotional, or other types of encumbrances needing constant care, "if one is a burden to others, then one's suicide will be for the benefit of others" (2009, 108). Yet considering Alexandria's perspective, neither Roy's planned death by morphine nor the violent suicide mission of his taleworld characters can be considered altruistic: Alexandria is traumatized both by the violent massacre in the tale and the old man's death she thinks is Roy's, and by managing to secure the morphine she would not merely witness but be fully implicated in his death.

In all these functions, stories can be seen to work as weapons in *Fall*. Yet they are also presented as holding transformative power, as Alexandria's influence and subversion of the tale causes Roy's healing. Lastly, considering *Fall* as the story, scholars study it as a heterotopic (Chung 2012) and transcultural (Greenhill 2020) film presenting Roy as an unreliable narrator (Stevens 2010) with the power to "complicate unilateral views of intercultural contract, exchange, and change" (Greenhill 2020, 70). Pauline Greenhill especially credits Alexandria's "mov[ing] between positions as focalizer, as co-narrator, and as intervening actor within the magical taleworld" (76), and argues it is the multiple viewpoints, partial perspectives, and situated knowledges brought by the weaving together of Roy's and Alexandria's viewpoints that make *Fall* a subversive and progressive fairy tale (91).

As Greenhill maintains: "Unpacking Roy's narrative flourishes means the audience must enact their own mental heterospatial moves, putting themselves in his and Alexandria's places, to understand not only why they see the world in different ways but also how their experiences have formed diverse ways of seeing" (2020, 91). It is the same multiplicity of perspectives, and their disruption of the familiar ways of representing difference and suicide, that I see exposing and challenging unilateral and potentially harmful views of gender, ability, and suicide. This is especially true regarding the "ableist suggestions that disability is a fate worse than death" (Kafer 2013, 2) and regarding the hypermasculine self-endangerment (Aaron 2014) presented in altruistic terms (Kosonen 2020a)—dominating ideas of a "good death" in opposition to suicide for reasons other than honor, often seen in terms of weakness, irrationality, and femininity.

Eventually, the multiplicity of perspectives can be argued to complicate simplistic understandings of suicide, suicidal individuals, and their moral standing (if suicide or suiciding individuals are simplistically "good" or "bad"). They can also be argued to serve social justice for the varied groups of people whose lives have been deemed "unlivable" (Butler 2004) by the conventional cinematic stories of egoistic suicide, juxtaposed with masculine altruism (Kosonen 2020b, 52). As Donna Haraway puts it: "It matters what stories we tell to tell other stories with.... It matters what stories make worlds, what worlds make stories" (2016, 12), and the truths of suicide and its gendered and moral implications are much more complex than the stories told over centuries have witnessed. *Fall*'s shared authorship between Roy and Alexandria, a white man invested with discursive power and a traditionally silenced child narrator, gives cues to how this justice-serving complexity in storytelling can be achieved.

NOTES

1. As with all rules based on generalization, there are exceptions. Tom Ford's *A Single Man* (2009), for instance, tells a story of a mourning-related death wish, although it does not end in its homosexual protagonist's suicide; in Robert Redford's Oscar-winning coming-of-age tale *Ordinary People* (1980), a young man and his family try to deal with the aftermath of his brother's suicide; and Mike Figgis's *Leaving Las Vegas* (1995) is a story of a suicidal alcoholic author's death by liquor.

2. According to Aaron, on-screen suicides can be divided into professional suicides (self-sacrifice "in the line of duty"), honorable suicides (enacting personal integrity), dishonorable suicides (avoiding guilt and/or humiliation), suicides avoiding dying (preempting pain and suffering), suicides avoiding living (willing the end of life), and mass suicides (collective) (2014, 42–47).

REFERENCES

Aaron, Michele. 2014. *Death and Moving Image: Ideology, Iconography and I*. Edinburgh: Edinburgh University Press.

Ahmed, Sara. (2004) 2014. *The Cultural Politics of Emotion*. New York: Routledge.

Baele, Stephane J., Lewys Brace, and Travis G. Coan. 2019. "From 'Incel' to 'Saint': Analyzing the Violent Worldview behind the 2018 Toronto Attack." *Terrorism and Political Violence* 33 (8): 1667–91.

Butler, Judith. 2004. *Precarious Life: The Powers of Mourning and Violence*. London: Verso.

Butler, Judith. (1993) 2011. *Bodies That Matter: On the Discursive Limits of Sex*. New York: Routledge.

Canetto, Silvia. 1993. "She Died for Love, He for Glory: Gender Myths of Suicidal Behaviour." *Omega: Journal of Death and Dying* 26 (1): 1–17.

Canetto, Silvia, and David Lester. 1995. "Gender and the Primary Prevention of Suicide Mortality." *Suicide and Life-Threatening Behavior* 25 (1): 58–69.

The Cell. 2000. Directed by Tarsem Singh. US/Germany: Radical/Media.

Chung, Hye Jean. 2012. "Media Heterotopia and Transnational Filmmaking: Mapping Real and Virtual Worlds." *Cinema Journal* 51 (4): 87–109.

Clum, John M. 2002. *"He's All Man": Learning Masculinity, Gayness, and Love from American Movies*. London: Palgrave.

Connell, Raewyn. 1993. "The Big Picture: Masculinities in Recent World History." *Theory and Society* 22 (5): 597–623.

Connell, Raewyn. 2005. *Masculinities*, 2nd ed. Berkeley: University of California Press.

Conner, Kenneth R., Peter C. Britton, Luke M. Sworts, and Thomas E. Joiner. 2007. "Suicide Attempts among Individuals with Opiate Dependence: The Critical Role of Belonging." *Addictive Behaviors* 32 (7): 1395–1404.

Durkheim, Émile. (1897) 1966. *Suicide: A Study in Sociology*. Translated by John A. Spaulding and George Simpson. New York: Free Press.

El Dorado. 1967. Directed by Howard Hawks. US: Paramount Pictures.

Emerald City. 2016–2017. Directed by Tarsem Singh. US: Shaun Cassidy Productions.

The Fall. 2006. Directed by Tarsem Singh. United States/South Africa/India: Googly Films.

Foster, Tom. 2003. "Suicide Note Themes and Suicide Prevention." *International Journal of Psychiatry in Medicine* 33 (4): 323–31.

Garland-Thomson, Rosemarie. 2002. "Integrating Disability, Transforming Feminist Theory." *Feminist Formations* 14 (3): 1–32.

Gran Torino. 2008. Directed by Clint Eastwood. US: Warner Bros.

Greenhill, Pauline. 2020. *Reality, Magic, and Other Lies: Fairy-Tale Film Truths*. Detroit: Wayne State University Press.

Haider, Syed. 2016. "The Shooting in Orlando: Terrorism or Toxic Masculinity (or Both?)." *Men and Masculinities* 19 (5): 555–65.

Haraway, Donna. 2016. *Staying with the Trouble: Making Kin in the Chthulucene*. Durham, NC: Duke University Press.

Hubbard, Phil. 2005. "The Geographies of 'Going Out': Emotion and Embodiment in the Evening Economy." In *Emotional Geographies*, edited by Joyce Davidson, Liz Bondi, and Mick Smith, 117–34. Aldershot, UK: Ashgate.

Immortals. 2011. Directed by Tarsem Singh. US/Canada/UK: Virgin Produced.

Inckle, Kay. 2014. "Strong and Silent: Men, Masculinity, and Self-Injury." *Men and Masculinities* 17 (1): 3–21.

Jaworski, Katrina. 2014. *The Gender of Suicide: Knowledge Production, Theory and Suicidology*. Aldershot, UK: Ashgate.

Joiner, Thomas. 2005. *Why People Die by Suicide*. Cambridge, MA: Harvard University Press.

Kafer, Alison. 2013. *Feminist, Queer, Crip*. Bloomington: Indiana University Press.

Kalish, Rachel, and Michael Kimmel. 2014. "Suicide by Mass Murder: Masculinity, Aggrieved Entitlement, and Rampage School Shootings." *Health Sociology Review* 19 (4): 451–64.

Kimmel, Michael S. 1987. "The Cult of Masculinity: American Social Character and the Legacy of the Cowboy." In *Beyond Patriarchy: Essays by Men on Pleasure, Power, and Change*, edited by Michael Kaufman, 235–49. Toronto: Oxford University Press.

Kimmel, Michael S. 1996. *Manhood in America: A Cultural History*. New York: Free Press.

Kimmel, Michael S. 2018. *Healing from Hate: How Young Men Get Into—and Out of—Violent Extremism*. Berkeley: University of California Press.

Kivel, Paul. 2010. "The Act-Like-a-Man Box." In *Men's Lives*, 8th ed., edited by Michael S. Kimmel and Michael A. Messner, 83–85. London: Pearson Education.

Kosonen, Heidi. 2020a. *Gendered and Contagious Suicide: Taboo and Biopower in Contemporary Anglophone Cinematic Representations of Self-Willed Death*. Jyväskylä dissertations 292: Jyväskylä: http://urn.fi/URN:ISBN:978-951-39-8313-0.

Kosonen, Heidi. 2020b. "Suicide, Social Bodies and Danger: Taboo, Biopower and Parental Worry in Films *Bridgend* (2015) and *Bird Box* (2018)." *Journal of Somaesthetics* 6 (2): 48–63. https://doi.org/10.5278/ojs.jos.v6i2.5739.

Kosonen, Heidi, and Pauline Greenhill. 2022. "'My Mother, She Butchered Me, My Father, He Ate Me': Vampires, Fairy Tales, and Feminist Filmmaking in *The Moth Diaries.*" *Journal of Folklore Research* 59 (3): 87–114.

Leaving Las Vegas. 1995. Directed by Mike Figgis. US: United Artists.

Leduc, Amanda. 2020. *Disfigured: On Fairy Tales, Disability, and Making Space.* Toronto: Coach House.

Lewis, Robin J., and George Shepeard. 1992. "Inferred Characteristics of Successful Suicides as a Function of Gender and Context." *Suicide and Life-Threatening Behavior* 22 (2): 187–96.

Mara, David. 2012. "Reformulating Masculinities: Renegotiating Masculinity After a Spinal Cord Injury." In *Canadian Men and Masculinities: Historical and Contemporary Perspectives*, edited by Christopher John Greig and Wayne Martino, 253–65. Toronto: Canadian Scholars' Press.

McDonough, Carla J. 1997. *Staging Masculinity: Male Identity in Contemporary American Drama.* Jefferson, NC: McFarland.

Mirror Mirror. 2012. Directed by Tarsem Singh. US/Canada: Relativity Media.

Nussbaum, Martha C. 2018. *The Monarchy of Fear: A Philosopher Looks at Our Political Crisis.* London: Simon & Schuster.

Ordinary People. 1980. Directed by Robert Redford. US: Paramount Pictures.

Plutchik, Robert. 1984. "In Search of the Basic Emotions." *Contemporary Psychology: A Journal of Reviews* 29 (6): 511–13. doi:10.1037/022979.

Russell, Nicholas. 2020. "Before Your Very Eyes: Tarsem's *The Fall.*" *Bright Wall/Dark Room* 80 (February). https://www.brightwalldarkroom.com/2020/02/17/tarsem-the-fall/.

Sabo, Don. 2010. "Masculinities and Men's Health: Moving toward Post-Superman Era Prevention." In *Men's Lives*, 8th ed., edited by Michael S. Kimmel and Michael A. Messner, 243–60. London: Pearson Education.

Salter, Anastasia, and Bridget Blodgett. 2017. *Toxic Geek Masculinity in Media: Sexism, Trolling, and Identity Politics.* London: Palgrave Macmillan.

Self/less. 2015. Directed by Tarsem Singh. US: Endgame Entertainment.

Shakespeare, Tom. 1999. "The Sexual Politics of Disabled Masculinity." *Sexuality and Disability* 17 (1): 53–64.

The Shootists. 1976. Directed by Don Siegel. US: Paramount Pictures.

Simpson, Mark. 1994. *Male Impersonators: Men Performing Masculinity.* New York: Routledge.

A Single Man. 2009. Directed by Tom Ford. US: Artina Films.

Space Cowboys. 2000. Directed by Clint Eastwood. US: Warner Bros.

Stack, Steven, and Barbara Bowman. 2009. "Pain and Altruism: The Suicides in John Wayne's Films." In *Suicide and the Creative Arts*, edited by Steven Stack and David Lester, 93–108. New York: Nova Science.

Stevens, E. Charlotte. 2010. "Telling the (Wrong) Story: The Disintegration of Transcultural Communication and Narrative in *The Fall.*" *Cineaction* 80:30–37.

Waldron, Ingrid. 1995. "Contributions of Changing Gender Differences in Behavior and Social Roles to Changing Gender Differences in Mortality." In *Men's Health and Illness*, edited by Don Sabo and David Gordon, 22–45. London: SAGE.

Weil, Kari. 2006. "Men and Horses: Circus Studs, Sporting Males and the Performance of Purity in Fin-de-Siècle France." *French Cultural Studies* 17 (1): 87–105.

Wise, Damon. 2008. "Final Fantasy." *Guardian*, October 4. https://www.theguardian.com/film/2008/oct/04/fall.tarsem.singh.

Yo Ho Ho. 1981. Directed by Zako Heskiya. Bulgaria: Boyana Film.

7

Post-Traumatic Soldier Stories

Speaking to Survive with Hope

JACK ZIPES

TRACES

When I was young, I loved to shoot guns: BB guns, plastic guns, wooden guns, branches made into rifles. My brother and I used to play soldiers with friends in a vacant lot near our house. This was during the 1940s. It was exciting—hiding behind bushes, climbing up trees, sliding into rock caves. If you were shot, you were dead and had to wait until everyone was shot except the victorious sharpshooter. Then we all bounced back to life and began our game again. It was so simple to bounce back to life again. World War II was about to end, and our favorite song was "Whistle while you work, Hitler is a jerk. All the Japs are saps, and Mussolini is a meanie!"

We all wanted to become soldiers and fight in the war. Fortunately, we were too young and nobody did. And fortunately, despite the fact that I had good training in the Cub Scouts and Boy Scouts, I was also too young to be drafted to serve in the Korean War. And thankfully, I tore the ligaments in my knee playing college soccer so that I was declared 4-F (unacceptable for combat) and did not have to serve in the Vietnam War. By that time, my opinions had already changed anyway. I thought those who wanted to fight in wars were the jerks, meanies, and saps. I did not have clear ideological reasons for this belief at that time. It was just that I could not imagine myself taking anyone's life. I have never killed or wanted to kill anybody or any animal. I have never shot a pistol or rifle. I am afraid of firearms.

My weapons are a pen, pencil, typewriter, or computer. I write and speak against wars of any kind. I have always wondered why anyone would ever want to become a soldier. A waste of time. A delusion. Yet, for many young patriotic men in America—and now patriotic women—soldiering is their duty, their way to show their dedication to their country, and also their only way to finance their education or get out of poverty. Some believe in all the flashing advertisements of soldiers, sailors, marines, and pilots fighting to defend America in some godforsaken part of the globe. The hype is drilled into them. They see themselves as protectors of free America. They register with recruiters and learn how to kill others and defend themselves. They learn all about weapons. They learn all about the necessary and diverse ways to kill.

I always ask myself whether we Americans are born or trained to kill other humans, not to mention the animals that surround us. Are we born to become killers? Does our American socialization transform us into cutthroat competitors and killers?

Emery Kelen, drafted by the Austro-Hungarian army in World War I, pretended to go insane so that he would not have to kill anyone. Later, as he once wrote, he became a "violent" pacifist for peace as a caricaturist. Paul Vaillant-Couturier, a poet who enlisted in the French army during World War I, also rejected killing. In the early 1920s he became a founder of the Communist Party in France and a fervent defender of peace until he died in 1937. Maurice Druon, a combatant in World War II, joined the Resistance against the Nazis. As a novelist and politician, he became a proponent for peace. He died in 2009.

All three writers, dedicated to peace, had their lives traumatically changed by war, and all three wrote fairy-tale books addressed to children and adults because, in my opinion, they suffered harrowing experiences during the wars in which they participated. Trauma pursued them and drove them to write and create new worlds filled with hope: *Jean sans pain (Johnny Breadless,*

1921) by Vaillant-Couturier, *Yussuf the Ostrich* (1943) by Kelen, and *Tistou les pouces verts* (*Tistou, the Boy with Green Thumbs*, 1957) by Druon.

As an antiwar and antifascist writer, I have published these books as well as Deirdre and William Conselman Jr.'s *Keedle, the Great: And All You Ever Wanted to Know about Fascism* (2020). All of these books have impelled me to think more about peace, war, and fascism, and they also drove me to share my thoughts about them with young and old readers.

To learn that you are worth nothing is traumatic. To learn that your body revolts against your killing other humans and animals for powerful elite groups is traumatic. To learn that patriotic stories are nothing but lies and that you cannot trust the people who tell them is traumatic. To reassemble your body and mind after you have killed without reason or justice, you must somehow learn to tell your own story. You may never overcome the trauma of killing so that you won't be killed, but at least you will speak and write with hope to cleanse your soul. Unfortunately, hundreds of thousands of young men and women continue to be sacrificed every year. We repress their stories and do not draw connections to the past. To provide hope that the chain of killing can be broken, we might do well to dig up past stories of soldiers who survived atrocities to speak on and in their own terms. It may seem flippant or fanciful to turn to folktales and fairy tales, but not to do so would mean ignoring traces of important messages that the original tellers left behind to warn us against war. As we well know, metaphors in fairy tales can help narrators distance themselves from deep personal wounds and allow them to address traumatic incidents. In this regard, wonder and folktales can alleviate pain, suggest ways to overcome exploitation, and heal wounds. As Sara Buttsworth and Maartje Abbenhuis remark in their excellent study *War, Myths, and Fairy Tales*: "It is not surprising . . . that fairy tales offer powerful propaganda in times of war. Equally importantly, they can also be useful in dealing with the aftermath of war and trauma, as they offer a medium through which children and adults alike can reflect on their wartime experiences. Wars can also become the subject matter of their own mythology—ultimately becoming their own fairy tales. It is the emotive and subjective content of the fairy tale that enables its multiplicity of uses and abuses in the equally emotive and subjective environment of violence, displacement, suffering, and grief present in time of war" (2017, 6).

I focus first on six gifted European folklorists of the nineteenth century—Jacob Grimm, Wilhelm Grimm, Johann Wilhelm Wolf, Alexandr Afanas'ev, Heinrich Pröhle, and Emmanuel Cosquin—who, among many other writers and folklorists in Europe, gathered soldier tales about war among other wonder folktales. Very few scholars have endeavored to understand and explain the trauma of soldiers and their wounds buried in these fairy tales. Nor have they explored the wounds of storytellers who were either negatively affected by war or who actually fought in a war. The stories about soldiers and war that the six folklorists collected or wrote reveal how the emotions of the body dictated the narratives. The trauma-related narratives are significant signs or traces of how art enables us to cope with wounds and devastation. It may seem that to focus on folktales and fairy tales when people are protesting on the streets and soldiers are daily losing their lives is a waste of time, but it is art, I argue, especially soldier tales, that can provide relief, understanding, and hope that we humans can overcome brutality, authoritarianism, corruption, and killing.

Given the immense number of tales and novels about war from 1800 to the present, I cannot include them all. Nor do I want to make vapid generalizations. Consequently, I limit my focus to small groups of significant tales collected by German, Russian, and French folklorists. I close by discussing four twentieth-century writers—Vaillant-Couturier, Hermynia Zur Mühlen, Lisa Tetzner, and Druon—to indicate how they coped with war and trauma in Europe and North America in different ways. I hope that by demonstrating how war wounds led these authors to create and communicate soldier tales to reading publics, other scholars may be inspired to join me in doing more research on this subject.

A BIT OF HISTORY MIXED WITH STORYTELLING

Among the important books and essays I have read that deal with the significance of folktales and fairy tales in enabling people to deal with inequities in a humane way are David Hopkin's astute and comprehensive *Soldier and Peasant in French Popular Culture, 1766–1870* (2002) and Eugen Drewermann's *Heimkehrer aus der Hölle: Märchen von Kriegsverletzungen und ihrer Heilung* (Returnees from Hell: Fairy Tales about War Wounds and Their Healing, 2010). Both authors deal with the trauma suffered by common soldiers and their communities from different perspectives. While there are other superb studies about the effects of war in Europe, I primarily deal with folktales and fairy-tale novels because we generally do not associate fairy tales with soldiers and wars. Yet they offer surprising and exceptional critiques of war and demonstrate the hope that the originators of these works had for peace and a more just society.

The Brothers Grimm: Jacob Grimm (1785–1863) and Wilhelm Grimm (1786–1859)

There are ten soldier tales in the *Kinder- und Hausmärchen* (Children's and Household Tales): "The Three Snake Leaves," "How Six Made Their Way in the World," "Brother Lustig," "Bearskin," "The Devil's Sooty Brother," "The Blue Light," "The Devil and His Grandmother," "The Worn-out Dancing Shoes," "The Boots of Buffalo Leather," and "The Grave Mound." If one includes "Herr Fix-It-Up," which was part of the 1812 edition and eliminated in 1819, there are eleven (Zipes 2014).

The sources for these tales vary greatly: Johann Friedrich Krause, a former soldier; Dorothea Viehmann, a peasant woman; the landed-gentry family the von Haxthausens; and books published by Friedmund von Arnim and Philipp Hoffmeister. The original sources of all ten tales were evidently soldiers themselves, and the relatively high percentage of soldier tales in the Grimms' collection is most likely a direct result of the Napoleonic Wars and the vast increase of soldiering as a profession in the European population. Storytelling enabled narrators and their listeners to address trauma with a sense of hope in transformation. Almost all these tales indicate that common soldiers must somehow discard their "superiors" to create a different, more humane or ideal world for themselves.

Ever since standing armies became widespread in the seventeenth century, more and more men from the peasantry and lower classes were recruited as common soldiers. The following remarks are based to a large extent on the findings of Jürgen Kuczynski (1981). By the eighteenth century there was a definite shift in the social and economic structure of the German principalities due to the rise of the military as a dominant political force. To keep standing armies and increase their power, the German sovereigns had to levy taxes on the populace at large. As the officer corps developed and played a role in the administration of different regions, the army elite formed a caste that exercised great influence in domestic and foreign policies. Moreover, the code of discipline and punishment and the actual regimentation within the army anticipated the type of control that would be used in schools, prison systems, insane asylums, and factories as society became more rationalized and institutionalized. The common soldier's lot was miserable. This was true not only in Germany but also in most countries and principalities throughout Europe.

Since the peasantry and the bourgeois town and city dwellers were obligated to house the soldiers and pay for their maintenance, there was a distinct antipathy toward both the military establishment and the soldiers, often considered the dregs of society. Indeed, even these so-called dregs themselves, the common soldiers, did not want to serve in the army and did not think highly of their military commanders. As soon as a soldier found a good reason to resign or desert, he did. Very rarely did a common soldier have anything good to say about the army as an institution. The major factors that kept most soldiers in a standing army were money (even if it was not much) and the threat of punishment.

Given these general conditions, it is not by chance that most of the Grimms' tales reveal the common soldier's dissatisfaction with the treatment he receives from his superiors. Moreover, the tales also incorporate the general anti-military sentiment common among the peasants and the bourgeoisie. Of the ten Grimm tales that focus on soldiers, eight deal with discharged or ex-soldiers who are down and out and want to gain revenge on the king or their former officers. One tale deals with a poor farmer who enlists and becomes a hero for the fatherland (perhaps a reference to the Napoleonic Wars), while another depicts three soldiers who desert. The general purpose in all these tales, the motive of the protagonists that stamps the action, is the struggle to overcome a desperate situation. The veteran wants to survive a bad experience as soldier because he has killed not with a purpose but with the desire to survive and also to find security.

None of the protagonists in the Grimms' soldier tales start their lives or careers with an idealistic goal. The last thing on their minds is rescuing or marrying a princess (although that might occur). On the contrary, all the ex-soldiers want is simply to get by and obviously, if possible, return to their homes and raise their social status. They are desperate to stay alive, and this is the reason that the soldier protagonist is, without exception, fearless. Yet bravery is not what society demands from a soldier if he wants to be reintegrated and accepted—especially when that society is hostile toward the military and expects correct behavior according to the Protestant ethic. So a soldier's integrity must be tested and tempted by evil forces if he is to survive his wounds. My favorite type of soldier tale is "How Six Made Their Way in the World" (ATU 513A) collected by the Grimms, and it is my favorite because it responds to corrupt superiors and demonstrates that greed and war can be conquered if one uses one's powers and cooperates with others to form a new, more just society.

I once wrote a long essay about this tale type, "How Super Heroes Made Their Way into the World of Fairy Tales: The Appeal of Cooperation and Collective Action from the Greek Myths to the Grimms' Tales and Beyond" (Zipes 2015, 131–51). It was based on the subtype "The Extraordinary Companions" (ATU 513).

After fighting many years for a king, a soldier receives nothing for his efforts and vows to get revenge on the king. Walking alone in a forest he meets five extraordinary men who have unusual talents: a strong man who can rip up trees and carry them on his back; a sharpshooter who can shoot flies from great distances; a runner who can run around the world in minutes; a wind blower who can propel wind sails from miles away and cool off people; and a listener whose sharp ears can hear anything people say from miles away. These men join the ex-soldier in a contest organized by the king: whoever beats his daughter in a race will be permitted to marry her and obtain half the king's kingdom. If he loses, he and his friends will be beheaded. Indeed, the king allows all five friends to help the ex-soldier, and they almost lose the race when the runner falls asleep at the halfway mark. However, the sharpshooter awakens him, and the runner wins. Nevertheless, the haughty princess refuses to marry the ex-soldier, and she and her father try to kill him and his friends. However, the six men easily protect themselves. Finally, the king offers the ex-soldier and his friends all the wealth and treasures they can carry from the castle. To his dismay, the six men empty the castle and demolish the soldiers who pursue them. In the end, the king is penniless.

As an ideal soldier tale that expresses the wounds and wish fulfillment of soldiers from the Greco-Roman period to the present, this story is highly significant because it indicates the grievance and hope of soldiers throughout the world. Whatever trauma soldiers experience in senseless wars can be a starting point for hope and peace (MacDonald 1992). The theme here is that cooperation is needed to outwit and defeat a corrupt king.

JOHANN WILHELM WOLF (1817–1855)

The Grimms' nineteenth-century collection of folktales and fairy tales was not the first nor the last to deal with the plight of common soldiers and the trauma that results from war. There are thousands if not millions of versions of soldier resentment and hopeful tales because there have been thousands and millions who have dealt with their experience in wars and written and spoken about them.

One of the most fervent followers of the Grimms was Johann Wilhelm Wolf, a German folklorist who spent his early years working as a merchant. In Belgium he collected Flemish folktales and published them as *Niederländische Sagen* (Dutch Legends) in 1843. Soon after he returned to Cologne, he joined his brother-in-law, the writer Wilhelm von Ploennies, to develop a better understanding of German popular culture, and together they collected folktales directly from soldiers in Odenwald, published as *Deutsche Hausmärchen* (German Household Tales) in 1851. Wolf also founded one of the first folklore journals in Germany, *Zeitschrift für Deutsche Mythologie und Sittenkunde* (Journal of German Mythology and Morals, 1853). In his important 1851 collection, he wrote that his trips into the Odenwald countryside to meet with former soldiers and peasants provided him with an incredible number of tales. In his introduction to *Deutsche Hausmärchen*, he says: "All of a sudden we encountered a rich source of new and familiar stories. Indeed, we were surrounded by thousands of storytellers whom we had not expected. Wilhelm, who was a lieutenant in the royal Hessian army, called for the soldiers to march and appear before us man after man and had them tell and sing whatever they knew—fairy tales, legends, sagas, incantations, superstitions, and songs. They were a godsend, and there were so many tales that we could not edit them there because our hands were full. We had to spend our time collecting and ordering them" (1851, 17, my translation).

Among the important soldier tales are "The Princess of Tiefenthal," "About the Eighteen Soldiers," "About the Evil Comrades," "The Golden Deer," "The Twelve Brothers," "Hare-Herd," "The Thread," and "The Thirteen Bewitched Princesses." Typically, many begin with starving and dissatisfied soldiers, as in "About the Eighteen Soldiers," which has an unusually stark opening: "Eighteen soldiers, namely a colonel, a sergeant, a corporal, a drummer, and fourteen common soldiers were gathered together to be sentinels on a lonely watch.

However, it was hard work to stand on guard duty, and they were treated poorly. So, the entire regiment decided to desert. Only the colonel, who was an older soldier and had fought in two campaigns did not want anything to do with desertion" (Wolf 1851, 47).

Yet shortly thereafter, the colonel joins the soldiers because he realizes that he might be severely punished for allowing the others to desert. On their way through a forest, the soldiers stop at a tavern, where they eat and drink to their hearts' content. When the innkeeper learns that they have no money to pay for the food and drink, he becomes angry but has no choice but to send them away, hoping that they will be killed by a devil in a nearby mountain. Once the soldiers go through a forest and reach the mountain, they cross three bridges until they arrive in the courtyard of an enchanted castle, in which everything they need is magically provided. The soldiers decide to make their home there, and once they set up guard duty and establish their own routine, a carriage arrives with a beautiful but cursed princess who explains to the colonel that every day a carriage with a beautiful cursed princess will arrive, and each time a soldier must marry her.

Everything goes well until the eighteenth soldier, too anxious to wait for his princess, leaves the castle to search for her. When he comes to the bridge that leads back to the tavern where the soldiers had annoyed the innkeeper, the devil is waiting and asks him why he wants to cross the bridge. The soldier answers: "I want to leave the mountain." The devil grabs him and twists his neck until he dies. When the princess of the castle learns that there are now only seventeen soldiers, she tells the colonel that the curse can be lifted only if there are eighteen soldiers for the eighteen princesses. Otherwise, they will all die.

Consequently, the colonel sends three soldiers to the tavern where they recruit a carpenter to join their regiment by giving him lots of gold from the castle. The eighteen soldiers gladly marry the princesses and become kings of different realms. Meanwhile, the greedy innkeeper and his wife, certain that there must be tons of gold in the castle, decide to cross the bridge in the mountain guarded by the devil. Unfortunately for them, the devil will not allow them to go to the castle. Instead, he twists off their heads. From then on, the devil stops twisting necks because he now has business in other parts of this realm.

This bizarre, somewhat comic soldier tale is notable for its inexplicable contents. We never learn why the castle is enchanted, why the princesses are cursed, and why the number eighteen is so important. In fact, there is something Kafkaesque about this particular tale. Little can be explained. Everything just happens. Nevertheless, like many soldier tales, the desertion is explained and somewhat justified, and the wish fulfillment of the narrator for a better life is clear.

ALEXANDR AFANAS'EV (1826–1871)

Afanas'ev was a prominent Russian folklorist, who held positions as lawyer, historian, and journalist before embarking on a major study of Russian folklore. His most important work is *Russkie narodnye skazki* (*Russian Folk-Tales*, 1855–1867). Inspired by the Brothers Grimm, this collection was published in eight fascicles and contained 640 stories. The tales, which came from over thirty provinces, were recorded largely secondhand from records and manuscripts of other people. In his late life, when he had been punished by the Russian authorities for publishing anticlerical and vulgar tales, Afanas'ev was prohibited from doing further research on folklore.

Like most of the major folklorists of the twentieth century, he included a number of soldier tales in his collections, such as "The Two Ivans," "A Soldier's Sons," "Soldier Simkin," "The Volunteer Soldier," "Soldier Erema the Crafty," "How Peter the First Rewarded a Soldier with an Old Saddle," "The Insulted Soldier and the Good Spirit," "The Soldier and the Robber," "The Peasant and the Soldier," "The Soldier and Death," "The Soldier and the Tsar in the Forest," "The Soldier's Riddle," "The Soldier-Fiddler and the Devil," "The Soldier-Fiddler and the Witch," "The Soldier-Fiddler and the Unclean One," "The Soldier and the Watch," "The Soldier, the Peasant, and the Woman," "The Soldier and the Landlord," "The Runaway Soldier," and "The General's Wife and the Merchant's Son."

These tales vary greatly, featuring soldiers gaining revenge on their superiors or being killed after twenty-five years of service to the tsar. In my opinion, the best tale that optimistically depicts how most soldiers in Russia felt during this period is "Soldier Erema the Crafty." It concerns a shrewd soldier and a wise tsar with a sense of humor.

> There was this soldier who served in the tsar's guards, and on account of his agility they called him Erema the Crafty. In those days soldiers served twenty-five years. And most of the officers were Germans. This Erema somehow got

acquainted with the son of an officer and started learning German from him. And after two or three years he spoke German tolerably well.

A soldier's duty was difficult—they were beaten and insulted. In short, the soldiers were badly maintained and poorly fed. At first Erema tolerated everything, but then he decided to get back at some officers and the brigadier. He waited for the right opportunity and then such an opportunity arose. (Afanas'ev 1974, 76)

Erema tricks two German officers, who are sent to prison by the tsar because Erema demonstrates that they were willing to sell half of Russia just to please the brigadier's beautiful daughter. Impressed by Erema's cleverness and courage, the tsar tells him he will provide him with the opportunity to wed the beautiful daughter under certain conditions. So after Erema is imprisoned with a millionaire whom the tsar dislikes, he solves three riddles, an accomplishment that sets him and the millionaire free. However, the tsar tells Erema that he will release him from the army only if he manages to marry the general's daughter, who is already engaged to a prince. Erema finds a way to climb into the daughter's room and, disguised as a German officer, he makes love to her. When the prince, her fiancé, discovers this, he commits suicide. Then Erema is allowed to wed the daughter, and dressed in disguise as a German general, he returns to Petersburg and has all the officers in his regiment punished. Once again, the tsar is impressed, and he sets Erema free—but not before he sentences the general to death for creating poor conditions in the army. Moreover, he grants Erema the general's estate.

This is an exceptional tale, for not many depict a king or tsar with a sense of justice. Despite the comic aspect, it is highly significant because, like other folktales, it shows how desperate common soldiers were for revenge and for the chance to determine their own fate.

HEINRICH PRÖHLE (1822–1895)

Pröhle was a teacher and folklorist who studied at the universities of Halle and Berlin, where he was strongly influenced by Jacob Grimm, who encouraged him to collect folktales in the region of the Harz forest. Thanks to the Grimms' encouragement, Pröhle published several important collections: *Kinder- und Volksmärchen* (Children's and Folktales, 1853), *Unterharzische Sagen* (Lower Harz Legends, 1856), *Harzsagen* (Harz Legends, 1859), and

Rheinlands schönste Sagen und Geschichten (The Rhineland's Most Beautiful Legends and Stories, 1886). There are five soldier tales in *Kinder- und Volksmärchen*: "Lorenz the Soldier," "The Tricky Soldier," "The Merchant's Wife as Colonel," "The Jumping Root and the Little Light," and "A Bluffer Lays out the Cards in a Favorable Way." Most stress the cleverness of soldiers and use traditional fairy-tale motifs to demonstrate how common soldiers must prove themselves to be courageous and compassionate. "Lorenz the Soldier" is a good example.

A common soldier encounters a ghost several times when he is on guard duty. On the third night the ghost tells him that he must leave the army and obey the ghost if he wants to become a king. On the fourth night the ghost demands that he obtain a release from the army, which he does. However, he wanders around the region, runs out of food, and doubts whether he should have listened to the ghost. One night he sleeps on a heap of ants that sting him. He starts killing them, but the ghost warns him to protect his folk (the ants), for they may be able to help him in the future. So, Lorenz stops killing the ants, and the next morning he continues on his way until he comes to a pond with many ducks. Lorenz catches one of the ducks, intending to eat it, but the ghost advises him not to kill it because the ducks might be of service to him in the future.

Lorenz keeps wandering and finally comes across two beautiful maidens bathing in a river. They shout: "Our savior has arrived!" It seems, though it is never explained, that these two maidens have been enchanted. So, with the help of the ants and the ducks, Lorenz is able to overcome the curses placed on the maidens, who are princesses. Also, the ants and ducks turn out to be servants at the castle of the maidens, and Lorenz weds one of the princesses to become a king.

This tale is significant because it emphasizes a theme concerning harmony with nature and collective action. To become a king the soldier must learn to protect and not to kill.

EMMANUEL COSQUIN (1841–1919)

Desperation and loneliness mark many tales that indicate to what extent a soldier is ready to gamble his life for a chance to find food and freedom. French folklorist Cosquin devoted most of his life to the study of European folklore and its origins. Between 1877 and 1881 he collected numerous tales from the region of Champagne that he published in the journal *Romania*. Each tale was fully annotated and demonstrated Cosquin's comprehensive knowledge of folktales and fairy tales. As a result of his research, he published *Contes populaires de Lorraine* (Folktales of Lorraine, 1886), which compared the folktales in this collection with other French and European tales. In *Contes*, "The Two Soldiers of 1689" serves as a dramatic illustration of the suffering of common soldiers in the nineteenth century. One might even call this story drastically traumatic despite a so-called happy ending.

Two friends are discharged from the army after long years of service. Since they receive next to nothing from an ungrateful king, and thus have no money or food, they decide to go begging. However, they do not have much success at first and decide to flip a coin to decide who will become a blind soldier. The loser of the coin toss has his eyes poked out so they can draw more pity and money from the people they encounter. After a year or so of begging, they have a disagreement because the soldier who can see has been taking the best food, deceiving his friend. Abandoned in a forest, the blind soldier climbs a tree during the night and overhears four animals beneath him talking about some magic water in a spring that can heal blindness and other injuries and diseases. In the morning they depart. The blind soldier descends the tree, manages to reach the spring, gathers the water, and can see again.

Then he goes to the king, whose daughter is sick and who has announced that anyone who can cure her can have her as wife along with half the kingdom. Of course, the blind soldier heals the princess and soon becomes king. His deceitful friend appears one day, and the new king forgives his friend and tells him how he survived his friend's desertion thanks to the animals. So the deceitful soldier goes to the forest, climbs the tree, and eavesdrops on the angry animals, who are arguing about who revealed their secret. Looking up to see the deceitful soldier on a branch, they catch him and eat him.

This tragic, if not traumatic, tale can be found in many other French and German collections, such as Angelika Merkelbach-Pinck's "Two Old Soldiers" in *Lothringer Volksmärchen* (Lorraine Folktales, 1961), published about 100 years later. We must imagine that these tales of soldiers who take drastic steps such as blinding each other to survive were told time and again by survivors of brutal wars and brutal treatment. It is an example that demonstrates how hazardous the world is for former—and current—soldiers, even if they have survived wars.

SOLDIERS' STORIES, IMAGINING PEACE

What better way to deal with trauma than to imagine a world in which there is justice and compassion, where happiness or happy endings simply mean peace? I don't want to talk only about the hundreds of folktales I have read that deal with war and revenge. I also want to note that numerous soldiers in the twentieth and twenty-first centuries have continued to deal with their traumatic wounds by imagining other worlds. So I want to discuss how four books for children and adults emerged from the horrors of World War I and World War II to alert their readers (children and adults) that war is not the answer to the inequalities and inhumanities caused by politicians, corporations, military brass, religious leaders, and authoritarian rulers in this world.

In Vaillant-Couturier's *Johnny Breadless*, a magical rabbit uses his ears as propellers to take the orphan Johnny on a tour of Europe during World War I to show him who has caused the war and how soldiers can fight for peace. At one critical point, Johnny takes part in the famous Christmas truce of 1914, when soldiers on both sides of the battle, on their own initiative, stopped the war to stop the killing. This moment of truce and peace is stamped on Johnny's mind forever.

In 1931 Lisa Tetzner adapted the book for the stage and as a novel, *Hans Urian oder Die Geschichte einer Weltreise* (Hans Urian; or, The Story of a Journey around the World). The context here is the Great Depression. Hans goes looking for bread for his mother and encounters a fairy-tale rabbit who takes him around the world and exposes Hans to the exploitation of common people. Aside from a few soldiers in this tale, a weapons manufacturer also appears. The rabbit scorns and condemns the brutal treatment of children he shows to Hans. The rabbit, who has often been maltreated and exploited wherever he goes, does not want to meet with Hans's mother or have anything to do with humans at the end of their adventures. The provocative ending reveals that humans have a lot to learn about compassion for animals and other species.

Finally, jumping to World War II, there are two other significant tales for children that are clearly related to soldier tales: Kelen's *Yussuf the Ostrich*

(1943) in which a young ostrich demonstrates his courage and friendship to humans in a battle in North Africa against the Nazis, and Druon's *Tistou les pouces verts* (1957), in which a boy from a rich family discovers that he has magical fingers that can protect the environment, and he uses his power to prevent a war and to bring about a peaceful green environment. Interestingly, both Kelen's and Druon's fairy-tale novels remain open in their conclusions. We do not know what will happen either to the ostrich or Tistou at the end.

Today there are thousands if not millions of different kinds of fairy tales and folktales that deal with war and traumatic experiences throughout the world. Yet very few scholars have investigated the positive role that folktales and fairy tales may have played or do play in symbolic narratives that enable sufferers of traumatic wounds to heal. These particular tales can bring psychological relief and can activate our hope for sociopolitical changes. They can inform children that war is not necessary, and that glory and rewards do not benefit anyone if killing is the way we engage with one another.

My brief analysis of soldier tales is a modest endeavor to encourage folklorists and other researchers to trace the history of such tales in various cultures so that we can learn how wars come about and how to react to the recruitment of humans to kill one another. There is no lack of spectacular advertisements of soldiers and war, especially in movie theaters, television shows, and commercials. This means that researchers of soldier tales must take a critical and ethical stance while they collect and publicize findings that reveal how soldiers have spoken for themselves and also demonstrate how veterans have been deprived of experiencing peace and compassion because the trauma of war never abates.

REFERENCES

Afanas'ev, Alexandr. (1855–1867) 1974. *Russian Folk-Tales*. Edited and translated by Leonard Magnus. New York: E. P. Dutton.
Buttsworth, Sara, and Maartje Abbenhuis. 2017. *War, Myths, and Fairy Tales*. Singapore: Springer.
Conselman, Deirdre, and William Conselman Jr. (1940) 2020. *Keedle, the Great: And All You Ever Wanted to Know about Fascism*. Minneapolis: Little Mole and Honey Bear.
Cosquin, Emmanuel. 1886. *Contes populaires de Lorraine*. Paris: F. Vieweg.

Drewermann, Eugen. 2010. *Heimkehrer aus der Hölle: Märchen von Kriegsverletzungen und ihrer Heilung*. Ostfildern: Patmos.
Druon, Maurice. 1957. *Tistou les pouces verts*. Paris: Del Duca.
Hopkin, David. 2002. *Soldier and Peasant in French Popular Culture, 1766–1870*. London: Royal Historical Society.
Kelen, Emery. 1943. *Yussuf the Ostrich*. New York: Hyperion.
Kuczynski, Jürgen. 1981. *Geschichte des Alltags des deutschen Volkes, 1650–1810*. Vol. 2. Cologne: Pahl-Rugenstein.
MacDonald, Margaret Read. 1992. *Peace Tales: World Folktales to Talk About*. Hamden, CT: Linnet Books.
Merkelbach-Pinck, Angelika. 1961. *Lothringer Volksmärchen*. Cologne: E. Diederichs.
Pröhle, Heinrich. 1853. *Kinder- und Volksmärchen*. Leipzig: n.p.
Pröhle, Heinrich. 1856. *Unterharzische Sagen*. Aschersleben: O. Fokke.
Pröhle, Heinrich. 1859. *Harzsagen*. Leipzig: Mendelsohn.
Pröhle, Heinrich. 1886. *Rheinlands schönste Sagen und Geschichten*. Berlin: Meidinger.
Tetzner, Lisa 1931. *Hans Urian oder Die Geschichte einer Weltreise*. Stuttgart: Gundert.
Vaillant-Couturier, Paul. (1921) 2019. *Johnny Breadless: a Pacifist Fairy Tale*. Edited and Translated by Jack Zipes. Minneapolis: Little Mole and Honey Bear.
Wolf, Johann Wilhelm. 1843. *Niederländische Sagen*. Leipzig: F. A. Brockhaus.
Wolf, Johann Wilhelm. 1851. *Deutsche Hausmärchen*. Göttingen: Dieterich.
Zipes, Jack, ed. and trans. 2014. *The Complete First Edition: The Original Folk and Fairy Tales of the Brothers Grimm*. Princeton, NJ: Princeton University Press.
Zipes, Jack. 2015. *Grimm Legacies: The Magic Spell of the Grimms' Folk and Fairy Tales*. Princeton, NJ: Princeton University Press.

8

Reimagining Evil

Justice and Magic in Disney's Fairy-Tale Live-Action Remixes

MING-HSUN LIN

Fairy tales have long addressed concepts of justice. But with Disney's current "cultural stranglehold" on the form (Zipes 1999, 333), scholars lambast its films' interpretations as retrograde and patriarchal for perpetuating gender-confining notions and binary perspectives. Jack Zipes, for example, argues that the heteronormative morality in Disney's fairy-tale films creates a dichotomous world in which character development and deeper understanding of good and evil are absent (1997, 93). However, in recent years, the sexist and reactionary ideology in Disney's early fairy-tale animations has been challenged in its live-action films, which endeavor to present a more inclusive idea of justice by providing insight into the complexity of evil. In response to criticisms of Disney's early animations, these live-action films humanize evil by twisting and subverting its illustrations of antagonists through a liberal feminist approach. This chapter focuses on Disney's fairy-tale films of the past decade, specifically *Maleficent*, directed by Robert Stromberg in 2014, *Cinderella*, directed by Kenneth Branagh in 2015, *Beauty and the Beast*, directed by Bill Condon in 2017, *Aladdin*, directed by Guy Ritchie in 2019, and *Maleficent: Mistress of Evil*, directed by Joachim Rønning in 2019.[1]

These blockbuster films, adapted from classic fairy tales, remix previous animations. A cinematic remix is a revision "wherein the conventional and innovative merge and blend. The spectator's pleasure results from predicting the familiar plot twists and turns and being pleasantly surprised to be both correct and incorrect" (Greenhill and Matrix 2010, 14). This chapter demonstrates how the results reshape a more inclusive justice by implanting backstories for the movies' antagonists, and elaborates on how, in most remixes, they are also the victims. I argue that magic serves as a test for the protagonists to demonstrate their capacity for love, which is the crucial characteristic that distinguishes good from evil. As its influence on justice diminishes, magic inevitably weakens and eventually departs.

JUSTICE IN TRADITIONAL FAIRY TALES

In many traditional versions of fairy tales, the notion of justice is primarily constructed by a clear dichotomy of good and evil. Yet compared with the diverse images of protagonists who represent goodness, antagonists who stand for evil are rather simplified.[2] Vladimir Propp identifies the villain as one of seven dramatis personae in fairy tales whose main function is to motivate the story by impeding the protagonist. Villainy, according to Propp, serves to "disturb the peace of a happy family, to cause some form of misfortune," and to initiate "a fight or other forms of struggle with the hero" (1968, 27, 79). Evil therefore is the force or behavior that breaks harmony, destabilizes the social order, and/or hinders self-fulfillment. Antagonists are defined by their actions instead of by their identities.

The lack of psychological underpinning and character growth contributes to the stereotyping of antagonists in fairy tales. Philip Pullman notes that fairy tales lack character development and psychological depth (2012). This is especially true with antagonists. Fairy tales offer little or no explanation of why these malefactors become wicked. Often they do not have names and are simply given nefarious titles. Miscreants like the wicked witch, the vicious stepmother, the evil queen, and the cannibalistic ogre loom large, greedy and jealous in nature, and evil to the core. Their static, flat characters make them not just the agents of evil but evil itself. The protagonists, on the other hand, become the manifestation of goodness, and their defeat of the antagonists signifies ultimate justice.

Traditional fairy-tale justice is deeply rooted in the belief that good should always prevail over evil, manifested by immediate reward and retributive punishment. The protagonist's fight against the antagonist represents the journey of setting things right, and the restitution at the end of the story restores order. The protagonist's rewards often come in the forms of marriage, fortune, or social status. Equal to, if not more important than, the protagonist's reward is the antagonist's punishment. The evil stepmother who kills and stews her young stepson is crushed to death by a millstone in "The Juniper Tree" (ATU 720); the stepsisters' eyes are pecked out by pigeons in "Cinderella" (ATU 510A); and the evil queen in "Snow White" (ATU 709) is forced to put on a pair of red-hot iron slippers and dance herself to death. Since antagonists represent wickedness itself and show no remorse for the evil they perpetrate, it seems justifiable to give them the most severe punishments.

One recurring plot sequence in fairy tales is the pattern of prohibition/violation. Often the protagonists must do exactly what they are asked not to do so the story can proceed. Whether straying from the path in the woods or opening the forbidden door, from trivial misconduct to serious offenses, the protagonists' violation of the interdiction is a necessary step for the completion of their journey and the key to their self-fulfillment. However, the consequences of transgression tend to be gender specific; male characters are acquitted of their transgression but female characters are denounced (Bottigheimer 1987, 81). Heroes are often set on the path of fortune because of their curiosity, while heroines are shamed and punished because of theirs. In "Faithful Johannes" (ATU 516), the prince disobeys his father and enters the room where the portrait of the Princess of the Golden Roof is hidden. His transgression nonetheless brings him neither misfortune nor death, but sets him on a quest that results in his happiness in the end.

On the other hand, curiosity about the secrets beyond the door, commendable in "Faithful Johannes," is a failure in "Bluebeard" (ATU 312). The heroine cannot hold back her inquisitiveness, opens the door to the forbidden chamber, and stains the key with blood. When her husband finds the gory evidence, she is brought to her knees to repent and only the timely arrival of her brothers saves her from decapitation by him. Maria Tatar comments on these two stories, "Clearly there is a double standard at work here in the moral order of the fairy-tale world" (2019, 167). When male curiosity induces the hero to violate an interdiction, it indicates courage, wisdom, or luck that is indispensable to his success. Unresisted female curiosity, on the other hand, is tainted with evil (Tatar 1992, 111). Fairy-tale heroines face the punishment of abasement and psychic or literal death for their transgressions. This pattern is repeated in the animated films that provide the sources for the remixes I discuss, but is altered to some extent in the live-action remixes.

REMIXES: PLOT OVERVIEW

Maleficent is very loosely adapted from the animated *Sleeping Beauty*, directed by Clyde Geronimi, Les Clark, Eric Larson, and Wolfgang Reitherman in 1959. Powerful winged fairy Maleficent (Angelina Jolie) defends the Moors and its magical creatures from the adjacent human kingdom. She falls in love with the human Stefan (Sharlto Copley), who later betrays her by stealing her wings so he can become the new king. For revenge, Maleficent curses Stefan's infant daughter Aurora (Elle Fanning) to prick her finger with a spindle on her sixteenth birthday and fall into an eternal sleep, only to be awakened by true love's kiss. Under Stefan's order, three good fairies raise Aurora in the countryside. Maleficent observes Aurora and gradually comes to care for her, eventually becoming her fairy godmother. Aurora meets Prince Philip (Brenton Thwaites) in the woods, and the two are attracted to each other. However, when Aurora discovers the curse, she tells Maleficent she hates her before returning to the castle and falling into an enchanted sleep. Maleficent abducts Philip and takes him to the castle in hopes that his kiss will break the curse. When he fails to awaken Aurora, Maleficent tearfully repents and kisses her forehead, reviving her unexpectedly. Aurora finds Maleficent's stolen wings in the castle and returns them to her. The two attempt to leave, but Stefan assaults Maleficent from behind and falls to his death during their struggle. Maleficent crowns Aurora queen of the Moors, thereby unifying both kingdoms.

The sequel *Maleficent: Mistress of Evil* (henceforth *Mistress*) begins five years after King Stefan's death. Ulstead, the home kingdom of Prince Philip (Harris Dickinson), still perceives Maleficent and the Moors as threats. Philip's father King John (Robert Lindsay) desires peace, but his mother Queen Ingrith

(Michelle Pfeiffer) secretly prepares weapons for war. Maleficent and Aurora are invited to dinner at Ulstead and Ingrith curses John with the spellbound spindle from the previous film in order to falsely implicate Maleficent. Enraged by Aurora's doubts about her innocence, Maleficent leaves Ulstead, but is wounded by Ingrith's servant. The fairy Conall (Chiwetel Ejiofor) rescues her and takes her to a hidden cavern of fairies. Ingrith invites the residents of the Moors to Philip and Aurora's wedding and proceeds to massacre them. Maleficent and the fairies start a war against Ulstead. In protecting Aurora, Maleficent is shot by Ingrith's arrow and turns into ashes. As Aurora mourns, her tears fall on the ashes and revive Maleficent in the form of a phoenix. In the end, Maleficent destroys the cursed spindle and transforms Ingrith into a goat, while Aurora and Philip's marriage brings peace to their kingdoms.

The live-action *Cinderella* is largely similar to the animated original, directed by Clyde Geronimi, Wilfred Jackson, and Hamilton Luske in 1950. The heroine, Ella (Lily James), is abused by her stepmother Lady Tremaine (Cate Blanchett) and her two stepsisters after her father dies. Ella encounters Prince Kit (Richard Madden) in the woods. Hoping to see her again, he holds a royal ball to which he invites every maiden in the kingdom. Ella, transformed into a princess by her fairy godmother (Helena Bonham Carter), dances with Kit at the ball. Upon leaving, she drops a glass slipper, leading the prince to search the kingdom for the girl whose foot fits it. Lady Tremaine discovers the second slipper in Ella's room. She offers to help Ella marry Kit in return for making her head of the royal household. Ella refuses, and Lady Tremaine breaks the glass slipper and locks the young woman in the attic. Fortunately, Kit overhears her singing and frees her. Ella puts on the slipper, and the two are happily married.

Beauty and the Beast (2017) is a close remix of the animated *Beauty and the Beast*, directed by Gary Trousdale and Kirk Wise in 1991. An enchantress (Hattie Morahan) transforms a prince (Dan Stevens) into a beast and his servants into living objects because he is devoid of love, then erases the villagers' memories of the prince and his servants. She leaves the Beast with an enchanted rose. To become human again, he must learn to love another and earn her love before its last petal falls. Heroine Belle (Emma Watson) becomes the Beast's prisoner when her father Maurice (Kevin Kline) steals a rose from the castle. Belle and the Beast become close, and eventually he frees her to return to her father. Upon her return home, Belle's arrogant suitor Gaston (Luke Evans) discovers her affection for the Beast and rallies the villagers to kill him. They attack the castle, and Gaston shoots the Beast from a bridge, but falls to his own death when it collapses. The Beast dies in Belle's arms and the last petal falls before she confesses her love. The enchantress reappears and undoes the curse, restoring the Beast and his servants to human form and returning the villagers' memories. The prince and Belle host a ball to celebrate their happiness.

Aladdin's (2019) storyline follows that of the animation, directed by Ron Clements and John Musker in 1992, telling the story of street thief Aladdin (Mena Massoud) who meets Princess Jasmine (Naomi Scott) in the marketplace and falls in love with her. He obtains a magic lamp from which a genie (Will Smith) grants him three wishes. With his first wish, Aladdin becomes Prince Ali to pursue Jasmine. He promises to release the Genie with his final wish, but refuses to do so when he gets the sultan's (Navid Negahban) permission to marry Jasmine. Jafar (Marwan Kenzari), the wicked royal vizier, steals the lamp, exposes Aladdin's identity, and takes control of the kingdom. Aladdin tricks Jafar into becoming a genie, resulting in him being confined to his lamp forever. Instead of using his last wish to become Prince Ali again, Aladdin frees the Genie, who becomes human and starts a family with Jasmine's handmaid (Nasim Pedrad). Jasmine becomes the first female sultan, abolishes the law that only princes can wed princesses, and marries Aladdin.

ANTAGONISTS' BACKSTORIES AND INCAPACITY TO LOVE IN DISNEY REMIXES

Disney's live-action remixes significantly redraw the binary values of good and evil. Only rarely do the original animations explain evil's origin and cause, and the antagonist is often its source. Through providing backstories, however, the remixes attempt to humanize evil and add psychological complexity, enabling viewers to understand how the character suffers. As Claudia Schwabe explains, the audience can thus identify the villain as a "misunderstood victim of society and social misfit," and further sympathize with such characters because they are just flawed individuals like everyone else (2019, 92). The live-action versions' feminist perspective challenges stereotypes of femininity and portrays patriarchy as an oppressive force. The remixes demonstrate that evil takes many forms, from gender inequality to violent aggression and patriarchal hierarchy, victimizing everyone, including the antagonists.

However, in remixes that closely re-create the narrative structure of the original animations, antagonists often become difficult to sympathize with as their backstories are rarely as compelling as their villainy. Nevertheless, the added information renders the antagonist and the protagonist as foils to one another, both of whom experience similar injustices. Antagonists incapable of loving anyone except themselves succumb to evil, whereas heroes and heroines prevail by sacrificing for love; justice is ultimately restored through love, while villainy is attributed to an inability to love.

Maleficent (2014) offers an example, successfully subverting the expected image of the unredeemable antagonist and disrupting the binary of good and evil. In the animation *Sleeping Beauty*, the witch Maleficent embodies pure evil, cursing Aurora due to not being invited to her christening. She is merely a catalyst to bring about the protagonist's struggle against her villainy, and her motivation is never the focus of the narrative. The live-action version, on the other hand, illuminates how Maleficent became evil and thus her villainy is understandable. Screenwriter Linda Woolverton achieved this goal by drawing inspiration from the animation's cursing scene. She explains: "I had to figure out what possibly could have happened to her to make her want to hurt an innocent baby. Something that would equal that act. In the animated movie, she had no wings. She just threw her robes open like wings. I thought, 'Is that it? Did someone take her wings?' They stole her soul and her heart had to turn cold" (quoted in *Women and Hollywood* 2014). Consequently, the remix depicts Maleficent's descent into evil after losing her wings, shifting the storyline to her avenging journey, not Aurora's plight.

Changing the narrative structure allows Maleficent to manifest various roles, from persecuted heroine to villain to rescuing hero. Initially, her story conforms to patterns of gender-specific transgression and punishment for fairy-tale heroines. She is deeply moved when the poor barn boy Stefan casts away his iron ring so his hand can hold hers. Yet the narrator observes that Stefan, the thief seeking fortune in the Moors, steals something far more precious than jewels. There is a subtle implication that Maleficent should not easily trust a man. The prohibition between Maleficent and Stefan is not rooted in the old hatred between humans and fairies, but rather in the virtue of chastity for fairy-tale heroines. On Maleficent's sixteenth birthday, Stefan gives her what he calls "true love's kiss," which, according to the narrator, is doomed to be a lie. Fairy-tale heroines are punished when they cannot resist sexual curiosity, and Maleficent, who falls for the false promise of love, is debased by losing her wings. During an interview with BBC Woman's Hour, Jolie clarifies how the scene of stolen wings evokes the date-rape narrative. She remarks, "We were very conscious, the writer [Woolverton] and I, that it was a metaphor for rape" (Rich 2014). In severing Maleficent's wings for the purpose of becoming the new king, Stefan demonstrates a man exerting power over a woman through sexual aggression. Maleficent's wings symbolize her identity as the fierce protector of the Moors, so Stefan's action represents patriarchal oppression that degrades powerful women.

Maleficent's abasement echoes the heroine's experience in Giambattista Basile's version of the tale, "Sun, Moon, and Talia" (2001). It depicts a married king discovering Princess Talia in the woods and having sex with her while she is in an enchanted sleep. Talia and Maleficent are both victims of sexual violence, but the former obeys her persecutor, while the latter rises to fight hers. *Maleficent* subverts the gender-specific punishment's discriminatory narrative in classic fairy tales and in the animation. It not only presents Maleficent's villainy as having a compelling motivation, but also endorses it as a part of women's struggle against male oppression.

Yet in taking revenge on Stefan's infant daughter instead of on the real culprit, Maleficent becomes an antagonist, much like Stefan, who sacrifices others for his own ends. When he kneels to plead for his daughter's life, Maleficent scornfully declares that the princess can be awoken only by true love's kiss, which neither believes exists. Maleficent's mockery further complicates the notion of female rivalry shown in the animated version. True love's kiss becomes a symbol of deception and the patriarchal mechanisms that defraud and deprive women. Cursing an innocent girl makes Maleficent complicit in acts of violence against other women, including herself.

Maleficent and Stefan resemble one another, both being antagonistic characters driven by hatred. However, as the film progresses, the two take divergent paths. Stefan strives to destroy his victim rather than atone for his crime, while Maleficent takes a path toward redemption. Stefan serves as her foil. He becomes cruel and hateful toward his family and people, revealing his inability to love as the source of his villainy. On the other hand, Maleficent demonstrates that she has regained the ability to love and awakens Aurora with her kiss, symbolizing the power of love to overcome injustice.

Maleficent transforms from antagonist to rescuing hero. By manifesting different roles, she transcends the barrier between good and evil. The remix further subverts the conventional delineation of true love, which Disney fairy-tale films initially defined as heterosexual "love-at-first-sight" (Wood 2015, 157), exclusive to heroes and heroines. By diminishing true love's romantic meaning, the film redefines it in maternal form. In addition to saving Aurora from eternal sleep, Maleficent's love allows her to break free from the prison she had placed herself in through hatred. When Aurora returns Maleficent's wings so she can defeat Stefan, the two become the epitome of solidarity that eradicates female rivalry as well as its pernicious roots in the patriarchal conditioning of women.

In both Disney *Cinderellas*, the reshaping of antagonists begins with their appearance. In the animation, the binary of good and evil manifests through the characters' looks. The stepmother and her daughters are unsightly and wicked, while Cinderella is fair and kind. The stepmother's mistreatment is explained by the narrator in the prologue: "Cold, cruel and bitterly jealous of Cinderella's charm and beauty, she was grimly determined to forward the interests of her own two awkward daughters." The stepmother forbids Cinderella to attend the ball and try on the slipper as her physically unappealing daughters stand little chance against Cinderella in a marriage match. The animation suggests that women's physical attractiveness determines their marriageability, and jealousy over looks leads to strife between them. The stepmother's acts to abuse Cinderella hence become the epitome of female rivalry. But the remix portrays stepmother and daughters as physically attractive; appearance does not mirror inner nature. Lady Tremaine, whom the narrator describes as having "refined tastes," shares her daughters' disdain for Ella's looks, indicating a deeper cause of female strife than jealousy over appearance.

In the remix, patriarchal oppression is the source of female enmity. In the animation, the dead father is exculpated from any share in his second wife's evil or his daughter's misfortunes. Nevertheless, he is partly blamed for destroying the family's harmony in the remix. Although Ella is contented and happy, her father is not satisfied with their life. He expresses a wish to marry Lady Tremaine, who, as he says, "finds herself alone, though still in the prime of her life." His explanation allows the audience to sympathize with Lady Tremaine as a widow who needs to rely on a man's support to survive.

Before departing for his last trip, Ella's father tells her that his new wife and stepdaughters "may be trying at times" and reminds her to cherish the house, as her dead mother is "the very heart" of the place. The stepmother overhears and walks away silently. Rebecca Gadd comments that "Ella's father is able to insult his new wife by reminding her that she has taken up a role which was never truly vacant in the first place" (2022, 126). While the scene encourages the audience to pity Lady Tremaine for being slighted, it also implies that she is flawed in personality and less virtuous than the first wife, rather than her equal. Margery Hourihan argues that patriarchy is the underlying cause of women's rivalry in stories such as "Cinderella," noting that "where status, comfort and security, perhaps survival itself, depend upon being chosen and valued by men, women's natural enemies are each other" (2005, 201). Since Lady Tremaine relies on her husband for her status and livelihood, her position is threatened as he views Ella as the rightful mistress. Lady Tremaine's act of imposing housework can be regarded as her attempt to degrade Ella to the position of maid. The remix thus illustrates how patriarchy contributes to the stepmother's mistreatment of her stepdaughter.

Lady Tremaine plays the roles of both persecutor and victim in the live-action film. She tells Ella that she first married for love, then for a living, and lost her husbands in both marriages. She mocks, "And so, I live unhappily ever after. My story would appear to be ended." Lady Tremaine sees her life as a fairy tale gone wrong. Her remark is especially sarcastic when considered in the context of Disney's fairy-tale films, characterized by the portrayal of young maidens finding true love, while old women are reduced to persecutors or helpers. As the fairy-tale stepmother, Lady Tremaine is unlikely to find the happily ever after she dreams about. Her account offers a bitter comment on how women must rely on marriage for happiness and survival. Her abuse of Ella does not directly stem from inherent evil, but rather from the cruelties that greeted her as a woman throughout the course of her life.

The remix further sheds light on why the stepmother transforms from victim to persecutor. When Ella asks Lady Tremaine why she is being so cruel, she glares at her and replies, "Because you are young, and innocent, and good." Because Lady Tremaine is none of the three, Ella's existence serves as a reminder of her forever-lost innocence and the hopes she had before she became the (wicked) stepmother. Hence, female jealousy leads to envy of those who remain hopeful. The film suggests that the oppressed may lose optimism and succumb to hatred, becoming a part of the system by oppressing others. Despite this, Lady Tremaine remains an unsympathetic character. Gadd notes that by the time the audience learns her story, "her evil-stepmother arc has been fulfilled, and there is very little that she can do to redeem herself" (2022, 126).

Lady Tremaine's backstory nevertheless strengthens her connection to Ella, since both lose loved ones and must survive without the financial support of men. Their true difference lies in their response to adversity (though they have faced different degrees thereof). To protect Kit, Ella refuses to allow Lady Tremaine to run the kingdom even at the potential cost of losing her marriage prospects. While her stepmother sees only the possibility of a trade, Ella is willing to make a sacrifice to protect those she loves. Justice in the remix is determined by love, which allows characters to make the difficult but right choice. Ultimately, Ella tells Lady Tremaine that she forgives her. In the end, the heroine triumphs over her evil stepmother, offering the possibility of female reconciliation, the hope of solidarity among women, and the end of patriarchal oppression.

Disney's *Beauty and the Beast* films portray male villain Gaston as a representation of malevolent masculinity. In the animation, he is a hunter whose "misogyny and egocentrism position him as the quintessential antagonist for the film's late-twentieth-century predominantly female viewers" (Haas and Trapedo 2018, 182). He criticizes women who read, and tells Belle that her greatest happiness should be to be his "little wife" and bear him children. Described by Belle as "primitive," Gaston embodies the patriarchal perspective that perpetuates conventional gender roles and impairs social progress. He falls to his death during his attempt to kill the Beast, illustrating how toxic masculinity leads to violence and destruction. However, Gaston's malignant masculinity is not explained in the animation; he appears to have been born vicious and brutal.

In contrast, the remix attempts to illuminate Gaston's villainous nature through his backstory. It portrays Gaston as a war hero who is, according to Evans, who plays him, "a broken human being," suffering from PTSD (Snetiker 2017). Gaston's traumatic past is vaguely hinted at in his conversation with his sidekick LeFou. When Maurice angers Gaston, LeFou attempts to calm him by recalling happy memories: "Go back to the war. Blood. Explosions. Countless widows." The scene implies that war can destroy a man's humanity, turning him into a bloodthirsty beast like Gaston. Nonetheless, without sufficient explanation of the trauma he suffered, what comes across on-screen is a sadistic monster who revels in shedding blood.

Gaston is crafted as a foil for the Beast, as both represent "extreme masculinity" (Gutierrez 2017, 186). The remix further strengthens their connection through their backstories. A brief flashback shows the Beast as a young boy being taken by his father from his mother's deathbed. The castle's housekeeper Mrs. Potts explains to Belle that when the prince lost his mother, his father twisted him into a cruel being like himself. The Beast, thus compelled to become a heartless monarch, also becomes a victim insensitive to emotion in accordance with the patriarchal masculine paradigm. Susan Jeffords argues that the Beast's story illustrates how "masculinity has been betrayed by its own cultural imagery," and becomes a curse for men (1995, 171). Gaston and the Beast are both victims who lost the ability to love as a result of fulfilling oppressive masculine roles.[3] Gaston, who exhibits no empathy or love and dies during his murderous attack on the Beast, is a lost cause. In contrast, the Beast exemplifies the redemption of masculinity through sacrificial love by freeing Belle and giving up his chance to break the curse. The Beast's transformation offers hope that trauma can be healed and masculine oppression rectified, if not completely eliminated, through love.

Both the animated and live-action versions of *Aladdin* depict Jafar, the male villain who resents being second best, as the embodiment of greed for power and wealth. Through his backstory, the remix further explains his abhorrence of subordinates as a result of a social hierarchy that reinforces dominance over oppressed classes. Jafar informs Aladdin that he, too, was once at the bottom of society and learned that only authority and money can make others see a person's value. He claims that the sultan and the princess continually remind him of his position and humble origins, which he believes prevent him from attaining greatness. In spite of Jafar's claim to be a victim of the social hierarchy, the remix does not showcase his past struggles, but instead depicts him as a persecutor who exploits the system by oppressing the underprivileged, such as Aladdin.

In the remix, evil's complexity is ultimately exhibited through the similarities between Aladdin and Jafar. Aladdin enters the cave to obtain the magic lamp after being convinced by Jafar that in order to succeed, commoners must steal and seize power and wealth. Aladdin becomes engulfed in power and ascribes greater value to title than to inner worth. After obtaining the sultan's permission to marry Jasmine, Aladdin refuses to release the Genie, declaring, "Aladdin is gone. I'm Prince Ali now." He appears to be following Jafar's path. Just as Jafar sacrifices others for the sake of power, Aladdin enslaves the Genie to achieve royal status. However, unlike Jafar, who cares for no one, Aladdin commits these wrongdoings primarily because of his love for Jasmine. Ultimately, his love empowers him to repent and right his wrongs by releasing the Genie. Aladdin's transformation in the remix offers a more humanized perspective on how evil can arise within good people for comprehensible reasons, and how love can help characters overcome their own evil and redeem justice.

Female villain Ingrith in *Mistress* is absent from the animated *Sleeping Beauty*, and her character was likely derived from the ogress who is the heroine's mother-in-law in Charles Perrault's "La belle au bois dormant" or "Sleeping Beauty in the Wood." Both Perrault's ogress and *Mistress*'s Ingrith are disguised as loving mothers, yet one orders the steward to kill and serve her Sleeping Beauty and her children, while the other curses her husband and kidnaps fairies for cruel experiments. Nonetheless, unlike the ogress, born wicked and bloodthirsty, Ingrith sees villainy as a legitimate means of opposing patriarchy. She recounts how her brother was sent to the Moors to seek assistance, only to be killed by the magical creatures there. Her loathing of these beings represents, as director Rønning notes, the "fear of the unknown" (quoted in Sandwell 2019). Ingrith further associates this dread of the other with the evil of male domination and ascribes her own tragedy to weak male rulers who seek peace. Upon her brother's death, her father was overthrown by his people. Ingrith remarks, "I was cast out. Forced by fate into marriage with King John of Ulstead. Another weak king speaking of tolerance and civility." As she spreads the evil story of Maleficent, she instills fear in her people, takes control of the throne, and slaughters the Moors. Ironically, Ingrith, a victim of fear and violence, becomes a persecutor who uses these same forces to tyrannize others.

The complexity of Ingrith's evil lies not in her victimized past but in her conviction in the cause she fights for. Her strong belief in justice leads her to create injustice. Unlike the antagonists discussed above, Ingrith is motivated not only by her own interests but also those of her people. After killing Maleficent, she tells Aurora, "I know you think I'm a monster. But what I did to the king, to Maleficent, to my son . . . I did for Ulstead." Ingrith considers her villainy necessary for the good of her people, making her something of a tragic figure. Even so, the film maintains a clear distinction between good and evil through the comparison between Ingrith and Maleficent. Maleficent, persecuted by humans, is also driven by hatred and wages war to protect the fairies. But while Ingrith ignores her son's pleas to stop the war, Maleficent lets go of her resentment due to her love for Aurora. Maleficent's maternal love enables her to overcome her hatred and end the cycle of violence, whereas Ingrith's lack of maternal love determines her villainy. The film distinguishes the good mother, Maleficent, from the terrible mother, Ingrith, applying normative ideals to define female villainy (Rowe 2022, 45). The film consequently draws a distinction between good and evil in terms of motherhood.

In these remixes, female villains receive less severe punishments than their male counterparts. Maleficent transforms Ingrith into a goat, while Lady Tremaine leaves the kingdom after her evil scheme is revealed. Male villains, on the other hand, pay heavily for their offenses. Gaston and Stefan both fall to their deaths, while Jafar is imprisoned in a lamp for eternity. The modified repercussions for villainy may be a result of feminist concerns. The death and incarceration of the male villains symbolize the fall of evil patriarchal domination, whereas the lenient punishments for the female villains display sympathy because it is caused by male oppression.

THE TEST AND DEPARTURE OF FAIRY-TALE MAGIC

In the live-action remixes, love is an essential characteristic that distinguishes good from evil, while the protagonists' choices and actions affirm their ability to love. This process results in a change from the originals. The animations feature magic as a reward for the protagonists' virtues, granting justice through a romantic happily ever after. However, magic in the remixes becomes a perilous force testing the protagonists' characters and their capacity for love, traits that enable them to make the right decisions so that justice prevails. But in the live-action films, magic fades as its impact on justice diminishes, and eventually departs once harmony and order are restored.

The spell of true love's kiss illustrates the subtle change in the nature of magic from the animated *Sleeping Beauty* to *Maleficent*. In *Sleeping Beauty*, the good fairies present the kiss's magic as a gift to Aurora, along with the blessings of grace and beauty. Magic predicts and fulfills the prophecy that Aurora will be rescued by true love. By enchanting Philip's sword and shield, the good fairies assist him in slaying the dragon Maleficent transforms into, demonstrating the power of magic to defeat evil. Aurora and Philip's happy ending depicts justice through the triumph of romantic love. In *Maleficent*, however, the spell is more than just a curse. Rather, as it represents Maleficent's hatred and her disbelief in love itself, true love's kiss becomes a test for her to regain her ability to love. When Maleficent believes that the curse can never be broken, she still ventures into the castle filled with deadly weapons and risks her life to save Aurora. After all hope seems lost, she vows to devote her remaining days to protecting the sleeping princess. When Maleficent shows her determination to break the curse and atone for her sin, her kiss that awakens Aurora demonstrates that she has passed the test of magic and learned to love again.

In *Maleficent*, justice is achieved not by magic but by Maleficent and Aurora's decisions. To restore peace, the two must choose love over hatred and overcome their resentment of those who wrong them. Ultimately, Maleficent's endeavor to redeem herself and crown Aurora as queen of the Moors, along with Aurora's forgiveness of Maleficent and the return of her wings, lead to female solidarity and the realization of justice. The subversion of the female villain's story into the heroine's tale in *Maleficent* further announces the withdrawal of magic. Subverting the animation's plot to portray Maleficent as a loving godmother essentially expunges the malicious winged dragon from the story.

In the *Cinderella* animation, magic rewards Cinderella for her beauty and kindness, enabling her to marry the prince, a victory over her evil stepfamily and the attainment of justice. In the live-action remix, magic becomes a trial. Ella faces the first test when her stepfamily calls her "Cinderella" because of the ashes on her face. The narrator says, "Names have power, like magic spells. And of a sudden, it seemed to her that her stepmother and stepsisters had indeed transformed her into merely a creature of ash and toil." The name evokes the debasing power of curses. Ella, angry and humiliated, rides off into the woods, meets Kit, and stops him from hunting a stag. When Kit asks about her family, she states that they treat her as well as they can. Even though Ella is abased, she shows compassion to others, including her abusers. Her acts reject the debasing power of magic, demonstrating her noble nature, which appeals to Kit.

While Cinderella's magical transformation at the ball is vital to her happy ending in the animation, it is a test that Ella fails in the remix. Unlike Cinderella, who was unaware of the prince's true identity, Ella realizes that Kit is the future king. She does not correct him when he assumes she is a princess, but rather warns him that once he discovers the truth about who she is, he will no longer regard her in the same way. The scene suggests that Ella's transformation is not only a gift from her fairy godmother but also a test to see if she can remain true to herself and appreciate her worth, regardless of her social status. When Ella questions her own humble origins, the magic that represents Cinderella's virtues in the animation becomes a challenge to Ella's character in the remix.

The confrontation between Ella and Lady Tremaine marks the third and final test of magic in the live-action film. The glass slipper, which allows Ella to present herself as the "mysterious princess" Kit seeks, represents the remaining magic from her transformation. Lady Tremaine, who finds Ella's slipper and asks her to sacrifice the kingdom for her own happiness, shows magic as temptation. To protect Kit, Ella refuses her stepmother and sacrifices for love. Ultimately, Ella passes the test and the trial of magic ends with Lady Tremaine breaking the glass slipper. The remix's happy ending does not depend on Ella fitting the shoe. Before putting it on, Ella asks Kit if he will accept her as an honest country girl who loves him. Consequently, the remix reduces magic's influence, rejecting the traditional portrayal that miraculously elevates Cinderella to princess status.

In the *Beauty and the Beast* remix, the curse-breaking scene again changes the portrayal of magic. In contrast to the animated version, in which Belle breaks the spell by confessing her love to the Beast, the live-action film shows him closing his eyes as the last rose petal falls and depicts the servants becoming lifeless furniture *before* Belle's revelation. It is instead the enchantress who casts a spell that restores and transforms the Beast and his servants. Kirsten Acuna claims that the enchantress's presence is unnecessary, and that the remix detracts from the magic of the original and reduces its emotional impact by moving the scene from Belle and the Beast's pivotal moment to a cutaway of servants becoming motionless objects before returning to Belle's confession (2017). However, according to Mike Reyes, the remix implies that salvation does not occur when the protagonists are taught an "emotionally charged lesson," but rather when the enchantress sees and recognizes the substantial change in the world and the characters (2017). By replacing Belle with the enchantress as the curse lifter, the film shows human judgment, rather than magic, determining justice.

The *Beauty and the Beast* remix ends with a subtle implication of magic's departure. The enchantress curses not only the castle's residents but also the villagers, trapping them and dividing the world in two. The servants become animated furniture, while the villagers lose their memories; neither world is real or normal. When the curse is broken, the castle is released from its winter confinement and the villagers regain their memories. Returning the kingdom to its original state, the remix implies that magic fades once happiness and justice are reinstituted.

Both the animation and remix of *Aladdin* feature magic as a test for the hero to demonstrate his worth without relying on its power. The remix further emphasizes the danger of magic's destructive effects. The Genie warns Aladdin that magic cannot satisfy desire: "Here's the thing about wishes. The more you have, the more you want." Magic, as the Genie explains, usually leads to depravation rather than fulfillment. Aladdin appears changed by his wish, and initially fails the test of magic. Even though the sultan grants his wish to marry Jasmine, Aladdin still desires magic, and refuses to free the Genie. In the animation, the Genie is angry with Aladdin for not keeping his promise. However, in the remix, the Genie urges Aladdin to tell the truth instead of living the magical lie. The Genie, devastated by Aladdin's corruption, says, "Well, kid, I don't care nothin' about that wish. This is about you, what's happening to you." Magic may elevate Aladdin's social status, but it also degrades his character and results in falsehoods and destruction. Aladdin's epiphany manifests in his warning, "You can't find what you're looking for in that lamp, Jafar. I tried and failed, and so will you." Eventually, Aladdin proves his good character by freeing the Genie and sacrificing his happiness for another's, passing the test of magic.

The *Aladdin* remix reveals justice not only through the genie's freedom, but also through social reform. The sultan undermines outdated laws and customs when he crowns Jasmine the first female sultan, and she abolishes the rule that only princes may marry princesses. The abandonment of magic symbolizes a new future. Unlike the animation's Genie, who retains his magic after being freed, in the remix he becomes human and loses his powers. The scene in which he sails away with his family indicates not only his liberation from enchantment, but magic leaving the human realm.

Mistress depicts magic as a manifestation of the mind that possesses the ability to bring about life and death. Magic has a reviving power when wielded with love, as Maleficent shows at the film's end when she restores the castle and makes the flowers bloom. Hatred, on the other hand, turns magic into a destructive force, as demonstrated by Ingrith, who uses enchanted weapons to slaughter fantastic creatures. Maleficent's test is not to harness magic, but rather to resist it. While the fairies believe that her magic can protect them from human persecution and bring justice, Conall advises Maleficent not to use it. As her heart fills with anger and animosity, waging magical war against humans can only bring death and destruction. Conall, convinced that only Maleficent's transformation will bring peace, says, "You transformed when you raised Aurora. When you found love, in the middle of your pain." This change reflects Maleficent's choice of love over hatred in *Maleficent*. It may explain why *Mistress* has Maleficent shield Aurora from Ingrith's arrow with her body, rather than killing Ingrith with her magic. By doing so, Maleficent successfully passes the test by rejecting the magic evoked by hatred, and demonstrating her capacity for love.

As in the remixes discussed above, justice is redeemed through the characters' actions and choices in *Mistress*. Ultimately, instead of Maleficent's magic, Philip and Aurora's decision to unite the two kingdoms brings peace. Magic eventually departs from *Mistress*, too. In the end, Aurora stays in Ulstead with Philip, while the fairies settle on the Moors. Though united, the two kingdoms' worlds remain physically separated. Maleficent bids farewell to the newlyweds and promises to visit at their child's christening—the potential beginning of another "Sleeping Beauty" story, but also the end of magic in Aurora's.

In the Disney live-action remixes, evil becomes explainable, and so does justice. While the antagonists' backstories provide insight into what causes evil and why it exists, the protagonists' struggles with the test of magic illustrate how evil resides within everyone. By depicting love as the essence that distinguishes good from evil, the remixes weaken magic's influence on justice and make it more realistic and accessible to all. In contrast to the animations, which magically bestow justice on only the bravest and fairest chosen ones, justice in the remixes comes from love, and is determined by the protagonists' choices. While far from perfect, the Disney remixes present a more just narrative, suggesting that anyone, young or old, rich or poor—or indeed good or evil—can achieve redemption and justice by finding love within themselves.

NOTES

1. *Mulan* (2020) is not adapted from classic Euro-American fairy tales but from a legend in a Chinese poem written during the Northern Wei Dynasty, and is therefore not included here.

2. To be more specific, I use the term "hero" for men, "heroine" for women, and "protagonist" for both, as well as "male villain" for men, "female villain" for women, and "villain" or "antagonist" for both.

3. The inability to love is marked as the essence of evil in both the animated and live-action *Beauty and the Beast*. In both, an enchantress transforms the prince into a beast because, as the narrator explains, "there was no love in his heart."

REFERENCES

Acuna, Kirsten. 2017. "*Beauty and the Beast* Makes a Big Change to the Movie's Ending that Takes Away from the Magic of the Original." *Insider*, March 18. https://www.insider.com/beauty-and-the-beast-new-ending-2017-3.

Aladdin. 1992. Directed by Ron Clements and John Musker. US: Walt Disney Pictures.

Aladdin. 2019. Directed by Guy Ritchie. US: Walt Disney Pictures.

Basile, Giambattista. 2001. "Sun, Moon, and Talia." In *The Great Fairy Tale Tradition: From Straparola and Basile to the Brothers Grimm*, edited by Jack Zipes, 685–88. New York: Norton.

Beauty and the Beast. 1991. Directed by Gary Trousdale and Kirk Wise. US: Walt Disney Pictures.

Beauty and the Beast. 2017. Directed by Bill Condon. US: Walt Disney Pictures.

Bottigheimer, Ruth B. 1987. *Grimms' Bad Girls and Bold Boys: The Moral and Social Vision of the Tales*. New Haven, CT: Yale University Press.

Cinderella. 1950. Directed by Clyde Geronimi, Wilfred Jackson, and Hamilton Luske. US: Walt Disney Pictures.

Cinderella. 2015. Directed by Kenneth Branagh. US, UK: Walt Disney Studios.

Gadd, Rebecca. 2022. "The Stepmother Problem: How an Information Deficit in Film Creates Female Villains." In *Gender and Female Villains in Twenty-First-Century Fairy Tale Narratives: From Evil Queen to Wicked Witches*, edited by Natalie Le Clue and Janelle Vermaak-Griessel, 117–28. Bingley, UK: Emerald.

Greenhill, Pauline, and Sidney Eve Matrix. 2010. "Introduction: Envisioning Ambiguity: Fairy Tale Films." In *Fairy Tale Films: Visions of Ambiguity*, edited by Pauline Greenhill and Sidney Eve Matrix, 1–22. Logan: Utah State University Press.

Gutierrez, Anna Katrina. 2017. *Mixed Magic: Global-Local Dialogues in Fairy Tales for Young Readers*. Amsterdam: John Benjamins.

Haas, Lynda, and Shaina Trapedo. 2018. "Disney Corporation." In *The Routledge Companion to Media and Fairy-Tale Cultures*, edited by Pauline Greenhill, Jill Terry Rudy, Naomi Hamer, and Lauren Bosc, 178–87. New York: Routledge.

Hourihan, Margery. 2005. *Deconstructing the Hero: Literary Theory and Children's Literature*. London: Routledge.

Jeffords, Susan. 1995. "The Curse of Masculinity." In *From Mouse to Mermaid: The Politics of Film, Gender, and Culture*, edited by Elizabeth Bell, Lynda Haas, and Laura Sells, 161–72. Bloomington: Indiana University Press.

Maleficent. 2014. Directed by Robert Stromberg. US: Walt Disney Pictures.

Maleficent: Mistress of Evil. 2019. Directed by Joachim Rønning. UK: Walt Disney Pictures.

Propp, Vladimir. 1968. *Morphology of the Folktale*. Austin: University of Texas Press.

Pullman, Philip. 2012. "The Challenge of Retelling Grimms' Fairy Tales." *Guardian*, September 21. https://www.theguardian.com/books/2012/sep/21/grimms-fairy-tales-philip-pullman.

Reyes, Mike. 2017. "Why the New Beauty and the Beast Ending is Better Than the Original." *CinemaBlend*, March 22. https://www.cinemablend.com/news/1638330/why-the-new-beauty-and-the-beast-ending-is-better-than-the-original.

Rich, Katey. 2014. "Angelina Jolie Confirms a Key *Maleficent* Scene Was About Rape." *Vanity Fair*, June 12. https://www.vanityfair.com/hollywood/2014/06/angelina-jolie-maleficent-rape.

Rowe, Rebecca. 2022. "A Tale of Two Mothers: Recombining Villainy and Motherhood in *Maleficent: Mistress of Evil* (2019)." In *Gender and Female Villains in Twenty-First-Century Fairy Tale Narratives: From Evil Queen to Wicked Witches*, edited by Natalie Le Clue and Janelle Vermaak-Griessel, 35–46. Bingley, UK: Emerald.

Sandwell, Ian. 2019. "*Maleficent 2* Star Michelle Pfeiffer Reveals Queen Ingrith's Villainous Plan." *DigitalSpy*, August 27. https://www.digitalspy.com/movies/a28820511/maleficent-2-cast-michelle-pfeiffer-villain-plot/.

Schwabe, Claudia. 2019. *Craving Supernatural Creatures: German Fairy-Tale Figures in American Pop Culture*. Detroit: Wayne State University Press.

Sleeping Beauty. 1959. Directed by Clyde Geronimi, Les Clark, Eric Larson, and Wolfgang Reitherman. US: Walt Disney Pictures.

Snetiker, Marc. 2017. "Luke Evans' Backstory for Gaston Is a Beauty." *Entertainment Weekly*, March 14. https://ew.com/movies/2017/03/14/beauty-and-the-beast-luke-evans-gaston-backstory/.

Tatar, Maria. 1992. *Off with Their Heads! Fairy Tales and the Culture of Childhood*. Princeton, NJ: Princeton University Press.

Tatar, Maria. 2019. *The Hard Facts of the Grimms' Fairy Tales: Expanded Edition*. Princeton, NJ: Princeton University Press.

Women and Hollywood. 2014. "*Maleficent* Writer Linda Woolverton on Adapting Fairy Tales for a New Generation." May 30. https://womenandhollywood.com/maleficent-writer-linda-woolverton-on-adapting-fairy-tales-for-a-new-generation-a85bb1d1478b/.

Wood, Naomi J. 2015. "Disney, Walt." In *The Oxford Companion to Fairy Tales*, edited by Jack Zipes, 154–59. Oxford: Oxford University Press.

Zipes, Jack. 1997. *Happily Ever After: Fairy Tales, Children, and the Culture Industry*. New York: Routledge.

Zipes, Jack. 1999. "Breaking the Disney Spell." In *The Classic Fairy Tales*, edited by Maria Tatar, 332–52. New York: Norton.

SECTION THREE

Seeking Justice

9

Queer Kinship in the Grimms' "The Three Spinning Women"

Challenging the Binary

KAY TURNER

OVERTURE

Consider the following from a *New York Times* review:

> Eliza Reid, the first lady of Iceland, was recently ignored in a newspaper caption, even though she was front and center in greeting the Prince of Denmark. Only the men in the picture were listed. I'm sure you are familiar with this kind of snub; perhaps you are a woman who like Reid has been erased from a caption or two, or from a job opportunity or two, or from a position of power or two. . . . Reid posted her annoyance on Facebook: "One man with a name came to dinner at another man with a name's house." She signed off using the hashtag: #dowomenexist. (Leive 2022)

Do women exist? An excellent question! Let it spin around and through the following discussion of a certain fairy tale's proposal that women do indeed exist, but it's rough going unless . . .

ENTER THE SPINNING ROOM

If fairy tales are the queerest of them all (Turner and Greenhill 2012, 3), some—such as the Grimms' "The Three Spinning Women"—are, I think, snap-worthy queer. The widespread tale, ATU 501, about supernatural helpers, is one of many that feature spinning as both a problem and a solution to various women's concerns. To address spinning's strategically queer qualities adds to feminist folklorists' work of decades ago (Rowe 1986; Bottigheimer 1987; Tatar 1987).

[let the spinning begin]

Spinning, along with weaving, evolved as a woman-centered metaphor for creation and creativity. Over the centuries, from antiquity to the early modern period to the age of industrialization, this symbol continued to code women's imagination and agency even as patriarchal history progressed to erode the artistic primacy of women's spinning arts into reductive labor. But the fairy tale protests such reduction. Because the actual onus of spinning, and its attendant repetitive injuries, exhaustion, and boredom, fell squarely on women, the female tellers of these tales dispensed more than mere entertainment. Spinning tales code women's displeasure with this demanding if necessary work (Bottigheimer 1987, 112–13, 116–17, 122). They also trace a singular and powerful antidote to the labor's negative physical and psychological effects: female bonding and friendship.

The entanglements of alterity, women, queerness, and the supernatural—their challenges to normativity, their elisions and revisions—undergird spinning in stories such as the one under discussion here. We are reminded that, as Marina Warner advised, "Fairy tale is essentially a moralizing form, often in deep disguise and often running against the grain of commonplace ethics" (1994, 25). If queerness is behind one of those disguises, let the mask fall.

For when we take spinning to heart as queer in itself, as a mode of dancing, conjuring, making, even of thinking and feeling, we experience the delirious whirl, the sensation of being off-kilter and open to something new. Spinning incites movement out of control, transgressive movement. Can we rethink the drudgery of the wheel to see it, guided by a woman's hand, powerfully transforming raw, messy flax into cooked thread for making something culturally new, and providing the rhythm for telling stories about that invention?

Can we see it as a source for energizing the tale magic that spins new ways of being?

[attach the spindle to the wheel]

I say yes, but first we must spin the patriarchal logic of our folklore forefathers to look afresh and aslant at conventional structuralist aspects of the fairy tale, perhaps to at last provide an answer to anthropologist Claude Lévi-Strauss's important and still relevant question: "how to make opposition, instead of being an obstacle to integration, serve rather to produce it" (1963, 89). Opposition cannot be integrated without the subversive entailments of queerness.

Over the past ten years or so I've been working on a book about the witch figure in folklore, history, and contemporary art. I have also presented performance works aimed at theatrically activating the history of ideas about witches.[1] I'm my own personal witch craze but with serious intent: the witch figure brings our attention to women's existence in both shattering and renewing ways. A core concept I've been exploring views witches and their associated magical outliers as deeply anti-patriarchal harbingers of the nonbinary, not only in the sense of gender transformation and fluidity but as central to a comprehensive epistemological project for helping unfasten the ties that bind people to binary logic and lives. The prospect, rich for exploration, is one that began for me by reopening the door I had closed years ago on my graduate studies interest in structuralism. (Well, perhaps it was always open a crack.)

My current fairy-tale work benefits from such retroactive interest because these stories, highly structural in form and function, are exemplary narratives in which to observe and interpret the play of oppositional signs. We own the fairy tale and the fairy tale owns us in this kind of serious play. Though weighted by conventional gendered oppositions, correspondences, and mediations, the fairy tale also offers illuminating figurations of perversity and queerness. Fairy tales challenge as much as they uphold the binary. When we invite queer theory to play with fairy-tale structuralism, what transformations of wonder transpire? Especially as they concern kinship, might some tales reveal queer ideals before history made them more concretely viable? Do fairy tales involve us in the "utopian and willfully idealistic practices of thought [that] are in order if we are to resist the perils of heteronormative pragmatism" (Muñoz 2009, 96)?

[the wheel starts to turn]

Largely, the fairy tale embroils kinship with class, status, age, gender, and sexuality to ask socially significant questions. Who wins in the kinship contest? What are the stakes? Who sticks with the old? Who invents the new? The fairy tale answers these questions in diverse and often profound ways that affirm kinship's basis in the social, not the biological. And because the tales promote a particularly dynamic version of kinship, they might also support anthropologist David Schneider's (1984) famous teaching, elaborated by Judith Butler, that kinship comprises doing rather than being (2004, 123).

Queer kinship is a kind of perverse doing, and I use the simple and broadest claim that queerness unsettles normativity; it is, as Eve Sedgwick asserted, "*troublant*. . . . Keenly, it is relational and strange" (1993, xii). The fairy tale invests both the relational and the strange; it offers an invitation to discover queer kinship arrangements. It disturbs normative binaries: blood relations/ nonblood relations; married/unmarried; suitable/unsuitable; legitimate/ illegitimate; and inherit/disown, to name some of the obvious. If a central structure of feeling expressed in the fairy tale is longing to belong, we can anticipate challenges to normative kinship prescriptions that draw the line between who belongs and who doesn't and who belongs to whom.

By custom and by law, conventional kinship defines symbolic genealogical imperatives that gird misogyny, colonialist violence, and racist ideologies. Blood is not just an emblem of relation but a weapon that polices inclusion/ exclusion. Kinship structures uphold heteronormative sex and gender prejudices within a framework of descent that privileges male dominance and male heirs. Literally and figuratively, women are pawns in this game of reproductive futurism. In its dissection of binary oppositions, starting with male/female and man/woman, classic structuralism justified this relational ideology as singular and inevitable. The goal here is to unloose contravening queer kinship patterns using the "The Three Spinning Women" as our model, queering structuralism.

[turning a bit faster now]

QUEERING STRUCTURALISM

A queered structuralism need not eliminate our interest in binary oppositions and their meaning-generating capacity. Oppositions mediated through substitution move a tale forward, but themselves remain immovable. A queer structuralism seeks out tertiaries: some third way that ruptures the falsely inscribed completeness of the dyadic. Here we owe a debt to Jacques Derrida's "distrust of oppositions as having a completeness in themselves" (Sturrock 2003, 141). Queer theorists (and common queer persons) convene on this distrust.

Our sense of thirdness, as much an embodied sensory as a cognitive way of knowing, avows the necessary impossibility of binary completeness, an impossibility that in both story and sociality fosters relational possibility. The queer call to rupture the absolute is inflected through erotic and emotional tendencies—desire and expression—that transgress bounded hierarchies inscribed in narrative and social binaries. Structuralist parameters expose the oppositional patterns that are—must be—interrupted by the diversity of human longings and aspirations. Not only do fairy tales anticipate this rupture, they lay down the communal narrative groundwork for imagining alternative forms of human relationship, now called "chosen families" (Weston 1997). Fairy tales take detours down irregular or forbidden third paths that are alien to the binary compulsions of the straight and narrow.

Queering structuralism for fairy-tale studies relaxes the rigidity of old theories, yet still engages their utility in identifying the salient binaries we wish to challenge. A transgressive approach upsets the certainty of oppositional paradigms captured, perhaps too neatly, for example, in folklorist Bengt Holbek's "cube," created to help describe the workings of Danish fairy tales. The cube graphically plots the tale moves between binaries male/female; adult/youth; and high/low status that "define the three categories of crises which occur in fairytales" (1987, 416–17). As the story progresses, interaction among these thematic axes produces solutions, the most essential of which for Holbek is an ending in heterosexual marriage. Like other structuralist paradigms, the cube provides insight into deeply rooted patriarchal ideas and ideologies. Granted, it is over thirty-five years old and its structural certitudes seem rather absurd now. Yet its power to assign relations is not depleted, and the glitter of its appeal continues to sparkle and destroy relational potential, especially as we still find its determinations playing out in the arena of heteronormative proscriptions that limit conceptions of marriage and the family.

[speeding up]

QUESTIONING THE NATAL FAMILY

Luckily, the contingencies of marriage and family construction figure as central fairy-tale themes. The *unmaking* of formulaic family structures is as much a fairy-tale aim as creating them. Even if the resulting new affinity pattern is momentary, ephemeral, enchanted, anomalous, ambivalent, or doomed, it nonetheless rises from the story to be given visibility, recognition, and interpretation. Sedgwick's critique of the natal family offers a great deal to our interest in cracking open the cube. A structuralist in method, a post-structuralist queer theorist in interpretation, she views the erotic as a site of multiform sexual alliances and individual agency. To argue this point, she works a rich catalogue of binary oppositions, some canonical, some not: male/female; homosexual/heterosexual; homosocial/homosexual; auto-erotic/alloerotic; sexual/nonsexual; active/passive; constructivist/essentialist; immanent/ extrinsic; knowledge/ignorance; innocence/ignorance; satiable/insatiable; natural/unnatural; natural/artificial, will/compulsion, and others (1993, 275–76).

Sedgwick counterposes structuralist categories with sex/gender and psychoanalytic ones to produce new sets of dynamic pairs, many of which are no doubt quite recognizable to fairy-tale scholars. Perhaps most critical for our purpose is the heavy slash Sedgwick draws between natal and avunculate, her recognition of aunts and uncles—whether blood-related or adopted kin—who serve as models for identity formation outside of parental control (1993, 63). Sedgwick's slash marks her deep suspicion of the natal family, the biological triad of father, mother, child. Her indictment of it prosecutes a closed sexuality system: "When 'the family' is stylized as the supposed biologically based triad . . . its heterosexist circumscription [is] guaranteed, if it is not already caused, by the fact that the closed system of 'the family,' within which all formative identification and desire are seen to take place, is limited by tendentious prior definition to parents—to adults already defined as procreative within a heterosexual bond. Within this ideological system, accounts of the desire of any child must in turn be disfiguringly ritualized" (63–64). Fairy-tale outcomes generally perpetuate this ideological system, landing the heroine in Holbekian heterosexual marriage. It is often the case, but not always. The formation of queer kinship bonds interrupts the functional heteronormative progress of maiden to wife, poor girl to princess, and may reroute the typical path from a troubled nuclear family to freshly created queer kinship.

[hear the whirring of the wheel]

QUEERING KINSHIP

Kinship has been on the minds of queer theorists for quite some time and takes many sides. My work falls into the potentiating view. As Taylor Bradway and Elizabeth Freeman summarize, for these theorists "the social order is not so much an *order* as an unfolding practice that fails to reproduce itself just as often as it succeeds. From those failures, queerness leaks out on all sides, rearranging and recalibrating the social in frequently surprising and always richly embodied ways. Kinship plays a role in this . . . precisely because it is a site to glimpse the emergence of new relational forms" (2022, 11).

Bradway points out that almost twenty years ago Judith Butler noted that the growing trend toward new sexual and kinship arrangements adopted by queers and nonqueers alike suggested "we are witnessing a queering of relationality itself" (2021, 713). If queering kinship opens modalities of inclusion, and not only within the context of LGBTQIA+ social worlds, it does so in part through what Bradway and Freeman call kin-aesthetics:

> As a philosophical term, kin-aesthetics, containing not only kin but also aesthetics and kinetics, concerns itself with how processes of *figuration*, whether they take place as social practice or in imaginative texts, de-form and reform the categories and genres by which we experience our relationships. Kin-aesthetic activities make and unmake the social field. Kinship needs kin-aesthetics, because kinship is a symbolic system as well as a set of practices. But kin-aesthetic practices are not epiphenomenal to a deeper and invariant structure of kinship; nor are they simply a floating discourse untethered from the material relations and conditions of belonging. Rather, kin-aesthetics are the site of kinship's renewal, transformation, and extension beyond the present. (2022, 4)

Bradway centers kin-aesthetics in "narrative as a form that fosters queer relationality. . . . Queerness is shaped by passionate attachments to certain forms, and certain forms make queer orientations available for readers and audiences" (2021, 712). Narrations of queer kinship arrangements have far-reaching consequences. They posit the creation of family as an act of agency and choice rather than destiny and obedience.

Unsurprisingly, it is within the realm of kin-aesthetics that the fairy tale shines. Not only does it expressively demonstrate queerness in unconventional kinship arrangements, it formalizes those connections in the genre itself. The heterogeneity of kinship identifies a central human problem the fairy tale grapples with, often as it is queerly construed within that fundamental, if ambivalent and shifting, binary structure of feeling: "belonging/exclusion" (Turner 2012, 248–49). Where this binary is in operation, a commitment to new relations is potentiated along the lines José Esteban Muñoz calls "belonging in difference": "the field of utopian possibility is one in which multiple forms of belonging in difference adhere to a belonging in collectivity" (2009, 20).

[pedal the treadle]

Where in a tale should we find the bloom of this heterogeneity, of differently belonging? From a queer perspective, our interest generally is not served by the oft-cited binary prescription for openings and endings of lack/lack liquidated, wherein initially troubled blood relations resolve in new blood relations installed through lineage-extending heterosexual marriage. Rather, a liberated kinship rearrangement plays out in the doings at the center of the story, the site of the queer tertiary, where nonblood, nonnormative, often ambiguous and anomalous but substantially motivating relationships are formed. In the muddled middle heightened desires, emotions, and stratagems combine to instigate new and different belongings.

QUEERING THE SPINNERS

Now let's come to "The Three Spinning Women" to see a particular kind of transgressive nonnormative relational formation in process. On the surface a story about the relentless hardships associated with spinning, it also makes some profound claims about blood versus nonblood and natal family versus adoptive kin relations inspired by an unusually queer breed of female bonding. The following summary relies on D. L. Ashliman's English translation (2001–2002) from the Grimms' seventh edition of *Children's and Household Tales* (1857):

There once was a girl who was lazy and hated spinning; she refused her mother's insistence that she perform the heinous task. Even her mother's severe beatings could not make her spin. One day, the girl's pained cries are heard by the queen as she passes by. Asked why she beats her daughter, the embarrassed mother lies, saying her daughter loves to spin, but they are too poor to provide enough flax. Immediately the queen whisks the daughter off to occupy three rooms filled from floor to ceiling with flax ready to be spun. Promising her eldest son in marriage if the girl completes the task, the queen leaves the girl alone. Afraid, she weeps that she can never finish the work, not even if she lived 300 years to do so. When the queen returns on the third day and asks why she has not begun to work, the girl feigns homesickness.

Looking out the window, she sees three old women coming toward her, all of whom are deformed from years of spinning. Still, they offer to assist the girl on the condition of a four-fold favor commanded in return: "If you will invite us to your wedding, not be ashamed of us, call us your aunts, and let us be seated at your table, we will spin all the flax for you." Not hesitating, the girl agrees, "With all my heart." The Spinners magically complete the work in short order. When the girl asks the queen and bridegroom if her "three wonderful aunts" may attend the wedding and be seated at the head table, consent is given.

The three odd-looking women enter the wedding feast dressed in bizarre costumes. Nonetheless, the bride sweetly greets them saying, "Welcome, dear aunts" then leads them to the head table. Disgusted by their appearance, the groom asks his bride, "How did you come to this hideous friendship?" He turns to the Spinners and asks them how they became deformed. They respond: a flat foot from treading, a large thumb from twisting thread, and a drooping lip from licking it. The alarmed prince declares his beautiful wife will never spin again and the girl is relieved forever from the dreaded task.

CHANCE MEETS STRUCTURE

Serendipity gets the story started. Chance meetings in the fairy tale promote the possibility of momentary, affectively charged experiences. Serendipity ignites the magic of relationship formation, bringing unlike together to discover likeness and liking of each other, or the opposite. It occasions a unique moment in time and space that rouses relational experience in unusual ways:

kismet. In "The Three Spinning Women" serendipity induces relationships between and among the central characters: the mother's with the queen and the girl's with the Spinners. If serendipity defines a spatio-temporal glitch with potentially charged social implications, Mark de Rond expands this accepted usage, emphasizing it as "capability" (2014, 342–45). Chance meetings in the fairy tale are always already full of such capability: the genre's form and functions dictate this. X meets Y; E (experience) occurs; and O (outcome) results. Some of these stimulate queer affections and affiliations. When strangers meet transgressive alternatives to the norm begin to spin. Queerness inhabits fairy-tale serendipity as a font of its mystery and magic, also its provocations and transformations.

[twisting, twisting]

In "The Three Spinning Women," serendipity produces new homosocial relations. Here the creation of a queer sororal family, founded in mutual consent, has the effect of raising the status and promoting the happiness of all its members. To reach this outcome, the tale puts paired female oppositions and correspondences into play: mother/daughter; mother/queen; girl/queen; queen/Spinners; girl/Spinners; mother/Spinners; daughter/aunts; and bride/spinsters. These interactive sets raise the potential for revised meanings concerning blood kin/nonblood kin and natal family/marriage family. Further, various physical, behavioral, emotional, affective, and moral binaries create tensions that alert the queer reader: youth/age; normal/abnormal; inclusion/exclusion; crucial/marginal; industrious/lazy; reward/punishment; institutional/personal; truth/deceit; dignity/shame; esteem/disgrace; forlorn/heartened; promise/renege; able-bodied/disabled; conventionally formed/deformed; and beautiful/ugly. These paired opposites do not so much structure the story as spin it. They are the flax made into thread, natural material taking shape in a new cultural form.

[licking, licking]

Our protagonists are an abused young girl exiled by her birth mother for refusal to perform normative women's work and a trio of marginalized old women who do nothing but perform this kind of labor, and have been physically deformed by the repetitive actions it requires. How these contrary characters come into relationship results from a secondary opposition between the mother and the queen. Five lowly women, one high. There's going to be a struggle to correct this imbalance. Yes, some magic will help.

Two mothers confront each other at the tale's start. One is beating her daughter as the other rides by and becomes alarmed at the child's screams. Caught in a vicious act, the one mother quickly turns the emotional table from rage to shame, then to sycophancy. Lying to the queen even as she sucks up to her, she effectively disowns her daughter by giving her for palace service in—where else—three large spinning rooms. There the exiled daughter will suffer in that intermediate place between her maidenhood and marriage, between her past and future. In this liminal, every woman's no-man's-land, the girl despairs. She faces an impossible spinning task made even more so by her determined disinclination, her queer failure to dutifully subscribe to this convention of female labor.

Little does she know that what seems to her a prison will become a site of magic. Like her mother, she lies to the queen about her disinterest, but the lie is uniquely fraudulent in suggesting that her inability to work emanates from sorrow at leaving her mother's side. In fact, this biological mother/daughter bond has already been broken; it will be replaced with a new one. The three women she encounters don't seem to know her yet, but in some sense they do. These outcast, deformed old Spinners, who have long endured the pain and privation of social shaming, meet a younger outcast. They share in having had quite enough of their worthlessness except as laborers at the wheel. Easily assuming a bond with the girl, they will claim their value on new and different terms. Once their agreement is made to help each other, the Spinners reveal their knack for magic and transform the dreary, oppressive spinning rooms into a busy site of enchantment.

[find the rhythm]

Intergenerational attractions and alliances between women manifest a figure of queerness in numerous fairy tales. Except by desire or need, menstruating girls generally don't mix with post-menopausal hags. Here the mutual support between young and old diminishes structural hierarchies that would usually keep them apart. Together they will seek a quite literal place at the table of their imminent elevation: the queen's table of wealth and status. Asking the girl to exchange their labor for something more dear to them than spun flax can measure, the Spinners immediately make their wishes known, and in no uncertain terms: "If you will invite us to your wedding, not be ashamed of us, call us your aunts, and let us be seated at your table, we will spin all the flax for you." A queer tempest brews in the teapot of possible utopian outcomes from these sweeping requests.

[spin harder now . . .]

WHO ARE THE THREE SPINNERS?

The Spinners comprise their own unique—we assume nonbiological—family of three hoary, unmarried women: spinsters, gossips, hags! Generative makers of thread (mythic in its own right as necessary for weaving the world), they stand in symbolic opposition to the orthodox reproductive trio: father, mother, child.[2] Insisting upon social recognition of their bond, they are not ashamed of their anomalous status; on the contrary, they aim to quite blatantly inject their queerness into the normative wedding scene. In a conventional sense, they ask the girl to be their conduit for a status move upward. But is this really what they seek? After all, these are supernatural beings. Yes, they magically assist the girl by spinning huge quantities of flax in short order, but at the same time they magically spin a strategic morality tale of queer recognition and inclusion.

Our Spinners are metaphorical and theatrical. They bear a compelling relation to other storied trios of magical women who activate moral, religious, and other inspirational outcomes in instructional myths and tales. Putting the Spinners in league with the Three Graces, Three Muses, Three Marys, Three Witches, and more closely with the fate-spinning Three Norns of Norse and Germanic mythology, we open a wider horizon for viewing their powerful legacy. All these trios compose figurations of a queer sisterhood associated with destiny and change manifested through the arts of spinning, weaving, conjuring, song, story, and drama combined with making magic, the potentiating feat of change.

That they are threesomes designates their symbolic relation to prime number three, held sacred and auspicious by Europeans at least since the ancient Pythagoreans named it the perfect number, representing wisdom, creativity, harmony, and understanding. From my perspective, three also gives us the middle zone, the diverging third path, the queer tertiary that troubles the binary. And of course, three became the fairy tale's magic number. The count of three realizes transformations, and threes populate tales as omens, in an enzymatic way stimulating the potential for magic to occur. In addition to our three Spinners, we tally three deformities, three days, three hundred years, three spinning rooms, and three questions asked by the prince. The Spinners inhabit the number and its charmed, moral, and queering properties. Magical and artful, they spin their skill, their appearance, their deformities, their low status, and their shame to teach both the girl and us a central lesson about how harmony and understanding can be achieved. The girl must join their sisterhood in order to make it so.

BINARY DOINGS AND UNDOINGS

It seems the girl will do anything to get out of spinning, and in a tale wherein deceit is commonplace, she might lie for advantage alone, just to get the help she needs, and in the end deny any kin relationship to the women. Her lack could still be liquidated: from lowly exiled girl to married princess. But here's where predictable binary oppositions and correspondences are reconfigured in favor of a different liquidated lack. New relational dispositions result from the vow made "with all her heart" to include the Spinners in the wedding party. She returns the women's pledge request with a vow that binds them, especially in her agreement to adopt them as her named aunts. In this heightened moment of relationship formation they originate a subversive family, a family of expedience, but also a queer family of choice. The girl's emotionally charged, performative vow changes the affective trajectory of the story from simply transactional to affectively affinal.

This move is not without risk. When the Spinners stride into the wedding scene wearing strange, inappropriate clothing, the prince questions his bride sharply, "How did you come to this hideous friendship?" She has already introduced them as her "aunts," but somewhat suspiciously he refers to them as "friends," potentially undermining their standing as family. This confrontational moment between bride and groom could go poorly for the Spinners, yet the bride does not dissemble or disavow. She simply remains silent, quietly confirming her relationship to them. He redirects his questioning to the aunts: "How did you become so deformed?" They answer truthfully, describing the physical consequences of endless work at the wheel, and the prince declares his bride will never spin again. Perhaps he even feels some sympathy for the old aunts. The wedding proceeds.

[pedal, twist, lick, and repeat; pedal, twist, lick, and repeat]

The homosocial vow made midway complements the heterosexual marriage vow made at the story's end. Both vows are taken seriously and both take effect. In combination, these performatives invent an open queer kinship arrangement: three aunts, one princess bride, one princely groom, and one queenly mother-in-law. Noticeably, both patriarchs, the girl's father and the king, are missing; and notably the girl's mother is not present at the wedding, nor is she likely to take part in the future of this new family. She who exiled her own daughter is herself rejected in the end. In contrast, her daughter finds a new home at the palace and the adopted Spinners see their stigma lifted by becoming members of the royal family. Refusing to see his beautiful bride disfigured, the none-the-wiser prince lets her off the spinning hook forever. Will the Spinners spin for the prince instead? I doubt it.

A DEEPER LOOK AT PLEDGES AND VOWS

Those chance meetings precipitate a series of lies that drive the tale's affective force. Mother lies to the queen; girl lies to the queen; and girl lies to the royal family on behalf of the Spinners, who have asked her to lie for them. Lying creates emotional tension in the characters in the form of uncomfortable feelings of guilt, shame, and insecurity. Yet deceit also proves to be a way of getting things done. Lies, lies, lies. How will a higher truth be spun from the flax of falsehood?

Structurally the lies are offset by claims made through pledges and vows that ultimately produce the truth of radical new emotional and social outcomes. Two transactional pledges, the mother's to the queen and the queen's to the girl, result in two significantly life-changing vows. The pledges execute the exchange basis for getting the work of the story done—the spinning work, that is. Not unusual in the fairy tale, mothers (and fathers) regularly rid themselves of benighted daughters or stepdaughters, or trade them for gain. The mother's lie promotes the worth, or use value, of her allegedly industrious daughter as a fit candidate to help the queen. The queen buys into it, later giving her pledge of an arranged marriage to her son, contingent upon the girl's spinning prowess.

But then the focus shifts dramatically to the meeting between the daughter and the Spinners, and the emotionally charged and unusually queer pledge asked of the young girl by the old women. She responds in an immediate, almost rapturous, agreement to guarantee the request. If heightened, determining affective experiences are often intense and momentary, the arc of this tale reaches its apex in the moment when the girl cries out, "With all my heart." The emotionally laden idiom refers to something felt earnestly and deeply and carries a sense of both vow and pledge, as in "Truly, I will," and "I will give the task all I've got." A pledge is an outward, often publicly declared commitment to duty, while a vow adheres to deeper emotional loyalties, such as devotion and love. Pledges are made while vows are kept. The girl intends both. Surely she wants those heaps of flax spun, but more is emotionally, morally, and queerly at stake than mere expedience will satisfy.

[the piles of flax diminish]

SHAME AND ITS EFFECTS

Deceit propels the story on its surface but shame motivates its deeper moral agenda. Sedgwick takes a broad view, seeing shame as central to any understanding of affect and identity:

> It seems very likely that the structuring of associations and attachments around the affect shame is among the most telling differentials among cultures and times.... Shame ... is not a discrete intrapsychic structure, but a kind of free radical that (in different people and also in different cultures) attaches to and permanently intensifies or alters the meaning of—of almost anything. Thus, one of the things that anyone's character or personality is is a record of the highly individual histories by which the fleeting emotion of shame has instituted far more durable, structural changes in one's relational and interpretive strategies toward both self and others. (2003, 62)

Following Sedgwick's exhortation, we see shame/guilt and shame/dignity operating forcefully in our story to leverage queer kinship strategies. Shame attaches to and intensifies behaviors and identities in several ways. Its negation also functions powerfully. Without it as a forceful affect to be reckoned with, creative reconfigurations of relations might not be realized.

Two typical types of shame bookend the story to intensify the lack/lack-liquidated function: the mother's shame turned to rage provoked by her daughter's laziness and obstinacy and the prince's prevention of the shame he would feel by forcing his wife's disfigurement.

Now, we can say that the girl has been shamed by her mother and by the queen for failure to obey her command, but she never takes shame on as part of her identity. She persists in her contrary ways of being, refusing to be chastened into performance of the task that is veritably the sign and function of woman. This girl sticks her thumb in the pie of gender conformity. The Spinners, too, know shaming, but they resist accepting abjection as their lot. For them, shame is something projected onto them by others. Still, they understand its universal sting and are particular in commanding the girl not to be ashamed of them. They preempt any prejudice that might derail their nobler cause. For they are not a group of common spinners, they are the Three Spinners, and they come with a mission. Their backstory helps us see this.

Though less developed, a variant of our tale called "Nasty Flax Spinning" (ATU 501) was the first to occupy position no. 14 in the earliest edition of *Kinder- und Hausmärchen* (1812/2014, 42–43). The story features a king, a queen, their three beautiful daughters, and three ugly old maids. The king loves spinning and requires his daughters to complete a large quantity of this work while he is away. They complain. So the queen summons the ugly spinsters to do the royal labors and then report to the king about their subsequent deformities. When the king hears this, he forbids the queen and his daughters from ever spinning again (Zipes 2014, 42–43).

What's important here? Three young, beautiful princesses oppose three ugly old spinsters, but these spinsters appear to be common women pressed into service. Their deformities, observed in real time, result from actual years spent at the wheel. The oppositional contrast is vividly observed through the patriarchal eyes of the king. He will forbid spinning in order to protect his queen's and daughters' physical assets. In effect, the old women are props for the queen's machinations: meant to work at her command, then soon sent back to the lowly life from which they came. They are not rewarded; they are used and used up. The king's interest aims at preserving his wife's status and the beauty and marriageability of his female progeny. He realizes the mistake of ordering his women to do the kind of punishing work that should be reserved for disposable old maids.

Consider these spinsters our Spinners' sister analogues and we gain a deeper understanding of their reason for exacting the threefold promise from the girl. Position in the feudal class hierarchy was determined by one's role in production. Both trios emblematize alienated labor. Kings and queens own the means and raw materials of production (large amounts of flax and a storehouse of wheels), and spinners extract value (thread) without compensation—or with very little—and without care for them as persons. Kings and queens hold the labor power and powerless spinners do the laboring. Visibly deformed and no doubt stigmatized, they exemplify what Ann Schmiesing says is the Grimms' use of disability to intensify depictions of the socially outcast Other (2014, 182). Othered and objectified, both sets of spinners also lack a safety net of sustaining social relations. Certainly they have each other, but in the big picture they are marked as unmarried, without kin, post-menopausal, old, and ugly. Considered odd, if not offensive pariahs, they have been shamed and shunned. There is no place for them except as anonymous, disposable workers.

[the skeins of thread increase]

The first-edition variant paints a convincing picture of the way old spinners are used: summoned when needed, but always treated as outsiders. No magical intervention relieves their plight. But our Spinners enjoy a camaraderie empowered with magic, and they take control. Cunning and clever, they strike at an opportunity to both raise their status and command a new vision of their kind: accepted as queer kin and also made visible as subjects of the court. They come to undo shame of a great and collectively damaging order: the centuries of shame heaped on an entire class of women whose persistent abjection, abetted and normalized through the social application of insidious sex, gender, and age binaries, has left them impoverished, isolated, unrecognized, and unrecognizable as persons.

Even though the prince gets the final word, and he reinforces misogynist stereotypes that privilege female beauty as a primary object of women's worth, the Spinners and the girl together assert a counterargument: female solidarity and intergenerational alliance bring queer relational power as a force to be reckoned with, and as a model for rewriting shame and disenfranchisement. The tale finds one of its most radical symbolic motives in a hailing of all spinners and spinsters as worthy to sit at the table of status and honor. Recall that this story falls under ATU 501, the type for supernatural helpers. In this tale help comes in the form of supernatural Spinners instigating justice, abetting the possibility of social reform embedded in unnatural bonds.

Now, you might be asking, is this for real? And I suggest that it is, if you will accept the performative nature and the basis in performance of the Spinners' achievement. Here I call once again on Sedgwick, who invokes what she calls "shame creativity" (2003, 63) expanding the definition of queer performativity to include "a strategy for the production of meaning and being, in relation to the affect shame" (61). Shame creativity constellates around queers, who are particularly attuned to shame and transform it through creative performances of activism (63–64). The Spinners are queer, not perhaps in their sexual orientation but in their eccentricity, in their willful perversity, and, yes, in their activist magic. Sedgwick gives us a way to understand them as figures kin-aesthetically capable of undoing shame and rejection through a bold performance of belonging. Enlisting the girl to partner with them in troubling traditional relational categories, they execute a performance of their bond at the wedding, the very social site that, institutionally geared to the formation of new families, ritually affirms the significance of affiliation. Asserting their queer kinship in the midst of this heightened heteronormative atmosphere, the young girl and the old women spin the thread that will bind them in belonging differently to each other and also change the nature of the new family coming into being at the marriage ceremony.

The birth mother's substitution by the "dear aunts" recalls Sedgwick's claim that in the move from "family" to "kinship" to "queer kinship" we find "the importance of residual, re-created, or even entirely newly imagined forms of the avunculate" (1993, 62), or in our case the aunt-specific "materteral." That they are named as such and assume the role of aunts brings greater intensity to the emotional truth rendered through their performance of queer kinship, and it may index a lasting effect. Through marriage, the girl will attain the princess power to grant a permanent status change for the Spinners.

[the wheel spins faster to complete the task]

Perhaps that's a stretch of the yarn? Well, then, let's just suggest that the performative power of the performance itself—even if not lasting—stands as an artful act of shame creativity that demonstrably brings a queer family into being and gives us a picture of its potential to affectively loosen the hegemonic grip of patriarchal hierarchies and binaries. Call it fairy tale. Call it theater. Even when the tale's telling finishes or the curtain comes down, we feel the emotional residue of art's creative power to change our hearts and minds, still caught up in the spin of the Three Spinners.

Exemplified in "The Three Spinning Women," the fairy tale defies absolutism by picturing—figuring in its queer kin-aesthetic way—an abundance of non-, even antinormative, familial types. Deploying strategies to overcome socially embedded binaries that consolidate and perpetuate normative kinship strictures, "The Three Spinning Women" performs a negation of shame attached to the most socially and politically poisonous binary of all: inclusion/exclusion. Now Holbek's cube becomes instead a rainbow-colored thread with boundless possibilities for weaving a truly broad broadcloth of relationships, identities, genders, and other ways of choosing to be human.

[now at last slowing down]

CODA: CIRCLING BACK TO THE BEGINNING

Let's not forget Eliza Reid. At the beginning of this chapter, in response to her hashtag #dowomenexist, I suggested that yes, we do, but it's rough going unless . . .

Unless women support each other in the face of our erasure.

The Supreme Court of the United States overturned women's constitutional right to medical abortion services on May 24, 2022. Women, especially those who are poor or otherwise marginalized, have been sent back to the cage of forced pregnancy, economic hardship, and unfulfilled dreams. Like being forced to spin, but much worse. Against this regression, the queer kinship of the Spinners and the girl offers both a lesson and a radically underestimated strategy: the power of women helping women.

I think of our Spinners, whose everyday magic may also have included midwifery, including ways to gain a pregnancy or end it. They spin in league with the pre–*Roe v. Wade* Janes of Chicago, a secret collective whose members learned how to perform abortions and gave thousands of women access to reproductive choice before they were shut down. Also spinning with us are the *Abortion Stories* collective, which today creates space for women to share the intricate and politically charged details of how and why they exercised choice in the *Roe* years from 1973 to 2022. Many more are spinning at wheels of protest, arguing against misogyny and male control over women's bodies in all its nastiness. When women suffer erasure, when our needs are denied, when our truths are ignored, women together with other women turn their occlusion toward the light of being seen by each other. Then we act. This story is not new. Once upon a time and right now it is told in different ways to show us the many ways women do and always will exist.

[the wheel keeps spinning, never stops]

NOTES

Thanks to Pauline Greenhill, Jennifer Orme, and Jeana Jorgensen. Versions of this essay were presented at the American Folklore Society (2009), the International Society for Folk Narrative Research (2021), and the University of Iceland (2022).

    1. Under the series title *What a Witch*, I have been performing aspects of the witch figure since 2012.

    2. Thanks to Valdimar Hafstein for pointing out this underlying salient opposition.

REFERENCES

Ashliman, D. L., trans. 2001–2002. "The Three Spinning Women" (KHM 14) by the Brothers Grimm. January 6, 2020. https://sites.pitt.edu/~dash/grimm014.html.

Bottigheimer, Ruth B. 1987. *Grimms' Bad Girls and Bold Boys: The Moral and Social Vision of the Tales*. New Haven, CT: Yale University Press.

Bradway, Tyler. 2021. "Queer Narrative Theory and the Relationality of Form." *Publications of the Modern Language Association* 136 (October): 711–27.

Bradway, Tyler, and Elizabeth Freeman. 2022. "Introduction: Kincoherence/Kin-aesthetics/Kinematics." In *Queer Kinship: Race, Sex, Belonging, Form*, edited by Tyler Bradway and Elizabeth Freeman, 1–22. Durham, NC: Duke University Press.

Butler, Judith. 2004. *Undoing Gender*. New York: Routledge.

de Rond, Mark. 2014. "The Structure of Serendipity." *Culture and Organization* 20 (5): 342–58.

Grimm, Jacob, and Wilhelm Grimm. 1812/2014. *The Complete First Edition of the Brothers Grimm*, translated and edited by Jack Zipes. Princeton, NJ: Princeton University Press.

Holbek, Bengt. 1987. *Interpretation of Fairy Tales: Danish Folklore in a European Perspective*. Helsinki: Academia Scientiarum Fennica.

Leive, Cindi. 2022. "Nordic Thriller," review of *Secrets of the Sprakkar: Iceland's Extraordinary Women and How They Are Changing the World* by Eliza Reid. *New York Times Sunday Book Review*, March 6, p. 17.

Lévi-Strauss, Claude. 1963. *Totemism*. Boston: Beacon.

Muñoz, José Esteban. 2009. *Cruising Utopia: The Then and There of Queer Futurity*. New York: NYU Press.

Rowe, Karen E. 1986. "To Spin a Yarn: The Female Voice in Folklore and Fairy Tale." In *Fairy Tales and Society: Illusion, Allusion, and Paradigm*, edited by Ruth B. Bottigheimer, 53–73. Philadelphia: University of Pennsylvania Press.

Schmiesing, Ann. 2014. *Disability, Deformity, and Disease in the Grimms' Fairy Tales*. Detroit: Wayne State University Press.

Schneider, David. 1984. *A Critique of the Study of Kinship*. Ann Arbor: University of Michigan Press.

Sedgwick, Eve Kosofsky. 1993. *Tendencies*. Durham, NC: Duke University Press.

Sedgwick, Eve Kosofsky. 2003. *Touching Feeling: Affect, Pedagogy, Performativity*. Durham, NC: Duke University Press.

Sturrock, John. (1986) 2003. *Structuralism*, 2nd ed. Hoboken, NJ: Wiley Blackwell.

Tatar, Maria. 1987. *The Hard Facts of the Grimms' Fairy Tales*. Princeton, NJ: Princeton University Press.

Turner, Kay. 2012. "Playing with Fire: Transgression as Truth in Grimms' 'Frau Trude.'" In *Transgressive Tales: Queering the Grimms*, edited by Kay Turner and Pauline Greenhill, 244–74. Detroit: Wayne State University Press.

Turner, Kay, and Pauline Greenhill. 2012. "Introduction: Once upon a Queer Time." In *Transgressive Tales: Queering the Grimms*, edited by Kay Turner and Pauline Greenhill, 1–24. Detroit: Wayne State University Press.

Warner, Marina. 1994. *From the Beast to the Blonde: On Fairy Tales and Their Tellers*. New York: Farrar, Straus & Giroux.

Weston, Kath. 1997. *Families We Choose: Lesbians, Gays, Kinship*. New York: Columbia University Press.

Zipes, Jack, ed. and trans. 2014. "Nasty Flax Spinning." In *The Complete First Edition: The Original Folk and Fairy Tales of the Brothers Grimm*, 42–43. Princeton, NJ: Princeton University Press.

10

Dead-End Genres, Hidden Wolves, and Misrecognition
Reading Promising Young Woman *through "Little Red Riding Hood"*

ANNE KUSTRITZ

Writer/director Emerald Fennell's *Promising Young Woman* (2020) won accolades for its many plot twists and brutally direct feminist critique of ripped-from-the-headlines incidents in contemporary rape culture. Yet it may come as a surprise that it also relies on the traditional story of "Little Red Riding Hood" (ATU 333) as a key intertext. The first three-quarters of *Promising Young Woman* vacillate between the structures of rape-revenge and romantic-comedy plots. It opens by framing its protagonist Cassandra/Cassie (Carey Mulligan) as a woman on a mission to extract retribution from would-be rapists, using her own faux-drunken body as bait. However, her mission takes a detour via a rom-com-inspired meet-cute with Ryan (Bo Burnham), a former classmate from medical school.

Their relationship becomes a litmus test for heterosexuality as Ryan's nice-guy character contradicts Cassandra's feeling that men are predators. Their relationship sours due to unearthed video evidence of his presence years previously at the rape of Cassandra's best friend Nina. The revelation sets the film on a different path, away from both rape revenge and rom-com into darker territory. While Cassandra initially takes on the figure of a foreboding avenging angel, Nina's rapist ultimately kills her and the work of justice is left to the men who survive. This unexpected turn highlights the film's key theme: for women, city streets, college parties, and bars are deep, dark woods, wolves wear disguises, and the huntsman arrives too late to prevent violence.

Reading *Promising Young Woman* through the intertext of "Little Red Riding Hood" makes sense of the film's ambiguous relationship to female power and victimization. Yet its return to one fairy-tale ending also intersects with long-standing debates over the feminist value of depicting violence against women and framing the agency of women who experience sexual assault. By emphasizing the brutality and pervasiveness of violence against women, the film does not offer a vision of actionable activism or politics. Rather, it attacks the misrecognition of violence caused by post-feminist arguments that inequality has been overcome and neoliberal mantras that all people are equal, autonomous agents fully responsible for whatever befalls them on the dark path through the woods. As such the film is a corrective that uses elements of "Little Red Riding Hood" to challenge audiences to see sexual violence more clearly.

FALSE FRIENDS: DEAD-ENDS OF THE ROM-COM AND RAPE-REVENGE GENRES

Charles Perrault appended the following moral to his version of "Little Red Riding Hood": "Children, especially attractive, well-bred young ladies, should never talk to strangers, for if they should do so, they may well provide dinner for a wolf. I say 'wolf,' but there are various kinds of wolves. There are also those who are charming, quiet, polite, unassuming, complacent, and sweet, who pursue young women at home and in the streets. And unfortunately, it is these gentle wolves who are the most dangerous ones of all" (1697/2018, 104).

As detailed below, in his 2016 decision to sentence Brock Turner to only six months in jail after his conviction for raping an unconscious woman, Judge Aaron Persky, then of the Santa Clara County Superior Court, stated that among other matters influencing him "is the likelihood that if not imprisoned, the defendant will be a danger to others. I think that he will not be a danger to others. I think he has a good chance of complying with the conditions of probation. The character letters suggest that up to this point he complied with social and legal norms sort of above and beyond what normal law-abiding people do" (Levin 2016).

After decades of feminist consciousness-raising and political action on the prevalence of rape and the pervasiveness of social beliefs that normalize and enable male violence against women (both cis and, even more commonly, transwomen) known as rape culture, it is well understood that men can be wolves. Yet at the same time, the seductive hope that not all men are implicated offers the possibility that romance can usurp or even heal the cultural and emotional wounds of sexual violence and restore heterosexuality's privileged position. This problematic between acknowledging rape culture and desiring heterosexual romance lies at the heart of *Promising Young Woman*. As such, its structure is a complex, postmodern mashup of genre conventions, allusions, and storylines that compete, collapse, and recur throughout the film, as if the story itself is desperately searching for answers but must discard most cultural commonsense resolutions as dissatisfying and unreliable false friends.

In language learning, a "false friend" refers to a word that sounds similar in two languages despite differing meanings. Likewise, in *Promising Young Woman* both revenge and romance may at first seem comfortingly familiar, but each betrays the heroine in turn. Like linguistic false friends, their opening salvos sound the same but they do not carry the meaning audiences expect. The film thus implicitly critiques both genres as inadequate imaginative tools to tackle the current situation faced by women. *Promising Young Woman* references contemporary discourses around male sexual violence, then invokes the rape-revenge and rom-com genres as potential narrative solutions, only to find both unsuitable dead-ends, ultimately turning to "Little Red Riding Hood" instead.

The film's title invokes contemporary feminist and popular critiques of rape culture because it ironically transposes the common phrase "promising young man," which often serves as an apologia for reduced sentences for, or dropping charges against, accused rapists. In a series of high-profile cases like the Turner decision quoted above, American lawyers and judges argued that "promising" white, wealthy men at elite universities who excel in sports do not deserve to have their future ruined by one boyish "indiscretion." Such rhetoric then posits that delivering the full punishment for rape inscribed in the law would unfairly undermine the "promising" future their achievements (and privileges) ensure. This logic repeats aspects of what Lauren Berlant (1997, 25–54, 83–144) and Lee Edelman (2004) call "futurity." Both argue that the use of children and fetuses in politics depends on an imaginary projection that all will inevitably mature into healthy citizens who will reproduce their civilization. These discourses of futurity position interventions into allegedly natural processes as inherently tragic and threatening to a nation's future. By extension, "promising young man" rhetoric assumes that absent the law's intervention, these privileged men's futures would unfold naturally into happy, productive, and successful adult lives. Thus, it eliminates their responsibility—that is, their agency in choosing to rape—and dismisses any possible consideration of the future that "promising young women" should have enjoyed before sexual violence diverted the unfolding of their lives.

Thus, in the Turner case reporters frequently framed him as "Stanford swimmer Brock Turner" rather than "suspected/convicted rapist Brock Turner," emphasizing his status as an elite college athlete rather than as a suspected then convicted criminal (LaChance 2016). Likewise, many commentators explained his extremely lenient sentence as a result of this tendency to soften the punishment of privileged white boys in sexual assault and rape cases (Gagnon and Grinberg 2016; Koren 2016). As in the judge's sentencing statement above, such patterns rely on a benefit of the doubt assumption that nice guys, those Perrault might term "gentle wolves," aren't really dangerous, just momentarily misguided or diverted.

Numerous commentators framed *Promising Young Woman* as a direct response to the Turner case and similar incidents (Chappet 2021). The film does indeed reflect at length on the divergent outcomes of sexual assault for young men and young women in order to indict the cultural value placed on men's futures at the expense of women's present trauma and prospective promise. Despite both women's top grades, demonstrating clear aptitude for a medical career, Nina's rape and subsequent ostracism during med school lead to her suicide and Cassie's withdrawal from college. Cassie ends up working at a café, single and living at home, trapped in sexual trauma. In contrast, the film shows classmates who participated in, witnessed, or helped to cover up the rape leading happy, fulfilling lives as doctors, spouses, and parents. What would Nina and Cassie's lives have become if there had been no wolf in their path? It appears painfully clear in *Promising Young Woman* that women's futures, bodies, and lives are disposable when the preservation of a privileged white man's expectations may be at stake. When asked if she intended the film to respond to the Turner case, Fennell replied: "I don't think that it was, but certainly that as a phrase is so commonly used when young men do something wrong.... There's always this inclination to be forgiving.... When you look at the phrase 'promising young woman' it's hardly ever used, and if it is used, it's usually to describe a girl who's no longer alive. You can only really be a 'promising young woman' when it's too late, when your promise is completely aborted" (Polowy 2020). As such, the film refers to broad Euro- and North American cultural patterns that stubbornly persist in erasing women's potential and pain to ensure the survival of the status quo system of white heteropatriarchy.

REVENGE!

Where, then, can a narrative turn after explicating this entrenched system of hierarchy and violence? Although not common in mainstream Hollywood films, solidarity with other women, the formation of feminist communities, and/or lesbian separatism form narrative solutions favored by many indie and international films such as *Antonia's Line* (1995), *Fire* (1996), and *Itty Bitty Titty Committee* (2007). However, *Promising Young Woman* harshly dismisses the possibility of solidarity as two major female characters are complicit in the rape. The narrative instead turns to revenge. Although Peter Robson (2021) notes that the Hays Code initially forbade the depiction of vigilantism in films set in the contemporary period, after its fall in 1968 revenge of all sorts became a popular theme in Hollywood. Carol Clover (1992) and Jacinda Read (2000) thus explain that the rape-revenge film emerged in the 1970s, most paradigmatically with the horror film *I Spit on Your Grave* (1978), wherein a woman hunts down and gruesomely murders four men who raped her. Bloody vigilantism now offers a stock narrative solution to the problem of sexual violence.

At first *Promising Young Woman* sets up a rape-revenge story with characteristic clichés and satisfactions—outrage followed by retribution. In the opening scene, a group of men at a bar spot a woman sprawled across a bench. They spout common misogynist clichés about rape and alcohol, including "That is just asking for it." The "nice guy" leaves "to see if she's okay." The woman slurs her words, slumps dizzily, and cannot find her phone. He calls an Uber for both of them, ostensibly to take her home, but redirects the driver to his apartment. Inside he gives the woman more alcohol and begins kissing her.

When she states that she needs to lie down, presumably due to sickness or dizziness, he brings her to his bedroom, lays her down in bed, and starts to undress, kiss, and fondle her. In a tentative, breathy voice she repeatedly asks, "Wait, what are you doing?" while he repetitively assures her, "It's okay, you're safe," as he removes her panties. Suddenly her sleepy eyes open wide, she sits upright, and in a loud clear voice she asks more forcefully, "Hey, I said what are you doing?" He stares back, dumbfounded. The woman, later introduced to viewers as Cassie, was never drunk. She used her seemingly pliant body to lure a man who would take advantage of a woman in order to orchestrate this moment of confrontation, a scene the film will repeat several times.

A hard cut to the opening credits interrupts so the audience never finds out exactly what revenge may follow. Will Cassie physically harm or even kill this man for trying to rape her, or is the shock and fear on his face when she confronts him the punishment she seeks? The answer remains ambiguous throughout the film; indicators point in both directions. The title sequence words "Promising Young Woman" appear in hot-pink block-capital letters, spattered in droplets of red that begin to run down like blood, an effect evoking the horror genre. The screen shifts from a pink background to a shot of Cassie walking down the street in the clothes she wore during the attempted rape, presumably the next morning. Red spatters running down her legs and white blouse mirror the bleeding letters.

The implication is that between these scenes someone bled. Since Cassie lacks obvious wounds, the logical conclusion is that it is the man who took her from the bar. However, the cameras pan up to reveal a doughnut in Cassie's fist, oozing red jelly. Does the dripping jelly account for the red spatters? Did she leave the man alive and unharmed? We don't know. Cassie repeats the ritual with several more men. The audience sees a notebook in which she records each incident as a new tally mark amid a plethora of red, black, and blue others. There is no resolution to the ambiguity of what she has done to these men, or if the variation in colors may indicate different forms of revenge.

Initially Cassie does not seem to target any particular man; Meaghan Allen notes it appears that, unlike most rape-revenge stories, "Cassie takes on rape culture as a whole" (2021). Rape-revenge films, like any vigilante story, "are about what ordinary citizens do when the justice system fails them" (Robson 2021, 75). Thus, while the opening of *Promising Young Woman* references the form, the film differs both because Cassie's action is so ambiguous and because structurally it lacks an initial specific inciting incident and thus lacks a clear endpoint. Most rape-revenge films maintain a clear count of the perpetrators who must be punished, both ratcheting up tension and allowing for complete closure and containment of danger at the end when the last rapist is punished. Because Cassie's quest indicts not specific men but men in general, the film threatens to undermine the boundaries and satisfactions of the rape-revenge structure. The danger exceeds any possible narrative closure if all men may be wolves.

ROMANCE?

At this point *Promising Young Woman* restarts, introducing a different narrative opening reminiscent of the romantic comedy. Ryan, a former med school classmate, walks into the coffee shop where Cassie works and the two banter in the adorably awkward manner of a typical "meet-cute" while the breathy pop sound of "Nothing's Gonna Hurt You Baby" by Cigarettes After Sex plays in the background. The film does not immediately commit to the romantic narrative path, cutting to another mini-revenge arc wherein Cassie picks up another guy who brings her to his apartment, forces drugs into her mouth, and tries to touch her sexually without consent. Yet soon the focus reverts to the coffee shop, where Ryan returns for more witty banter and the promise of a lunch date. The two chat over shakes at a 1950s diner, then the scene cuts to them joking and laughing as they stroll home after dark.

In a jarring interruption, Ryan, faux-surprised, "notices" that they have arrived in front of his apartment building and invites Cassie up for a drink. The moment parallels the opening rape-revenge sequence. Suddenly Ryan transforms from a rom-com hero into a potential rapist and the rom-com and rape-revenge genres begin the long wrestling match sustained throughout. Cassie freezes then agrees but Ryan, noticing her hesitation, apologizes and goes into his apartment building alone. He turns back into a romantic hero and Cassie kicks a trash can in frustration with herself for her momentary misrecognition. Maybe there are good men after all? Maybe heterosexuality can be as safe, fun, and fulfilling as the romantic comedy genre promises? Acting like an awkward rom-com heroine taking a chance on love, Cassie shows up at Ryan's medical practice the next day, apologizes with wit and dark humor, and asks to see him again.

The romance element may seem like an illogical or even disturbing set of narrative and social conventions for resolving a story that began with rape. However, many feminist literary critics argue that the interpretation and diffusion of male violence forms the central problem of the genre. Janice Radway (1984) and Tania Modleski (1982) write that archetypes from gothic romances, Jane Austen, and the Brontë sisters structure the modern romance genre around a formula that begins with a male character treating the heroine rudely, disrespectfully, even violently. She must withstand this cruel behavior and reinterpret it as a sign of love in order for her devotion and goodness to reform the hero and improve his actions toward her. Indeed, part of the reason Ryan and Cassie's first meeting reads as a clear opening to romance is that they insult each other. Likewise, Cassie's momentary assumption that Ryan may be about to rape her may seem an unlikely premise for a love story, yet it is not uncommon in romances that, in the Austen tradition, involve discerning between a respectable man and a rake who may molest or take sexual advantage of women, such as John Willoughby in *Sense and Sensibility* or George Wickham in *Pride and Prejudice*. Such romance plots often require women to actively consider which men they are safe with.

Thus, *Promising Young Woman* takes up the well-worn premise that heterosexual success involves choosing a good man from among a crowd of bad ones. In deciding to believe that Ryan is the former, Cassie falls into a romance trope that resolves the specter of male sexual violence when the heroine finds a worthy gentleman. However, almost immediately the film's plot structure reveals a shadow of doubt. At their next date Ryan mentions that he still hangs out with their old classmates, saying, "They're not that bad—they really aren't," and relates that one, Al Monroe (Chris Lowell), recently returned from London to get married and another, Madison (Alison Brie), just had twins. Cassie stiffens, although the reason is not revealed to the audience until later; Al is Nina's rapist and Madison spread rumors that the rape allegations were false. This reminder that the rapist never received any punishment punctures the possibility that the film could end with the heroine's successful heterosexual coupling with a good man, which would paper over male sexual violence. Instead, the romantic storyline cannot replace the revenge narrative; Cassie cannot accept a "happy ever after" ending with Ryan until those involved with Nina's rape receive punishment.

The plot turns to a traditional rape-revenge goal. With a set number of people involved in Nina's rape, the film counts them down by placing a bright pink tally mark at the beginning of each remaining revenge scene. Because Cassie now focuses on a specific number of people, it becomes conceivable that they could all be accounted for. This goal may unite the genre structures and satisfactions of both the romantic-comedy and the rape-revenge story. Perhaps once Cassie deals with the perpetrators, she could lay aside her traumatic fixation with bad men and accept the love of a good man, represented by Ryan. That Cassie's revenge objects are both men and women also undermines the strict association between men and the perpetuation of sexual violence implied by the earlier revenge ritual at bars. This decoupling creates more space to fully imagine Ryan, and by extension heterosexual romance, as not inherently implicated in rape culture. Since those responsible for a social system that enables sexual violence are not invariably male, Cassie may accept a man as love object without compromising her principles, thereby setting up a potentially fulfilling and happy hetero-romantic ending.

Yet the film cannot sustain this balance. Cassie forgets a date with Ryan and, when he asks where she was, she tells him she needs rest. But instead of returning home, she slips back into her earlier pattern and goes to a bar. Ryan catches her leaving it draped against her latest target. "If you weren't interested you could have just told me," Ryan says, breaking off their nascent relationship. A narrative crisis opens as Cassie must choose whether to invest in Ryan and the notion of redeemable heterosexual romance or to stick with revenge.

Two incidents tilt Cassie's path toward romance. First, with a large pink "III" across the screen indicating the third person on her revenge list, Cassie confronts the lawyer, Jordan (Alfred Molina), who defended the rapist and publicly attacked Nina's reputation. Yet, instead of the outrage, defiance, and confusion the audience has witnessed from Cassie's other targets, Jordan immediately admits his guilt, acknowledges Cassie's right to punish him, remembers Nina's name, and asks for forgiveness. He explains that in the intervening years he quit his job and wants to make amends. In stunned surprise Cassie forgives him, then walks out of his house to tell a man waiting by her car that his services are no longer needed. Presumably he would have exacted some form of revenge against the lawyer. The incident marks the first time Cassie sees anyone explicitly acknowledge the harm inflicted on women by sexual violence and rape culture, which again works toward decoupling an essentialist definition of men as wolves, inherently driven toward violence against women.

The next scene reframes Cassie's revenge within a developmental rather than heroic context. A considerable volume of scholarship frames rape revenge as empowering for raped women in particular and all women in general because it makes them active agents rather than passive victims (Allen 2021; Clover 1992; Read 2000; Schorn 2013). Yet there is relatively little critique of the feasibility of lone vigilantes as a valid social solution. With some exceptions, films frame rape-revenge protagonists as tough, physically and mentally dominant, and masterful, much like male action stars. Such films end immediately after the last perpetrator is vanquished, before the heroine must face any social, psychological, or legal consequences (Robson 2021). Likewise, the focus often remains on a simplistic idea that individual acts of revenge can give equivalent retribution for the harms of sexual assault, after which no further healing or social change are necessary (Henry 2013).

Promising Young Woman makes a different argument about revenge's inadequacy and futility. Although in revenge scenes Cassie does indeed appear tough, intimidating, dominant, and even frightening, otherwise her primary traits are childish. She dresses in pastels and rainbows, lives with her parents in her childhood bedroom, repeatedly views childhood photos of herself and Nina, and secures her revenge notebook with a colorful scrunchie. These signs suggest that Nina's rape trapped Cassie in childhood and prevented her maturation into a heterosexual adult capable of entering into a reproductive relationship. Ryan confirms this impression when he mentions that although he and Cassie have been on several dates, she refuses to kiss or touch him.

The condemnation of revenge as childish comes together directly after Cassie confronts Jordan when she visits Nina's mother (Molly Shannon). As Cassie sips from a juice box, another form of infantilization, they reminisce about funny childhood incidents. Nina's mother breaks the mood, asking, "Why are you here? . . . You need to stop this. It isn't good for any of us. It's no good for Nina. It isn't good for you. Look, I know you feel bad that you weren't there, but you gotta let it go." Cassie says, "I'm just trying to fix it." Nina's mother responds, exasperated, "Oh, come on, you can't. Don't be a child, Cassie. . . . Move on. Please. For all of us." She represents revenge as a simplistic worldview that attempts to imaginatively undo a past wrong. Yet Cassie cannot bring Nina back and no act of revenge, punishment, or repentance will repair the damage. Imagining otherwise is recast not as the act of a tough, strong, heroic feminist avenger, but instead as the deluded magical thinking of a child.

Thereafter, Cassie must put aside revenge to accept that an unproblematic, nonviolent relationship with a man is possible and desirable. She deletes her "Friender" (Facebook) account where she had been cyberstalking her next target—Al, Nina's rapist. She discards her revenge notebook, goes to Ryan's apartment, apologizes, and recommits to their relationship. A series of typical rom-com hijinks follow as the couple kiss, banter, dance to Paris Hilton's "Stars Are Blind" at a pharmacy, meet Cassie's parents, have sex, and say they love each other. The romance triumphs! All that is left to secure heterosexual closure is marriage and pregnancy.

AN EMPTY RETURN TO REVENGE

Yet ultimately, romance cannot fully suture the trauma and danger evoked by male sexual violence. Just as revenge was exposed as an inadequate, childish solution, romance likewise proves to be an overly simplistic bandaid. Both narrative conventions lead to dead ends in the search for symbolic solutions to male sexual violence. After Cassie led Madison to wrongly believe that someone may have raped Madison while she was intoxicated, just like Nina, Madison comes to ask Cassie what really happened. Cassie explains that she only wanted to scare Madison. Relieved but shaken, Madison acknowledges her culpability in smearing Nina's reputation and admits that she knew the rape accusations were true. She gives Cassie a video of the rape that "everyone" had sent to each other at the time. She tells Cassie not to watch it, but she does so and cries; the audience cannot see but hears male laughter and cheering. Cassie visibly shudders and gasps as Ryan's voice says, "Oh, my god, woah. This is insane. Hey, don't film me. [*laughs*] Jesus Christ, Al," and she and the audience together realize his complicity. Romance has been fully foreclosed. Ryan is a wolf. Because he stood in for good men, all men are wolves. Danger is everywhere.

The narrative veers sharply back to revenge; yet at this point in the story, Cassie's desire for revenge has been classified as the result of trauma and a stumbling block to full maturation, rather than heroic. Likewise, Ryan's complicity invalidates the notion that those implicated in rape culture can be recognized, quantified, and vanquished. All options typical of the revenge and romantic genres now lack the ability to create full narrative closure. Cassie confronts Ryan, severs their relationship, and extracts the location of Al's bachelor party under the threat of sending the rape video to Ryan's family, patients, coworkers, and friends. A pink "IIII" appears on the screen, indicating the fourth target as she arrives at the party dressed as a "sexy nurse" stripper in an ironic reference to the doctors she and Nina might have become.

This setup opens the possibility that the film may still conclude with the partial satisfaction of seeing Cassie take revenge against Al; yet it rejects even this incomplete closure. As she attempts to carve Nina's name into Al's stomach with a scalpel after handcuffing him to a bedframe, he breaks one hand free and murders her. This reversal of fortune parallels the absolute negation of the expected romantic resolution. Ryan is an accomplice rather than a romantic hero; Cassie rather than Al is dead.

What follows is a grim, stomach-churning depiction of Al's friend Joe (Max Greenfield) finding Al still handcuffed in the morning, assuring him he did nothing wrong, and helping him to burn Cassie's body. The police begin to investigate her disappearance but Ryan does not reveal her presence at the bachelor party. The scene cuts to Al's wedding, a vacuous, over-the-top spectacle of wealth, cliché, and heteronormativity. A text message from Cassie, timed to send in the event of her death, surprises Ryan at the reception, synched with the nondiegetic song "Angel of the Morning" by Juice Newton, which sets off a flashback montage. Clips show Jordan receiving a package from Cassie with the rape video, details of her bachelor party revenge plan, and instructions to contact the police if she goes missing. "You didn't think this was the end, did you?" reads the text as sirens sound in the distance.

Four bright pink tally marks and a fifth slash intersecting them appears on the screen, indicating one last act of revenge the lawyer performs on Cassie's behalf, as police appear and arrest Al for her murder. Pre-scheduled texts continue on Ryan's phone: "It is now. Enjoy the wedding! Love, Cassie & Nina ;)." A kind of revenge is achieved, but at what cost? Al presumably goes to prison but so many others escape punishment, including Joe, Ryan, and countless men in bars, while Cassie and Nina are gone forever. *Promising Young Woman*'s concluding revenge evades full closure because it cannot offer restitution for all the wrongs done throughout the film, nor contain the generalized dangers of rape culture that it unearthed. The romantic ending might have been salvaged had Ryan shown up at the bachelor party to save Cassie from Al in the nick of time, or if Ryan, rather than the lawyer, sought retribution after her death. Instead *Promising Young Woman* refuses the rom-com and undercuts rape revenge.

"LITTLE RED RIDING HOOD" AND *PROMISING YOUNG WOMAN*: NEOLIBERALISM AND MISRECOGNITION

By withholding the satisfactions of a traditional romantic or rape-revenge ending, *Promising Young Woman* implicitly critiques both. Although untenably nihilistic and grim as a basis for political or cultural action, the conclusion nonetheless suggests a resonant narrative corrective to both genres' tendency to posit overly simplistic individual solutions to complex social problems. While second-wave feminism transformed allegedly personal issues like rape, domestic violence, and sexual harassment into political issues with cultural causes, and liberal feminism offered legal and legislative solutions, what scholars such as Angela McRobbie (2004) call "post-feminism" undertakes a neoliberal reversal, making sexism back into a personal problem resulting from individual weaknesses and failures.

Both romance and the rape-revenge resolutions to stories about sexual violence provide what Berlant terms "privatized" solutions to collective problems (1997). Such notions imply that one marriage between a good woman and a good man restores faith that deserving people find happiness in hetero-coupledom and that revenge against individual perpetrators can contain the sexual violence that pervades society. Such private, specific solutions redirect political concerns about social justice, underestimate the real scope of sexual violence, and undermine solidarity among classes of people subjected structurally to similar harms. Thus, for *Promising Young Woman*, bringing in "Little Red Riding Hood" as an additional if less obvious intertext helps to elucidate the critical edge to what may initially appear to be a devastatingly antifeminist and disempowering ending.

The film's "Little Red Riding Hood" structural and thematic references and allusions are telling. Most directly, the bachelor party scene begins with Cassie walking down an unlighted path in the woods. Trees dominate the screen and swallow her body as she walks into the darkness. Although she wears a white nurse costume, her high heels provide a bright splash of red when she arrives at the cabin door. Like Little Red Riding Hood, Cassie walks alone through the dangerous woods. Jack Zipes argues that the tale may metaphorically deal with rites of passage between childhood and womanhood, when women often must first confront aggressive and sometimes violent sexual advances (1983). Little Red starts the story innocent and confused about the dangers posed by wolves loitering in the woods and, if she survives the story, gains more fully adult knowledge of the threats women face. As a result, Steven Kohm and Pauline Greenhill (2014) argue that the tale offers a template for stories about adult men's predation on girls and young women, and in some versions their efforts to turn the tables and exact revenge against rapists and pedophiles. Although dark woods remain a resonant symbol, especially in the horror genre, the home, bars, and school grounds are all more common contact zones for an actual first experience of sexual predation (Hickman and Muehlenhard 1997). As such, like "Little Red Riding Hood," *Promising Young Woman* reflects upon how girls' and women's first encounter with sexual violence and aggression may alter their path through life and form a structural part of the maturation process shared by many female-identified and female-identifying people.

Further, the film and "Little Red Riding Hood" fundamentally center cultural misrecognition surrounding patriarchal violence. Numerous versions of the tale repeat two absurd moments of misrecognition when Little Red fails to comprehend a danger that audiences clearly understand. First, she has no fear of the wolf when she meets him in the woods and takes his advice that she should dally there. Second, when she meets him disguised as her grandmother, she makes ever more bizarre observations: "What big ears you have, what big eyes you have, what big teeth you have." Audiences understand the ridiculous contrast between the average appearance of a grandmother and a wolf. Putting the two incidents together, something is seriously wrong with Little Red's insight and understanding, or some social or psychological element explains why she cannot recognize a wolf when she sees one.

Radway (1984) observes that part of the pleasure for romance readers derives from knowing more than the heroine. Her research sample group preferred a young, naïve, and almost unfailingly virginal heroine. The older, more sexually and socially experienced readers therefore shared a knowingness about male behavior and heterosexual courtship rituals and norms that the heroine slowly develops throughout the story. Radway thus classifies romance novels similarly to Zipes's discussion of "Little Red Riding Hood" as stories about loss of sexual innocence, not as loss of virginity but loss of ignorance about the world of male desire, male violence, and (hetero)sex. Little Red cannot recognize a wolf because she has been kept innocent (and ignorant) of the realities of sexuality and patriarchal norms that enable male sexual violence.

In contrast, the misrecognitions in *Promising Young Woman* often stem from a more deliberate form of suppression and double-talk. Characters know about the past but do not behave or speak in ways that reflect that shared truth. Though the entire film revolves around a rape and shows many other attempted rapes, the word *rape* is spoken only once, when Al denies raping Nina; instead, characters substitute phrases like "sex you don't want," "accusations," or simply "We did not . . . you know." This strange elision exemplifies the film's underlying tension between competing versions of reality as the narrative struggles to force characters and the audience to admit that what they witnessed is rape (Greenhill and Kohm 2013).

Like the Cassandra of Greek mythology who knows the future but is not believed, Cassie alone discerns and accepts the truth of what happened to Nina and what that means about the prevalence of male sexual violence and the world's complicity in it. As a result, unlike readers of "Little Red Riding Hood," the audience of *Promising Young Woman* does not begin from a position of superior knowingness but must instead take the journey of coming to consciousness about sexual violence along with the characters. Thus, the film's critique of the conventions and pleasures of a romantic or heroic revenge ending also functions as a performative critique of the audience's own expectations and willingness to invest in cultural stories that explain away and seek neat and tidy closure to sexual violence against women. The refusal of full pleasurable closure for the audience mirrors Cassie's refusal to allow the characters around her to move on with their lives unchanged by and unreconciled to the truth of what happened to Nina and to so many other women and girls around them.

Therefore, most revenge scenes in *Promising Young Woman* undermine characters' ability to continue to suppress and deny that Nina was raped and that they know men can be sexually violent toward women. Cassie drugs and manipulates Madison to believe she may have been raped while intoxicated just like Nina and leads the med school dean to believe her drunk high school daughter is alone in a dorm room with male college students. These situations crack the two women's suppression of their own knowledge of male sexual aggression. Both were initially dismissive of Nina's claims based on their professed belief that women claiming they have been raped are merely, according to Madison, "crying wolf" (Weiser 2017).

Yet when Madison herself and the dean's daughter are intoxicated and alone with men their immediate panic reveals that on some level they knew the truth all along. It also lifts a form of false consciousness because it reminds them that they are women and that women as a class in patriarchal societies are vulnerable to male sexual violence.[1] Cassie's revenge undermines their ability to continue their complicity with patriarchal institutions and norms, whether for their own gain or as a defense mechanism, inviting them back into solidarity with other women and girls.

The unexpected outcome of Al murdering Cassie at the end of the film likewise functions as a similar form of revenge against the audience's potential genre-based suppression of knowledge about male violence against women. In an interview, Fennell says what should be painfully obvious about Cassie's revenge quest: "Any woman who watches this film will understand that what she's doing is incredibly dangerous" (Cole 2021). Yet the film's narrative twists function well only if they come as a surprise. Given that the audience knows that Ryan was friends with Al in med school and still likes and spends time with him in the present, why would they expect Ryan to be different? Given that so many men try to rape Cassie and Al was sexually violent with Nina, why would it come as a surprise that he overpowers and harms Cassie at the end? This suppression of knowingness, enabled by experience in viewing rom-com and rape-revenge films, brings the audience into painful complicity with *Promising Young Woman*'s characters and postfeminist neoliberal ideologies that explain away and individualize rather than collectivize rape risk and sexual violence.

Bringing in "Little Red Riding Hood" as an intertext clarifies *Promising Young Woman*'s critique and connects with a long-standing debate among feminist scholars and activists about women's agency and empowerment. Cassie's murder mirrors versions of "Little Red Riding Hood" like Perrault's, wherein Little Red and her grandmother end the story dead, inside the belly of the beast. Zipes characterizes this form of the tale as the least feminist and most disempowering, especially with the addition of Perrault's victim-blaming "moral" (1983). He likewise criticizes versions like the Grimm brothers' (1812/2014), in which Little Red and her grandmother must be saved by a man, and emphasizes the female ingenuity and solidarity celebrated by earlier versions of the story from the French oral tradition.

Zipes's analysis echoes many feminist concerns that fictional and nonfictional depictions of women as victims of male violence requiring male protection reinforce the notion of female bodies as inherently weak and inferior (Hollander 2016). In particular, female sexual victimization has historically been used as a patriarchal tool to undermine women's own sense of security and self-efficacy and to legitimate brutal racist regimes of segregation and violence in the name of protecting white women from men of color (Stoler 1991). As a result, some feminist scholars and activists champion strong, empowered, and even violent female characters. Like Zipes, they may thus classify stories of female protagonists who end up dead as inherently anti-feminist. This line of reasoning suggests that *Promising Young Woman* cannot serve a feminist function because Cassie does not survive.

However, this stance alternatively has the potential to enhance neoliberal notions that the individual rather than the state is ultimately completely responsible for everything that happens to them, and thus reinforces victim-blaming. If women are fully capable of revenging or preventing violence, then neoliberal logic suggests they are at fault when they do not violently fight back and successfully repel an attack. Taking on this contradiction, Bell Murphy argues that feminist self-defense training must both "acknowledge and encourage women's capacity to resist sexual violence while also holding a compassionate, blame-free space for victims and maintaining focus on perpetrators as the only people responsible for violence" (2018, 79).

Yet Murphy admits this tightrope is difficult to walk, given that "the notion that women should 'empower' themselves to avoid risks to their safety is highly compatible with neoliberal governments' goals to relieve themselves of responsibility for the costs and consequences of social problems" (2018, 76). Thus, Alyson Cole argues that the pervasiveness of such neoliberal logic makes it difficult for otherwise critical feminists theorizing "vulnerability" to rid themselves of an underlying disgust for women who fall prey to violence and become "victims" (2016). She maintains that discomfort with the idea of victimization leads many well-intentioned feminist theorists to make the workings of injustice more difficult to publicly recognize when they attempt to undermine essentialist equivalences between the female body and weakness by arguing that all people are equally vulnerable.

The return to "Little Red Riding Hood"'s most dire outcome for a girl who walks alone into the woods may then represent an important corrective to genre conventions, ideologies, and theoretical legacies alike that erase ongoing collective struggles against still all too common sexual violence. Cole writes, quoting and critiquing Martha Albertson Fineman and Anna Grear (2013), "It seems that the ostensible absence of agency or any generative qualities makes theorists uneasy. Fineman and Grear write: 'This vulnerable self is not a victim . . . he/she can act, both individually and collectively'" (2016, 270). As "uneasy" as audiences and theorists may feel about their fate, the dead Nina and Cassie and the swallowed Little Red clearly cannot act by the end of the story, nor can the many intoxicated and unconscious victims of assault the film references. Although *Promising Young Woman* attempts to provide Cassie with a form of agency and closure from beyond the grave by visualizing her pre-scheduled texts to Ryan, her revenge quest must be taken on by Jordan. The pleasure of watching a strong, agentive female avenger in a rape-revenge story thus evades discomfort with the idea of victimization, a solace *Promising Young Woman* brutally withholds.

In its indictment of the legal system via Cassie's interrogation of both the dean, who undermines justice within the school, and Jordan, who confesses to the way male privilege and wealth corrupt the formal criminal justice system, the film destabilizes the notion that individual restitution is possible or desirable. This institutional critique combines with scenes showing the many attempted rapists Cassie targets at bars and the numerous incidental moments of gendered aggression throughout the film, such as catcalling. Together they paint a picture of far broader institutional and cultural work yet to be accomplished that no single heroine can be expected to combat alone. Although *Promising Young Woman* does not provide a hopeful vision of the community of solidarity and sustained political work necessary to take on this behemoth, it does take a first step by envisioning the problem and cutting off solutions that draw potentially politicized feminist subjects back into privatized stasis.

PROMISING YOUNG LITTLE RED

By returning to what may be the most conservative ending of "Little Red Riding Hood," *Promising Young Woman* undermines misrecognition and suppression of the extent of male sexual violence against women in contemporary society and seductive cultural conventions for containing that danger. The displeasure and discomfort that may remain for audiences at the end of the film thus require new solutions that exceed the privatized domains of neoliberal heterosexual coupling and individual acts of self-improvement, agency, toughness, and revenge. Although *Promising Young Woman* does not imagine solutions, it challenges audiences to recognize the problem of sexual violence as a collective, pervasive, institutional, and cultural issue centered in the political realm. Characteristic features of "Little Red Riding Hood" that present sexual danger as a commonplace part of women's life course help to bring the persistently constitutive experience of sexual danger to the forefront. As such, although not immediately obvious, using "Little Red Riding Hood" as an intertext exposes the pleasures of rape-revenge and rom-com genre structures as political dead ends and offers telling insights for the interpretation of *Promising Young Woman*'s feminist critique.

NOTE

1. On this point I am indebted to conversations with Dr. Anna Poletti.

REFERENCES

Allen, Meaghan. 2021. "Her Body, Herself: Rape-Revenge and the Desire for Catharsis." *The Final Girls*, March 24. https://www.thefinalgirls.co.uk/bloody-women/violation.

Antonia's Line. 1995. Directed by Marleen Gorris. Netherlands: Bergen, Prime Time, and Bard Entertainments.

Berlant, Lauren. 1997. *The Queen of America Goes to Washington City: Essays on Sex and Citizenship*. Durham, NC: Duke University Press.

Chappet, Marie-Claire. 2021. "Why Do We Protect Promising Young Men over Promising Young Women?" *Harper's Bazaar*, April 12. https://www.harpersbazaar.com/uk/culture/a35519409/promising-young-woman-comment/.

Clover, Carol. 1992. *Men, Women, and Chain Saws: Gender in the Modern Horror Film*. Princeton, NJ: Princeton University Press.

Cole, Alyson. 2016. "All of Us Are Vulnerable, but Some Are More Vulnerable Than Others: The Political Ambiguity of Vulnerability Studies, an Ambivalent Critique." *Critical Horizons* 17 (2): 260–77.

Cole, Geri. 2021. "OnWriting Live: Emerald Fennell." *Writers Guild of America East*. Accessed October 3, 2023. https://www.wgaeast.org/onwriting/onwriting-live-emerald-fennell-promising-young-woman/.

Edelman, Lee. 2004. *No Future: Queer Theory and the Death Drive*. Durham, NC: Duke University Press.

Fineman, Martha Albertson, and Anna Grear. 2013. "Introduction: Vulnerability as Heuristic—An Invitation to Future Exploration." In *Vulnerability: Reflections on a New Ethical Foundation for Law and Politics*, edited by Martha Albertson Fineman and Anna Grear, 1–11. Burlington, VT: Ashgate.

Fire. 1996. Directed by Deepa Mehta. Canada: Trial by Fire Films Inc.

Gagnon, Janette, and Emanuella Grinberg. 2016. "Mad about Brock Turner's Sentence?" *CNN*, September 4. https://www.cnn.com/2016/09/02/us/brock-turner-college-athletes-sentence/index.html.

Greenhill, Pauline, and Steven Kohm. 2013. "*Hoodwinked!* and *Jin-Roh: The Wolf Brigade*: Animated 'Little Red Riding Hood' Films and the Rashōmon Effect." *Marvels & Tales* 27 (1): 89–108.

Grimm, Jacob, and Wilhelm Grimm. (1812) 2014. "Little Red Cap." In *The Complete First Edition: The Original Folk and Fairy Tales of the Brothers Grimm*, edited and translated by Jack Zipes, 85–87. Princeton, NJ: Princeton University Press.

Henry, Claire. 2013. "Challenging the Boundaries of Cinema's Rape-Revenge Genre in *Katalin Varga* and *Twilight Portrait*." *Studies in European Cinema* 10 (2–3): 133–45.

Hickman, Susan E., and Charlene L. Muehlenhard. 1997. "College Women's Fears and Precautionary Behaviors Relating to Acquaintance Rape and Stranger Rape." *Psychology of Women Quarterly* 21 (4): 527–47.

Hollander, Jocelyn A. 2016. "Teaching about Gendered Violence without Disempowering Women." In *Teaching Gender and Sex in Contemporary America*, edited by Kristin Haltinner and Ryanne Pilgeram, 85–92. Cham: Springer.

I Spit on Your Grave. 1978. Directed by Meir Zarchi. United States: Barquel Creations.

Itty Bitty Titty Committee. 2007. Directed by Jamie Babbit. United States: Power Up Films.

Kohm, Steven, and Pauline Greenhill. 2014. "Little Red Riding Hood Crime Films: Critical Variations on Criminal Themes." *Law, Culture and the Humanities* 10 (2): 257–78. https://doi.org/10.1177/1743872111416328.

Koren, Marina. 2016. "Why the Stanford Judge Gave Brock Turner Six Months." *Atlantic*, June 17. https://www.theatlantic.com/news/archive/2016/06/stanford-rape-case-judge/487415/.

LaChance, Naomi. 2016. "Media Continues to Refer to Brock Turner as a 'Stanford Swimmer' Rather Than a Rapist." *Intercept*, September 2. https://theintercept

.com/2016/09/02/media-continues-to-refer-to-brock-turner-as-a-stanford-swimmer-rather-than-a-rapist/.

Levin, Sam. 2016. "Stanford Sexual Assault: Read the Full Text of the Judge's Controversial Decision." *Guardian*, June 14. https://www.theguardian.com/us-news/2016/jun/14/stanford-sexual-assault-read-sentence-judge-aaron-persky.

McRobbie, Angela. 2004. "Post-Feminism and Popular Culture." *Feminist Media Studies* 4 (3): 255–64.

Modleski, Tania. 1982. *Loving with a Vengeance: Mass-Produced Fantasies for Women*. Hamden: Archon Books.

Murphy, Bell. 2018. "Fighting Back on Feminist Terms: Empowerment Through Self-Defence Training in Neoliberal Times." In *Orienting Feminism: Media, Activism and Cultural Representation*, edited by Catherine Dale and Rosemary Overell, 71–94. Cham: Palgrave Macmillan.

Perrault, Charles. (1697) 2018. "Little Red Riding Hood." In *The Complete Fairy Tales*, edited and translated by Chistopher Betts. New York: Oxford University Press.

Polowy, Kevin. 2020. "'Promising Young Woman': Carey Mulligan and Emerald Fennell Talk Sexual Assault Revenge Thriller, Title's Similarity to Brock Turner Case." *Yahoo!News*, December 22. https://ca.news.yahoo.com/promising-young-woman-metoo-sexual-assault-revenge-brock-turner-case-title-160055320.html.

Promising Young Woman. 2020. Directed by Emerald Fennell. United States: Focus Features.

Radway, Janice. 1984. *Reading the Romance: Women, Patriarchy, and Popular Literature*. Chapel Hill: University of North Carolina Press.

Read, Jacinda. 2000. *The New Avengers: Feminism, Femininity, and the Rape-Revenge Cycle*. Manchester: Manchester University Press.

Robson, Peter. 2021. "Developments in Revenge, Justice and Rape in Cinema." *International Journal for the Semiotics of Law* 34: 69–88.

Schorn, Johanna. 2013. "Empowerment through Violence: Feminism and the Rape-Revenge Narrative in *The Girl with the Dragon Tattoo*." *Gender Forum* 41: 8–17. https://www.proquest.com/scholarly-journals/empowerment-through-violence-feminism-rape/docview/1400449156/se-2.

Stoler, Ann. 1991. "Carnal Knowledge and Imperial Power: Gender, Race, and Morality in Colonial Asia." In *Gender at the Crossroads of Knowledge: Feminist Anthropology in the Postmodern Era*, edited by Micaela di Leonardo, 51–95. Berkeley: University of California Press.

Weiser, Dana A. 2017. "Confronting Myths about Sexual Assault: A Feminist Analysis of the False Report Literature." *Family Relations* 66 (1): 46–60.

Zipes, Jack. 1983. "A Second Gaze at Little Red Riding Hood's Trials and Tribulations." *The Lion and the Unicorn* 7:78–109.

11

Margery's Miscellany; or, What "All the World Must Allow"

Children's Citizenship, Goody Two-Shoes, and the Fairy-Tale Public Sphere

ALLISON CRAVEN

Goody Two-Shoes—real name Margery Meanwell—began life as the titular character in an influential children's book produced by the English publisher John Newbery in 1765: *The History of Little Goody Two-Shoes with the Means by Which She Acquired Her Learning and Wisdom, and in Consequence of Her Estate (Goody Two-Shoes* 1981).[1] Newbery was a pioneer of children's publishing (Darton 1966, 72–81), and *Little Goody Two-Shoes* was among his best sellers (G. Brown 2006, 356; O'Malley 2003, 23), becoming a "staple of Anglo-American children's publishing" for 150 years (Crain 2016, 19). Margery's story is told from orphaned childhood to her career as a teacher of the alphabet, her marriage, and her death, and her reputation is extolled as a friend to the poor and a moral exemplar for children and curmudgeon elders alike. Dale Townshend notes the book's wild ambiguity between nursery tale and novel (2008), and Patricia Crain likens it to a "baby bildungsroman" (2006, 2016, 19). While the story is barely known today, it is regarded as the "very foundation of the Moral Tale" and the "virtue-is-its-own reward . . . type of story" (Darton 1966, 131).

Little Goody Two-Shoes did not originate as a fairy tale or magical narrative or derive from folklore. Instead, it appeared in the clay-footed realm of didactic literature at a time in England when fairy tales, especially for children, were greatly disparaged within the prevailing Puritan sensibility. As I explain, while elements of the story are fantastical (Crain 2006, 2016; Fergus 2006; Selwyn 2010), its reputation as a children's fairy tale emerged during the nineteenth century as its puritanism became eroded within that century's burgeoning mass entertainments for children. This passage from moral tale to fairy tale is at issue in Crain's definitive discussion of the heroine's emblematic position in the eighteenth-century print public sphere as an exponent of literacy and hence citizenship. In the first section of this chapter, I follow and extend her account in exploring Margery's relationship then and since to what Courtney Weikle-Mills calls "imaginary citizenship" (2008, 2012).

The late eighteenth century in Britain and Europe is widely recognized as a period in which modern ideas of the child, childhood, and books for children all emerged concurrently. This history is contemporaneous with Jürgen Habermas's theory of emergence of the modern, rational public sphere, although this model has attracted extensive criticism as a "segment, restricted to 'an educated male bourgeoisie and enlightened nobility'" (Hartley 2002, 107). Historians of children's culture question the separation of public and private spheres and the equation of "citizenship with public debate" through the figure of the child (Weikle-Mills 2008, 58). Children's books, in particular, foster forms of literary or "imaginary" citizenship (Weikle-Mills 2012). Newbery's books propagated social ideology espoused by the emerging middle class (O'Malley 2003; Fergus 2006) and cultivated John Locke's ideas about the social contract (Crain 2016). Weikle-Mills, in particular, illuminates how "the evolving concept of childhood helped to define the limits . . . and boundaries of citizenship" (2012, 4).

If a citizen in the modern sense is a "member of a political community with obligations and entitlements and some measure of political agency" (Weikle-Mills 2012, 2) (that may or may not extend to suffrage), "imaginary citizenship" is not simply "make-believe," nor merely "a token or symbolic form of mini-citizenship for children" (6–7). Nor are children exclusively or even primarily addressed as imaginary citizens in literary works (4). Rather, "imaginary citizenship" can "overlap," "resemble," and "inform" legal notions through "powerful cultural work" that "supplement[s] . . . dominant notions of citizenship" (6–7).² In *Little Goody Two-Shoes*, this idea of imaginary citizenship is immanent, I argue, in Margery's dedication to civic welfare and the public good. This is despite the paradox noted by Weikle-Mills that girls were excluded from "civic rights on the basis of both gender and age," and that the equation of the "obedient child" as "ideal subject" in Locke's theories is "fraught with contradictions" (2008, 36–37).

This situation is not greatly changed today, as children in Western societies are typically denied citizenship (Phillips et al. 2019, 30). Social policy on, for, or about children focuses largely on protection (Wyness 2000), with children seen to belong to the "'private' worlds of play, domesticity and school" (Roche 1999, 479).³ Yet abundant critical and creative practices demonstrate the activist, political, and social uses of fairy tales (for instance, Labrie 2018; Bacchilega and Orme 2021). Furthermore, as Cristina Bacchilega and Jennifer Orme suggest, fairy-tale scholarship at times must navigate "disparaging" presumptions that fairy tales are "'just' for children" (2021, ix). Conversely, the history of children's literature shows that even the most cogent address to children is typically couched in an adult voice or with an older readership marginally implied. Weikle-Mills's notion of "imaginary citizens" and the case study of Goody Two-Shoes can suggest vulnerability to the vagaries of the narrative voices in children's fiction and the residual fictionality of the child citizen as well as the marginality of fairy tales as vehicles of agency.

To this end, in what follows, I examine Goody Two-Shoes's emergence in the late eighteenth-century public sphere, the character's transition to fairy tale, and how the ambiguities of this evolving subjectivity resonate today. Despite Margery's moral heroism and model contribution to the public good, a "Goody Two-Shoes" today is an idiom for a person with an ambiguous relationship to virtue and agency. The expression is profusely applied in tabloid journalism and commentary about stars and celebrities and relates to perceived dissonances between their public personas and private lives, or on their stances on public causes. Emma Watson is a particular example for the persistent allusion to her child-self through the "goody two-shoes" legacy of her role as Hermione Granger in the *Harry Potter* films, which even haunts her feminist activism. The paradoxes of imaginary citizenship are only marginally adjusted when considering activist children such as Greta Thunberg and Malala Yousafzai, although Thunberg was a teenager when she entered the public sphere and both are now well advanced in young adulthood. I consider the "juvenile ageism" (Bergmann and Ossewaarde 2020) that accompanies their media coverage, and how it inflects allusions to Goody Two-Shoes and their own rhetorical uses of wonder and folktales for the imaginary citizenship they embody and inspire.

With the worldwide spectacle of children mobilizing in public demonstrations for climate action, education rights, or gun control in the United States,[4] the larger purpose is to reflect on children's voices and agency for social change and the residual challenges of the fictionality of this mode of citizenship. The fluctuating legacy of Goody Two-Shoes, I suggest, holds an enduring place in the fairy-tale public sphere: an idea that pertains to the role of wonder in arenas of public debate and to the potential—imaginary and literal—of children as citizens.

HER STORY AND HER PUBLICS: GETTING TO KNOW EIGHTEENTH-CENTURY GOODY TWO-SHOES

The History of Little Goody Two-Shoes opens with an "Editor's Preface" describing Margery and her brother Tommy's orphaned poverty following the deaths of their parents, Mr. and Mrs. Meanwell, which were hastened by persecution from the cruel landlords Gripe and Graspall. The homeless pair is taken in by a clergyman who arranges a career at sea for Tommy and a new pair of shoes for Margery, who has only one shoe. The excited announcements by Margery of the arrival of her "Two Shoes" leads to her eponymous nickname. Later, Gripe and Graspall's hounding of her benefactors leads to Margery being turned out again. Undaunted, she teaches herself to read and then becomes a "trotting tutoress" (*Goody Two-Shoes* 1981, 28), teaching spelling to poor farmers' children. With "ten Setts [sic]" of her hand-cut wooden alphabet letters, she travels to lessons with "these Rattle-traps in a basket" and teaches using "the Game, as they called it" of arranging words from the letters, a process visualized in the typesetting and illustrations of the tiny book. Margery's novel teaching method was a progressive feature of the book, modeling Locke's ascendant prescription to make reading into "'Play and Recreation to Children'" (cited in G. Brown 2006, 352).

Margery eventually replaces the retiring mistress as "President of the A, B, C College" (*Goody Two-Shoes* 1981, 66). She teaches with assistance from various rescued and gifted animals, among them Ralph the Raven, who learns to read and spell, and Jumper the Dog, who heroically delivers all the children to safety when Margery's school falls down. Beyond the classroom, Margery counsels citizens using her own invention, a "Considering Cap" (115), and she consults on crops and weather with a barometer. Resentment arises in a neighboring village when the crops fail, and, with added suspicion regarding her animal familiars, Goody Two-Shoes is accused of being a witch. The magistrate, Sir William Dove, condemns these "absurd and foolish Notions" of witchcraft as "Folly and Ignorance" (129), and publicly thanks Margery for her good works. One Sir Charles Jones is so enamored he proposes marriage, and she becomes Lady Jones and continues her dedicated work for the poor until the story concludes with her death, which is greatly mourned.

This moral tract of Margery's life is in the eighteenth-century form of a miscellany (Fergus 2006, 151) in which Margery's adventures are liberally accompanied by prayers, scriptures, epithetic wisdoms, songs, and other embellishments. With its "puffs," or advertising, *Little Goody Two-Shoes* is "merrily self-conscious" of its "status as a print commodity" (Crain 2016, 30). Yet the messages, firm and stern, are delivered mostly in the voice of the anonymous narrator who relays Margery's speeches. They denounce superstition and belief in magic, and when Margery is accidentally locked in a church and hears strange noises (a dog, in fact), the narrator praises her "good *Sense*" in not indulging in thoughts of "*Ghosts*, *Witches* and *Fairies*" (*Goody Two-Shoes* 1981, 56; emphases in original). When the schoolhouse collapses (an allusion to an actual incident, according to Darton 1966; Grenby 2013), and with another twist in the "protean" narration (Fergus 2006, 144), the Man in the Moon praises Jumper and admonishes governments to "guard against Accidents of this Sort" by "having a public Survey . . . of all the Houses in every Parish" (*Goody Two-Shoes* 1981, 100).

The schoolhouse collapse is not wholly adventitious in the narrative but accords with Margery's larger mission for the public good. She "laid every possible Scheme to promote the Welfare and Happiness of all her Neighbours, and especially of the Little Ones . . . and all those whose Parents could not afford to pay for their Education, she taught for nothing but the Pleasure she had in their Company" (*Goody Two-Shoes* 1981, 66). The public good, as Jane Johnston argues, is a complex concept that has "evolved as ambiguous and mutable" and "contextually determined" (2019). As a progressive teacher of spelling, advocate for free education, and practitioner of kindness to tormented animals (expressing the era's growing social sentiment toward prevention of cruelty), Margery upholds the concept in a recognizably modern way.

Yet, as an early modern child, Margery was on the cusp of transition from the idea of children as "Lilliputian people," or "scaled down adults," which transformed with the emergence of the middle class (Iskander 1988, 166). Eighteenth-century children's books, Newbery's especially, promulgated "the virtues . . . espoused to promote social reform and individual improvement—'sobriety, obedience, industry, thrift, benevolence and compassion'" (O'Malley 2003, 6). Goody Two-Shoes was not the only good fairy-tale citizen, as Newbery co-opted traditional heroes like Jack the Giant Killer and Tom Thumb. Jack was "greatly reformed" to espouse "reading and obedience" as a pathway to "successful adult[hood]" rather than "robbing and killing giants" (21–22). Goody Two-Shoes, on the other hand, was an invention of her time, without any apparent folktale or fairy-tale heritage.

The digressive narration and obtrusive interlocutors in *Little Goody Two-Shoes* have raised queries about the exclusive address of the story to children. If the primary purpose was to instill good behavior and teach reading (Selwyn 2010, 144), it shares the "riches . . . to rags to riches" trajectory and "episodic, digressive narrative" (Crain 2016, 20–21) that typified eighteenth-century fiction, and the story is "full of general satire on human behaviour as well as specific satire against legal chicanery and land enclosure" (Fergus 2006, 148). Some critics note the Editor's allusion (in the Preface) to "children of six Feet high" (*Goody Two-Shoes* 1981, 11), as if "a child reader alone cannot satisfy the author's needs" (Kertzer 1984, 20), or the book supposes an adult reader of the Preface (Selwyn 2010, 146). But, as several critics argue, the shifting child and adult subjectivities are emblematic in the heroine's own name(s): the nickname "Two-Shoes" replaces her patronymic Meanwell (Crain 2016, 25); while "Goody"—the medieval contraction of "good-wife," a "sign of lower-class status, not a moral tag," as Jan Fergus notes (2006, 139)—"supplants her Christian name" and makes the child Margery into a "mini-woman" (Crain 2016, 26). Fergus counts seventeen names attributed to the heroine, as her appellation changes with events of her life (2006, 149).

"Goody Two-Shoes," however, stands as her public self, her persona, as the term is used in studies of celebrity (see Rojek 2001), and it carries formidable power. Crain notes that "Goody Two-Shoes" is given to her by the parish people, and hence it is "the metonym that her public gives her by acclamation" (2016, 26). By this name she inhabits the "commons": "she belongs to no one and to everyone" (Crain 2006, 217). The book's opening line—"All the world must allow, that Two-Shoes was not her real Name"—bespeaks, Crain argues, the status of this character as a product of the eighteenth-century public sphere and the "here and now of life lived out in public" (2016, 21). Her social remit was considerable, as this imaginary celebrity embodied the democratization of print as well as changing ideas of childhood itself, which entailed a "new relation to books and reading" (1) as well as citizenship.

Beyond the instrumental aims of teaching spelling and reading, Crain imagines Goody Two-Shoes as a mouthpiece for literacy as a commodity that represented a new form of cultural capital (2016, 7). While, as she notes, in the eighteenth century it is "anachronistic to speak of literacy" and in *Little Goody Two-Shoes* it "manifests as the mechanics of alphabetization" (20), she argues that the promise of literacy channeled Locke's ideas about citizenship. Beyond morals and spelling, eighteenth-century children's books, as Gillian Brown (2001) argues, were "Lockean manuals for 'promoting consensual individuals'" that cultivated children as "the new subjects of the social contract" (Crain 2016, 5). Thus Margery's citizenship and her threshold position in the print mass medium created from movable type are iconically refracted in the little wooden letters that she carries to her lessons. These emblematic props of her model citizenship are the spectacle and substratum of the print public sphere of which she was herself a product. Her alphabet remained a feature of the story well into the nineteenth century and accompanied her transformation into wider media and the fairy realm.

HER PASSAGE TO FAIRY TALE AND BEYOND

Despite its pronouncements against witches and fairies, *The History of Little Goody Two-Shoes* has not gone unremarked for its "'genuine fairy tale quality'" (Ronald Paulson, cited in Fergus 2006, 149). Aside from the potential to be equated with a Calvinist version of "Cinderella" (ATU 510A), for what Andrew O'Malley terms the "'coach and six' reward system" for moral virtue (2003, 22), Crain suggests that Margery's shoes and her letters evoke the marvelous (2016, 28). The letters are said to make up "all the Words in the

World" (*Goody Two-Shoes* 1981, 25), and Margery's way of "materializing of the letters, bringing them into the world of bread, turnips, and apple pies," enters the "fantastic" (Crain 2016, 28). Indeed, Margery's letters—along with her orphanhood, her two shoes, her teaching, her animal helpers, and some of her adventures—remained features of subsequent iterations of the story, which was quickly swept into the market for piracy and reproduction in the rising eighteenth- and nineteenth-century tides of children's entertainments (Crain 2016; O'Malley 2003, 27; Stone 1940, 16–17).

These editions exploited her liminal subjectivity anew: she appeared in picture books (ranging from juvenile travesties to Walter Crane's splendid editions) and alphabet tutors for young children, and in games, spelling books, verse novels, and plays for older ones. "Old Goody Two Shoes" was co-opted as a Mother Goose–type storyteller in fairy-tale anthologies. She is depicted multifariously as a child, preteen, and old woman. Her death disappeared as a story element while her marriage became a culminating highlight. Her literacy and goodness remained hallmarks, although Fergus observes that "to identify Newbery's character with a simple, earnest virtue is possible only by reading nineteenth-century redactions, not the 1765 original" (2006, 139).

For Crain, this passage represents degradation and loss of the character, as "the nineteenth century redactions . . . repudiated" Goody Two-Shoes and she was "treated as a fairy tale" (2016, 42). She refers to this phase as her "afterlife" in which she became a "meme" and a "brand" who was "evacuated of her political and narrative complexity" and "of her girl and child power" (38–40). Indeed, the polemics and politics all but disappeared. But the story was also ensnared in the eighteenth-century "quarrel" over fairy stories and the effects on children of "supernatural events" and "imaginary beings" that consumed this era of early children's literature (Darton 1966, 99, 97). By Victorian times, fairies and fairy tales had resurged in British popular culture as folk traditions "flooded back and swamped" the Puritan theology (Briggs 2002, 66). Goody Two-Shoes is right there among them, prospering through the transition, although much adapted from her first didactic editions.

By the 1830s, "Goody Two-Shoes" was no longer an alias but an exclusive persona who stepped out as a romantic heroine in the Victorian repertoire of what Jennifer Schacker terms "fairy-tale pantomimes" (2018). Within this carnivalesque theater with its marvelous dramaturgy of transformation, Margery's child-self was banished. She became an adolescent icon of sweet femininity whose love life eclipsed her alphabet, and who was wildly paired with nursery-tale lovers in breeches parts, like Little Boy Blue in *Little Goody Two-Shoes; or, Harlequin and Cock Robin* (Blanchard 1862). In a climactic dream sequence, she transformed into a fairy and was enthroned as the Queen of the May. Reprised as a "children's pantomime," a form devised with an all-child cast to limit risqué content (Varty 2008), it became *Little Goody Two Shoes; or, Harlequin a Little Boy Blue* (Blanchard 1876).[5] Elsewhere, Goody Two-Shoes was matched with Tom the Piper's Son and appeared among the immortals, performing her eldership in the Victorian fairy-tale pantomime pantheon.

Goody Two-Shoes pantomimes continued well into the twentieth century in increasingly vaudeville modes, and they remain a parodic staple of British panto theater.[6] But the Victorian spectacle remains its high point, which harbored, unlike the less ordered repressions of the Puritan moral tract, the moral extremities and "underlying Manichaeism" that Peter Brooks aligns with the nineteenth-century "melodramatic imagination," an aesthetic, he argues, that connected the spectator with "the conflict of good and evil played out under the surface of things" (1976, 4). Somewhere in the pantomime's moral occult, with its dark scenes and glittering transformations, Margery was severed permanently from her book-character persona. By the end of the nineteenth century, Goody Two-Shoes had been spectrally reconstituted into vernacular English as an idiomatic "catchphrase," a phase of her afterlife that Crain terms the novel's "residue" (2016, 19).

While its precise history is "difficult to trace," Crain suggests it "probably evolved from pantomimes and sentimental versions of the novel" into "an oddly vital element of popular speech" (2006, 233). *The American Heritage Dictionary of Idioms* defines "goody two-shoes" as a "prudish, self-righteous individual, a goody-goody" (Credo Reference 2022), while an internet source that attributes its origin to Newbery's book defines it as someone "who is virtuous in a coy, smug or sentimental manner" (The Phrase Finder n.d.). A "negative expression," according to one online language tutor, it covers a "person who wants everyone to think that he or she is a good person," "someone who merely acts like a good person," or "someone who actually is a good person but who makes others feel inadequate in comparison" (Writing Explained 2022).

This idiom is ubiquitous today in Web forums. Discussion on Quora.com over several years since 2017 has grappled with the pros and cons of people who are "goody two shoes," and generated a range of gender-inclusive descriptions: "over achieve[r]," "perfect angel," "fake," "never authentic," "showing fake modesty," "too nice," "superior," "too good to be true," and so on (Quora, Inc. 2022). While some contributors see a "goody two-shoes" as exclusively "negative," others defend them as "not bad people" or "hated" (Quora, Inc. 2022). This forum is among results Google searches returned on "Goody Two-Shoes," of which the most consistent is the 1980s pop hit by New Romantic musician Adam Ant. There, "Goody Two-Shoes" is a lyric that parodies the (hetero)sexual stresses of a (male) rock star's press-hounded life. Margery, the fantastic rattle-traps, and the driven little girl with joyous pleasure in her "two shoes" are far away.

HER RESIDUE: THE PERSONA OF A MORAL BAROMETER

"Whether you fell in love with her as the straight-talking, *goody-two-shoes* Hermione in Harry Potter or as the woman-saviour she became during her infamous epic HeForShe UN speech, you're likely familiar with her empowering way with words" (Osmanski 2020; my emphasis). The object of this ambivalent praise, Emma Watson, child star, Hollywood celebrity, and feminist activist, was appointed in 2014 as a UN Goodwill Ambassador to the HeForShe campaign for gender equality (heforshe.org) (UNWomen n.d.). Her public persona has been haunted for years by the fictional child Hermione whom she played in the *Harry Potter* films, who, in turn, is ineffably remembered as the "goody two-shoes of Hogwarts" (Johnson 2008). Stephanie Osmanski's barbed tribute in *Parade* on Watson's thirtieth birthday assigns virtue to the fictional Hermione while deeming the actor's first performance for the UN "infamous" (2020). I shall return to Watson and the reception of her activism, but celebrity comparisons with Goody Two-Shoes are in no way unique to her (or Her/mione).

Twenty-first-century Web celebrity gossip abounds with examples, usually (but not exclusively) pertaining to women stars. Mostly it chastises putative dissonances in their public personas, but sometimes it affirms their disciplined, "square," or unglamorous private lifestyles, such as Nicki Swift's praise for Taylor Swift because she "bakes," and her "goody-two-shoes image" is "carefully-crafted and all over her Instagram feed" but "also feels insanely genuine" (2017). Self-use of "goody two-shoes" by celebrities is also common: Keira Knightley says of her schooldays, "I didn't get into any trouble ... I was absolutely a goody two-shoes" (Brimson 2014), while Natalie Portman is noted as having "cultivated" a "straightforward" image while a young actor and a Harvard undergraduate by "often describing herself as a 'goody two-shoes'" (Daly 2005). When *Cosmopolitan* disclosed that she had "smoked weed," it noted the consequent loss of her "'goody two-shoes images' [*sic*]" (Cosmo Gossip 2011).

Elsewhere, celebrity "goody two-shoes" are simply not what they seem. A feature in *The Richest* titled "20 Goody Two-Shoes Celebrities Who Are Actually Very Different" lists ten men and ten women, all major American screen and music stars, who are alleged to be "enormous hypocrites." These people's offenses are that they *are not* "goody two-shoes" either because, like Bill Cosby, who heads the list, they have been convicted of criminal offences,[7] or their public personas are deemed dissonant with their activist stances or expressed principles. These range from Gwyneth Paltrow's promotion of shoddy health products (no. 3) to Madonna's alleged misleading of the Malawian father of two children she adopted (no. 12) to Leonardo DiCaprio's (no. 18) commendable environmental activism that is contradicted by his alleged taste for "private jets and mega yachts." Multiple (female) stars are cited for alleged hypocritical views about industry sexual offenders (Rose McGowan, Kate Winslet, and Demi Lovato) (Elizabeth 2018).[8]

Going way back, Watson is the most persistent inheritor of the Goody Two-Shoes residue and its child/woman liminality due to journalism's pattern of attention to the actor's age (her birthday is reported every year) and the character of Hermione. Photographed alongside "bad girls" Dita Von Teese, Lily Allen, and Katy Perry at Paris Fashion week in 2008, "the goody two-shoes of Hogwarts, her alter ego Hermione Granger, would probably frown at the mere thought of associating with such troubled company" (Johnson 2008). On her twenty-fourth birthday, Fraser McAlpine reflected that Watson "spent the years since Harry Potter ... putting as much clear water between herself and her goody-goody image as Hermione Granger as is humanly possible (while also studying for her degree, just like Hermione would)" (2014). On her twenty-fifth, without directly mentioning Goody Two-Shoes, Meghan O'Keefe noted that "Hermione Granger is a quarter-century old" while asking, referring to Watson's breakout role in *The Perks of Being a Wallflower* (2012) whether she "can ... be taken seriously as a 'bad girl'?" (2015).

Osmanski's tribute to Watson on her thirtieth birthday differs in the attention to her inaugural speech to the UN, which is compared unfavorably to "straight-talking goody-two-shoes Hermione" (2020). Watson's UN profile (which describes her as an "actor" and university graduate) notes that, at the time of her appointment at "just 24 [sic]," Watson had a record of humanitarian activism for fair trade, organic clothing, and promoting girls' education in Africa (UNWomen n.d.). This public feminism converged oddly with Watson's starring role in Disney's *Beauty and the Beast* (2017), for which she herself cultivated the narrative of her "coming of age" (at twenty-seven) from "childhood playing Hermione to entering womanhood as Belle" (Blasberg 2017). In publicity for the film she described Belle as her childhood "role model" and claimed to portray the character as an "activist in her own community" (Huver 2017). In one sense it was typical of her persona, as Laura Mattoon D'Amore cites Watson as exemplary of "celebrities" who use their "influential platforms for a social-equality-based feminism," whose "feminist rhetoric" is "deeply intertwined with their relationship to the personal" (2017, 389). Watson, she argues, also appeals to "younger generations" because she "invites men to the table" (389–90) and the HeForShe campaign strives for a "level playing field with men" (390).

The ambivalences toward her public feminism and her career coming of age, and the oscillations of her reputational debt to Hermione/Goody Two-Shoes all coalesced in a 2017 *Vanity Fair* article, "Rebel Belle," that promoted the release of *Beauty and the Beast* (Blasberg 2017). Derek Blasberg questions the actor's feminist mentor Gloria Steinem about Watson's activism, asking if "there's a risk of becoming, well, annoying to the general public. Is she too much of an ethical Goody Two-Shoes?" Steinem, who either did not get the Hermione allusion or ignored it, replies: "Let me ask you something: If you did a story on a young male actor who was very private and involved in activism, would you think he was too severe or serious? . . . It's possible to be both serious and fun, you know" (quoted in Blasberg 2017). The article was soon followed by a Twitter campaign criticizing Watson for appearing "topless" in *Vanity Fair*, which was deemed hypocritical for a feminist (A. Brown 2017). Annie Brown, who reported this incident tongue-in-cheek as "news just in from 1965," reproduced Blasberg's exchange with Steinem about Goody Two-Shoes and observed that the critics' "outrage is a hiss at women who advocate for causes."

Tabloid concern about "seriousness" can hardly be taken seriously or regarded as a reliable monitor of public importance or activist worth. The unedifying extension of this tabloid discourse in, as it were, more serious journalism bespeaks not only the fragility of Watson's efforts to reconcile her screen persona with social commitment but also the terminal paradoxes of children's imaginary citizenship. Watson's persona is haunted by the hyperreal residues of Hermione, Goody Two-Shoes, and the nagging hegemony of fictional measures of moral goodness that they both represent. Meanwhile, the chastising gossipy press—a miscellany as didactic as the excesses of any eighteenth-century children's book—which obsesses over Watson's age and ambivalently chips at her authority as public figure, demonstrates its own child/adult liminality by identifying with the child audience for *Harry Potter* films, for which Hermione remains an imaginary peer. It offers a perverse and inverse index of the social discomfiture generated when real children—teenagers, at least—command authority as global activists.

DARING: GRETA, MALALA, AND WHO'S NOT (AGEIST ABOUT) GOODY TWO-SHOES

The collective force of child, teen, and young-adult activism for climate change and education rights has resulted in unprecedented twenty-first-century global movements. Their youthful figureheads, Greta Thunberg and Malala Yousafzai, are seen as "girl heroes of social activism" (Bergmann and Ossewaarde 2020). A significant amount of commentary and academic research has been generated regarding both, although direct comparisons are fairly rare. Thunberg has attracted more quantitative analysis of the so-called "Greta effect" on attitudes to climate change (Jung et al. 2020; Sabherwal et al. 2021). Furthermore, Yousafzai came to prominence in Pakistan nearly ten years before Thunberg and within a different sphere of activism, and, aged eleven, was much younger at this point in her public life.

Yet Zoe Bergmann and Ringo Ossewaarde, while observing that research on ageism overrepresents the effect on older populations, highlight how both Thunberg and Yousafzai are affected by "juvenile ageism" in media coverage (2020, 269), and not simply because so much coverage relates to their perceived childhood or youth.[9] I suggest that the way Goody Two-Shoes hovers around them in English-language commentary, and the fact that both

Thunberg and Yousafzai have established their respective personas with reference to fairy tale and folktale, are aspects of this juvenile ageism.

In turning first to the residue of Margery, the allusions are not uniformly defensive or offensive. Rather, where commentary is favorable toward either Thunberg or Yousafzai, Goody Two-Shoes is referenced offensively regarding contenders who do not meet the heroines' benchmarks. James Plested on the Socialist Alternative website (*Red Flag*) praises Thunberg's "wonderful, intransigent attitude" and reserves the critical "goody two-shoes" slur for inferior local contenders: "All we [Australians] . . . have is . . . high-achieving goody two-shoes whose desire to actually change society in any radical way . . . weigh[s] little against their personal ambition to join . . . the 'influencer' class" (2021). Similarly, Jake Wilson's comments about Yousafzai refer favorably to her portrayal in the documentary *He Named Me Malala* (2015): "an extremely likeable young woman . . . in short, anything but a goody-two-shoes figurehead" (2015). Negative connotations of "Goody Two-Shoes" are sometimes directed toward Thunberg, who is generally more ambivalently regarded than Yousafzai, and more prone to ageist criticism.

Thunberg is "arguably the most popular climate activist of our time" (Sabherwal et al. 2021, 330). She was fifteen when she gained prominence in 2018 by demonstrating in front of the Swedish parliament. The worldwide school strike that followed in more than 120 countries involved an estimated 1.6 million children (Jung et al. 2020). The risks of environmental activism on any front are well known and, as Bergmann and Ossewaarde point out, activists are vulnerable because they target a "patriarchal regime that enacts vested interests and climate skepticism" (2020, 270). Based on their critical discourse analysis of German news media, they claim that "ageist" coverage of Thunberg extends to the FridaysForFuture movement to reinforce the "hegemony" of the "established environmental governance regime" and to "delegitimize" the "youth climate movement" (270).

The highlights of Thunberg's ascendancy have been her potent speeches about political inaction on climate change at global forums and her censures of world leaders, notably her impassioned "How dare you" to the UN. The international media coverage of the strike and the speech led to Thunberg becoming "a leader and a target at the same time" (Jung et al. 2020, 1). Researchers have noted the contrariness of the responses to an "inspirational youth figure" who receives "fierce criticism and ad hominem attacks" (Sabherwal et al. 2021, 322), from being named *Time*'s Person of the Year in 2019 (Alter et al. 2019) to advice from her arch critic Donald Trump to work on "'her anger management problem'" (quoted in Luscombe 2020). Thunberg and her family have been attacked by "conservative commentators, far-right politicians and 'online haters'" and conspiracy theorists (Urban, Pehoski, and Stroud 2020, 3), and conservative politicians have identified her as a victim of the misuse of children in politics (Collett 2019). She has consistently subverted such rancor, adopting Trump's patronizing ridicule in her Twitter biography,[10] and responding to vilification that she is "disturbed" (Andrew Bolt, quoted in Collett 2019) by proclaiming Asperger's syndrome as her "superpower."

While Thunberg's rhetoric is characterized by factuality and embrace of "science" (Alter et al. 2019), the superhero self-characterization is not an isolated allusion to wonder in her public discourse. While criticizing governments for telling "fairy tales" about climate, Thunberg mobilized nursery tale in her rhetoric at Davos and the UN by figuring the planetary home—"Our house is on fire"—with seeming allusion to the nursery rhyme "Ladybird, Ladybird." This stirring phrase also titles Thunberg's coauthored book (with her family), *Our House Is on Fire* (Thunberg et al. 2020).[11] Wonder emerges from commentary as well, whether favorable or critical, such as Robinson Meyer's description of Thunberg's "Pippi Longstocking braids" (2019). Goody Two-Shoes materializes in a parodic opinion piece that invokes Thunberg's response to a fictional question: "Greta, why so angry?" Thunberg's imagined reply conjures the age barrier between the activist and her critic: "Because . . . we are the generation that watches . . . the Kardashians, not The Oprah Show. . . . Action comes from influence. And influence does not come from being Miss Goody Two-Shoes" (Nag 2020). The imaginary encounter ends with "Greta" disappearing like magic.

"Thunberg is 16 but looks 12" (Alter et al. 2019). From the *Time* profile (which also refers to her "braids") to all variety of global media flotsam, the coverage views Thunberg's discourse of wonder through the lens of juvenile ageism and positions her as a liminal figure. Debapriya Nag's fantasy opinion piece situates Thunberg outlandishly as a "generation[al]" product of media consumption, while Meyer's essay, "Why Greta Makes Adults Uncomfortable" ("Especially in private, she sounds . . . like . . . a teenager"), fixates paternalistically on her youth. Meyer draws attention to Thunberg's dress style and her anxieties about being (in her own words) "the center of attention" while attributing her "influence" to her "extreme teenager-ness," and observing that she "often" refers to herself in speeches as a "child" (2019). Patriarchally speaking, it is not unusual for female authority figures to be trivialized through attention to their bodies, although Meyer's ageism inflects Thunberg's criticism of climate "'fairy tales'" as the province of a child's perspective on adult governments.

Whereas Thunberg is criticized for being young or a child, Yousafzai has been praised for being "mature beyond her years" (Hesford 2013, 412). In further contrast to Thunberg, Phyllis Ryder argues, coverage of Yousafzai in the United States and Europe is "unabashedly doting" (2015, 175). While her activism is for girls in the Global South, Yousafzai is seen as "an exceptional role model for girls in the west" (Hesford 2013, 412). Wendy Hesford attributes this predominantly favorable Western media coverage to Yousafzai's "appealing" subjectivity within the "imaginary" of "Liberal internationalism" (407). It "eagerly adopts certain narratives," she argues, including "the individual defender of children's rights and the exceptional child with ordinary needs narrative" (409). Nevertheless, Ryder detects criticism of the "white saviour" narrative (the saving of a "native girl" by white men) in some Western media coverage, a view that more accords with ambivalent reception in Pakistan (2015, 178). Habib Qazi and Saeeda Shah, in their critical discourse analysis of Pakistani English-language news, found that editorials and readers' responses ranged from proclaiming Yousafzai a "'courageous' girl" to calling her a "drama queen," the "daughter of a good PR manager," and a "west groomed Pakistani daughter" who is "'silent on Kashmir and Palestine'" (2018, 1606).

In navigating the tensions in the Western and Pakistani perspectives, Ryder supports Omid Sati's view of Yousafzai's indomitable agency, arguing that "even as Malala relies on Western media to circulate her message, she persistently disrupts its dominant messages" (2015, 176). Ryder invokes Antonio Gramsci and Gayatri Spivak, who "remind us to focus on the potential agency of subaltern voices," and she recognizes "the many layers of cultural hegemony that get in the way" (184). Indeed, as voices of the subaltern child, both Yousafzai and Thunberg are divided from their diverse publics by layers of culture, language, media platforms, and cultural discourses of wonder as well as childhood.

Yousafzai became a transnational public figure in 2009 when she began an anonymous blog for BBC Urdu following the takeover by the Taliban of her home in the Swat Valley, Pakistan (Yousafzai and Lamb 2014; Qazi and Shah 2018, 1598). She had been publicly active for girls' education since 2008 when, aged eleven, she gave a speech in Peshawar entitled: "'How Dare the Taliban Take Away My Basic Right to Education?'" (quoted in Kids Rights 2022). The Taliban death threat was issued thereafter, and Hesford says she became a target because she was a "symbol of western culture" and her advocacy for education was deemed "obscenity" (2013, 410). Yousafzai survived an assassination attempt to found her Malala Fund (Malala.org) and become the youngest Nobel Laureate, sharing the Peace prize in 2014, and receiving several humanitarian awards.[12] Subsequently, she published an autobiography, *I Am Malala: The Girl Who Stood Up for Education and Was Shot by the Taliban* (Yousafzai and Lamb 2014), cowritten by the British journalist Christina Lamb, who also cowrote the documentary *He Named Me Malala* (2015). Yousafzai was seventeen at the time of the book's publication.[13]

Folk heroes and child legends coalesce in Yousafzai's recollection of the formation of her public persona in a way that both nationalizes and Westernizes her heroism and her imaginary citizenship. Malala's given name commemorates an Afghan teenage woman hero, Malalai of Maiwand, a Pashtun "Joan of Arc," who died resisting the British occupation (Yousafzai and Lamb 2014, 10). As a blogger, Yousafzai was known as "Gul Makai," a Pashtun folk heroine (130). Gul Makai's story is about forbidden lovers whose attraction causes a tribal war. The war ends, not with the deaths of the lovers, but with Gul Makai persuading her elders to end the war so the lovers can unite. The implication, as Ryder explains, is that the girl's knowledge of the Quran enables her to persuade her elders to change (2015, 182). Yousafzai likens the story to William Shakespeare's *Romeo and Juliet* but without the tragic ending (Yousafzai and Lamb 2014, 130).

The name Gul Makai was provided by the BBC Urdu journalist Abdul Hai Kakar, who recruited Yousafzai to write a diary of her life under the Taliban, and who "told me about Anne Frank" and her diary (Yousafzai and Lamb 2014, 129). Yousafzai did not write her diary herself, though; she spoke by phone with Hai Kakar, who wrote her words for the website, and recordings by the BBC used "another girl's voice" (130). Thus, like the legends that subtend this persona, the girl hero entered the global commons speaking anonymously for anyone and everyone denied an education. But the guise of anonymity did not keep her or her imaginary constituency of girl citizens safe; after her first daring speech she was targeted by assassins.

Unlike Thunberg's "How dare you" to the UN, the threat deemed to be posed by Yousafzai was not mitigated by her age or the juvenile ageism of an adult forum. Thunberg's imagined age and lack of legal citizenship defuse the threat she poses—beyond the risk of elder outrage—as long as the perception of her childhood is maintained and despite the imaginary citizenry that mobilizes around her. Comparison between Thunberg and Yousafzai shows at the very least how—like the public good—the boundaries of childhood are mutable, and culturally and contextually determined. It shows, too, how in the West, what Weikle-Mills refers to as the "boundaries of childhood" in debates about (American) citizenship (2012, 11) represent a fixation with the age of the child while their repertoire of folktales, fairy tales, and nursery tales contribute to their identities as children regardless of their chronological ages. Unlike the case of Watson, their sparse encounters with Goody Two-Shoes contain their liminality and affirm their girlhood, even though, chronologically, it is in the past. Goody Two-Shoes is a girl again but—alas for Margery—not the girl hero.

THE FAIRY-TALE PUBLIC SPHERE

Goody Two-Shoes is not alone among fairy-tale characters in representing the cultural production of childhood, with its undulating rhetorics of the child as moral subject and its repression of the child as political agent. Margery, the forgotten identity in the persona of Goody Two-Shoes, is feisty, forthright, and esteemed for her pedagogy and moral fortitude—and spoken for by an anonymous narrator. Her idiomatic residue (however despondently Crain [2016, 42] derives this characterization from Margery's nineteenth-century fairy-tale otherness) lives on as an arbitrary and peripatetic measure of the fictionality of virtue in the hysterical didactics of celebrity journalism, where moral goodness is a burden, not a virtue or any reward of its own. Meanwhile, for the imaginary citizens who are followers of Thunberg and Yousafzai, childhood is the frustrating limit of enfranchisement that makes their daring merely a dream of what might be different if children could vote in elections. It is what the world would allow if Margery, Ralph, and Jumper were to have a say.

NOTES

1. The author is unknown but was possibly Newbery himself (see Iskander 1988; Crain 2006; Fergus 2006).

2. Weikle-Mills's idea of imaginary citizenship is derived from wider debates about literary citizenship and formulated in her account of these issues in the context of the early American republic and the alignment of American citizens "with children" and the nation "imagined as a child" (2012, 2). Weikle-Mills and others utilize some British works, despite the differences of contexts and the colonial relationship of Britain to early America.

3. Alternatively, Jonathan Todres argues that "from a children's rights perspective, agency and the need for protection are not mutually exclusive," referring to the UN Convention on the Rights of the Child, which "reflects both ideas, emphasizing the essential role that parents and families play in the lives of children and establishing that children have a distinct right to be heard" (2020, 28; see also 27–31).

4. Todres also notes children's participation in the US civil rights movement and the South African anti-apartheid movement (2020, 32).

5. For more on children's pantomimes, see Anne Varty (2008), who notes the prominent child stars in this show: Connie Gilchrist as Goody Two-Shoes and Harry Grattan as Boy Blue.

6. See, for instance, *Goody Two Shoes: A Pantomime* (Hills 1995) and *Goody Two Shoes* (Reakes 2007).

7. Cosby's conviction and long prison sentence for sexual assault were later overturned on appeal.

8. In May 2021, Lovato came out as nonbinary (see Lovato 2021).

9. They follow Jack C. Westman's (1991) categories of juvenile ageism in their analysis of German news media, including (and I condense): "being ignored," "segregation of children in public spaces and media," "denigration of parenting," children treated as "adults," and systems of child care that do not service child interests (Bergmann and Ossewaarde 2020, 269).

10. "'A very happy young girl looking forward to a bright and wonderful future'" (quoted in Urban, Pehoski, and Stroud 2020, 3).

11. Although the content of the book does not suggest the authors' consciousness of this connotation, or contain any reference to the nursery rhyme.

12. The Nobel Prize was shared with Kailish Satyarthi, an advocate against child labor and slavery (Nobel Prize Outreach 2022).

13. A "Young Readers Edition" coauthored with Patricia McCormick is differently titled: *I Am Malala: How One Girl Stood Up for Education and Changed the World* (Yousafzai and McCormick 2015). Todres notes further retellings "in a number of

children's books" and suggests the versions coauthored with Lamb and McCormick target adult and child readerships respectively (2020, 32–33).

REFERENCES

Alter, Charlotte, Suyin Haynes, Justin Worland, and Evgenia Arbugaeva. 2019. "*Time* 2019 Person of the Year: Greta Thunberg." *Time.* Accessed July 19, 2022. https://time.com/person-of-the-year-2019-greta-thunberg/.

Bacchilega, Cristina, and Jennifer Orme. 2021. "Introduction." In *Inviting Interruptions: Wonder Tales in the Twenty-First Century*, edited by Cristina Bacchilega and Jennifer Orme, ix–xxv. Detroit: Wayne State University Press.

Beauty and the Beast. 2017. Directed by Bill Condon. USA: Walt Disney Pictures/Mandeville Films.

Bergmann, Zoe, and Ringo Ossewaarde. 2020. "Youth Climate Activists Meet Environmental Governance: Ageist Depictions of the FFF Movement and Greta Thunberg in German Newspaper Coverage." *Journal of Multicultural Discourses* 15 (3): 267–90. https://doi.10.1080/17447143.2020.1745211.

Blanchard, E. L. 1862. *Little Goody Two-Shoes; or, Harlequin and Cock Robin.* London: Music-Publishing.

Blanchard, E. L. 1876. *Little Goody Two Shoes; or, Harlequin a Little Boy Blue.* Manuscript, British Library, London. (Pantomime first performed at the Adelphi Theatre, London).

Blasberg, Derek. 2017. "Emma Watson, Rebel Belle." *Vanity Fair*, February 28. https://www.vanityfair.com/hollywood/2017/02/emma-watson-cover-story.

Briggs, Katharine. 2002. *The Fairies in Tradition and Literature.* London: Routledge.

Brimson, Hannah. 2014. "Keira Knightley Reckons She Was a Boring Child and a Goody Two-Shoes." *Heatworld*, October 22. https://heatworld.com/celebrity/news/keira-knightley-reckons-boring-child-goody-two-shoes/.

Brooks, Peter. 1976. *The Melodramatic Imagination.* New Haven, CT: Yale University Press.

Brown, Annie. 2017. "Emma Watson Called a 'Hypocrite' for 'Topless' Photo in *Vanity Fair.*" *Sydney Morning Herald*, March 2. https://www.smh.com.au/entertainment/celebrity/emma-watson-called-a-hypocrite-for-topless-photo-in-vanity-fair-20170302-guoskt.html.

Brown, Gillian. 2001. *The Consent of the Governed: The Lockean Legacy in Early American Culture.* Cambridge, MA: Harvard University Press.

Brown, Gillian. 2006. "The Metamorphic Book: Children's Print Culture in the Eighteenth Century." *Eighteenth-Century Studies* 39 (3): 351–62.

Collett, Michael. 2019. "Greta Thunberg, the Teen behind Climate Strikes, Hits Back at Andrew Bolt Column." *ABC News*, August 2. https://www.abc.net.au/news/2019-08-02/thunberg-hits-back-after-being-called-deeply-disturbed/11376724.

Cosmo Gossip. 2011. "Natalie Portman: 'I Smoked Weed.'" *Cosmopolitan*, April 8. https://www.cosmopolitan.com/uk/entertainment/news/a111710/natalie-portman-i-smoked-weed-3/.
Crain, Patricia. 2006. "Spectral Literacy: The Case of Goody Two-Shoes." In *Childhood and Children's Books in Early Modern Europe 1550–1800*, edited by Andrea Immel and Michael Witmore, 213–42. London: Routledge.
Crain, Patricia 2016. *Reading Children: Literacy, Property, and the Dilemmas of Childhood in Nineteenth Century America*. Philadelphia: University of Pennsylvania Press.
Credo Reference. 2022. "goody two-shoes: from *The American Heritage Dictionary of Idioms*." Accessed January 10, 2022. https://search-credoreference-com.elibrary.jcu.edu.au/content/entry/hmidiom/goody_two_shoes/0.
Daly, Steven. 2005. "This Portman Life." *The Age*, January 9. https://www.theage.com.au/entertainment/movies/this-portman-life-20050109-gdzb09.html.
D'Amore, Laura Mattoon. 2017. "Vigilante Feminism: Revising Trauma, Abduction, and Assault in American Fairy-Tale Revisions." *Marvels & Tales* 31 (2): 386–405.
Darton, F. J. Harvey. 1966. *Children's Books in England: Five Centuries of Social Life*. Cambridge: Cambridge University Press.
Elizabeth, Hilary. 2018. "20 Goody Two-Shoes Celebrities Who Are Actually Very Different." *The Richest*, March 23. https://www.therichest.com/lifestyles/20-goody-two-shoes-celebrities-who-are-actually-very-different/.
Fergus, Jan. 2006. *Provincial Readers in Eighteenth-Century England*. Oxford: Oxford University Press.
Goody Two-Shoes: A Facsimile Reproduction of the Edition of 1766 with an Introduction by Charles Welsh. (1881) 1981. Tokyo: Holp Shuppan.
Grenby, M. O. 2013. *Little Goody Two-Shoes and Other Stories: Originally Published by John Newbery*. Basingstoke, UK: Palgrave Macmillan.
Hartley, John. 2002. *Communication, Cultural and Media Studies: The Key Concepts*. 3rd ed. London: Routledge.
He Named Me Malala. 2015. Directed by Davis Guggenheim. United States/UAE: Imagenation/Participant Media.
Hesford, Wendy S. 2013. "Introduction: Facing Malala Yousafzai, Facing Ourselves." *JAC: Journal of Advanced Composition* 33 (3–4): 407–23. http://www.jstor.org/stable/43854561.
Hills, Richard. 1995. *Goody Two Shoes: A Pantomime*. Northampton, UK: Jasper.
Huver, Scott. 2017. "Emma Watson Says *Beauty and the Beast*'s Belle Was Her Role Model." *CBR.com*, March 15. https://www.cbr.com/emma-watson-beauty-and-the-beast-belle/.
Iskander, S. P. 1988. "'Goody Two-Shoes' and *The Vicar of Wakefield*." *Children's Literature Association Quarterly* 13 (4): 165–68.
Johnson, Chris. 2008. "What Would Goody Two Shoes Hermione Say? Emma Watson Hangs with Bad Girls at Paris Fashion Week." *Daily Mail Online*, Septem-

ber 30. https://www.dailymail.co.uk/tvshowbiz/article-1064540/What-goody-shoes-Hermione-say-Emma-Watson-hangs-bad-girls-Paris-Fashion-Week.html.

Johnston, Jane. 2019. "Whose Interests? Why Defining the 'Public Interest' Is Such a Challenge." *The Conversation*, January 23. http://theconversation.com/whose-interests-why-defining-the-public-interest-is-such-a-challenge-84278.

Jung, Jieun, Peter Petkanic, Dongyan Nan, and Jang Hyun Kim. 2020. "When a Girl Awakened the World: A User and Social Message Analysis of Greta Thunberg." *Sustainability* 12 (7): 2707. https://doi.org/10.3390/su12072707.

Kertzer, Adrienne E. 1984. "Inventing the Child Reader: How We Read Children's Books." *Children's Literature in Education* 15 (1): 12–21.

Kids Rights. 2022. "2013—Malala Yousafzai (16), Pakistan." Accessed July 13, 2022. https://www.kidsrights.org/advocacy/international-childrens-peace-prize/winners/malala-yousafzai/.

Labrie, Vivian. 2018. "Activism: Folktales and Social Justice: When Marvelous Tales from the Oral Tradition Help Rethink and Stir the Present from the Margins." In *The Routledge Companion to Media and Fairy-Tale Cultures*, edited by Pauline Greenhill, Jill Terry Rudy, Naomi Hamer, and Lauren Bosc, 93–103. New York: Routledge.

Lovato, Demi. 2021. Twitter post, May 19. https://twitter.com/ddlovato/status/1394913215994155009.

Luscombe, Richard. 2020. "'Chill!' Greta Thunberg Recycles Trump's Mockery of Her as He Tries to Stop Votes." *Guardian*, November 6. https://www.theguardian.com/environment/2020/nov/05/greta-thunberg-donald-trump-twitter-chill.

McAlpine, Fraser. 2014. "Happy 24th Birthday Emma Watson: Five of Her Most Startling Roles." *BBC America*. Accessed January 10, 2022. https://www.bbcamerica.com/anglophenia/2014/04/happy-24th-birthday-emma-watson-five-startling-roles.

Meyer, Robinson. 2019. "Why Greta Makes Adults Uncomfortable." *Atlantic*, September 24. https://www.theatlantic.com/science/archive/2019/09/why-greta-wins/598612/.

Nag, Debapriya. 2020. "Engaging the New Gen; or, Who Says Millennials Are Entitled and Selfish?" *Business Connect India*, April 16. https://businessconnectindia.in/engaging-the-new-gen-or-who-says-millennials-are-entitled-and-selfish/.

Nobel Prize Outreach. 2022. "Kailish Satyarthi—Biographical." *The Nobel Prize*. Accessed July 13, 2022. https://www.nobelprize.org/prizes/peace/2014/satyarthi/facts/.

O'Keefe, Meghan. 2015. "Can Emma Watson Be Taken Seriously as a 'Bad Girl'?" *Decider*, April 15. https://decider.com/2015/04/15/emma-watson-forever-hermione/.

O'Malley, Andrew. 2003. *The Making of the Modern Child: Children's Literature and Childhood in the Late Eighteenth Century*. New York: Routledge.

Osmanski, Stephanie. 2020. "Emma Watson's 50 Most Empowering Quotes to Celebrate Her 30th Birthday." *Parade*, April 15. https://parade.com/1024971/stephanieosmanski/inspiring-emma-watson-quotes/.

Phillips, Louise Gwenneth, Jenny Ritchie, Lavina Dynevor, Jared Lambert, and Kerryn Moroney. 2019. *Young Children's Community Building in Action: Embodied, Emplaced and Relational Citizenship*. London: Routledge.

The Phrase Finder. n.d. "The Meaning and Origin of the Expression: Goody Two-Shoes." *Phrases*. Accessed November 11, 2020. www.phrases.org.uk/meanings/goody-two-shoes.html.

Plested, James. 2021. "Why Greta Thunberg Is Cooler Than You." *Red Flag*, October 5. https://redflag.org.au/article/why-greta-thunberg-cooler-you.

Qazi, Habib, and Saeeda Shah. 2018. "Identity Constructions through Media Discourses: Malala Yousafzai in Pakistani English Newspapers." *Journalism Studies* 19 (11): 1597–1612. https://www.tandfonline.com/doi/full/10.1080/1461670X.2017.1284574.

Quora, Inc. 2022. "Why Do People Hate So Called Goody Two Shoes and Know-It-Alls?" *Quora*. Accessed July 19, 2022. https://www.quora.com/Why-do-people-hate-so-called-goody-two-shoes-and-know-it-alls.

Reakes, Paul. 2007. *Goody Two Shoes*. New York: Samuel French.

Roche, Jeremy. 1999. "Children: Rights, Participation and Citizenship." *Childhood* 6 (4): 475–93.

Rojek, Chris. 2001. *Celebrity*. London: Reaktion.

Ryder, Phyllis Mentzell. 2015. "Beyond Critique: Global Activism and the Case of Malala Yousafzai." *Literacy in Composition Studies* 3 (1): 175–87. https://doi.org/10.21623/1.3.1.14.

Sabherwal, Anandita, Matthew T. Ballew, Sander van der Linden, Abel Gustafson, Matthew H. Goldberg, Edward W. Maibach, John E. Kotcher, Janet K. Swim, Seth A. Rosenthal, and Anthony Leiserowitz. 2021. "The Greta Thunberg Effect: Familiarity with Greta Thunberg Predicts Intentions to Engage in Climate Activism in the United States." *Journal of Applied Social Psychology* 51 (4): 321–33. https://doi.org/10.1111/jasp.12737.

Schacker, Jennifer. 2018. *Staging Fairyland: Folklore, Children's Entertainment, and Nineteenth-Century Pantomime*. Detroit: Wayne State University Press.

Selwyn, David. 2010. *Jane Austen and Children*. London: Bloomsbury.

Stone, Wilbur Macey. 1940. *The History of Little Goody Two-Shoes: An Essay and a List of Editions*. Worcester, MA: American Antiquarian Society.

Swift, Nicki. 2017. "Celebrities Who Are Total Squares." *Nicki Swift*, July 10. https://www.nickiswift.com/2953/celebs-youd-never-guess-total-squares/.

The Perks of Being a Wallflower. 2012. Directed by Stephen Chbosky. USA: Mr Mudd Productions.

Thunberg, Greta, Svante Thunberg, Malena Ernman, and Beata Ernman. 2020. *Our House Is on Fire: Scenes of a Family and a Planet in Crisis*. Translated by Paul Norlen and Saskia Vogel. London: Penguin Random House UK.

Todres, Jonathan. 2020. "Children's Right to Participate: Insights from the Story of Malala." In *Literary Cultures and Twenty-First-Century Childhoods*, edited by Nathalie op de Beeck, 25–40. Cham: Springer International.

Townshend, Dale. 2008. "The Haunted Nursery: 1764–1830." In *The Gothic in Children's Literature: Haunting the Borders*, edited by Anna Jackson, Karen Coats, and Roderick McGillis, 15–38. London: Routledge.

UNWomen. n.d. "UN Women Goodwill Ambassador Emma Watson." *UN Women*. Accessed 11 July 2022. https://www.unwomen.org/en/partnerships/goodwill-ambassadors/emma-watson.

Urban, Michaela, Justin Pehoski, and Scott R. Stroud. 2020. "Greta Thunberg and Her Harsh Critics." Austin: Center for Media Engagement, Moody College of Communication, University of Texas. https://mediaengagement.org/research/greta-thunberg-and-her-harsh-critics/.

Varty, Anne. 2008. *Children and the Theatre in Victorian Britain: "All Work and No Play."* Basingstoke, UK: Palgrave Macmillan.

Weikle-Mills, Courtney. 2008. "'Learn to Love Your Book': The Child Reader and Affectionate Citizenship." *Early American Literature* 43 (1): 35–61.

Weikle-Mills, Courtney. 2012. *Imaginary Citizens: Child Readers and the Limits of American Independence*. Baltimore, MD: Johns Hopkins University Press.

Westman, Jack C. 1991. "Juvenile Ageism: Unrecognized Prejudice and Discrimination against the Young." *Child Psychiatry Human Development* 21 (4): 237–56.

Wilson, Jake. 2015. "Review: *He Named Me Malala* Shows Campaigner for Female Education as a Remarkable Individual." *Sydney Morning Herald*, November 14. https://www.smh.com.au/entertainment/movies/review-he-named-me-malala-shows-campaigner-for-female-education-as-a-remarkable-individual-20151111-gkvglt.html.

Writing Explained. 2022. "What Does Goody Two-Shoes Mean?" *Writing Explained*. Accessed 11 July 2022. https://writingexplained.org/idiom-dictionary/goody-two-shoes#:~:text=Goody%20Two%20Shoes%20Meaning&text=This%20expression%20can%20be%20used,others%20feel%20inadequate%20in%20comparison.

Wyness, Michael G. 2000. *Contesting Childhood*. London: Falmer.

Yousafzai, Malala, with Christina Lamb. 2014. *I Am Malala: The Girl Who Stood Up for Education and Was Shot by the Taliban*. London: Weidenfeld & Nicholson.

Yousafzai, Malala, with Patricia McCormick. 2015. *I Am Malala: How One Girl Stood Up for Education and Changed the World*. New York: Hachette Children's Books.

12

The Horror of Crime

Representing (In)Justice in Canadian Indigenous Crime Films

STEVEN KOHM

CRIME AS HORROR OR THE HORROR OF CRIME?

The wondrous, the magical, the monstrous, and the ghostly are worlds seldom explored by criminology. Yet scholars across the social sciences and humanities have embraced a turn toward the metaphysical and spectral for several years now. For example, analyses have employed haunting and ghosts to explore cultural memory and the impact of past traumas and injustices on current social realities (Dziuban 2019). Avery F. Gordon (2020) asserts that "haunting is one way in which abusive systems of power make themselves known and their impacts felt in everyday life, especially when they are supposedly over and done with" (para. 10). Trauma and memory are central features of the experience of crime and (in)justice, and criminology could likewise benefit from taking up the interrelated concepts of monstrosity, haunting, and horror in its analyses. In particular, there is no more traumatic issue of injustice than the "crime of all crimes," genocide (Rafter 2016), experienced in Canada by Indigenous peoples as an ongoing feature of colonialism.

https://doi.org/10.7330/9781646425853.c012

Yet, most criminologists have been reluctant to interrogate genocide as a crime, and in general, Canada has largely remained in what criminologist Stanley Cohen would describe as a state of denial about its genocidal foundations (2001). Nevertheless, cultural criminology appears well positioned to seriously take up these issues, given its long-standing and serious engagement with culture and the emotional entanglements of crime and victimization (Ferrell 1992, 2004; Kohm 2009). Cultural criminology might take a cue from literary scholars who have critically interrogated Canada's colonial history using "gothic metaphors of monstrosity and haunting" (Turcotte and Sugars 2009, xvii). However, criminology is only now beginning to take up the spectral and the monstrous in its analyses of the intersections of crime, culture, and justice, as well as related issues of trauma, colonization, and cultural memory.

I begin by considering the ghostly and the monstrous in recent criminological work and what these concepts might reveal about the origins of crime and the responses of the state and individuals to acts of injustice, including cultural genocide and colonialism. This emerging cultural criminological scholarship offers help in establishing a theoretical and methodological schema for those who want to use these concepts in analyses interrogating crime and injustice that cut across history and generations. However, nearly all cultural criminological work positions the ghost or monster as a broad metaphor for social, political, and economic arrangements in society and/or the operation of the criminal justice system itself—in particular the police and the carceral apparatus. To date, there has been little interest within cultural criminology in examining horror film itself, or, more specifically, cinema that uses familiar horror tropes and motifs to critically interrogate the colonial violence and trauma upon which Canada was founded as a settler-colonial state.

I explore two Canadian horror films that deal directly or indirectly with postcolonial trauma for Indigenous peoples: *Clearcut* (1991) and *Blood Quantum* (2019). I argue that these films are productive in terms of generating and/or subverting popular myths or ideology (Rafter 2006) about Indigenous peoples, crime, and the Canadian state. Additionally, they offer potentially cathartic fantasies of retribution and revenge for historic and ongoing injustices.

In *Clearcut*, audiences wrestle with an ethical dilemma through the eyes of a white protagonist who initially calls for violent retributive justice in response to historic and ongoing acts of oppression of Indigenous peoples and the over-exploitation of the environment. However, the audience and the protagonist are later horrified to see this wish for vengeance granted by a malevolent Indigenous spirit of the forest. While mainly sympathetic to the struggles of Indigenous peoples, *Clearcut* lacks meaningful participation by Indigenous peoples behind the camera and appropriates Indigenous culture and experiences. The film is therefore framed by what Christopher Gittings calls "the white camera eye" (2002, 198). As Miléna Santoro puts it, "The cinematic gaze on Indigenous lives is clearly that of a non-native, at worst imbued with superiority and at best with ethnographic or ideological intentions" (2013, 267).

In contrast to *Clearcut*, more recent films make Indigenous peoples and their experiences central. *Blood Quantum*, directed and written by Indigenous filmmaker Jeff Barnaby (Mi'kmaq), provides counternarratives about crime and justice in Indigenous communities and offers critical political and cultural engagement with colonial trauma through the use of cinematic horror tropes, including ghosts, zombies, and the monstrous. Unlike in *Clearcut*, audiences see the ongoing intergenerational trauma of colonization through Indigenous eyes. I conclude by calling on cultural criminology and interdisciplinary scholars of justice to take horror film seriously as a cultural site that reflects and refracts the haunting traumas of the past, present, and future for Indigenous communities in Canada, while offering cultural vehicles for decolonization, resistance, and catharsis.

I am a non-Indigenous, settler scholar of mixed European ancestry, born and currently residing on traditional territories of the Anishinaabeg, Cree, Dakota, Dene, Métis, and Oji-Cree Nations in what is now Winnipeg, Canada. Although this land was taken from Indigenous peoples using the legal framework of a treaty with British colonizers in the late nineteenth century, those who reside here today are multiply haunted by the ghosts of a colonial project that continues to unfold. I write this chapter because I too am haunted by the colonial foundations of this nation and this city, which have brought me and my settler ancestors great benefit while displacing and erasing Indigenous people. This chapter is but a small reflection of my commitment to reconciliation and reckoning with colonialism, and it is my hope that the following analysis demonstrates the role that film and criminology can play in a process of decolonization.

HAUNTING CRIMINOLOGY

What place is there in criminology for the ghost or the monster? As Jock Young (2004) has colorfully argued, contemporary criminology adopts a detached and scientific approach to its subject that tends to drain the humanity away from the vivid and often visceral experience of crime, justice, and crime control. Adopting Young's playful style, perhaps criminology could itself be conceived metaphorically as a vampire or zombie—an academic field that sucks the lifeblood of human experience away and transforms crime and emotion into "unreadable and table-turgid" scientific prose (Ferrell, Hayward, and Young 2008, 161). For Young, criminology is a special type of monster, a hulking "datasaur" whose huge statistical gut devours and digests human experience (2011, 15). A tiny, underdeveloped theoretical brain and inconclusive tail round out the criminological beast. Yet, if the ascendance of true crime as entertainment is any indication, many people appear to be fascinated—some say obsessed—with the traumatic, the visceral, and the emotive and affective dimensions of crime and punishment—the pain, loss, hurt, or humiliation of victimization and the voyeuristic thrill of watching others hunted, subdued, and punished (Horeck 2019; Stoneman and Packer 2021).

The horror of crime in visual culture is intertwined with pleasure and the voyeuristic thrill of penal spectatorship (Brown 2009). Reality TV, news as infotainment, social media, and true-crime documentary present audiences with a steady diet of commodified violence and trauma for pleasure as well as extra-legal vengeance beyond the justice system (Stoneman and Packer 2021; Kohm 2009). Nevertheless, most mainstream criminology avoids direct engagement with these emotive and affective dimensions of crime and punishment, preferring instead to reduce them to Likert scales measuring fear of crime and abstract measures of public punitiveness. Perhaps criminology is haunted by the ghosts of its subjects who have been buried alive under the terse and distanced scientific language of quantitative criminology. Conversely, cultural criminology has sought to reorient scholarly discussion toward the visceral, the emotive, and even the metaphysical experiences associated with crime and transgression (Ferrell, Hayward, and Young 2008; Hayward 2016; Hayward and Young 2004). This scholarship looks to awaken the dead and reanimate the subjects of criminology largely through examination of the lived experiences of those most directly affected by crime, but also by examining aspects of popular culture that celebrate crime. To untangle some of the analytic threads that link cultural criminology's interest in the experience and representation of crime I look to the ghostly, the monstrous, and the supernatural.

If the so-called spectral turn implies an interest in the way past traumas metaphorically haunt the present, Claire Valier's essay on the power of horror anticipates this intellectual movement. She argues that a renewed interest in the emotive and visceral aspects of punishment in contemporary penality is underpinned by "gothic seductions." She explains, "Gothicism, typified by gruesome injury and trauma, and menacing shadowy figures, is a prominent feature of the discourses of public protection and vengeance" (2002, 320). Valier applies Julia Kristeva's concept of "abjection" (1982) to "the horror of that which breaches borders" (Valier 2002, 321). Following Kristeva, Valier argues that crimes against children are particularly abject. The boundary-transgressing character of crime against children thus gives rise to horror, because horror emerges "as the edges between things collapse and their contents flow out and mingle, threatening both defilement . . . and engulfment" (333). Valier's analysis of the power of horror is suggestive of the temporal and spatial dislocation that is at the heart of "hauntological" analyses in more recent criminological works (Fiddler 2019). The metaphorical and metaphysical ghost exists liminally, at the edges of things, between the spaces and places of the past and present, and as a reminder of past traumas, crimes, and injustice. The border-transgressing features of horror are very much in evidence in the films I analyze.

ZOMBIES AND CRIME, OH, MY! MONSTERS, STATE VIOLENCE, COLONIALISM, AND THE CARCERAL

The current cultural fascination with the zombie has given rise to a number of sometimes playful and frequently metaphoric applications in criminology. For example, Jamie Peck creatively invoked the metaphor of the zombie in his analysis of crime control in the United States: "Neoliberalism may indeed have entered its zombie phase. The brain has apparently long since ceased functioning, but the limbs are still moving, and many of the defensive reflexes seem to be working too. The living dead of the free-market revolution continue to walk the earth, though with each resurrection their decidedly uncoordinated gait becomes even more erratic" (2010, 109).

In a recent prophetic analysis of zombie cinema, Robert Wonser and David Boyns (2016) argue that the flesh-eating monster of popular culture provides a compelling vehicle for examining sociological theory and concepts relating to the risk society and disease pandemic. Similarly, Tammy Garland, Nickie Phillips, and Scott Vollum (2018) use the popular American cable network AMC television series *The Walking Dead* to critically examine gendered violence, patriarchy, and stereotypes relating to crime and society. The use of the zombie as an evocative cautionary metaphor in media and popular culture to represent the ravages of drugs, ranging from synthetic marijuana to methamphetamines, has been documented by Whitney Marsh, Heith Copes, and Travis Linnemann, who argue that "methamphetamine users appear in the public's imagination as diseased, zombie-like White trash . . . degenerate, atavistic throwbacks" (2017, 52–53). Moreover, Linnemann and Tyler Wall link the spectral to the zombie, noting that "like spectral 'shadow people' the punitive imagination of meth as criminal transgression . . . appears as images of zombie-like corporeal ruin" (2013, 316).

And while much cultural criminological work on drug use in America tends to reduce the zombie to a cultural metaphor, Linnemann, Wall, and Edward Green have provocatively argued that "it is important to be clear that we do not conceive the walking dead simply as metaphor, but rather the literal embodiment of those dispossessed and socially dead others borne of late-capitalism" (2014, 519). Focusing on the process of *"zombification*—the politico-cultural production of . . . *walking dead"* (507), those who have not achieved the status of the living, or the so-called socially dead—they argue that "zombies are endlessly mimetic—everyone and no one at all, everywhere and nowhere—a ghostly, spectral, monstrosity" (517).

If the zombie can function as both the metaphorical and literal embodiment of the monstrous, criminal Other, the criminal justice system itself may likewise be viewed as monstrous and horrific. A few cultural criminologists have productively invoked horror and the monstrous to explore the interconnections between contemporary crime and control and the horror of violence, abuse, and incarceration at the hands of the criminal justice state. While Steven Kohm and Kevin Walby (2022) argue that the surgically assembled monster in *Human Centipede III* is a metaphor for the monstrous late modern American carceral apparatus and the grim embodiment of political and economic rationales underpinning Western crime control, Linnemann,

Wall, and Green invoke the figure of the zombie as a flexible analytic device to critically interrogate American policing in the early twenty-first century. They regard the zombie as "a spectral sort of monstrosity that obscures and justifies police violence and state killing" (2014, 506). They argue that vast segments of the American population are cut off from mainstream society and marginalized due to legal and socioeconomic status and racialized difference. These groups are conceptualized as socially dead and therefore killable by forces of law and order in America. Racialized Others, illegalized migrants, and convicted sex offenders fill the ranks of the socially (un)dead who roam the back regions of society unable to assert more than a tenuous claim to bare life—what Giorgio Agamben refers to as *homo sacer* (1998): those deemed by the state to be biologically alive but unable to assert any claim to political or social citizenship.

The linking of the zombie—whether literal or metaphorical—to the socially (un)dead echoes nascent work by Jeff Ferrell (2015) on ghost ethnography. He argues that whole categories of people denied the conditions of full social life, such as illegalized migrants, drug addicts, the homeless, and sex offenders, lead a life of enforced invisibility. The task of ghost ethnography is to be able to see what is no longer there, or what may be hidden from view. Such methodological engagement with the spectral and ghostly focuses on "the affective and atmospheric 'resonances' left behind in places now abandoned, isolated or forgotten: 'the spectral presence of people no longer there'" (Kindynis 2019, 29).

Aside from these methodological applications, the rise of the ghost presents "a conceptual metaphor" or a "theoretical motif" (Kindynis 2019, 31). Building from Michel de Certeau (1984), Jacques Derrida (1994), and more recent work by Mark Fisher (2012, 2014), Theo Kindynis argues that a key concern of so-called hauntology is the "dialectic interplay of absence/presence" and "a sense of *temporal dislocation* or 'time out of joint'" (2019, 32). For Fisher, spectral encounters occur "when a place is stained by time, or when a particular place becomes the site for an encounter with broken time" (2012, 19). Thus, for Kindynis, "hauntology concerns a crisis of space as well as time" (2019, 32). Cultural geographer Steve Pile (2005) links the destabilization of time and space and argues that hauntings and ghosts are productive of some urban places. Linking the haunting of spaces and places to the cultural production of true crime, Linnemann (2015) invokes the ghosts of notorious crimes and criminals to map the shifting American social imaginary in the postwar period. During this time, the cultural specter of dangerous strangers moving freely across the United States, visiting random violence on unsuspecting innocents, provided a convenient focus for broader societal anxieties about the changing shape of American society. Thus, the ghosts of past grisly crimes and retributive state punishment leave spectral strains and traces on the communities forever changed by these violent and traumatic events. In this way, the ghost acts as a conceptual tool for the analysis of the ongoing effects of violent crimes on particular places and people, while indexing broader cultural shifts over time and society.

These conceptual and analytical threads help me to consider how this emerging body of cultural criminological work on the spectral, the monstrous, and horror can be used productively in an analysis of Canadian horror films to explicate issues of crime and justice for Indigenous peoples in Canada. Scholars of crime and criminal justice in Canada have too often regarded Indigenous peoples as a problem to be explained by academic theory or a target for public policy intervention (e.g., Lithopoulos and Ruddell 2016). However, Indigenous criminologist Lisa Monchalin (2016) instead identifies the Canadian criminal justice system itself as the issue because it is fundamentally rooted in colonialism. This work joins a growing international literature seeking to reimagine criminology and criminal justice studies within a critical framework of decolonization and anticolonialism (e.g., Cunneen and Tauri 2016), including the analysis of culture and art (Cunneen 2010). Crime films about Indigenous peoples in Canada have at times reflected dominant colonial tropes, while more recently, a handful actively resist and rework these framings, taking up the work of decolonization (Kohm and Richtik 2018). The two films I discuss here straddle the line between horror film and crime film, reflecting and refracting issues of colonial violence and genocide for Indigenous peoples in Canada. Horror films, particularly those that depict monstrous Others, reflect the cultures that produce them (Briefel 2005). Therefore, the Canadian horror films about Indigenous peoples analyzed in this chapter say a lot about the settler-colonial contexts of oppression and resistance that have fostered them. For Aalya Ahmad, "the very question of a 'Canadian' identity is founded upon settler cultures that have persistently represented indigenous people as hauntingly Other, whether monstrous or desirable (or both simultaneously)" (2015, 50). I turn first to *Clearcut*.

CLEARCUT (1991)

This 1991 horror-thriller, directed by Ryszard Bugajski and based on the Governor General's Award–winning novel *A Dream Like Mine* (1989) by M. T. Kelly, focuses on the struggles of an Indigenous community in Northern Ontario threatened by a logging company bent on destroying their traditional lands. Indiscriminate resource exploitation threatens both the environment and the Indigenous people who have relied on the land for millennia. Both novel and film present audiences with a metaphysical ethical dilemma about violent vigilantism. However, the film sidelines Indigenous characters by placing a white lawyer from Toronto at the center of the narrative.

The film opens with dramatic underwater footage and ominous otherworldly shrieks and howls. The camera moves through the water and rises up to the surface, acting as a sort of "monster cam" (Ahmad 2015, 59), its movement mimicking that of the creature itself. Aerial shots of a pristine northern lake are intercut with the underwater monster cam footage foreshadowing the awakening of a malevolent spirit. Peter Maguire (Ron Lea) is himself a fish out of water in the rugged Canadian wilderness far from his comfortable Toronto law office. Shots of endless wilderness are disrupted when the aircraft flies over a large section of forest that has been recently clear-cut. Maguire quips: "Looks like the moon on a bad day," to which the pilot retorts: "Looks like money to me." This exchange highlights the film's tension between the economic imperatives driving resource extraction and the negative impacts on the environment and Indigenous peoples. Thus, *Clearcut* may be initially read as a popular criminological text exploring issues of environmental (in)justice.

The tiny floatplane lands at an isolated rocky shoreline with no signs of settlement or development in view. The eerie wailing sounds resume, accompanied by a tracking shot moving quickly across the grassy shore. Maguire cautiously steps out of the plane, clutching his briefcase. "Are we in the right place?" Another tracking shot with ominous sound moves the view quickly from the shoreline and into the trees, indicating that the awakened spirit has moved from the water onto the land. Maguire asks the pilot again: "You wouldn't shit me, now, would you?" The plane abruptly takes off, leaving Maguire alone at the edge of the lake. As he struggles to walk through the dense forest, the sense of foreboding and isolation build.

With nothing but bush and the sounds of wildlife around him, Maguire starts to panic.

Then, all at once, a young Indigenous girl, Polly (Tia Smith), appears with a cigarette and asks Maguire for a light. She cautions: "Never go into the woods without matches." This unsettling exchange further adds to the increasing sense of foreboding and the feeling that Maguire is entering a land far from white settler civilization, where the spirit world intersects. The wild, untamed Indigenous land is fraught with potential danger precisely because it remains *unsettled*. However, the sounds of shouting and heavy machinery intrude into the wilderness, and Maguire quickly comes upon a violent clash between Indigenous protesters, police in riot gear, and logging company employees wielding chainsaws and driving bulldozers. A television news crew captures the scene, tactlessly taunting protesters to "say cheese" and smile for the camera. The intrusion of capitalist, settler industry into this land represents a different sort of horror for Indigenous peoples, who shout at Maguire: "Your fuckin' white courts did this!"

During the protest, the audience learns that Maguire is a lawyer representing the Indigenous community, which opposes the construction of a logging road by a local pulp mill. He has lost the court case, and is pessimistic about an appeal. As he explains the bad news to some of the men engaged in the melee, the otherworldly howls rise up over the din of the machinery and protest. Protester Tom Starblanket (Tom Jackson [Cree]) and Maguire pause, turning their heads to listen to the unsettling sounds. The view cuts to massive machines ripping and tearing at logs while chainsaws cut easily and quickly through trees, bringing them crashing to the ground. The violence against the forest foreshadows the violence that will later be brought to bear on those responsible for the environmental injustice.

Maguire hitches a ride with the TV news reporter (Rebecca Jenkins), hoping he can quickly get a flight back to Toronto and file an appeal to temporarily halt the environmental destruction. However, the reporter detours to the pulp mill to get a comment from the mill manager, Bud Rickets (Michael Hogan). The eerie wailing sounds rise up again as Maguire steps out of the car, and Indigenous activist Arthur (Graham Greene [Six Nations]) walks wordlessly through the foreground of the frame. Immediately the view cuts to large circular saw blades ripping through logs, followed by a view inside a massive tumbler that violently removes the bark from the cut logs.

The violence of the sawmill is juxtaposed against the battle waged in the courts by Maguire and the mysterious Arthur, who is seen for the first time in this scene.

The pulp mill manager is a thoroughly despicable character. He arrogantly introduces himself to Maguire as "Bud Rickets, filthy industrialist." Then he derisively asks Maguire: "Where's your halo?" He defends the clear-cutting of the forest as necessary to support jobs in the local community. He further claims to be a pillar of the (white) community because he coaches little league baseball. But as the film progresses, it becomes clear that Rickets is a bigot and a racist. Later, when confronted by Arthur, he calls him a "dumb drunken Indian." And even after being kidnapped and tortured, he continues to mock Indigenous people and their traditional way of life, affecting an offensive accent and claiming, wrongly, that reserve communities enjoy a high standard of living because of colonization.

Unable to get back to Toronto, Maguire visits Indigenous elder Wilf Redwing (Floyd Red Crow Westerman [Dakota Sioux]). After explaining his pessimistic outlook regarding the appeal, Maguire angrily expresses his frustration: "I feel like somebody has to pay, somebody has to hurt!" Redwing encourages Maguire to take part in what is represented as a traditional Indigenous sweat ceremony. Redwing claims the ceremony will provide Maguire with insight, and allow him to "find out what you really want . . . look inside for what you really want." During the ceremony, Maguire slips into a dream, and experiences fragmented visions including Indigenous rock petroglyphs, a tangle of twigs and branches, and blood flowing across the exposed rocks of the Canadian Shield. At the end of the bizarre series of visions, Arthur appears sitting inside the sweat lodge.

After the ceremony, Maguire splashes water on his face as he interacts with Arthur at the edge of a lake. Arthur asks: "What does a man who talks for us, do for us. . . . What's next?" Maguire responds sarcastically, "Blow the place up? Tie up the mill manager and skin him alive?" This offhand remark sets up a series of events culminating in the kidnapping and torture of Bud Rickets by Arthur, who also drags Maguire along to witness the violence deep in the wilderness—violence that Maguire himself claimed to desire as punishment for the injustice experienced by his Indigenous clients. Arthur takes the captives by boat to a remote area in the forest, where he enacts equivalent symbolic violence on the mill manager, including removing the skin from his legs—"debarking," according to Arthur. By inflicting equivalent violence on Rickets for his crimes against the Earth, Arthur's vigilantism suggests a sort of lex talionis, or a retributive eye-for-an-eye equivalent measure of punishment. This allegorical approach to punishment is driven home by vivid visions and dreams by Maguire throughout the ordeal in the wilderness, such as when he envisions blood running down tree trunks. Near the climax of the film, Maguire drives a large hunting knife into a birch log, causing sap to flow out of the wound like blood. In this way, the film asks the audience to equate the violence inflicted on the forest to the violence enacted on the "filthy industrialist" who is also a racist and a staunch defender of colonialism.

The film positions Arthur as the embodiment of a malevolent Indigenous trickster spirit that Maguire conjures during his vision quest. The ordeal in the wilderness is, according to Ahmad, "a rite of passage toward full manhood" for Maguire (2015, 63). The elder Redwing appears in the midst of the violence in the forest to explain this: "I would like to tell you a story about Wisakedjak, the deceiver." When Maguire asks how he can stop the horror, Redwing tells him that "the dream will end," implying that it is all part of the ritual begun in the sweat lodge the previous day. The appearance of the Wisakedjak in the form of a violent environmental activist is directly tied to Maguire's ambivalence about violence, and an indictment of his manhood. Despite his sublimated desire to use violence to make bad men like Rickets pay for their crimes against the environment, Maguire clings to an ideology of pacifism and nonviolent intervention in his own personal affairs, as well as in his fight on behalf of his Indigenous clients. When Maguire tries to dissuade Arthur from kidnapping Rickets, imploring: "Violence will accomplish nothing!" Arthur retorts: "Who are you lying to?" Redwing too, clarifies that Maguire brought on the violent activist because it was his desire—his dream—clarified through the sweat ceremony. Arthur taunts Maguire by presenting several opportunities to stop his violent rampage in the woods, but only if Maguire himself resorts to violence. In the end, only through a violent altercation can Maguire drive Arthur back to the bottom of the lake, thus ending his dream and saving Rickets from his awful fate.

The origin and eventual exit of the Wisakedjak in the lake exemplifies the centrality of water—the lifeblood of the environment—in the narrative of *Clearcut*: "The film is punctuated by shots of water—motel pools, lakes, waterfalls, the 'V' of the boat carrying the main characters and the rivulet trickling from between the thighs of the pictographic Earth Mother during the final part of Arthur's ceremony. When asked where he is from, Arthur replies teasingly 'Recently?' and trails his hands in the water, flicking it into his interlocutor's face" (Ahmad 2015, 59).

Through these multiple representations of water and the linking of white settler industrial expansion in the forest to the torture of the body of the villainous mill manager, *Clearcut* uses its setting in the Canadian wilderness to *unsettle* audiences. The fear that Maguire experiences when he first finds himself alone in the woods is amplified when Arthur forces him deeper into uncharted, or *unsettled*, territory in search of retribution. This trope mirrors the fraught relationship of the settler state to the untamed wilderness of the colonized Other. The terror of being kidnapped by the Indigenous Other and spirited deep into the woods where reality shades into a Kafkaesque nightmare strikes at the heart of the white settler psyche, and projects fantasies about the metaphysical and the Indigenous.

While clearly sympathetic to the suffering caused by colonial and environmental violence, *Clearcut* is nevertheless the creation of a white director who adapted a story by a white Canadian novelist to explore issues of violence and pacifism, leading some critics to compare it to Sam Peckinpah's *Straw Dogs* (1971). *Clearcut*'s representation of Indigenous people and their struggles for justice in the early 1990s received a mixed response from commentators and reviewers. For example, Ted Jojola described it as part of "a new wave of Indian sympathy films" (1998, 17) that followed after the success of *Dances with Wolves* (1990). He called the plot "as surreal and bizarre as a Salvador Dali painting." However, he also conceded that "Native actors finally got to act out unabashed their colonially induced angst" (17). Ahmad described the film as "environmental horror" revolving around "boundary transgressions between nature and the human" (2015, 48).

In this way, *Clearcut* aligns with the boundary-breaching horror of crime described by Valier (2002). As a crime film, it could be described as a cautionary tale about the limits of extralegal justice and vengeance. Invoking an otherworldly Indigenous spirit, or specter, as a narrative vehicle to examine the sublimated guilt and rage of a white settler firmly positions the film within Gittings's schema of films fetishizing and romanticizing Indigenous culture (2002). The use of the spectral or monstrous Wisakedjak affirms rather than subverts settler-colonial tropes about the horrors of the Indigenous Other.

Conversely, the film discussed in the next section counters these very same tropes but vehemently rejects romanticism or fetishization of the Indigenous Other, opting instead for a sustained critique of colonization through a reimagining of the zombie genre.

BLOOD QUANTUM (2019)

Mi'gmaq director Jeff Barnaby has been widely acknowledged for bringing an Indigenous perspective to genre cinema and using film to make broader political commentary about issues of colonization and trauma for Indigenous peoples (Santoro 2013). His debut feature film *Rhymes for Young Ghouls* (2013) centered on the intergenerational trauma and criminogenic effects of Canada's residential school system (Woolford and Gacek 2016; Miller 2017; Nagy and Sehdev 2012). Yet the film took up many themes and conventions of more typical Hollywood fare. According to Barnaby: "It's a revenge/heist movie about this young girl who topples the Indian agent who runs the reserve with an iron fist. It's so simple, I'm surprised nobody had thought of it yet" (DVD special features 2013). Barnaby's follow-up project *Blood Quantum* takes up the familiar generic conventions of the zombie apocalypse film, called "a searing indictment of colonialism—and also a zombie flick, full of squelchy gore, chainsaws, machetes, and buckets of blood" (Vowel 2020). The film is also distinctly Canadian; the undead are called "zeds" within the film, "by those who know how that letter is supposed to be pronounced" (Knight 2020). Yet despite Barnaby's nod to conventional horror genre cinema, his films epitomize a new wave of Indigenous filmmaking that "teaches us something about what it means to be Indigenous in Canada today, and what it means to tell stories about the past from a distinctly Indigenous point of view" (Stewart 2021, 166). Additionally, Barnaby embraces the wondrous and the monstrous in his films and in so doing "upset[s] the Eurocentric distinction between the real and the imagined" (Varga 2022, 10).

Released just prior to the COVID-19 pandemic, the film gained new cultural relevance during the public health emergency. However, as Barnaby noted in a recent interview, the association of the zombie apocalypse with a worldwide pandemic driven by a virus provides a sense of cultural continuity with the experience of colonialism for Indigenous peoples: "The weird thing about being native and making a comment on viruses in particular is the history of the pandemics and the colonization of America.... Once you put a native person in a zombie film, you immediately start thinking that it's a virus. It's one of the benefits of being a native film director: You have so much history to riff on. It exists in history and in our society and in the history of our cinema and literature" (Yamoto 2020).

The setting on the fictional Red Crow reserve in Eastern Quebec in 1981 also has particular historical resonance for Indigenous people and their struggle for justice. In the film, an early warning sign of the zombie apocalypse occurs when an Indigenous fisher discovers that the salmon he harvested from the river continue to live after being gutted. The link to the salmon fishery evokes events in 1981, when Quebec Provincial Police raided the Indigenous community of Restigouche (now known as Listuguj) in a dispute over salmon fishing. The event was chronicled in the NFB documentary *Incident at Restigouche* (1984), by Abenaki director Alanis Obomsawin. Barnaby had his cast watch this film prior to production of *Blood Quantum*. The police raids are described by Chelsea Vowel: "In the first raid, approximately 500 police officers, fisheries officers, and game wardens descended on the small community, beating and arresting Mi'gmaq and seizing their nets. Listuguj Mi'gmaq mobilized and erected barricades, preventing outside access to the community; another raid followed just over a week later. It was an astonishing show of state violence that most Canadians are completely ignorant of" (2020).

In *Blood Quantum*, the Red Crow reserve is similarly barricaded and fortified against incursions—this time by white zombies. Indigenous people are immune to the virus causing the monstrous outbreak. The outbreak can be seen as an allegory for the very act of colonization itself. Indeed, zombies and cannibals are apt "metaphors for the consequences of colonialism" (Varga 2022, 20). In a particularly ironic twist, white refugees from the zombie apocalypse seek shelter and protection within the Indigenous community. As well, in yet another visual nod to Canada's fraught relationship with its Indigenous peoples, the gates of the fortified compound are marked by a zombie in chains, wearing a period military uniform and helmet. Evoking the armed confrontation at Oka, Quebec in 1990, Barnaby frames a shot of an Indigenous man face-to-face with the zombie solider, re-creating the most iconic news image from the Kanesatake resistance standoff (De Bruin, McIntosh, and Doerr 2020; see also Harper 2020; Varga 2022).

Events in the first part of the film establish the impending zombie outbreak. The discovery of monstrous salmon that do not die after processing prompts Indigenous fisher Gisigu (Stonehorse Lone Goeman) to contact his son, local reserve police chief Traylor (Michael Greyeyes [Nêhiyaw]). That same morning, Traylor euthanizes a dog belonging to his ex-wife Joss (Elle-Máijá Tailfeathers [Blackfoot, Sámi]), who informs him that their son Joseph (Forrest Goodluck [Dine, Mandan, Hidatsa, and Tsimshian]) is in jail for vandalism in the nearby off-reserve community of Hollarbaster, along with his half brother, nicknamed Lysol (Kiowa Gordon). Warning signs of the zombie apocalypse occur when the dog, shot by Traylor, comes back to life in the trunk of the police cruiser. Similarly, Joseph and Lysol are attacked by a non-Indigenous man in the police holding cell who bites Joseph's arm. Later, Traylor responds to a domestic call on the reserve at the home of Shooker (William Belleau) and his white girlfriend. She attacks and bites Traylor and he struggles to fight off the petite woman, hitting her repeatedly in the head with the butt of his shotgun.

The film abruptly shifts from these early scenes of confusion at the onset of the outbreak to a post-apocalyptic world six months later. Red Crow has been transformed into a fortified compound with walls constructed of shipping containers and other remnants of the fallen civilization. The community provides shelter for a number of non-Indigenous residents, including Joseph's white girlfriend Charlie (Olivia Scriven), who is close to giving birth to their child. The film's title refers to a colonial practice of assessing Indigenous identity according to the amount of Indigenous blood. The unborn child provides a cultural echo of this exercise as Charlie and Joseph speculate. While it may have immunity due to the father's Indigenous heritage, Charlie is not immune, and when she is bitten near the climax of the film, the fate of mother and child are uncertain.

Discord breaks out when Lysol and Moon (Gary Farmer [Cayuga]) become frustrated by other community members allowing white refugees to take shelter in the fortified compound. Lysol sabotages the camp by letting a zombie loose. Traylor sacrifices his life to allow Joseph, Charlie, and Joss to escape. Later, Lysol and Moon threaten to kill a group of white survivors in a nearby church. Joseph, Gisigu, and others foil Lysol's plan, but in the process, Charlie is bitten by a zombie. Charlie, Joss, and Joseph flee by boat as Gisigu remains behind to hold off the zombie onslaught. Later,

Charlie gives birth to a healthy baby in the boat, but slowly succumbs to the zombie bite, requiring Joseph to shoot her before she can completely turn. The film ends with Joseph, Joss, and the newborn facing an uncertain future.

In most ways, the film faithfully replicates the standard plots, themes, and motifs of the zombie genre. It is set in an apparently realistic world where the impossible is nevertheless possible. Zombies, the reanimated corpses of human beings, are driven only by their base impulse to eat the flesh of the living. For non-Indigenous people, a bite from one results in an infection that will turn them into the undead. In keeping with the standard generic conventions, the only way to stop a zombie is by destroying the brain. Thus, the film is replete with beheadings, bludgeonings, and gunshots to the head. However, the immunity of Indigenous peoples to the virus causing the zombie outbreak offers a vehicle to metaphorically invert the violence of colonization. Rather than Indigenous people succumbing to alien viruses brought to the so-called "new world" by European colonists, it is the latter who lack immunity. The zombie also provides a broader metaphor to represent the ongoing damage of colonialism to Indigenous communities and people; the film depicts masses of white zombies literally overwhelming the Indigenous community, threating to destroy their way of life, and displacing them from their traditional land.

However, by couching political and social commentary within a fast-paced horror-thriller, Barnaby connects with audiences at two levels. Commenting about this approach within *Rhymes for Young Ghouls*, producer John Christou explains that Barnaby's films are first and foremost designed for audiences. As genre films filled with action and dramatic elements, they can be enjoyed on a superficial level. However, they are also "inherently political," leaving open the possibility that "audiences might walk away with a different view of what life is like on reserves" (DVD special features 2013). According to Barnaby, the most important distinction between his own and the genre films that inspired him is the inclusion of Indigenous people behind the camera: "I think the perspective of the Native person behind the lens has been the missing part of cinema . . . and I think the progression we are starting to see is part of the sweep of change" (DVD special features 2013).

The horror of a world overwhelmed by a destructive virus that turns otherwise peaceful human beings into relentless killing machines not only speaks volumes to the cultural anxieties of a world shaped by the COVID-19 pandemic, it also clearly resonates with one coming to terms with the crimes of colonialism. The genocidal actions of Canadian colonial authorities constructed Indigenous peoples as not only *uncivilized* but also *inhuman*. And like Linnemann, Wall, and Green's (2014) invocation of the zombie in their analysis of the policing of socially (un)dead segments of the American population, Barnaby's zombie is an apt construct to analyze and explicate the horrors of colonial crime and the ongoing mistreatment of Indigenous peoples by Canada's justice system.

The winter 2022 events in Canada surrounding the so-called "freedom convoy" that saw large numbers of non-Indigenous protesters occupy downtown Ottawa and other Canadian capitals and blockade critical border crossings while police apparently stood by and posed for photographs with protesters (Molina 2022) stand in stark contrast to militarized reactions to Indigenous protest in Canada from Listuguj to Oka to the present. The Canadian state and its forces of law and order have reacted to assemblies of Indigenous peoples in protest as if they posed the same threat as an approaching zombie apocalypse. Just as zombies are constructed in culture as disposable, killable bodies lacking any soul or humanity, Indigenous peoples have long been similarly constructed by the state. Barnaby's use of the zombie genre in *Blood Quantum* adeptly reverses the socially constructed dichotomy between settler and Indigenous, revealing the ongoing and toxic effects of colonialism in Canada, always threatening to break through the superficial veneer of official policies of tolerance and multiculturalism. The specter of past injustices by the Canadian state, such as Listuguj and Oka, linger in *Blood Quantum*, just as the ghosts of residential schools and genocide echo in the hordes of white zombies bearing down on the fortified Red Crow reserve. In short, the ghost and monster have much to reveal about the crimes and the injustices of colonization, past and present.

Clearcut and *Blood Quantum* are separated by three decades. And while the former provides a sympathetic but at times fetishistic and romantic image of Indigenous struggles for justice, the latter most fully exploits the tropes and themes of horror genre cinema to confront the lingering ghosts of past and ongoing colonial trauma for Indigenous peoples. Cultural criminology must take up and make central the cultural representation of Indigenous issues of justice and crime stemming from colonialism. Films are powerful vehicles to connect political and social commentary about justice to audiences, which may engage in these films on several levels. By excavating the ghosts of injustices past and present (e.g., Fiddler 2019) that are cleverly woven into films like *Clearcut* and *Blood Quantum*, cultural criminology can be an ally to Indigenous peoples looking to decolonize art, culture, and society more broadly.

REFERENCES

Agamben, Giorgio. 1998. *Homo Sacer: Sovereign Power and Bare Life*. Stanford, CA: Stanford University Press.

Ahmad, Aalya. 2015. "Blood in the Bush Garden: Indigenization, Gender, and Unsettling Horror." In *The Canadian Horror Film: Terror of the Soul*, edited by Gina Freitag and André Loiselle, 47–66. Toronto: University of Toronto Press.

Blood Quantum. 2019. Directed by Jeff Barnaby. Canada: Prospector Films.

Briefel, Aviva. 2005. "Monster Pains: Masochism, Menstruation, and Identification in the Horror Film." *Film Quarterly* 58 (3): 16–27.

Brown, Michelle. 2009. *The Culture of Punishment: Prison, Society, and Spectacle*. New York: NYU Press.

Clearcut. 1991. Directed by Ryszard Bugajski. Canada: Cinexus Capital.

Cohen, Stanley. 2001. *States of Denial: Knowing about Atrocities and Suffering*. Bristol, UK: Polity.

Cunneen, Chris. 2010. "Framing the Crimes of Colonialism: Critical Images of Aboriginal Art and Law." In *Framing Crime: Cultural Criminology and the Image*, edited by Keith Hayward and Mike Presdee, 115–37. New York: Taylor & Francis.

Cunneen, Chris, and Juan Tauri. 2016. *Indigenous Criminology*. Bristol, UK: Polity.

Dances with Wolves. 1990. Directed by Kevin Costner. USA: Orion.

De Bruin, Tabitha, Andrew McIntosh, and Audrey D. Doerr. 2020. "Kanesatake Resistance (Oka Crisis)." July 9. *The Canadian Encyclopedia*. https://www.thecanadianencyclopedia.ca/en/article/oka-crisis.

de Certeau, Michel. 1984. *The Practice of Everyday Life*. Berkeley: University of California Press.

Derrida, Jacques. 1994. *Spectres of Marx: The State of the Debt, the Work of Mourning and the New International*. New York: Routledge.

DVD special features. 2013. In *Rhymes for Young Ghouls*, directed by Jeff Barnaby. Canada: Entertainment One Films.

Dziuban, Zuzanna, ed. 2019. *The "Spectral Turn": Jewish Ghosts in the Polish Post-Holocaust Imaginaire*. Memory Cultures, vol. 6. Bielefeld: Transcript.

Ferrell, Jeff. 1992. "Making Sense of Crime: Review Essay on Jack Katz's *Seductions of Crime*." *Social Justice* 19 (2): 110–23.

Ferrell, Jeff. 2004. "Boredom, Crime and Criminology." *Theoretical Criminology* 8 (3): 287–302.

Ferrell, Jeff. 2015. "Ghost Ethnography: On Crimes against Reality and Their Excavation." Paper presented at "Crimes against Reality" common session, University of Hamburg, June 2. https://lecture2go.uni-hamburg.de/l2go/-/get/v/17693.

Ferrell, Jeff, Keith Hayward, and Jock Young. 2008. *Cultural Criminology: An Invitation*. Los Angeles: SAGE.

Fiddler, Michael. 2019. "Ghosts of Other Stories: A Synthesis of Hauntology, Crime and Space." *Crime Media Culture* 15 (3): 463–77.

Fisher, Mark. 2012. "What Is Hauntology?" *Film Quarterly* 66 (1): 16–24.

Fisher, Mark. 2014. *Ghosts of My Life: Writings on Depression, Hauntology and Lost Futures*. Winchester, UK: Zero Books.

Garland, Tammy S., Nickie Phillips, and Scott Vollum. 2018. "Gender Politics and *The Walking Dead*: Gendered Violence and the Reestablishment of Patriarchy." *Feminist Criminology* 13 (1): 59–86.

Gittings, Christopher. 2002. *Canadian National Cinema: Ideology, Difference and Representation*. New York: Routledge.

Gordon, Avery F. 2020. "Revolutionary Feminisms." *Verso Books*, September 2. https://www.versobooks.com/blogs/4842-revolutionary-feminisms-avery-f-gordon.

Harper, Rachael. 2020. "*Blood Quantum* Review: Indigenous Zombie Thriller Brings Guts and Politics." *SciFiNow*, April 29. https://www.scifinow.co.uk/reviews/blood-quantum-review-indigenous-zombie-thriller-brings-guts-and-politics/.

Hayward, Keith. 2016. "Cultural Criminology: Script Rewrites." *Theoretical Criminology* 20 (3): 297–321.

Hayward, Keith, and Jock Young. 2004. "Cultural Criminology: Some Notes on the Script." *Theoretical Criminology* 8 (3): 259–73.

Horeck, Tanya. 2019. *Justice on Demand: True Crime in the Digital Streaming Era*. Detroit: Wayne State University Press.

Human Centipede III. 2015. Directed by Tom Six. USA: Scream Factory.

Incident at Restigouche. 1984. Directed by Alanis Obomsawin. Canada: National Film Board.

Jojola, Ted. 1998. "Absurd Reality II: Hollywood Goes to the Indians." In *Hollywood's Indian: The Portrayal of the Native American in Film*, 2nd ed., edited by Peter C. Rollins and John E. O'Connor, 12–26. Lexington: University Press of Kentucky.

Kelly, M. T. 1989. *A Dream Like Mine*. Toronto: General Paperbacks.

Kindynis, Theo. 2019. "Excavating Ghosts: Urban Exploration as Graffiti Archaeology." *Crime Media Culture* 15 (1): 25–45.

Knight, Chris. 2020. "*Blood Quantum* Is a Zombie Movie with First Nations Politics on the Brain, Says Chris Knight." *Telegram*, April 23. https://www.saltwire.com/newfoundland-labrador/lifestyles/entertainment/blood-quantum-is-a-zombie-movie-with-first-nations-politics-on-the-brain-says-chris-knight-441294/.

Kohm, Steven. 2009. "Naming, Shaming and Criminal Justice: Mass-Mediated Humiliation as Entertainment and Punishment." *Crime Media Culture* 5 (2): 188–205.

Kohm, Steven, and Taylor Richtik. 2018. "Representing Justice in Indigenous Canadian Crime Films." *Annual Review of Interdisciplinary Justice Research* 7:68–95.

Kohm, Steven, and Kevin Walby. 2022. "Deforming Justice: Representing Punishment in *The Human Centipede III: Final Sequence*." *Crime Media Culture* 18 (1): 85–104.

Kristeva, Julia. 1982. *Powers of Horror: An Essay on Abjection*. New York: Columbia University Press.

Linnemann, Travis. 2015. "Capote's Ghosts: Violence, Media and the Spectre of Suspicion." *British Journal of Criminology* 55: 514–33.

Linnemann, Travis, and Tyler Wall. 2013. "'This Is Your Face on Meth': The Punitive Spectacle of 'White Trash' in the Rural War on Drugs." *Theoretical Criminology* 17 (3): 315–34.

Linnemann, Travis, Tyler Wall, and Edward Green. 2014. "The Walking Dead and Killing State: Zombification and the Normalization of Police Violence." *Theoretical Criminology* 18 (4): 506–27.

Lithopoulos, Savvas, and Rick Ruddell. 2016. "Crime, Criminal Justice, and Aboriginal Canadians." In *Criminal Justice in Canada*, 5th ed., edited by Julian Roberts and Michelle Grossmann, 185–98. Toronto: Nelson.

Marsh, Whitney, Heith Copes, and Travis Linnemann. 2017. "Creating Visual Differences: Methamphetamine Users' Perceptions of Anti-Meth Campaigns." *International Journal of Drug Policy* 39: 52–61.

Miller, J. R. 2017. *Residential Schools and Reconciliation: Canada Confronts Its History*. Toronto: University of Toronto Press.

Molina, Kimberley. 2022. "OPP Officer Lets Protesters Take Photos in Back of Police Cruiser." *CBC News*, February 11. https://www.cbc.ca/news/canada/ottawa/opp-cruiser-used-as-photo-booth-protesters-1.6348592.

Monchalin, Lisa. 2016. *The Colonial Problem*. Toronto: University of Toronto Press.

Nagy, Rosemary, and Robinder Kaur Sehdev. 2012. "Introduction: Residential Schools and Decolonization." *Canadian Journal of Law and Society* 27 (1): 67–73.

Peck, Jamie. 2010. "Zombie Neoliberalism and the Ambidextrous State." *Theoretical Criminology* 14 (1): 104–10.

Pile, Steve. 2005. *Real Cities: Modernity, Space and the Phantasmagoria of City Life*. London: SAGE.

Rafter, Nicole. 2006. *Shots in the Mirror: Crime Films and Society*. 2nd ed. New York: Oxford.

Rafter, Nicole. 2016. *The Crime of All Crimes: Toward a Criminology of Genocide*. New York: NYU Press.

Rhymes for Young Ghouls. 2013. Directed by Jeff Barnaby. Canada: Prospector Films.

Santoro, Miléna. 2013. "The Rise of First Nations' Fiction Films: Shelley Niro, Jeff Barnaby, and Yves Sioui Durand." *American Review of Canadian Studies* 43 (2): 267–82.

Stewart, Tyson. 2021. "Truth and Reconciliation Cinema: An Ethico-Political Study of Residential School Imagery in Contemporary Indigenous Film." *AlterNative: An International Journal of Indigenous Peoples* 17 (2): 165–74.

Stoneman, Ethan, and Joseph Packer. 2021. "Reel Cruelty: Voyeurism and Extra-Juridical Punishment in True-Crime Documentaries." *Crime Media Culture* 17 (3): 401–19.

Straw Dogs. 1971. Directed by Sam Peckinpah. USA: Cinerama.

Turcotte, Gerry, and Cynthia Conchita Sugars. 2009. "Introduction: Canadian Literature and the Postcolonial Gothic." In *Unsettled Remains: Canadian Literature and the Postcolonial Gothic*, edited by Gerry Turcotte and Cynthia Conchita Sugars, vii–xxvi. Waterloo: Wilfrid Laurier University Press.

Valier, Claire. 2002. "Punishment, Border Crossings and the Powers of Horror." *Theoretical Criminology* 6 (3): 319–37.

Varga, Darrell. 2022. "Screen Zombies, Alien Settlers, and Colonial Legacies." *American Review of Canadian Studies* 52 (1): 9–28.

Vowel, Chelsea. 2020. "Notes from an Apocalypse." *The Walrus*, July 6. https://thewalrus.ca/terra-cognita-notes-from-an-apocalypse/.

The Walking Dead. 2010–2022. Created by Frank Darabont. USA: AMC Studios.

Wonser, Robert, and David Boyns. 2016. "Between the Living and Undead: How Zombie Cinema Reflects the Social Construction of Risk, the Anxious Self, and Disease Pandemic." *Sociological Quarterly* 57 (4): 628–53.

Woolford, Andrew, and James Gacek. 2016. "Genocidal Carcerality and Indian Residential Schools in Canada." *Punishment and Society* 18 (4): 400–419.

Yamoto, Jen. 2020. "How Indigenous Zombie Horror Film *Blood Quantum* Became Prescient in the Pandemic." *Los Angeles Times*, May 8. https://www.latimes.com/entertainment-arts/movies/story/2020-05-08/blood-quantum-indigenous-horror-zombie-pandemic-jeff-barnaby.

Young, Jock. 2004. "Voodoo Criminology and the Numbers Game." In *Cultural Criminology Unleashed*, edited by Jeff Ferrell, Keith Hayward, Wayne Morrison, and Mike Presdee, 13–27. London: GlassHouse.

Young, Jock. 2011. *The Criminological Imagination*. Cambridge: Polity.

Afterword

JENNIFER ORME AND PAULINE GREENHILL

We write this afterword to *Just Wonder: Shifting Perspectives in Tradition* in spring 2023. The pleasure of watching buds appearing like magic upon trees that were bare yesterday and little green shoots pushing up and through what was snow last week creates in us wonder and hope for summer after a *very* long, dark, and snowy winter in Winnipeg and Toronto. At the same time, Canada's worst wildfire season of the century so far rages. In June smoke from fires in eight provinces and two territories traveled as far away as New York City and even moved into Europe ("Wildfire Maps" 2023). And a recent provincial election confirms that even climate catastrophe cannot dislodge the ideology of the political and social Right in one of the two worst-hit provinces. Sometimes it seems that the world is simply unredeemable. Witnessing the return of exuberant life in nature and human-caused hardship simultaneously can be confusing and jarring, but neither aspect of that uncomfortable juxtaposition should be ignored.

We began *Just Wonder* by asking where hope can be found in the current physical, cultural, social, and political environment. Perhaps the essays we

https://doi.org/10.7330/9781646425853.c013

collect here will offer our readers optimism, but we fully realize these writings won't be the immediate cause of more justice. Yet they may suggest an intellectual antidote to desperation in the face of the many challenges to human and nonhuman sovereignty and dignity from the past and into the future. Our original questions led us and the chapters' authors to look at relations, practices, and narratives not often considered from these perspectives. This book is deliberately very heterogeneous in terms of types of justice and injustice discussed, texts and practices engaged, and methods and approaches for examining them. It is our wish and expectation that *Just Wonder* will add to a flood of moves in a range of areas of endeavor for academics, activists, and artists. The chapters point to how imagination plays an important role in finding ways to respond to injustice. They show that far from being mere escapism, wonder offers tools and approaches for examining, understanding, and responding to events and conflicts in the everyday real world.

Together, the chapters also demonstrate that addressing injustice from one quarter may seem to overlook it in another. Not all the perspectives, arguments, and desires of those seeking justice in a difficult and complex world will be commensurate with all others. They will sometimes contradict each other. As Eve Tuck and K. Wayne Yang demonstrate, "Solidarity is an uneasy, reserved, and unsettled matter that neither reconciles present grievances nor forecloses future conflict" (2012, 3). For example, Veronica Schanoes confronts antisemitism embedded in the Grimms' traditional fairy tales while Kay Turner reads the Grimm version of one specific tale from a queer feminist direction the Brothers would never have imagined. The queer love of Turner's reading cannot alleviate the hate that Schanoes exposes in the Grimm canon, but including both reflections in the book creates space for difficult but important discussions.

The texts, traditions, and practices addressed by contributors don't provide easy solutions to current injustices. But facile answers are not needed today or in years to come. The world needs as many ideas as possible: experimentation, questions, attempts, and failures from multiple directions and points of view. Activist scholar Bryan Kamaoli Kuwada and criminal justice scholar Steven Kohm both show how different Indigenous sovereignty looks from Indigenous perspectives than it does from mainstream white ones. Their work fosters appreciation for the importance of valuing the former.

Yet we deliberately include varied topics, approaches, and voices in this volume because above all, we believe that heterogeneity, rather than compromised unity, is where solutions will derive from. Solidarity does not demand total agreement on every point. Some worthy goals for one group may not be fully endorsed by others. Conflict is inevitable.

The authors in *Just Wonder* do not argue that they know what justice will look like in every case. Anne Kustritz discusses a film unpacking feminist and antifeminist reactions to violence against women, while Andrea Braithwaite turns to novels that also explore women's power but implicate the role of fairy tales in both creating and addressing oppression and wrongs. Wondering about justice means asking difficult questions and discovering that the answers are rarely easy—and sometimes impossible. Yet as tricky as some interrogations are, this collection stresses that justice does not need to be tedious or lacking in humor. An Icelandic Yule Lad can raise public consciousness about inclusion for disabled folks, as Eva Þórdís Ebenezersdóttir and Stekkjastaur point out, and a television show about seeking treasure illuminates ecological issues, as Marek Oziewicz shows. Sometimes lighthearted approaches are called for. After all, we welcome a supernatural coauthor as happily as we receive both established and up-and-coming scholars.

Affirming the powers of the weak is important for several contributors. It is central to Jack Zipes's discussion of soldier tales, but also to Ming-Hsun Lin's consideration of Disney villains. Both attend to backstories and what actually happens to characters within stories, but also affirm how context engenders meaning. It matters how stories are used, but also where. The power of children—generally understood as less influential than adults—to effect change is thematically central to both Heidi Kosonen's discussion of the fictional film *The Fall* and Allison Craven's discussion of young women activists, too often downplayed or even dismissed by the mainstream. Both show how young people's well-founded fear and anger are more powerful than grown-ups can often see or accept—and that adult resistance can be all too effective.

Schanoes admits: "I don't think scholarship *can* restore or repair damage. I don't think that's what it's for. Scholarship doesn't provide justice; it asks, and sometimes answers, questions." We have by no means exhausted the possibilities. We call for more wondering about wonder and just thinking about justice in all areas of endeavor. We look forward to interdisciplinary scholarship and collaborations between academics, artists, activists, and supernatural folks (and all combinations thereof) finding ways to think and act and create together across difference and diverse points of view. Our hope is that this collection will inspire further discussion of the types of methods taken up by the contributors. We encourage readers to explore forms of wonder and areas where justice is being sought—especially when those areas need more light, air, and food for thought to grow.

REFERENCES

Tuck, Eve, and K. Wayne Yang. 2012. "Decolonization Is Not a Metaphor." *Decolonization: Indigeneity, Education, and Society* 1 (1): 1–40.

"Wildfire Maps 2023: Tracking Fires and Air Quality across Canada." 2023. *Globe and Mail.* June 13, updated September 6. https://www.theglobeandmail.com/canada/article-wildfire-map-air-quality-canada/.

Index

Aarne, Antti, 100
Aarne-Thompson (AT) Index, 94, 100; use in *Indexing* and *Indexing: Reflections*, 101, 102, 103–104, 105
Aarne-Thompson-Uther (ATU) index, 100, 112n1, 112n2
Aaron, Michele, 119, 132n2
Abad, Kēhaunani, 79, 80–81
Abbenhuis, Maartje, 138
abortion, 193
"About the Eighteen Soldiers" (Wolf), 143
"About the Evil Comrades" (Wolf), 143
activism, 3, 8, 23, 226, 228; celebrity, 226–34; disability, 35; environmental, 54, 227, 230, 252; feminist, 219; social, 229; wonder and, 9
Acuna, Kirsten, 167
adoptive kin, natal family versus, 182
advocacy, 22, 65
Afanas'ev, Alexandr, 139, 145–46
affections/affiliations, queer, 184
Agamben, Giorgio, 247

ageism, 229–34; juvenile, 220, 229, 234, 235n9
agency, 94, 199, 220; elemental, 75; female, 106, 107, 197; male, 130; political, 218
Ahmad, Aalya, 248, 252, 253
ʻāina, 70, 71, 76, 77, 78, 85, 86; kānaka and, 81–82; pono and, 72, 82, 83; wonder and, 71–75, 80–84, 81
akua, 73, 75, 76, 82, 83, 84
Aladdin (Disney): epiphany of, 168; identity of, 157; social status of, 168
Aladdin (film), 152, 157; animation of, 168; remix of, 168–69
alcohol, misogynist clichés about, 200
Allen, Lily, 227
Allen, Meaghan, 201
aloha, 71, 76
aloha ʻāina, 71–74, 77, 79, 85
AlterNative (periodical), 13n1
altruism, masculine, 130, 131
American Heritage Dictionary of Idioms, The, 225
"Among the Thorns" (Schanoes), 62, 64

268   INDEX

"Angel of the Morning" (Newton), 207
animation, 153, 157, 158, 159, 160, 162, 166, 167, 168, 169, 170; fairy-tale, 152
Ant, Adam, 226
Anthropocene, 56; discourse of, 44; fantasy for, 10, 41, 43, 45; urgencies of, 40
anthropocentrism, 40, 44, 51–52
anticolonialism, 248
antisemitism, 10, 60, 62, 63, 65, 264
Antonia's Line (film), 200
"Armless Maiden, The," 59
Árnason, Jón, 24, 25
art, 6, 77; analysis of, 248; decolonizing, 259
Ashliman, D. L., 182
assimilation, 13n2, 63
Asperger's (Autism Spectrum Disorder), 36n2, 231
AT Index. *See* Aarne-Thompson Index
Attebery, Brian, 41, 42–43
ATU Index. *See* Aarne-Thompson-Uther Index
Austen, Jane, 203
autonomy, 94, 108; women's, 106

Bacchilega, Cristina, 9, 72–73, 219; wonder and, 8
backstories, antagonists', 157–65, 169, 265
Bailey, Halle, 65
Barnaby, Jeff, 254, 255, 257, 258; counternarratives and, 243
Basile, Giambattista, 159
BBC Urdu, 233
BBC Woman's Hour, 159
"Bearskin" (Brothers Grimm), 140
Beauty and the Beast (film), 16, 66, 152, 156, 162, 170n3; remix of, 168; Watson and, 228
Beckford, William Thomas, 60
Belleau, William, 256
Benjamin, Lucy, 45
Bergmann, Zoe, 229, 230
Berlant, Lauren, 199, 208
Bill, Leo, 116
binaries, 152, 182; gendered, 122; heterosexual, 12; male/female, 179; normative, 178; socially and politically poisonous, 193
binary oppositions, 178–79, 180, 187

Björnsson, Árni, 24, 26, 34, 36n5
Bjúgnakrækir, 25, 26
Blanchett, Cate, 156
Blasberg, Derek, 228
Bleach, Julian, 116
Blodgett, Bridget, 123, 129
blood relations versus nonblood relations, 182
blood libel, 61
Blood Quantum (film), 12, 242, 254–59; cultural criminology in, 259; Indigenous peoples and, 243; production of, 255; zombie genre in, 258
Blue Fairy Book, The (Lang), 60, 62, 64
"Blue Light, The" (Brothers Grimm), 140
"Bluebeard," 154
"Bluffer Lays out the Cards in a Favorable Way, The" (Pröhle), 147
bonding, 12, 176, 180; female/queer, 182
"Boots of Buffalo Leather, The" (Brothers Grimm), 140
Bowman, Barbara, 119, 120, 130
Boyns, David, 246
Bradway, Taylor, 181
Braithwaite, Andrea, 7, 11
Branagh, Kenneth, 152
Brie, Alison, 203
"Bright Sun Will Bring It to Light, The," 60
British Museum, 48
Brontë sisters, 203
"Bronze Ring, The," 61, 65, 260; word Jew in, 62–63
Brooks, Peter, 225
"Brother Lustig" (Brothers Grimm), 140
Brothers Grimm, 4, 12, 65, 86, 142, 143, 176, 182, 212, 264; Afanas'ev and, 145; antisemitism and, 10; disability and, 191; Jews and, 63; tales of, 141. *See also* Grimm, Jacob; Grimm, Wilhelm
Brown, Annie, 228
Brown, Jeffrey, 108, 109
Bugajski, Ryszard, 249
Burnham, Bo, 196
"Burning Girls" (Schanoes), 62
Butler, Judith, 178, 181
Buttsworth, Sara, 138

California Institute of Technology, 69–70
Callard, Rebecca, 50
Caltagirone, Daniel, 116
Canetto, Silvia, 121
"Carrier Bag Theory of Fiction, The" (Le Guin), 41
Carter, Helena Bonham, 156
Casar, Paul, 51
celebrities, 219, 222, 226–227, 228, 234
Cell, The (film), 117, 118
Chalice and the Blade, The (Eisler), 41
chance meetings, structure and, 183–86
Charlie, Lianne Marie Leda, 79
Children's and Household Tales (Brothers Grimm), 182–83. See also Kinder- und Hausmärchen
children's books, 218, 222, 223, 236
Christmas, 20, 23, 36n3, 48; Yule Lads and, 27
Christmas beer, 27
Christou, John, 257
Cigarettes After Sex, 202
Cinderella, 59, 97, 100, 160, 161; magic and, 166, 167
Cinderella (film), 64, 152, 156, 160–162; animation of, 166; Disney and, 160
"Cinderella," 154; Calvinist version of, 223
cinema, 10, 11; Anglophone, 118; history of, 255; suicide, 119
citizenship, 12; children's, 217–34; imaginary, 193–94, 218–19, 220, 234, 235n2; legal, 234; literary, 235n2; model, 223; notions of, 219; political, 247; social, 247
civic welfare, 219
civil disobedience, 54
civilization, 199, 256; ecocidal, 56; ecological, 41, 43, 44; life-sustaining, 54; white-settler, 250
Clark, Les, 155
Clark, Timothy, 53
Clearcut (film), 12, 242–43, 248, 249–54, 258; colonization and, 243; cultural criminology in, 259; Indigenous peoples and, 243
Clements, Ron, 157
climate change, 3, 10, 55, 220; attitudes on, 229; hyperobjectivity of, 41

Clover, Carol, 200
Clum, John M., 120
Clute, John, 43
Cohen, Stanley, 242
Cole, Alyson, 212, 213
Collins, Patricia Hill, 4
colonialism, 12, 73, 74, 85, 241, 242, 245–48, 251, 252, 257; consequences of, 255; critique of, 254; fairy tales and, 8; indictment of, 254; Indigenous peoples and, 254–55; justice/crime and, 258; trauma of, 243
Comedy of Survival, The (Meeker), 41
compassion, 147, 149, 150, 167, 212
Condon, Bill, 152
Connell, Raewyn, 121, 129
Conselman, Deirdre, 138
Conselman, William, Jr., 138
consent, 22, 103, 183, 184, 202
conservation, 69, 70, 75
conte de fées, 8
Contes populaires de Lorraine (Cosquin), 148
Copes, Heith, 246
Copley, Sharlto, 155
Cosby, Bill, 227, 235n7
Cosmopolitan (periodical), 227
Cosquin, Emmanuel, 139, 147–49
COVID-19 pandemic, 254, 257–58
Crain, Patricia, 217, 218, 223, 225, 234
Crane, Walter, 224
Craven, Allison, 6, 12, 265
Creswell, John, 22
crime, 5; against children, 245; control, 244, 245; dimensions of, 244; fairy-tale, 93; fighting, 99; horror of, 241–43, 244; metaphysical experiences of, 244; representation of, 245; true, 247; victimization and, 242; victims of, 97; violent, 248; zombies and, 245–48
crime films, 248
crime stories, 93, 95, 98, 99–101, 106–11; fairy tales and, 94, 96; hard-boiled, 100
criminal justice system, 6, 7, 242, 246, 248; indictment of, 213
criminology, 7, 241; cultural, 242, 243, 248, 258, 259; haunting, 244–45; quantitative, 244; reanimation of, 244

crises, fairy-tale, 179
Crist, Eileen, 43
Crook, Mackenzie, 44
cultural concepts, 28, 96, 123
cultural concerns, Hawaiian, 82
cultural hegemony, 152, 232
cultural memory, 241, 242
cultural practices, revitalization of, 74
cultural values, 85, 95
culture, 64, 70, 74, 80, 208; analysis of, 248; children's, 218; decolonizing, 259; dominant, 63; Euro/North American, 55; fairy-tale, 66; folklore and, 61–62; Hawaiian, 82; Icelandic, 22; Indigenous, 243, 253, 258; participation in, 34; science and, 71; traditional, 4; visual, 244; western, 233. *See also* popular culture
Curry, Patrick, 52, 55

Dali, Salvador, 253
D'Amore, Laura Mattoon, 228
Dances with Wolves (film), 253
Dark Ecology (Morton), 53
Darwin, Charles, 66; as fictional character in *The Fall*, 116, 125, 127
datasaur, 244
Davies, Alexa, 47
Dawkins, Richard, 96
Dayton, Kevin, 80
de Certeau, Michel, 247
de Rond, Mark, 184
death: good, 131; honorable/dishonorable, 129. *See also* suicide
decolonization, 13n1, 85, 243, 248, 259
Deconstructing the Hero (Hourihan), 42
Delingpole, James, 44
Derrida, Jacques, 179, 247
Detectorists (television show), 41, 44, 45, 49, 51, 53, 55, 56
Deutsche Hausmärchen (Wolf), 143
Deutsche Mythologie und Sittenkunde (periodical), 143
"Devil and His Grandmother, The" (Brothers Grimm), 140
"Devil's Sooty Brother, The" (Brothers Grimm), 140

DiCaprio, Leonardo, 227
Dickinson, Harris, 155
disability, 11, 191; awareness of, 10, 21; cultural construction of, 21; experience of, 23, 35, 36n2; femininity and, 122; identity and, 122; narration of, 33; representation of, 28, 34; understanding, 19, 21
Disability before Disability (DbD) research project, 36n10
disability rights movement, slogan of, 21
disability studies, 19, 21, 23, 33, 34, 122
disabled people, 23, 28, 33; dehumanizing, 34; gendered expectations of, 118–22; social/cultural reality of, 35; stereotypical understandings of, 31
discipline, 95; army code of, 141
discourse, 5, 21, 43, 65, 102, 108, 181, 199, 231, 245; antisemitic, 61; censorship and, 118; contemporary, 198; critical, 230, 232; cultural, 232; gender, 106; sexuality, 106; tabloid, 229
Disney, 64, 65, 152, 161, 162, 169–70, 228, 265; princess industry and, 66; remixes by, 11, 153, 155–158, 160–170
diversity, 4, 6, 28, 179; human, 19, 27, 35
do Rozario, Rebecca-Anne C., 66
D'Onofrio, Vincent, 118
Donskoy, Daniel, 46
doomscrolling, 3
Dream Like Mine (Kelly), 249
Drewermann, Eugen, 139
Druon, Maurice, 137, 139, 150
Dundes, Alan, 61–62
Durkheim, Émile, 119

Earth Mother, 253
Eastwood, Clint, 119–20
Ebenezersdóttir, Eva Þórdís, 6, 7, 19, 29, 31, 32, 36n10, 36n12, 265; critical folklore/disability studies and, 34; poster by, 32f; studies of, 20
ecocentrism, 44, 45, 51–52, 56
Ecocriticism on the Edge (Clark), 53
eco-disasters, 10
ecoliteracy, 45, 53–54, 55
ecological crisis, 10, 44

ecological systems, 4, 70, 71
ecotage, 51
Edelman, Lee, 199
education: free, 222; place-based, 54; rights, 220
Edwards, Aimee-Ffion, 46
Eisler, Riane, 41
Ejiofor, Chiwetel, 156
Emerald City (television show), 118
Emmerson, Phil, 44
emotional tendencies, 179, 188
emotions: forbidden, 122–28; volatile, 122–28
enchantment, 185; language of, 52; liberation from, 169; origin/nature of, 55
ethnicity, 6, 11, 66
Evans, Luke, 157
evil: good and, 153, 158, 160, 165; justice and, 154
"Extraordinary Companions, The," 142

Facebook, 26, 74, 76, 78, 99, 175, 206
fairy-tale public sphere, 6, 12, 217–20, 223, 234
fairy tales, 11, 12, 45, 61–62, 64, 65, 95, 107, 108, 112, 138, 139, 140, 143, 148, 152, 178, 182, 186, 218, 223–26; antisemitism in, 10; bureaucratizing, 102–4; classic, 153, 159; climate, 232; colonial settings and, 8; crime fiction and, 94, 96; Danish, 179; as discursive forces, 97; documenting, 102–4; Euro-American, 9; feminist arguments and, 65; framing, 111; Jews in, 61; justice in, 153–55; marginality of, 219; plot sequences in, 154; rough justice and, 59; structure of, 177; traditional, 5; white supremacy and, 66; writing, 137
"Faithful Johannes," 154
Fall, The (film), 11, 115, 123, 124, 129, 131, 265; gendering of, 120; hypermasculine tales and, 117; origin story behind, 122; as subversive/progressive fairy tale, 130; toxic masculinity and, 119
family: chosen, 179, kinship and, 192; queer, 187, 192–93; structures, 180
Fanning, Elle, 155
fantasy, 44, 46, 53, 55, 64, 218; fairy-tale, 94; gendered, 94; as imagined order, 42; literary/filmic, 41, 43; potential of, 45; story system of, 40; wonder and, 9
Fantasy and Myth in the Anthropocene (Oziewicz, Attebery, and Dědinová), 42
Farmer, Gary, 256
Farnaby, Simon, 51
femininity, 106, 119, 131; disability and, 122; opposition to, 122; stereotypes of, 157
feminisms: liberal, 208; public, 228; queer, 264; second-wave, 208; social-equality-based, 228
Feminist, Queer, Crip (Kafer), 35
femme fatale, 106, 107, 108
Fennell, Emerald, 196, 211
Fergus, Jan, 222, 224
Ferrell, Jeff, 247
Fiedler, Leslie A., 62
Fifty Years of Mismanaging Mauna Kea (video), 80
Figgis, Mike, 131n1
Fineman, Martha Albertson, 213
Fire (film), 200
Fisher, Mark, 247
Flores, Kalani, 83, 84
Fo, Kaiolohia, 76
folklore, 4, 8, 21, 23, 33, 218; disability, 31, 34; human culture and, 61–62; Icelandic, 24, 36n8; role of, 62; studies, 21, 34; witch figure in, 177; Yuletide, 29
folkloristics, 4, 6, 19, 34, 36n2, 62
folklorists, 4, 26; disabled, 35; feminist, 176; German/Russian/French, 139; supernatural beings and, 34
folktales, 8, 65, 103, 138, 140, 148, 149, 220, 234; antisemitism in, 10; Flemish, 143; wonder, 139
Ford, Tom, 131n1
Forsyth, Isla, 54
Foster, Tom, 124
framings, 45, 47, 48, 71, 81, 82, 111, 196, 197, 248; fantasy, 44
Frank, Anne, 233
freedom, 106, 147, 168, 258
Freeman, Elizabeth, 181
FridaysForFuture movement, 230
friendship, female, 12, 176, 187

Gadd, Rebecca, 161, 162
Gaia concept, 53
Garland, Tammy, 246
Garland-Thomson, Rosemarie, 28
Gencarella, Stephen Olbrys, 21
gender, 6, 11, 120, 131, 162; equality, 226; imbalance, 27; inequality, 158; suicide and, 129
gender studies, 6
"General's Wife and the Merchant's Son, The" (Afanas'ev), 145
genocide, 241, 242, 248, 258
genres: crime, 94–96, 106; cultural hero, 123; fantasy, 42, 43; horror, 258; zombie, 246, 254, 257, 258
Geronimi, Clyde, 155, 156
ghosts/ghostly, 147, 241, 242, 243, 244, 245, 246, 247, 248, 259, 259
Gilchrist, Connie, 235n5
Gilroy, Dan, 115
Gittings, Christopher, 243, 253
Goeman, Stonehorse Lone, 256
"Golden Deer, The" (Wolf), 143
"Goldilocks and the Three Bears," 98
Gonzalez, Ryan "Gonzo," 77, 79, 81, 83
good, evil and, 153, 158, 160, 165
"Good Bargain, The," 60
Goodluck, Forrest, 256
Goody Two-Shoes, 12, 217, 219, 222, 224, 225, 226, 234; ageism and, 229–34; allusions to, 220; celebrities as, 226–27; definition of, 225–26; eighteenth-century, 220–23; as fairy-tale citizen, 222; as idiomatic catchphrase, 225; as moral barometer, 226–29; child-self of, 224; citizenship of, 223; civic welfare and, 219; moral heroism of, 219; pantomimes and, 225; public good and, 219, 221, public self of, 222–23; self-use of, 226–27
"Goody Two-Shoes" (Adam Ant), 226
Gordon, Avery F., 241
Gordon, Kiowa, 256
Gramsci, Antonio, 232
Gran Torino (film), 120
Granger, Hermione, 219, 226, 227, 228, 229
"Granny Rumple" (Yolen), 62

Grattan, Harry, 235n5
"Grave Mound, The" (Brothers Grimm), 140
Grear, Anna, 213
"Great Turning," 54
Green, Edward, 246, 247, 258
Greene, Graham, 250
Greenfield, Max, 207
Greenhill, Pauline, 130, 131, 209
Greyeyes, Michael, 256
Grimm, Jacob, 139, 140–42, 146
Grimm, Wilhelm, 139, 140–42, 143
Grimms. *See* Brothers Grimm
Grýla, 23, 24, 25
Gul Makai, 233
Gunnell, Terry, 24, 35

Habermas, Jürgen, 218
Hafstein, Valdimar, 194n2
Hans Urian oder Die Geschichte einer Weltreise (Tetzner), 149
Hansel and Gretel, 59
happy endings, 97, 100, 117, 126, 128, 148, 149, 166, 167
Harari, Yuval Noah, 42
Haraway, Donna, 131
"Hare-Herd, The" (Wolf), 143
Harry Potter (films), 219, 226, 229
Harzsagen (Pröhle), 146
hate speech, 10
hauntology, 245, 247
Hawai'i State Supreme Court, 71, 75
Hawaiian Renaissance, 74, 85
Hawaiian Studies, 82
Hawks, Howard, 120
Hays Code, 200
He Named Me Malala (film), 230
HeForShe campaign, 226, 228
Heimkehrer aus der Hölle: Märchen von Kriegsverletzungen und ihrer Heilung (Drewermann), 139
heroes: heroines and, 160; term, 170n2
heroines: action, 109; fairy-tale, 159; heroes and, 160; term, 170n2
heroism, 122, 129, 219
"Herr Fix-It-Up" (Brothers Grimm), 140
Hesford, Wendy, 232, 233

heteronormativity, 5, 152, 178, 180, 192, 207
heterosexuality, 27, 180, 196, 200, 202–4, 207, 210; neoliberal, 214
Hilton, Paris, 206
history, 52, 80; patriarchal, 176; storytelling and, 139–42
History of Little Goody Two-Shoes with the Means by Which She Acquired Her Learning and Wisdom, and in Consequence of Her Estate, 217, 220, 223
Hjaltalín, Egill, 31
hō'ailona, 76, 82, 83
Hobart, Hi'ilei, 75
Hoffmeister, Philipp, 140
Hogan, Michael, 250
Holbek, Bengt, 179, 193
Hollywood, 120, 129, 200, 254
Holocaust, 60, 65
homelessness, 220, 247
homosocial relations, 12, 188
hope, 12, 43, 77, 115, 137, 138, 139, 140, 142, 150, 162; wondering about, 3–4, 263
Hopkin, David, 139
horror films, Canadian, 242, 248
Horses of Iceland (website), 31
Hostina, Emil, 116
Hourihan, Margery, 41, 161
"How Dare the Taliban Take Away My Basic Right to Education?" (Yousafzai), 233
"How Peter the First Rewarded a Soldier with an Old Saddle" (Afanas'ev), 145
"How Six Made Their Way in the World" (Brothers Grimm), 140, 142
"How Super Heroes Made Their Way into the World of Fairy Tales: The Appeal of Cooperation and Collective Action from the Greek Myths to the Grimms' Tales and Beyond" (Zipes), 142
Hubbard, Phil, 126
Human Centipede III (film), 246
human-nonhuman relations, 7, 10, 41, 45, 52–54, 264
Hurðaskellir, ADHD and, 28
hyperobjects, 41
Hyperobjects (Morton), 53

I Am Malala: The Girl Who Stood Up for Education and Was Shot by the Taliban (Yousafzai and Lamb), 33
I Spit on Your Grave (film), 200
Iceland 24 (travel guide), 30
Icelandic Meteorological Office, 26
Icelandic National Broadcasting Service, 26
identity, 74, 110, 157, 159, 167, 189, 190, 234; Canadian, 248; disability and, 122; forms of, 44, 180; gendered, 94, 121; Indigenous, 256; shame and, 190; understanding of, 189
ideology, 180, 242, 252, 263; ethnic, 66; racial, 66, 178; reactionary, 152; relational, 178; social, 218
Ige, David, 80, 81
imagination, 129; gendered, 119–20; melodramatic, 225
Immortals (film), 117
Incident at Restigouche (film), 254
Indexing (McGuire), 11, 93, 94, 98, 102, 103, 106, 109, 110, 111; fairy tales/crime fiction in, 96; publication of, 95
Indexing: Reflections (McGuire), 94, 95, 99, 105, 107, 111
Indigenous community, 11, 255, 257
Indigenous peoples, 12, 241, 248, 249, 250, 255, 256; erasing, 243; inclusion of, 257; mistreatment of, 258; technologies/foods by, 13n1
Indigenous wonderworks, 9, 77, 82, 85
industrial growth, 54, 176, 253
infantilization, 6, 205
injustice, 7, 9, 158, 213, 241, 259, 264; criminal, 10; environmental, 250; love and, 160; past, 245
"Insulted Soldier and the Good Spirit, The" (Afanas'ev), 145
Intragovernmental Panel on Climate Change, 43
irrationality, 123, 130, 131
Íslenzkar þjóðsögur og ævintýri (Árnason), 24–25
Itty Bitty Titty Committee (film), 200

Jack the Giant Killer, 222
Jackson, Tom, 250
Jackson, Wilfred, 156

Jacobs, Joseph, 65
James, Lily, 156
Jaworski, Katrina, 121, 130
Jeffords, Susan, 163
Jenkins, Rebecca, 250
Jermyn, Deborah, 108
"Jew in the Bush, The," title change for, 63
"Jew in the Thornbush, The," 59–60, 61, 62, 64
Jews, 61, 62–63, 64, 65; assimilation of, 63; European Christian image of, 60; hostility for, 63; stereotyped, 63
Johnny Breadless (Vaillant-Couturier), 138, 149
Johnston, Jane: public good and, 221–22
Jojola, Ted, 253
Jólameyjar, 25
Jólasveinar, 10, 20, 23, 24, 25, 26, 32
Jolie, Angelina, 155, 159
Jólin Koma: Kvæði Handa Bornum (Kotlum), 25
Jones, Toby, 44
Jones, Tommy Lee, 119–20
"Jumping Root and the Little Light, The" (Pröhle), 147
"Juniper Tree, The," 154
just, term, 5–7
justice, 61, 62, 63, 64, 65, 71, 111, 138, 158, 166, 242, 244, 264, 265; bestowing, 170; conception of, 72; determining, 168; diminishment of, 165; ecological, 7; enacting, 9–10; environmental, 250; evil and, 154; extralegal, 253; fairy-tale, 5, 95, 153–55; Indigenous struggles for, 258; instigating, 192; meanings of, 5; pono and, 86; redeeming, 164, 169; reinstitution of, 168; restorative, 6; re/viewing, 9, 10–11; rough, 59; scholarship and, 66; seeking, 4, 9, 11–12; social, 4, 6, 19, 21, 34, 131, 208; system, 5, 244; ultimate, 154. See also criminal justice system
Justice, Daniel Heath, 72, 73; on fantasy, 9; Indigenous wonderworks and, 77, 82, 85

Kafer, Alison, 35
Kahaunaele, Kainani, 78
Kāhea: The Hawaiian-Environmental Alliance, 80
Kakar, Abdul Hai, 233
Kāko'o Haleakalā, 78, 79, 80
Kanaeokana, 78, 80
kānaka, 'āina and, 81–82
Kānaka Maoli, 75
Karlsson, Fannar Örn, 31; drawing by, 32f
Keedle, the Great: And All You Ever Wanted to Know about Fascism (Conselman and Conselman), 138
Keighren, Innes M., 44, 45
Kelen, Emery, 137, 138, 149–50
Kelly, M. T., 249
Kenzari, Marwan, 157
kia'i, 69, 70, 74, 75, 76, 77, 79, 80, 81, 82, 83, 85
Kimmel, Michael, 120
kin-aesthetics, 181, 182, 192, 193
Kinchen, Jaynee-Lynne, 118
Kinder- und Hausmärchen (Brothers Grimm), 140, 190. See also *Children's and Household Tales*
Kinder- und Volksmärchen (Pröhle), 146, 147
Kindynis, Theo, 247
Kingsley, Ben, 118
kinship: arrangements, 181, 182; conventional, 178; family and, 192; heterogeneity of, 182; level of, 42; normative, 178; queer, 11, 177, 178, 180, 181–82, 188, 189, 191, 192; structure of, 178
Kivel, Paul, 123
Kline, Kevin, 156
Knightley, Keira, 227
knowledge, 22, 64, 78, 96, 104, 106, 109; Indigenous, 8; institutional, 103; organizational, 102; police, 103; social construction of, 105
Kohm, Steven, 7, 12, 209, 246, 264
Kosonen, Heidi, 6, 7, 11, 265
Kötlum, Jóhannes úr, 25, 26
Kowalski, Walt, 120
Krause, Johann Friedrich, 140
Kristeva, Julia, 245
Kuczynski, Jürgen, 140
Kustritz, Anne, 7, 12, 265
Kuwada, Bryan Kamaoli, 7, 10, 264

"La belle au bois dormant" (Perrault), 164.
    See also "Sleeping Beauty"
labor, 101; female, 185; reductive, 176
Labrie, Vivian, 21
Lady from Shanghai, The (film), 107
"Ladybird, Ladybird," 231
Lamb, Christina, 233, 236n13
Lang, Andrew, 60, 64
languages, 6, 8, 52, 80, 100; English, 13n1; Hawaiian, 74
Larson, Eric, 155
Lau, Kimberly, 66
law enforcement, 75, 76, 79, 99, 102, 108
Le Guin, Ursula K., 41
Lea, Ron, 249
Leaving Las Vegas (film), 131n1
Leduc, Amanda, 36n2
Leppalúði, 23, 24
Lester, David, 121
Lévi-Strauss, Claude, 177
Lewis, Robin, 123
lies/deceit, 5, 50, 123, 148, 183, 184, 185, 187, 188, 189
Lilinoe, 75, 83
lilinoe (mist), 84
Lin, Ming-Hsun, 7, 11, 265
Lindsay, Robert, 155
Linnemann, Travis, 246–47, 247–48, 258
Listuguj, 255, 258
literacy, 218, 223, 224
literary studies, 6, 10
literature: didactic, 218, 224, 229, 234; history of, 255; Indigenous, 73
Little Goody Two-Shoes, 222, 223; imaginary citizenship and, 219; origins of, 218; "puffs" of, 221
Little Goody Two-Shoes: or, Harlequin a Little Boy Blue (Blanchard), 225
Little Mermaid, The (film), 65
Little Red Riding Hood, 209, 210, 213
"Little Red Riding Hood" (Perrault), 12, 59, 196, 197, 198; cinematic variations on, 5; *Promising Young Woman* and, 208–13, 214
live-action, 156, 170n3
Locke, John, 218, 219, 223
Lockwood, Jennifer, 98

Lopez, Jennifer, 118
"Lorenz the Soldier" (Pröhle), 147
Lothringer Volksmärchen (Merkelbach-Pinck), 148
Lovato, Demi, 227, 235n8
love, 158; capacity for, 153, 157–65, 169; injustice and, 160; suiciding for, 123
Lovelock, James: Gaia concept and, 53
Lowell, Chris, 203
Luske, Hamilton, 156

Macy, Joanna, 54
Madden, Richard, 156
Madonna, 227
magic, 166, 183; abandonment of, 169; debasing power of, 167; destructive effects of, 168; as diminishing force, 11; fairy-tale, 165–70; influence on, 169–70; as moral test, 11; reality and, 5; test/departure of, 165–70; withdrawal of, 166
Magnússon, Guðmundur, 32, 33
Maguire, Peter, 249, 250, 251, 252, 253
Malalai of Maiwand, 233
Maleficent (film), 152, 155, 158, 159, 166, 169
Maleficent: Mistress of Evil (film), 153, 155, 164, 169
Mangauil, Lanakila, 74–75, 83
Mara, David, 121
marginalization, 23, 65, 193
marriage, 154, 185, 192; heterosexual, 180, 182, 206
Marsh, Whitney, 246
Martinez, Natalie, 118
martyrdom, 116
masculinity, 119; bodily ability and, 121; compulsive, 126, 130; hegemonic, 118; models of, 121, 122, 123; phallic, 120; redemption of, 163; suicide and, 129; toxic, 122–28; Western, 122
Massoud, Mena, 157
Maunakea, 10, 69, 70, 73, 74, 75, 76, 77, 78, 79, 82, 83, 84, 85; historical mismanagement of, 81
Maunakea Access Road, 74
McAlpine, Fraser, 227
McBain, Ed, 95

McCormick, Patricia, 236n13
McDonough, Carla J., 121
McGowan, Rose, 227
McGuire, Seanan, 11, 93, 97, 99, 106; crime story and, 101, 111; on *Indexing*, 94; work of, 100–101
McRobbie, Angela, 208
media, 6, 129; children in, 235n9; digital, 78, 82; engagement with, 103; kia'i, 79; pono and, 85; team, 79, 82. *See also* social media
Meeker, Joseph W., 41
"Merchant's Wife as Colonel, The" (Pröhle), 147
Merkelbach-Pinck, Angelika, 148
Mertens, Donna M., 23
metaphors, 149, 245; conceptual, 247; woman-centered, 176
methamphetamines, 246
Meyer, Robinson, 231–32
Mirror Mirror (film), 117
"Miser in the Bush, The," 63
misogyny, 125, 126, 162, 178, 191, 194, 200
misrecognition, 197, 202, 214; neoliberalism and, 208–13
Modleski, Tania, 203
Molina, Alfred, 204
Monchalin, Lisa, 248
monsters, 245–48
moʻolelo, 73, 83
Moore, Colin, 80
Morahan, Hattie, 156
moral tract, 221, 225
morality, 12, 107, 189
Morton, Timothy, 41, 53
MTV Cribs (television show), 81
Mühlen, Hermynia Zur, 139
Mulligan, Carey, 196
multiculturalism, 116, 258
mundane, 72, 101; narratives of, 84; wonder and, 7, 8, 10, 74–77
Muñoz, José Esteban, 182
Murphy, Bell, 212
Musäus, Johann Karl August, 60
Musker, John, 157
myopia, anthropocentric, 42

mythology, 138; Greek, 210; Norse/German, 186; popular, 242

Nag, Debapriya, 231
narratives, 41, 46, 56, 84, 96, 97, 111, 116, 139, 158, 203, 249; common, 108; digressive, 222; disability, 33; folk, 65; heroic, 123; heteronormative, 5; Indigenous, 8; individualistic, 112; kin-aesthetics in, 181; magical, 218; popular, 8; revenge, 204; wonder, 4, 8, 85
"Nasty Flax Spinning," 190
natal family: adoptive kin versus, 182; questioning, 180–81
National Museum, 24
National Trust UK, 56n1
Nazis, 61, 137, 150
Neemia, Tracy Leinaala Kapali, 76
Negahban, Navid, 157
neoliberalism, 245; misrecognition and, 208–13
Nesbit, E., 61
New Age, 45
New York Times (periodical), 175
Newbery, John, 217, 218, 222, 224, 225, 235n1
Newton, Juice, 207
Niederländische Sagen (Wolf), 143
Nodelman, Perry, 63
Norcup, Joanne, 44, 45
Northern Wei Dynasty, 170n1
"Nothing About Us Without Us," 21–22, 34
"Nothing's Gonna Hurt You Baby" (Cigarettes After Sex), 202
Novik, Naomi, 62, 65
nursery rhyme, 50, 234, 235n11

Obomsawin, Alanis, 255
O'Keefe, Meghan, 227
"Old Goody Two Shoes," 224
O'Malley, Andrew, 223
Once Upon a Time (television show), Jews in, 63
Oprah Show, The (television show), 231
Ordinary People (film), 131n1
Orme, Jennifer, 9, 219
Osmanski, Stephanie, 226, 228
Ossewaarde, Ringo, 229, 230

Other, 191; colonized, 253; criminal, 246; Indigenous, 253, 254
Our House Is on Fire (Thunberg), 231
Oziewicz, Marek, 4, 7, 10, 265

Pace, Lee, 115, 116
Paltrow, Gwyneth, 227
pantomimes, fairy-tale, 224, 225, 235n5
Parade (periodical), 226
patriarchy, 65, 157, 158, 161, 163, 164, 188, 193, 210, 211, 246
peace, 138; imagining, 149–50
"Peasant and the Soldier, The" (Afanas'ev), 145
peasantry, 140, 141
Peck, Jamie, 245
Peckinpah, Sam, 253
pedophiles, revenge and, 209
Pedrad, Nasim, 157
Pele, 84
Perks of Being a Wallflower, The (film), 227
Perrault, Charles, 59, 164, 197, 212
Perry, Katy, 227
Persky, Aaron, 197
Pfeiffer, Michelle, 156
Phillips, Nickie, 246
physical embodiment, 6
Pile, Steve, 247
pledges and vows, 188–89
Plested, James, 230
Pocahontas, 66
Poli'ahu, 74, 75, 76, 83, 84
#PoliahuProtectingMaunakea, 70
police, 75, 95, 103, 108, 112n2, 207, 242, 250, 255, 256, 258; investigations, 99; stories, 98, 99–101; violence by, 247
political action, 95, 198, 208
political Right, ideology of, 263
pono, 72, 76, 81; 'āina and, 82, 83; justice and, 86; media and, 82, 85; push for, 74, 83; wonder and, 73
popular culture, 4, 6, 29, 108, 126, 129; German, 143; zombies and, 245, 246
Portman, Natalie, 227
power, 108; discriminatory, 11; discursive, 131; dynamics, 107; queer relational, 191; recursive, 84–85

Prahlad, Anand, 36n2
prejudice, 190; gender, 178; heteronormative, 188; sex, 178
Pride and Prejudice (Austen), 203
Princess and the Frog, The (film), 66
"Princess of Tiefenthal, The" (Wolf), 143
privatization, 208, 213, 214
Pröhle, Heinrich, 139, 146–47
Promising Young Woman (film), 12, 196, 197, 198, 199, 207–8; feminist function and, 212; heterosexual success and, 203; "Little Red Riding Hood" and, 208–13, 214; rape revenge and, 200–201, 205, 208, 210–11, 213; rom-com and, 202, 208; sexual violence and, 214; solidarity and, 200
Propp, Vladimir, 153
prosthetics, 20, 22, 23, 30–39
Protect Maunakea, 70, 79, 80
protectors, 10, 66, 69, 76, 85, 137, 159
protests, 3, 12, 50, 80, 82, 139, 194, 250, 258; fairy tale as, 176
public good, 219, 221–22
Public Policy Center, 80
public sphere, 218; children in, 235n9; fairy-tale, 12, 220, 234
pule, 70, 76, 77
Pullman, Philip, 153
punishment, 5, 154, 165, 206, 252; code of, 141; dimensions of, 244; gender-specific, 158; state, 248; threat of, 141; visceral aspects of, 245
puritanism, 218, 224
Pu'uhonua, 82
Pu'uhuluhulu University, 75, 78, 81
Pythagoreans, 186

Qazi, Habib, 232
Quebec Provincial Police, 255
queer theory, 179, 181
queerness, 12, 177, 181, 184, 186; demonstrating, 182
queers, 181; common, 179
Quora.com, 225–26

race, 65, 66
racialized Others, 247

racism, 212, 252
Radway, Janice, 203, 209–10
Rafter, Nicole, 7
Rankin, Ian, 95
rape: attempted, 210; cases, 199; claiming, 211; metaphor for, 159; misogynist clichés about, 200; punishment for, 198–99; risk of, 211. *See also* sexual assault
rape culture, 196, 207, 208; harm inflicted by, 205
rape revenge, 196–97, 200–201, 208, 209, 213, 214; dead-ends of, 197–200; inadequacy/futility of, 205; rom-com and, 204, 211; vigilantism and, 202, 205
Read, Jacinda, 200
reality, 9; magic and, 5; rewriting, 97; small-town, 44
Reality TV, 244
"Rebel Belle" (*Vanity Fair*), 228
recognition, 33, 54; bond of, 29; queer, 186; social, 186; social justice of, 21
Red Flag (website), 230
Redford, Robert, 131n1
redress, 7, 9, 11; finding, 4
Reid, Eliza, 175, 193
Reitherman, Wolfgang, 155
relationship, 52, 179, 183–84; formation, 183, 187; kin, 187; motivating, 182
remixes, 4, 97, 167, 168; cinematic, 153; Disney, 157–65; live-action, 11, 155, 157, 158, 165, 166, 169– 70; plot overview for, 155–57
renormalization, 85; linguistic/cultural, 74
reproductive choice, exercising, 193
resistance, 3, 6, 64, 85, 107, 137, 243, 255, 265
responsibility, 26, 53, 66, 199, 212; understanding, 45; web of, 84
revenge, 200–202, 205, 206–7, 209, 210–11; mini, 202
revitalization, 85; linguistic/cultural, 74
Reyes, Mike, 168
Reykjavik Grapevine (periodical), 30
Reynolds, Ryan, 118
Rheinlands schönste Sagen und Geschichten (Pröhle), 147
rhetoric, 198, 199, 220, 231, 234; feminist, 228; symbolic, 99

Rhymes for Young Ghouls (film), 254, 257
Riches, Adam, 45
Richest, The (periodical), 227
"Richilde" (Musäus), 60
Ritchie, Guy, 153
Robson, Peter, 200
Roe v. Wade, 193
romance, 198, 202–6, 208, 209–10
Romania (periodical), 148
romantic comedy (rom-com), 196–97, 203, 206, 208, 214; dead-ends of, 197–200; rape revenge and, 204, 211
romanticism, 123, 254
Romantics, 8
Romeo and Juliet (Shakespeare), 233
Rønning, Joachim, 153, 164
Rozan, S. J., 59
"Rumpelstiltskin," 59, 62
"Runaway Soldier, The" (Afanas'ev), 145
RuPaul's Drag Race: All Stars (television show), 5
Russell, Nicholas, 123
Russkie narodnye skazki (Afanas'ev), 145
Ryder, Phyllis, 232, 233

sacred, 48, 71, 75, 76, 186
Saga Jólanna (Björnsson), 24
Salter, Anastasia, 123, 129
Santoro, Miléna, 243
Sati, Omid, 232
Satyarthi, Kailish, 235n12
Schacker, Jennifer, 224
Schanoes, Veronica, 7, 10, 265; antisemitism and, 264; on justice, 6
Schmiesing, Ann, 191
Schneider, David, 178
scholarship, 64, 66, 265–66
Schwabe, Claudia, 157
Scott, Naomi, 157
Scriven, Olivia, 256
Sedgwick, Eve, 178; natal family and, 180; on shame, 189, 192; structuralist categories and, 180
self-endangerment, 116, 131
self-fulfillment, 153, 154
self-pity, 125, 128

Self/less (film), 117, 118
Sense and Sensibility (Austen), 203
separation, 40, 43, 54, 218
serendipity, 52, 183–84
settler-colonialism, 4, 11, 66
sexual assault, 159, 199, 205, 211, 235n7. *See also* rape
sexual offenders, celebrity, 227
Shah, Saeeda, 232
Shakespeare, William, 122, 233
shame, 188; behavior/identity and, 189; creativity, 192; effects of, 189–93; identity and, 190; types of, 189–90
Shannon, Molly, 205
Sheep-Cote Clod, 35–36n1. *See also* Stekkjastaur
"Sheep-Cote Clod Turns Down Össur Prosthetic" (*Reykjavik Grapevine*), 30
Shepeard, George, 123
Shootist, The (film), 120
Siegel, Don, 120
Simpson, Mark, 120
Singh, Tarsem, 11, 115, 117–18, 122–23
Single Man, A (film), 131n1
sisterhood, queer, 186, 187
Skyrgámur, 25
Sleeping Beauty, 59, 97, 98, 164, 169
Sleeping Beauty (film), 155, 158, 164, 166
"Sleeping Beauty in the Wood" (Perrault), 164. *See also* "La belle au bois dormant"
Smith, Michelle J., 66
Smith, Robin, 116
Smith, Rochelle, 66
Smith, Tia, 250
Smith, Will, 157
Snow White, 59, 60, 97, 104; crime story, 106–11; gendered expectations of, 108
"Snow White," 60, 65, 117, 154
Sobel, David, 54
social change, 21, 34, 205, 220
social discomfiture, index of, 229
social imaginary, 94, 247–48
social media, 4, 10, 27, 86, 244; connection and, 77–84; Jólasveinar and, 26, 27; pono and, 82; technology and, 78; wonder on, 74–77, 84–85

social movements, 74, 77
social norms, 111, 198
social order, 110, 112, 181
social problems, 208, 212
social reform, 168, 192, 222
social sciences, 6, 241
social status, 26, 141, 154
Socialist Alternative website. *See Red Flag*
"Soldier and Death, The" (Afanas'ev), 145
Soldier and Peasant in French Populist Culture, 1766–1870 (Hopkin), 139
"Soldier and the Landlord, The" (Afanas'ev), 145
"Soldier and the Robber, The" (Afanas'ev), 145
"Soldier and the Tsar in the Forest, The" (Afanas'ev), 145
"Soldier and the Watch, The" (Afanas'ev), 145
"Soldier Erema the Crafty" (Afanas'ev), 145
"Soldier-Fiddler and the Devil, The" (Afanas'ev), 145
"Soldier-Fiddler and the Unclean One, The" (Afanas'ev), 145
"Soldier-Fiddler and the Witch, The" (Afanas'ev), 145
"Soldier Simkin" (Afanas'ev), 145
soldier stories, 140, 141, 143, 149–50; comic, 144–45; ideal, 142; power of, 11
"Soldier, the Peasant, and the Woman, The" (Afanas'ev), 145
soldiers, 150; trauma for, 142
"Soldier's Riddle, The" (Afanas'ev), 145
"Soldier's Sons, A" (Wolf), 145
solidarity, 7, 160, 162, 200, 208, 211, 212, 213, 264, 265; decolonizing, 13n1; female, 166, 191
Soultanakis, Nico, 115
sovereignty, 65, 71; Hawaiian sovereignty, 74, 83; human/nonhuman, 264; Indigenous, 264
Space Cowboys (film), 119–20
spinners, 184, 185, 187, 188, 191; common, 190; queering, 182–83
Spinners, The Three, 189, 191; achievement of, 192; described, 187–88; magic of, 193; queerness of, 192; spin of, 193

spinning, 183, 186, 188, 190; room, 176–78, 187; tales, 176
Spinning Silver (Novik), 62
Spivak, Gayatri, 232
Stack, Steven, 119, 120, 130
"Stars Are Blind" (Hilton), 206
staurfætur, 20, 35–36n1
Steinem, Gloria, 228
Stekkjastaur, 6, 7, 10, 20, 23, 25, 36n5, 36n12, 265; disability and, 28, 31, 35; narrative of, 33; portrayal of, 30; poster of, 32f; representation of, 33; role of, 21; staring at, 27–34; as supernatural being, 22, 34. *See also* Sheep-Cote Clod
stereotypes, 63, 246; feminist, 157; misogynist, 191
Sterne, David, 46
Stevens, Dan, 156
Stirling, Rachael, 47
stories: ancestors', 79; patterns/themes of, 94; power of, 129–32
Stormfront, 62
Story of the Treasure Seekers, The (Nesbit), 61
storylines, 157, 158, 198, 204
storytelling, 11, 86, 102, 103, 105–6, 129, 224; history and, 139–42; institutional, 101; oral, 117; rhythm for, 176–77; serial, 94–96; techniques of, 7; Western, 42
storyworld, 96, 116, 125
Strategies of Fantasy (Attebery), 41
Straw Dogs (film), 253
Stromberg, Robert, 152
structuralism, 42, 54, 177, 180; classic, 178; queering, 178–79
structure, chance meetings and, 183–86
Stúfur, 29
suicidality, 116, 119, 122, 124, 127, 129
suicide, 11, 119–20, 122, 123, 126, 127; altruistic, 119, 120, 127, 128, 130, 131; egoistic, 119, 131; gender and, 119, 129, 130; honorable, 132n2; masculinity and, 124, 129; mass, 132n2; methods of, 121; notes, 124; on-screen, 128; predictors of, 130; representation of, 118; taboo-laden, 119; tale of, 117; truths of, 131; warnings against, 125
"Sun, Moon, and Talia" (Basile), 159

supernatural beings, 10, 19, 20, 21, 22–23, 31, 73, 76, 187, 191, 224, 226; disabled, 35; entanglements of, 176; folklorists and, 34
Sutton Hoo, 56, 56n1
Swift, Taylor, 226
Symphony No. 7 (Beethoven), 115

Tagé Cho Hudän, 78–79
Tailfeathers, Elle-Máijá, 256
taleworld, 119, 122, 124, 126, 127, 130; narrative, 116, 123
Tandy, Adam, 46, 56
Tangled (film), 63
Tarsem. *See* Singh, Tarsem
Tatar, Maria, 154–55
Taylor, Edgar, 63
telescopes, 69–70, 71, 75
tertiary (power of three), 182, 186
Tetzner, Lisa, 139, 149
"Thirteen Bewitched Princesses, The" (Wolf), 43
Thirteen Lads, 26. *See also* Yule Lads
Thirty Meter Telescope (TMT), 69–70, 75, 76, 79, 80, 81, 82; construction of, 71
Thomas, Jake, 118
Thompson, Sophie, 48
Thompson, Stith, 100
"Thread, The" (Wolf), 143
"Three Snake Leaves, The" (Brothers Grimm), 140
"Three Spinning Women, The" (Brothers Grimm), 12, 176, 178, 182, 184, 193
Thunberg, Greta, 219–20, 229–34; ADHD as superpower of, 231; ageism and, 230; ascendancy of, 230–31; criticism of, 231, 232; Goody Two-Shoes and, 230, 231; juvenile ageism and, 229; persona of, 230; public of, 232; UN speech by, 234; Yousafzai and, 230, 234
Thwaites, Brenton, 155
Time (periodical), Thunberg and, 231
Tistou les pouces verts (Tistou, the Boy with Green Thumbs) (Druon), 138, 150
Titchkosky, Tanya, 28
TMT. *See* Thirty Meter Telescope
Todres, Jonathan, 235n3, 235n4, 235–36n13

Tolkien, J.R.R., 40
Townshend, Dale, 217
Trachtenberg, Joshua, 60
transformation, 21, 43, 72, 77, 86, 184; dramaturgy of, 224; gender, 177
transformative research, 21, 22–23, 72, 94
transgressions, 176; gender-specific, 158; metaphysical experiences of, 244
trauma, 11, 137, 138, 139, 142, 143, 149, 150, 163, 206, 242, 244, 245, 254; addressing, 140; colonial, 243, 258; intergenerational, 12, 243; past, 241; sexual, 199
"Tricky Soldier, The" (Pröhle), 147
tropes, 97, 99, 101, 106, 123, 258; fairy-tale, 100; fantasy, 44; horror, 242, 243; narrative, 11, 42; romance, 203; settler-colonial, 248, 253–54; television, 101
Trousdale, Gary, 156
true crime, 11, 12, 244; cultural production of, 247
Tuck, Eve, 264
Turner, Brock, 197, 198, 199, 200
Turner, Kay, 7, 264
"20 Goody Two-Shoes Celebrities Who Are Actually Very Different" (*Richest*), 227
"Two Ivans, The" (Wolf), 145
"Two Old Soldiers" (Merkelbach-Pinck), 148
"Two Soldiers of 1689, The" (Cosquin), 148
Types of International Folktales: A Classification and Bibliography, The (Uther), 100

UN Convention on the Rights of the Child, 235n3
Untaru, Catinca, 115, 117, 123
Unterharzische Sagen (Pröhle), 146
US Supreme Court, 193
Uther, Hans-Jörg, 100

Vaillant-Couturier, Paul, 137, 139, 149
Valier, Claire, 245, 253
Vanity Fair (periodical), 228
Verma, Jeetu, 116
victimization, 197, 212, 213, 244
Viehmann, Dorothea, 140
vigilantism, 200, 249, 251; rape revenge and, 202, 205

villain, 158, 164; female, 165, 170n2; male, 165, 170n2
violence, 64, 123, 138, 159–60, 252, 253; colonial, 41, 178, 248; cycle of, 165; depicting, 197; environmental, 41; fueling, 121; gender, 41, 198, 246; hierarchy and, 200; male, 198, 210, 212; preventing, 197; racial, 41; random, 248; resisting, 212; sexual, 11, 197, 198, 200, 203, 204, 205, 206, 209–14; state, 245–48
Vollum, Scott, 246
"Volunteer Soldier, The" (Afanas'ev), 145
von Arnim, Friedmund, 140
von Ploennies, Wilhelm, 143
Von Teese, Dita, 227
Vowel, Chelsea, 255
vulnerability, 98, 126, 130, 212, 219

Waddell, Justine, 117
Walby, Kevin, 246
Waldron, Ingrid, 124
Walking Dead, The (television show), 246
Wall, Tyler, 246, 247, 258
War, Myths, and Fairy Tales (Buttsworth and Abbenhuis), 138
Warner, Marina, 8, 176
Watson, Emma, 156; activism of, 226, 228; as "goody two-shoes," 219, 226, 227, 229, 234; HeForShe and, 226; social commitment of, 229; tribute to, 226, 228; UN speech by, 226, 228
Wayne, John, 120
Weikle-Mills, Courtney, 219, 234; imaginary citizenship and, 218, 219, 235n2
Welles, Orson, 107
Wesley, Marcus, 116
Westerman, Floyd Red Crow, 251
Westman, Jack C., 235n9
"What Can We Do About Fagin? The Jew-Villain in Western Tradition" (Fiedler), 62
White Falcon (periodical), 36n1
whiteness, valorization of, 66
"Why Greta Makes Adults Uncomfortable" (Meyer), 231
Wilson, Jake, 230
Wilson, Michael D., 71
Winslet, Kate, 227

Winter and Night (Rozan), 59
Wisakedjak, 252, 253
Wise, Kirk, 156
witches, 177, 221, 223
Wizard of Oz (film), 118
Wolf, Johann Wilhelm, 139, 143–45
wolves, 5, 197, 199, 206, 209, 210
wonder, 56, 220; activism and, 9; 'āina and, 81; fantastic, 9, 41, 55; harms and, 11; intellectual, 12; invitation to, 84–86; mundane, 10, 74–77, 84; narratives of, 4, 8, 85; poetics of, 72; politics of, 8; pono and, 73; potential of, 45; relationship of, 70–74, 84; on social media, 74–77, 84–85; struggle for, 70–74; tales of, 84, 85; term, 79; transformations of, 41
wonderworks. *See* Indigenous wonderworks
Wonser, Robert, 246
Woolverton, Linda, 158, 159
"Worn-out Dancing Shoes, The" (Brothers Grimm), 140
wounds, 119, 120, 127, 130, 138, 139, 142, 156, 201, 252
Wundermärchen, 8

Yang, K. Wayne, 264
Yo Ho Ho (film), 115
Yolen, Jane, 62, 65
Young, Jock, 244
Young, Kalani, 76
Younging, Gregory, 13n1
Yousafzai, Malala, 219–20, 229–34; Goody Two-Shoes and, 230; juvenile ageism and, 229, 234; public of, 232–33; Thunberg and, 234
youth climate movement, 230
Yule family, 29, 31, 34, 35; history, 24–27
Yule Lads, 4, 10, 20, 23, 24, 28, 30, 34, 265; Christmas and, 27; events for, 25–26; favorite, 29
Yule Lasses, 25, 27, 28
Yunkaporta, Tyson, 48
Yussuf the Ostrich (Kelen), 138, 149–50

Zipes, Jack, 7, 152, 209, 210, 212; fairy tales and, 96; soldier stories and, 11
zombie apocalypse, 254, 255, 256, 258
zombies, 243; crime and, 245–48; cultural fascination with, 245; white, 255, 257

About the Authors

Andrea Braithwaite is a Senior Teaching Professor of Communication and Digital Media Studies at Ontario Tech University, Canada. Her research examines gendered discourses of sociability and belonging in pop culture. She looks at gender, crime, and detection stories across media, especially Canadian. She also discusses representations of and responses to feminist activism in online and gaming communities.

Allison Craven is Associate Professor of English and Screen Studies at James Cook University, Australia. She is the author of *Fairy Tale Interrupted: Feminism, Masculinity, Wonder Cinema* (2017) and *Finding Queensland in Australian Cinema: Poetics and Screen Geographies* (2016), and coeditor of *Monstrous Beings and Media Cultures: Folk Monsters, Im/Materiality, Regionality* (2023). She is an editor of the Anthem Film and Culture series.

Eva Þórdís Ebenezersdóttir is a PhD candidate in Folkloristics at the University of Iceland with a BA and MA in folkloristics from the same university. Her interests lie in legends and folk belief, which she approaches via folkloristics and disability studies. Her PhD research explores how archived Icelandic legends understand disability and portray people viewed as different or abnormal.

About the Authors

Pauline Greenhill is Professor of Women's and Gender Studies at the University of Winnipeg, Canada. Her recent books include *Fairy-Tale TV* (2021, with Jill Terry Rudy) and *Clever Maids, Fearless Jacks, and a Cat: Fairy Tales from a Living Oral Tradition* (2019, with Anita Best and Martin Lovelace). She has published in *Signs*; *parallax*; *Theoretical Criminology*; *Marvels & Tales*; *Studies in European Cinema*; *feral feminisms*; *Narrative Culture*; *Law, Culture and the Humanities*; and others.

Steven Kohm is a full Professor in the Criminal Justice department at the University of Winnipeg, Canada. His research focuses on media, popular culture, and crime, and his work has been published in such leading journals as *Crime Media Culture*, *Theoretical Criminology*, and *Critical Criminology*. He is coeditor of *Screening Justice: Canadian Crime Films, Culture and Society* (2017), and coeditor of *The Annual Review of Interdisciplinary Justice Research*.

Heidi Kosonen is postdoctoral researcher in Contemporary Culture at the University of Jyväskylä, Finland. She has published bilingually on suicide cinema and television, including case studies on the productions *13 Reasons Why*, *Annihilation*, *Bird Box*, *Bridgend*, *Midsommar*, *The Moth Diaries*, *Vanilla Sky*, and *Unfriended*. Her research expertise also includes varied phenomena dealing with difficult emotions and societal structures, such as death-related taboos and gendered hate speech.

Anne Kustritz is an Assistant Professor in Media Studies at Utrecht University, Netherlands. Her scholarship focuses on fan communities, transformative works, digital economies, and representational politics. Her forthcoming *Identity, Community, and Sexuality in Slash Fan Fiction* documents the slash fan fiction community's digital transition around the turn of the millennium and the pockets of counterpublic space they constructed for reimagining gender, sexuality, and relationality. Her articles have appeared in *Camera Obscura*, *Feminist Media Studies*, and *Sexualities*.

Bryan Kamaoli Kuwada is a writer, poet, photographer, and Assistant Professor at Hawaiʻinuiākea School of Hawaiian Knowledge. He uses Hawaiian traditional knowledge and stories to navigate and imagine Hawaiian futures. He has published fiction and poetry in ʻŌlelo Hawaiʻi, the Hawaiian language, and in English in *The Offing*, *Bettering American Poetry*, vol. 2, *Yellow Medicine Review*, *Black Marks on the White Page*, and *The Dark Magazine*. Find his surf photography (@waterbearfoto) in *Pacific Longboarder Magazine*.

Ming-Hsun Lin is Assistant Professor at Feng Chia University in Taiwan. She received her PhD in Drama from the University of Manchester, UK. Her research interests include fairy tales, fantasy, children's and adolescent literature, and film adaptations. She is currently researching the reinterpretation of culture and magic in modern adaptations of Asian fairy tales.

Jennifer Orme is an independent scholar, editor, and writer in Toronto, Canada. She coedited the creative anthology *Inviting Interruptions: Wonder Tales in the Twenty-First Century* (2021) with Cristina Bacchilega. She has published on fairy tales in academic journals and books, as well as feature magazine articles, multi-sensory ghost and adventure tales, and creative nonfiction.

Marek Oziewicz is Professor of Literacy Education, Director of the Center for Climate Literacy, and Sidney and Marguerite Henry Professor of Children's and Young Adult Literature at the University of Minnesota–Twin Cities. His current research is on the Anthropocene as a challenge to our story systems. He is the Senior Editor of *Climate Literacy in Education* and Editor in Chief of *Climate Lit*, a resource hub for teaching climate literacy with children's literature and media.

Veronica Schanoes is an Associate Professor in the Department of English at Queens College–CUNY. Her first book is *Fairy Tales, Classical Myth, and Psychoanalytic Theory: Feminism and Retelling the Tale* (2014). Her second is *Burning Girls and Other Stories* (2021). Her current project is on Jewish representation in the English-language fairy-tale tradition.

Stekkjastaur is a Jólasveinn (Yule Lad), which is both a profession and an identity. He has gone from infamous and horrid to a celebrated and delightful bringer of joy and gifts. Despite being traditional in his mindset, he is willing to try new things, such as working in cahoots with an academic. His primary concerns are the well-being of children and his role as an important figure to them. He also really loves sheep and sheep milk.

Kay Turner is an artist and scholar working across disciplines including performance, writing, music, exhibition curation, and public and academic folklore. She is noted for her feminist and queer writings and performances on subjects such as women's home altars, fairy-tale witches, and historical goddess figures. She is the coeditor, with Pauline Greenhill, of *Transgressive Tales: Queering the Grimms* (2012) and author of *Before and After: What the Witch's Nose Knows . . .*, with photographer Zini Lardieri (2021).

Jack Zipes is Professor Emeritus of German and Comparative Literature at the University of Minnesota. Some of his recent publications include *Grimm Legacies: The Magic Spell of the Grimms' Folk and Fairy Tales* (2015), *The Sorcerer's Apprentice: An Anthology of Magical Tales* (2017), and *Buried Treasures: The Power of Political Fairy Tales* (2023). He has also translated the first 1812/15 edition of the Grimms' tales, *The Original Folk and Fairy Tales of the Brothers Grimm* (2014).

www.ingramcontent.com/pod-product-compliance
Lightning Source LLC
Chambersburg PA
CBHW020405040426
42333CB00055B/491